A History of

SILSOE

By Roger Bradshaw

Published by Roger Bradshaw

Published by Roger Bradshaw, October 2011,
Glen Farm, Great Lane, Clophill, Bedfordshire MK45 4BQ

Printed by All Print Solutions,
Desborough, Northants, NN14 2UD

ISBN 978-0-9570446-0-9

Cover design by Elwyn Owen.

Contents

List of plates
List of abbreviations
Foreword
About the author
Acknowledgements

List of Plates.

The following plates are reproduced with the kind permission of Ordnance Survey from maps of the following dates, Plates 1/1, 3/1 & 13/2 1860, Plate 1/2 1901, Plate 10/1 1902 & Plate 11/8 1917.

Plates 1/4, 1/5, 10/8, 10/9, 12/5, 13/3, 14/6, 15/5, 15/6, 15/7 & 17/5 are from photographs by Ken Scott, provided by his executor, David Swain. Plate 17/5 is available in several places but the original may well be held by BLARS.

Plate 3/2 is taken from a sketch provided by Mrs K Shattock of Newbury Manor.

Plates 3/3, 3/4, 4/1, 5/5, 9/1, 11/2, 11/3, 11/4, 11/6, 11/7, 11/10, 11/11, 12/1, 12/2, 12/4 & 16/1 are photos or tracings from documents held by the Bedfordshire and Luton Archives and Records Service and we are pleased to record their permission to use these copies.

Plate 4/1 was originally sourced from Wikipedia.

Plates 4/2, 4/4, 5/4, 7/1, 9/2, 14/1, 15/2, 15/3, 17/2, 17/3 & 17/4 are photographs by the author.

Plate 4/3 was provided by English Heritage to whom thanks are due.

Plates 5/1 & 5/2 are photographs, taken by Elwyn Owen, of the pictures which hang in Silsoe Church.

Plates 5/3 & 5/7 were kindly supplied by Barbara Frazer.

Plates 8/2, & 14/8 are photographs by Elwyn Owen.

The cover photo is from Anderson, Series 132 and Plates 1/3, 8/1, 12/3, 14/4 and possibly 4/5 are also from postcards by Anderson. The current copyright holders have not been traced.

Plate 8/3 is a photo by Douglas Collyer. Courtesy of Stuart Antrobus, author of "We wouldn't have missed it for the world: the Women's Land Army in Bedfordshire, 1939 - 1950" Book Castle, 2008.

Plates 9/4 & 14/5 are from photos supplied by Ian Lilley, believed to be originally from JHC glass negatives. Plates 9/3, 15/1 the title page and the fly leaf were also supplied by Ian Lilley. The current copyright holders have not been traced.

Plates 10/5 & 10/7 are taken from William Treacher's booklet on Silsoe, originally of 1899 but re published about 1910.

Plate 10/6 is from a JHC glass negative.

Plate 13/1 is from the Luton Museum 1972 book The Turnpike Age, courtesy of Luton Culture.

Plate 14/2 is from the Henman collection, at Bedfordshire Libraries.

Plates 14/7 is reproduced courtesy of the Luton News

Plate 15/4 is from the Silsoe Drama Club.

Other plates are graphs etc. compiled by the author of photos or documents held by him.

Every effort has been made to trace copyright holders. The publisher will be glad to rectify in future editions any errors or omissions brought to their attention.

List of Abbreviations

BBC	Bedford Borough Council
BCC	Bedfordshire County Council, the County Council until 2009.
BHRS	Bedfordshire Historical Record Society
BLARS	Bedfordshire and Luton Archives and Records Service.
CBC	Central Bedfordshire Council, as from 2009
MBDC	Mid Bedfordshire District Council, existed until 2009.
OS	Ordnance Survey
VCH	The Victoria County History which was founded in 1899 and originally dedicated to Queen Victoria. It is an encyclopaedic record of England's places and people from earliest times to the present day.

Foreword

Reminiscing about his time at Silsoe in the 1830s Alfred Russel Wallace, the great naturalist and explorer, noted, 'this very small village is an appanage [adjunct] of Wrest Park, the seat of Earl de Grey'. Though it would be hard to argue today that Silsoe is 'very small', thanks to substantial house-building in the second half of the 20th century, the close relationship with Wrest Park has endured. Through telling the story of Silsoe and its people from prehistory to the present this book draws attention again and again to the continuing bond between village and estate. The owners of Wrest, the de Grey family were the main landowners in the parish, they provided employment for many villagers, rebuilt the parish church, supported local charities and the village school, and laid on entertainments from time to time. When they left in 1917 Wrest Park continued to serve as a focus for the village, initially as the residence of northern industrialist John George Murray, who provided a new village hall, and more recently as the home of an agricultural research institute. Now cared for by English Heritage the house, gardens and new visitor centre provide a valuable amenity for the local community.

There were, though, many other influences on Silsoe's development, as this book makes clear. The farmland was productive, there were opportunities for employment, particularly for women, in straw plaiting and hat making, and the village offered a convenient stopping-off point on an important thoroughfare – the road from London to Bedford. More than anything, however, Silsoe was shaped by the everyday lives of its people, chronicled here by Roger Bradshaw in intricate detail, based on years of painstaking research. A book on the history of Silsoe is long overdue, and one that is as comprehensive as this not only provides a fascinating account of life in the village over more than a millennia, it will also be a valuable resource for the local historians of the future.

Dr Andrew Hann, English Heritage

About the Author

The original idea for the writing of *A Silsoe Village History* came about by the author innocently wondering when and why the stone walls that are dotted around the older parts of Silsoe, actually came about. Little did he realise the size of the task that would ensue!

When embarking on the writing of *A Silsoe Village History*, Roger Bradshaw faced an intrinsic disadvantage because he was not born or brought up in Silsoe, or even Bedfordshire. He came from Canterbury in Kent, where he was born in 1941 and educated at Simon Langton Grammar School, and later studied Civil Engineering at, what is now, City University in London. After several years in the construction industry, he came to Bedfordshire to work for Local Government, mainly to provide uninterrupted schooling for his children, and moved to Silsoe in the late 1970's. Whilst living in Silsoe, he became involved in village life and served on several committees.

It always helps to have a background knowledge of local families and customs when a project such as *A Silsoe Village History* is begun, but Roger did not have that, and therefore has had to gratefully rely on some of the more mature residents to fill him in, with their experiences and often highly amusing, reminiscences of Silsoe life in the 20th Century. Unfortunately, some valuable knowledge has passed away with the people who had it, and even sadder still, some declined to help. It has to be acknowledged that as a result, there must be much which would have made very interesting reading that is absent.

Roger has with his insouciant writing style, created a book that took hundreds of researching hours, into an easy-read for all ages. *A Silsoe Village History* will provide a good starting point for many school or college projects, whilst expanding the general local knowledge of all.

Roger's own recent history has involved a permanent move in 2009 with his wife, Linda, to Poulx, France to help with the New Frontiers Church nearby. Having failed to learn any lessons, he is currently working on his maternal family tree.

Caryl Mossop
April 2010

Acknowledgements

A great deal of thanks is due to the staff at the now Bedfordshire and Luton Archives and Records Service in Bedford, and especially to James Collett-White whose knowledge of the Lucas documents was both impeccable and authoritative, and who allowed me the use of his personal papers on the fields of Silsoe. Dr Richard Smart, former Head of History at De Montfort University, was also of great assistance in reading the final document and providing his comments.

Dr Andrew Hann of English Heritage has also been of immense assistance in applying his expert knowledge, particularly to the Wrest Park section, and by providing advice on other sections. He also kindly agreed to write the foreword to the book.

I would also like to thank the members of the small group which started in 2005 to help process this book, unfortunately it has taken longer than expected, in that context Miles Greenhalgh, David Swain, Jill and Ray Norwich all helped in one way or another. In addition, Jill Burrows, Alan Denton and Elwyn Owen have been of enormous assistance in the process of getting the project finalised and printed.

Others such as Barbara Frazer, John Mackey, Tony Burton, Maureen Williams, Des Brazier and Ian Lilley have either provided information or commented on the draft.

Caryl Mossop has also been of invaluable assistance in transcribing her interviews with some of the ladies of Silsoe, in writing the 'Military' chapter and in proof reading the drafts. In addition, Anne Jarvis supplied several paragraphs on the development of the agricultural research institutions at Wrest park.

I would also like to thank the Bedfordshire Historical Record Society for allowing us to print the reminiscences of Violet Armstrong originally published in 1984 in the Bedfordshire Magazine.

Sources such as the National Archives were especially useful, and that body also provided copies of Wills of Silsonians for a small fee. The Wildlife Trust at the Priory Country Park Visitor Centre at Bedford also kindly supplied a great deal information on the wildlife sites in the parish.

However, some of the more elderly of the villagers were asked for their memories of Silsoe either individually, or at the village SOS meetings. I would particularly like to thank those who agreed to be interviewed, and whose information appears in the People and Families section.

I apologize for any omissions but whoever you are and wherever you are, thank you for your invaluable help.

Chapter 1 - Introduction

Introduction

If you wander into any of the local libraries, you will find there many histories written about villages in Bedfordshire, and considering the events and history that have formed our village both from the estate owning families and others, it is surprising that there is not already one for Silsoe.

There is a huge amount of information in the Bedfordshire and Luton Archives mainly from thousands of papers of the Wrest families, deposited there by Lady Lucas in the 20th century; but also there are other collections which refer to the village, along with papers deposited there by the parish Council and the Church. Documents are also available at the National Archives in London and other places, and the *Victoria County History* and Joyce Godber's *History Of Bedfordshire* are also valuable sources of information.

Unfortunately most of the older information is about land, and thus those people that are mentioned are the major landowners, or someone who was lucky enough to have a small field that he was selling. The average agricultural labourer or villager rarely got a mention until the advent of the ten yearly censuses in the 19th century.

Most of the local archive sources have been tapped and many old documents read to enable this book to be written, while in addition many villagers have kindly made their memories available for incorporating here.

Finally, there is much variation found in documents both in the spelling of the village name and also of people's names. It was not so important to spell 'correctly' before the 20th century, and so there will be found some variation in names and places throughout this book.

The Village Name

Villages usually have one or a combination of good practical reasons for their existence; they grew up at a river crossing, a spring, a natural harbour, a crossroads, a natural defensible stronghold, or were associated with a family which managed to become important.

It is suggested that Silsoe's name originates as Sifel's hoh or hill[1] probably of Anglo Saxon derivation thus suggesting perhaps a clearance on a prominence of some kind where Sifel lived. The name may then have been used to refer to a grouping of farms or manors to the east of Flitton, within which parish it was included, when parish boundaries were established. The name Flitton is probably also of Anglo Saxon origin, the suffix 'ton' being a house or farm.

---

[1] Beds Magazine, Mary Phillips,

Many different ways of spelling the village name have been found in the old documents, as the way it has been spelt in the past depended not only upon who was writing it down, (they may not have heard it pronounced before), but also on the accent of the person speaking the name. There was also not so much political correctness then about getting your spelling 'correct'.

Thus in one early document of the 12th century Swelesho is written; within the first decades of the 1300's there is Swyvelesho, Cyvelesho, Selvessso and Sevelsho. A hundred years later Syvelesho, Sevlesho, Sivelso and Syllesho all appear, and in the 1500's Sevelshoo, Sylshoo, Shevilsho, Sylshow all turn up, while in the 1600's Syvylshooe, alias Sylshoe appear. Most of the early names have three syllables but it is evident that these have been contracted to two in usage when the use of 'alias' gives the alternative pronunciations. From the 17th century the name becomes standardised as Silsoe, although the occasional 'y' occurs or the 'e' disappears.

The centre of Silsoe became established near the intersection of the north/south Luton to Bedford road and one of the east/west routes from Dunstable to Shefford and also where other radiating tracks connected easily to Brabury, Newbury and Upbury Manors plus West End and Fielden. In that location a small chapel to St Lawrence was built, perhaps initially for the adjacent manor, but which was eventually used to provide a more convenient place of worship for the population.

Although never very large, the village grew over the centuries as a location from which the manors of Wrest, Newbury and others could find the necessary labourers to work their land. The reduction in the farming workforce due to mechanisation and other changes, meant that people had to leave or find other work, and the proximity of Luton enabled many, mainly women and girls, to find work in the straw hat industry, by making straw plait at home.

After the 19th century, better transportation enabled some to find work at Bedford or Luton or elsewhere and by the end of the 20th century, Silsoe had almost turned into a dormitory village, with jobs and occupations predominantly being found outside the village, some as far away as London.

Some English villages had in the past sent their sons away to find their fortune in the colonies where they prospered and even named settlements after themselves. Whether life in Silsoe was too comfortable for many to leave, with Wrest Park providing much of the work and succour for the poor, is arguable, but only one other 'Silsoe' settlement has been found, a station[2] near Longreach in Queensland, Australia of a mere 6.5 million hectares, about half the size of England!

---

[2] In Australia a station generally means a large farm which in Queensland could be many thousands of acres.

When he died there in 1884 aged 56, Daniel Williams owned the property and he left it to his brother David Lewis Williams, who passed away only 2 months after Daniel. Both Daniel and David were born and raised in Luton which may have had an influence on naming the station. No direct connection with Silsoe has been found with them or their parents, John and Caroline Williams. Caroline was born in London while John was a builder based in Luton, although probably originally from Wales, who owned a great deal of property in Bedfordshire.

The Parish Boundary

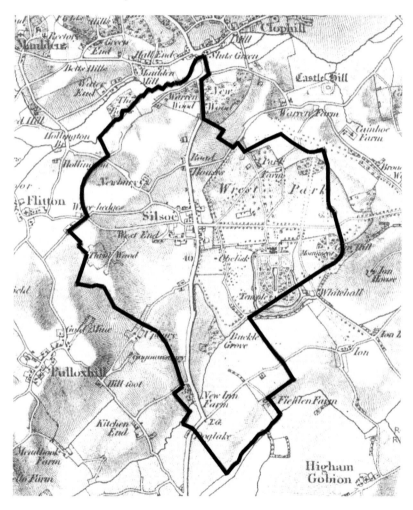

Plate 1/1 - Old Silsoe Parish Boundary on 1860 OS Base map

The area which is the subject of this book relates primarily to what lies within the current parish boundary but, as no man is an island, neither is a parish.

People travelled across the boundary then, for work as they do now, and a farm or manor's land holdings frequently straddled the boundary.

There is a good example in Silsoe where a detailed plan of 1801 has the parish boundary between this village and Barton, running through Fielden House. This house, originally of 17th century origin[3], must therefore have been built on the boundary, which must consequently have been there before the house was built.

In some parishes the boundaries have been found through archaeology following territorial boundaries dating back to the late Bronze Age, some 3000 years ago[4]. Those boundaries were respected during the Roman period and have descended unchanged to this day. Thus, it may well be that where in Silsoe the current boundary makes turns for no apparent reason, or cross through the middle of a field where there is now no hedge, nor even one on the 18th century plans, that it is following a very ancient line. The boundary north of the site of the old Manor of Upbury also seem to follow no obvious line as, from north of Sand Land through to Thrift Wood, it runs across the centre of fields far away from any existing hedge line.

As both Newbury Manor and what became Wrest are said to be in Silsoe at the time of the great survey of 1086, the implication is that the parish of Flitton-cum-Silsoe had become established well before then. No other manor is said to be in Silsoe at that time, and so the other manors described below must have been created after that time.

Unfortunately there seems to be no record of any local tradition of *'beating the boundary'* in Silsoe as there is elsewhere; where villagers led by the Vicar, walked the whole length of the boundary on Rogation Day, and where in some cases the young of the village were ceremonially bumped on the markers, to establish in their minds, its location!

The boundary described below is taken from a description of the hamlet of Silsoe in a document of 1845, at the time when the parish was being separated from the 'Flitton-cum-Silsoe' parish. It is interesting to note that there were then several obvious boundary markers which have no doubt by now disappeared:-

This boundary commences at Clophill Bridge situate at the most northern extremity of the said Hamlet and proceeds from thence in a southwardly direction along the Clophill & Silsoe road about a quarter of a mile to a certain boundary mark[1] at the Warren Wood, thence eastwardly across that Wood to a boundary mark in the Hedge at Herring (otherwise Heron) pond field and Young's field, thence southwardly along the fence of the said Wood about two chains, thence eastwardly to the north west corner of Young's

---

[3] Date from schedule prepared when the building became a Listed Building. Schedules with MBDC.
[4] British Archaeology, Issue 49, 1999

Field, thence southwardly, eastwardly and northwardly to the north west corner of Wrest Park, thence proceeding eastwardly and north eastwardly to a boundary mark in Bean Close, thence northwardly to the south-western corner of Park Field[2], thence southeastwardly to the north side of Cain Hill thence southwardly past the south side of the Pavilion to the north corner of Fielding Meadow[3] thence eastwardly through a spinney across the road leading from Fielding to Gravenhurst and proceeding in the same direction to the north west corner of Little Field thence southwardly and eastwardly to and thro' a certain Farm House of Thomas Flint Field Esq. called Fielding Farm House in his own occupation to a brook which divided the hamlet of Silsoe aforesaid from the parish of Higham Gobion thence in a southwestwardly direction along the said brook to the south corner of Old Balky Ground thence in a westerly direction to the Turnpike Road leading from Silsoe to Barton thence northwardly for a short distance and then westwardly across the said road to a certain boundary mark in Blundell's Close near a Brook thence northwardly to New Inn Farm from which it proceeds in a westerly direction to the north side of Upbury Farm at a boundary mark in a close known by the name of Greens Close [4] thence westerly across Warden Hills and Clay field to a point in Low Croft hedge thence northwestwardly to the south east corner of the Thrift Wood[5] from thence westwardly to the road leading from Shefford to Dunstable at a certain boundary mark thence northwestwardly to Ward Hedges[6] thence northwardly to Beaumont's tree situate at the side of the road leading from Silsoe to Ampthill and thence westwardly to a certain brook dividing the parishes of Flitton cum Silsoe and Maulden to Clophill Bridge first started from. [5]

Comments

[1] Mark probably obliterated by the Silsoe bypass works which was opened in early 1981.

[2] The boundary has since been changed so as to run along the Shefford – Dunstable and then the Clophill – Gravenhurst roads up to Cainhoe Manor.

[3] The boundary here runs in a straight line from Cain Hill through the Wrest Park gardens and the Pavilion to a point on the brook. There must have been a good reason for an ancient boundary to be that straight, especially as in this location there is a stream which could have been used as a boundary for at least half of the distance.

[4] This close appears on a map of 1768 but even then, the parish boundary did not follow any obvious field boundaries between the A6 and Thrift Wood apart from a field division shown on the 1718 map in Kitchin Field around New Inn Farm which the parish boundary appears to have followed.

[5] There have been subsequent boundary changes around Thrift Wood presumably to follow new field edges.

[6] At Ward Hedges the boundary then followed a track between the houses and the Jolly Cooper which remains today only as a hedge line.

---

[5] BLARS L27/54

Since then there have been minor boundary changes at Wardhedges and a larger one near Warren Farm taking the boundary out to the Shefford and Gravenhurst Roads, but broadly speaking the boundary today is the same as it was in 1845.

The area of the parish used in the 2001 census calculations totals 927 Hectares, or 2290 acres, whereas the 1890 *Bedfordshire Directory* had the area at 2063 acres.

The Appearance of the parish

Topography

Silsoe is situated on a low ridge between the valley to the north created by the River Flit, and the clay vale to the north which abuts the chalk hills of the Chiltern escarpment. The centre of the village is approximately 212 ft (64.6m) above sea level, but the land rises in the west to the highest point in the parish at Thrift Wood where the top is 307 ft (93.6m) above sea level. Conversely the lowest level appears to be an almost equal match between the most northerly part of the parish at the A6, with 171ft (52.1)[6] or the land at the south of the Wrest Park Estate by the New Inn stream where a level of 164 ft (51m) is shown at the eastern corner of Buckle Grove.[7]

Hydrology

The River Flit, which forms part of the northern boundary to the parish, has its main sources at Chalton, north of Luton and to the west of Steppingley. From Flitwick through to Clophill its valley is flat, and several peat moors have been formed in the past. It is not very wide on the boundary, being about 4 metres, but there is a reasonable fall on this stretch, and mills at Maulden, Clophill and Cainhoe have been recorded.

A spring arises in the small valley mid-way between Newbury Farm and Wardhedges which was historically called Edmunds Well. This fed the fish ponds and moats at Newbury Manor, and since 2006 runs into a new fish pond or nature reserve near the source. After Newbury it continues eastwards passing behind the houses of Newbury Lane, before crossing the A6 to run on the south edge of Warren Wood eventually joining the Flit, south east of Clophill

The lakes and water systems of Wrest Park are fed by the stream that flows in a culvert under West End Road and which originates in several field ditches to the east of Thrift Wood. No obvious spring heads can be found and it does tend to dry out in the summer. The water passes under the A6 before joining the Old Park water on the west side of Wrest Park.

---

[6] OS first edition circa 1834 1" = 1 mile
[7] OS map Explorer 193 1:25000 scale

It is quite likely that Wrest Park itself is the location of a spring as it is situated in a low valley which rises to the north east. The spring is currently thought to have been near the bath house south west of the present mansion. An account book of 1701-1705 refers to " … making a place to lay the pipes from the canal in the chapel garden to the millpond …" suggesting a mill local to the old Wrest Park house[8]. The water system in the park joining the various lakes is complex, and even now the full details of this are being investigated with the taking over of the park by English Heritage. From the park, the water outfalls into a stream at Whitehall before continuing between Gravenhurst and Shillington, to join the Flit at Shefford.

Entering the parish at New Inn another stream, called variously New Inn Brook (1826), Kitchin Brook, Southillford Brook or Fielden Meadow Brook, runs alongside Buckle Grove before joining the previous stream at Whitehall. Its source appears to be in the hills to the south east of Harlington.

Finally there is another brook which before 1778 was called variously Fielden Brook or Fann Brook, but is now Barton Brook, and which forms part of the parish boundary between Silsoe and Barton, south of Fielden House. It originates in springs at the foot of the Sharpenhoe Clappers. The name Fann is very old, in 1439 it was also called "le Fannebroke,"[9] and the name probably derives from 'fen' indicating how wet this area used to be. This is emphasised in a 1597 document where a 'Fanne Brook alias Barton Brook cawseye" or causeway is mentioned[10].

In 1806 a treatise on mineral waters in the area was written which recorded that:-

"… several springs are known to be impregnated with various minerals, but none of them have acquired much celebrity. The ingenious Dr. Yeats, physician to the Infirmary at Bedford, who has bestowed considerable attention to this subject, has favoured us with a list of the places where mineral springs have been pointed out to him, and the result of his analysis of a few of them. The springs enumerated are at …… Silsoe (at a farm called New Inn); …… and the spring which supplies the cold bath in Wrest-gardens. Dr. Yeats has analysed the water from Clapham, Wrest-gardens, Bromham, Oakley, and Turvey. "The two first evidently contain iron. In the Wrest-garden water, iron appears to be held in solution by the carbonic acid; in the Clapham water, by the vitriolic acid forming the ferrum vitriolatum. They both of them contain also the sulphate and muriat of lime, as likewise the sulphate of magnesia, or Epsom salts.".[11]

---

[8] BLARS L31/289

[9] BLARS L Jeayes756

[10] BLARS CRT 130 Sils 34

[11] Extracts from Lysons' Magna Britannia being a concise topographical account of several counties of Great Britain by the Rev. Daniel Lysons, A.M., F.R.S. F.A. and L.S. Rector of Rodmarton in Gloucestershire and Samuel Lysons, Esq., F.R.S. and F.A.S. Keeper of His Majesty's Records in the Tower of London, 1806.

As far as is known, no one was entrepreneurial enough to bottle the water for sale as was done at Flitwick Moor.

Wells

Water is of course essential, and with Silsoe being sited on a hill, it is fortunate in that wells could be sunk to a reasonable depth to find such a valuable resource.

As mentioned elsewhere, there was a well at the spring head in the valley opposite Newbury, which probably supplied the manor and the associated housing there. The old mansion at Wrest Park also had an internal well, and other large houses would also have had a pump in the scullery or kitchen. In the account books, there are several references to work on the spring such as "2 millwrights laying the great pipe to the spring, ramming it down, & stopping the water" so there was probably one near the old house.

By the time we get to the early 20th century, wells are still important enough to need mention in the sale documents of the Wrest Park Estate break-up. Several times, access to wells in other peoples property is guaranteed, such as when Mrs A Mann bought a house behind The Alma, she was guaranteed access to the well across the road in Mr Case's garden, at No 10 West End Road.

Also, the Ordnance Survey map for 1901 helpfully shows a great number of wells and pumps, and probably some of the larger houses had a pumped supply from a well in the scullery. The exterior wells and pump locations culled from plans and sale documents, are shown on Plate 1/2. There are no doubt many others, but they remain unrecorded.

The Bedfordshire Historical Records Society in its Wells Survey of 1933, said that the public draw well in Silsoe stood recessed alongside the main road in the village. There is no obvious location or evidence that remains today of this, but there was a well, or pump, situated between numbers 30 & 32 in the front garden which on maps dated to the turn of the 19th century is seen to be in a small enclosure with access off the road and this may well be it. An alternative may be the well between the Star and Garter and the churchyard which is easily accessible off the High Street.

Plate 1/2 - Locations of Pumps and Wells

In the same decade that the public pump was noted, piped water came at last to Silsoe, so that every house could have a safe water supply. In fact in 1937, only 34 of the 120 parishes in Bedfordshire had running water, making Silsoe one of the first.

Geology

Broadly speaking, the geological strata under the parish dip about 5 degrees to the south. Thus the chalk hills which are exposed at Barton lie on top of the gault clay, which in itself lies on top of the lower sandstone, which is exposed in the Maulden Hills and in the old quarry at Silsoe.

To the south of the parish the gault clay, which forms the low areas, was created during the Lower Cretaceous period about 100 million years ago. When freshly quarried, the clay appears to contain no fossils, but as it weathers a diverse and rich fauna is slowly revealed. The fossils of the gault clay include many of the groups familiar in the Jurassic period. Ammonites are still common but some have now started to grow straight shells. The gault clay also contains layers of small phosphatic nodules which were formed during times when sediment deposition was slow. The clay has been used for the manufacture of bricks, pipes and tiles.

The Silsoe ridge itself is sandy, as witnessed by the old quarry at its centre now occupied by 'The Maples', and has been separated from the main lower Greensand strata to the north by the erosion of the Flit. The sands were formed at the bottom of a shallow sea during the Lower Cretaceous period 120 million years ago, and although the sands are poor in fossils they do contain signs of formed life, through disturbances caused by the digging and burrowing of marine organisms. The sands also show cross bedding formed by the flow of water in the ancient sea.

The quarry in the village is found on all maps from 1718 onwards, but was probably used for building stone many years before that. Most stone for Wrest, other stone buildings and the stone walls came from that source, and it is said that St John's at Moggerhanger was part-built of that stone, in 1860.
[12]

Just to the north, between Cainhoe and Clophill in the Flit Valley, have been found beds of fullers earth which are the product of ash from a volcanic explosion. This was used originally for cleaning or 'fulling' woollen cloth. During the 20th century, the uses of fullers earth expanded, with the most important applications being a bonding agent for foundry sands, in civil engineering, and as oil well drilling fluids, for pet litter, water stable carriers for pesticide and herbicides, for refining edible oil and fats, the manufacture of carbonless copy paper and as a fibre and filler retention aid in papermaking. The accessible earth has now been extracted with the resulting holes being allowed to fill with water to create lakes.

The soil in and around Silsoe varies and it was this mix of soil types that was one of the influences in the establishment of agricultural research organisations here. The central ridge overlying the sandstone gives rise to a lighter sandy soil, while to the north and south of this ridge there are clay based soils of varying types.

Landscape

While Bedfordshire is not, generally, a well wooded county, Silsoe has a pleasant rural feel to it, due to the remaining woods and hedging. The area would have been much more wooded in the past, a 13th century document[13] speaks of new "assarts" and "inlonds", areas cleared of trees, between Wrest and Silsoe Chapel and other areas and in addition, when the Wrest estate was broken up early in the 20th century, the area allotted for parkland was reduced and many trees felled, while at Fielden, the farm was bought for its timber, which was then removed and the farm sold on.

Entering the village from the north, the A6 climbs to pass between Simpsonhill Plantation in the west, and Warren Wood at the east, after which

---

[12] The Gentleman's Magazine, 1861
[13] BLARS L Jeayes 652

the village and its church can be seen between the trees to the south west, and the fields of Home Farm to the east.

To the east, Home Farm, the largest farm in the parish, runs a dairy herd and there are consequently many acres of pasture land surrounding the farm, with fields of varying size. The remainder of the land in this area of the parish is arable although a certain amount of market gardening takes place in the north west of the parish.

The land from Simpsonhill towards Flitton is fairly undulating and open, while west of the Maulden/Ampthill Road the fields in the small valley have recently been re-fenced and hedged to provide paddocks for horses. In addition, the old pond adjacent to the old well has been enlarged to form a small environmental area. The road to Wardhedges, The Avenue, was once lined with elms, but when the elm bark beetle arrived in the second half of the 20th century, the elms were cut down. The wide verge has been allowed to scrub up with saplings, and additional planting has been put in; all of which contributes to form an attractive wooded approach to the village from the west, and which will eventually reinstate the avenue aspect.

Thrift Wood set on the highest point, of the parish dominates the west of the parish. From the permissive footpath on its eastern side, there is an open view eastwards from which the village can be seen, with the poplar plantation on the western side of the old Cranfield University site, providing a useful screen. Looking southwards towards the Upbury Manor site there are many good hedges surrounding fields, where some individual tree planting has taken place.

From this view point the specimen trees surrounding and within Wrest Park, once the seat of the Earls of Kent can be seen in the distance. The French style Wrest Park house together with its 380 hectare landscaped park and garden buildings, is the most important feature of the parish. It also includes most of the open water in the parish with its ornamental ponds and lakes. The whole park and house is now managed by English Heritage, and there is a possibility that the landscaping may be extended into its old park area, and north of the house, to replicate an earlier layout.

Unfortunately some of the buildings associated with the now departed Silsoe Research Institute at Wrest, which were permitted to be built to the north-west of the mansion are of a design which does not reflect that of the mansion and its stables, and these detract from the general attractiveness of the open country thereabouts.

South of the village and between the eastern side of the A6 and Wrest Park, lies Buckle Grove, an ancient woodland which together with planting within and to the southern boundary of the park gives a heavily wooded aspect from the Portway, and the Gravenhurst road.

South of the Park and Buckle Grove up to the boundary with Barton le Clay and Gravenhurst, lie the flat fields of Fielden through which runs the road from the A6 to Gravenhurst. There is little hedging, apart from alongside the road and around Fielden House and farm, and the feel is very different from the rest of the parish.

The Environment

Before the 19th century not much interest was taken in the abstract concept of recording wildlife by observation, and any records that do occur relate mainly to collecting – by using a gun. Most ordinary people were more concerned with where the next meal was coming from, and those who did have more leisure time had other areas of interest, or just wanted to shoot whatever moved and remove any wild plants that were not productive.

However, this mindset slowly began to change and there were some who began to observe and write down what was seen; and there are individual observations of plants or animals from an early age and also from the 16th century; at which time there would have been considerably more to see of both plants and animals. More land would have been pasture right up until the Second World War with fertilising carried out only using natural manure and until the 20th century none or little spraying would have been carried out.

LUTON ROAD SILSOE (from the Church)

**Plate 1/3 – View South from the Church early in the 20th century.
Note the large number of trees.**

No general or specific records of the environment of the parish have been found, but some indications as to the environmental richness at the turn of the 19th century can be found in the photographs taken from the church tower, early in the 20th century which, show mature trees growing throughout the village and especially in the park. At that time, Wrest Park truly was a park and much larger than it is today. Maps from the turn of the century show trees planted throughout the area enclosed by the stone walls, both north and west of the mansion with small copses also being abundant. It would have been similar to Woburn Park as that is today, with deer wandering about, isolated specimen trees and large flocks of birds flying from tree to tree, or foraging in the cropped turf.

West of the village the scene would have appeared similar to today's landscape, but there were more copses along boundaries or at field corners; and hedges would have been more extensive. The woods at the north of the parish and adjacent to the southern end of Wrest Park, have probably not changed, although they may then have had more mature trees in them.

Flora

There were only isolated records of flora in the County until the 18th and 19th centuries, when people with a more profound interest in the plants of the fields and woods emerged. Locally the most notable of those recording their natural surroundings, was William Crouch who lived at Cainhoe Manor, and both he and his brother James Frederick, became clergymen while retaining an interest in botany throughout their lives. As William had a living at Lidlington Church and resided at Cainhoe, he could indulge in his hobby when riding between those places.

Then, in the latter half of the 20th century, John Dony increased our knowledge of the local flora considerably writing both the *Flora of Bedfordshire* and the *Flora of Hertfordshire*[14]. He not only collated records of species and produced his own surveys, but in his book on Bedfordshire he carried out Habitat Studies of selected locations in the county, three of which were in Silsoe, namely Thrift Wood, Simpsonhill Plantation and the roadside near Clophill. He also listed individual records of plants found in the parish, but which he found outside the study locations.

So for example, we know that in 1950 at Simpsonhill, when he carried out his surveys, there was short turf grazed by rabbits (descendants of the original warren?), at the intersection of two wide paths in the sweet chestnut plantation, which has now disappeared through the quarrying operations. At that point he recorded 31 species, of which 14 were rare, and which included the Mouse Ear Chickweed, the Lesser Yellow Trefoil and the Yorkshire Fog Grass.

The other two Habitat Studies similarly produced records of plants at those locations and his book has also many references to specimens of plants and fungi recorded in the parish, none unfortunately, being of great rarity.
Currently, in 2008, there are eight County Wildlife Sites (CWS) which are in, or contiguous with the parish.[15] From the south the first to be found is Buckle Grove CWS, which is important as part of a damp 'ancient woodland'

---

[14] John G Dony; Flora of Bedfordshire; 1953, Rep 1978; EP Publishing

containing ash trees, coppiced hazel and many other plants, including wild garlic.

Wrest Park grounds are also similarly designated, as they contain a great variety of habitats on gault clay together with many ponds and lakes. The grassland contains many herbs such as ox eye daisy and cowslips.

Part of Thrift Wood is also an ancient wood, and contains species indicating this, such as field maple, hawthorn, hornbeam, yew, hazel and bluebells. There is also a thriving rookery, and badgers have been seen there.

Silsoe pit, the depression evident in the fields behind what was the Lord Nelson and the Clophill Road, contained some ponds but also is a good example of neutral grassland. There is a rabbit population and buzzards have been seen sitting on posts nearby, keeping an eye on their next dinner.

At Warren Wood there was a roadside nature reserve due to the appearance there of mouse eared chickweed plus other plants which like the neutral/acid soil on the Greensand Ridge. The site does need more intensive maintenance however, to preserve the interesting flora, as there is a lack of appropriate maintenance.

Simpsonhill Plantation which contains the sand quarry is also listed as an ancient woodland, and is dominated by sweet chestnut coppice. The wood probably developed from adjacent copses when it ceased to be a warren for Newbury Manor and, as the soil was poor, it could not be used for farming. Warren Wood on the opposite side of the A6 is also of a similar nature, but contains more variety of species.

Right on the northern boundary of the parish runs the River Flit and this and its associated wet areas are an important natural feature of Mid-Bedfordshire, with many moisture loving species and animals living along its banks.

Fauna

Before records were kept of animals or birds, there are only a few ways by which we can find what wildlife was around before the advent of industrial farming. One of these is the way that names of animals were allocated to places or fields. Thus, a 1562 lease of much of Upbury has a field called Storkesnest Slade which was near Storkesnest Furlong, probably an indication that storks once nested there.

Jannion Steele-Elliott, a native of Bedford, was the first major figure to study the fauna of Bedfordshire and intended to write a book on the subject. He unfortunately only completed the section on birds,[16] but this does provide an indication of the richness of the environment at the end of the 19th century

---

[15] For more details of the County Wildlife Sites contact The Wildlife Trust, Priory Country Park Visitor Centre, Barkers Lane, Bedford, MK41 9SH.

and interestingly from our point of view, there are several references to Silsoe.

The following incorporates his remarks but is only a brief comment on the birds of Silsoe. Many others species have been seen but no comprehensive 'bird list' for the parish is believed to exist.

The Red Kite is making a comeback in the England as a result of less persecution and introduction, but it is recorded that one of the last pairs that nested in the county built in Silsoe woods; typically for that period, both the old birds were destroyed. Another bird of prey, the honey buzzard, was provided to a taxidermist for stuffing in 1870, having been taken alive at Silsoe. (Hopefully it had died by the time it was stuffed.)

Reports of barn owls sightings are still made, mainly at the Fielden end of the village, and they also used to nest in Wrest Park. Steele-Elliott records that they inhabited parks such as Wrest, especially if protection was offered.

The tawny owl is still in the area and until its tree blew down in 2006, a family nested in a large poplar tree on the east side of the verge opposite the Waterslade allotments. They were evidently less common than barn owls in the 19th century.

Nightingales were 'very common' according to Steele-Elliott and occasionally they still set up here in the spring. A few years ago, two males were heard singing in Buckle Grove in the spring. Wheatears are occasionally seen early in the spring, flitting from stump to stump or clod to clod, and one winter several hundred golden plover were having a stopover in the Old Park area of Wrest.

We treasure skylarks for their song, and there are still a good number around the fields west of West End Farm or in Wrest Park. However, in the 19th century they were so abundant that they were taken as food and it was estimated that 48,000 were taken annually at Dunstable Downs.

Surprisingly, ravens were not uncommon at that time, but Steele-Elliott says that there was a superstitious awe in killing these birds, and sometimes even when instructed by the gamekeeper, no one would kill them. A pair nested in Silsoe park every year in the elms on top of Cain Hill but the young were frequently taken by the servants and sold in London – perhaps our birds are the ancestors of the Tower of London ravens.

One of the pleasures of Silsoe is the numbers of jackdaws that still frequent the village, no doubt upsetting some through their habit of nesting in chimney pots. If we still had the mature trees around they would probably prefer those, as they did earlier at Wrest.

---

[16] "The Vertebrate Fauna of Bedfordshire", J Steele-Elliott, 1897-1901, Repr 1993 Beds Natural History Society

Great spotted woodpeckers still visit the village trees and occasionally the green woodpecker; but in Steele-Elliott's days the green was more common, he says that in Silsoe it was known as the "Whetile".

To be confidant of seeing a wryneck nowadays you need to go to Mallorca but they were common here, as were many other species that have unfortunately declined in numbers due to a lack of food, or suitable habitat. Thus if a nuthatch is seen it is likely to be in Wrest Park due to the trees; they were there in the 19th century.

Nightjars prefer sandy heaths with scattered trees, and they used to frequent Maulden Woods in the 1980's before the plantations grew up. It is probable that they used the warren areas of Silsoe or Clophill at Warren Wood or Simpsonhill Plantation in the past, as they were said to be relatively frequent.

Finally the pheasant is still reared for game here and it is recorded that Silsoe had a reputation for providing very large bags during the season.

Of the non-feathered fauna, it is quite common to see muntjac deer in the fields in the early morning; and hares, of which I counted some 10 together at the east end of Wrest Park Drive one morning some years ago. foxes are also common and we find Lady Amabel de Grey of Wrest discussing both foxhunting and hares in the [17]1770's when in December 1774, due to the snow, they had been unable to go foxhunting, and in 1775 she said that her husband "is too good a friend to the Sport, to destroy the Enemies of his Poultry-Yard by any other way than the fair War of Hunting". It seems from another letter that Wrest Park had its own kennels for foxhounds and there is a view of them in Earl de Grey's sketchbook.

Grey squirrels still abound in the gardens of the village and, of course, the occasional rat and house mouse can be found, with hedgehogs seen in gardens and, unfortunately, flattened on the roads.

With the availability of nesting and roosting sites both in trees and buildings in Wrest Park and elsewhere, bats are also often seen around the mansion and the village.

The draining of the Wrest Park canals for dredging in 2007 exposed many dozens of huge fresh water mussels, probably swan mussels, and it is known that there is a good selection of fresh water fish in the lakes there.

---

[17] BLARS L30/13/12/30 etc

Chapter 2 - The Early History of Silsoe until the 17th century

In the beginning

Some 10,000 years ago the ice age had ended, the ice sheets had left Britain and vegetation such as birch trees, willow and aspen spread northwards from the continent. With the plants came animals such as deer, wild boar and aurochs (the wild ox) and of course these were preyed on by carnivores such as wolves, bear and others.

Following the retreating ice, Mesolithic men crossed what is now the North Sea to hunt with flint tipped arrows and spears, and supplemented their fare with nuts & berries. The climate improved over several centuries so that the temperatures were not that different from today's and this encouraged forest of oak and hazel to develop.

Some time around then, a group of these men camped on the south bank of the River Flit, on the sandy prominence of what is now, Warren Wood. They may have walked there or possibly used a dugout canoe, similar to one found further away in the River Lea; but once there they prepared some flint tools. Flint pieces from this work were found during sand quarrying operations there and they, together with flint objects found in the subsoil of Red Field during preparatory work for a research project in 2005, provide the earliest indication of human activity in the parish.

No doubt they soon moved on to find more food, but later the nomadic lifestyle slowed down when it was found that some animals could be tamed and bred, and crops could be planted and harvested. So small farms developed by clearing the forest in areas where the soil could be easily turned, near water, and where some form of defence against marauders and wild animals could be erected.

Farming had virtually replaced hunter-gathering by the Neolithic Age, the period between 4000 to 2000 BC. It is reasonable to suppose that farming settlement took place at Silsoe, as a late Neolithic/early Bronze Age flint arrowhead was found in an archaeological trench excavated on the north-west corner of the Church, for the new toilet facilities in 1984.

However, communities were probably still fairly mobile, so permanent settlement may not have taken place for some time, and even if early farming took place in Silsoe, most evidence has probably been destroyed by the development of the village, in the ensuing centuries.

It seems likely that the Flit Valley south of the sand hills to the north of Silsoe, would have been very wet and boggy, and would have created a barrier to north–south movement except perhaps opposite Clophill, where there is a narrowing of the Valley. With an east–west route along the top of the chalk hills just to the south of Barton, Silsoe could have been a backwater, which may account for the lack of evidence of strong occupation, both at this time and later.

However, there have been many finds on the Chiltern Hills just to the south, with domestic sites also having been seen. There are also some associated flints found at Ruxox near to Flitwick. In addition there was at Leagrave, a large Neolithic henge, Walluds Bank, and there are also concentrations of Neolithic finds at Fenlake near Bedford; so a route between the two may have been established at that early date.

The Neolithic Age segues into the Bronze Age with the probable invasion from the continent, of people of who are called the Beaker folk, due to the inclusion in burials of a particular type of pottery. That the Bronze Age did not completely pass Silsoe by, is shown by the discovery in 2005 of a well preserved barbed and tanged arrowhead, together with a thumbnail scraper in Red Field, which were suggested to be of the early Bronze Age.

In addition, a bronze axe has been found in the village, (although it is not known where), of a type known as "Palstave" which would date from perhaps 1200 BC. According to the *Bedfordshire Archaeological Journal* it was lent to the Luton Museum who subsequently mislaid it!

After the Bronze Age, and leading into the Roman occupation, came the Iron Age with the most spectacular nearest evidence being the hill top forts, notably at Ravensburgh above Hexton, with another further away at Maiden Bower, Dunstable. It is probable that most of the population lived in small farming centres or hamlets, and only retreated to the forts in times of trouble and invasion. Evidence of their farming occupation would be small, as they lived in wooden shelters, but a series of linear ditches and a possible oven or kiln feature uncovered in Red Field, together with a few pot sherds, have been tentatively dated to the Iron Age or Saxon periods.

The Romans

After the imposition of their civilisation on the country, and suppressed rebellions, the Roman way of life proved attractive to the local population. Their standards of living improved by emulating their conquerors in ways such as housing and farming, and of course by using their roads, in addition to the many earlier trackways, which already criss-crossed the country.

A stater (coin) of Cunobelinus, British King of most of the south east of England, was found in 1863, possibly in the Wardhedges/Newbury Farm area. Cunobelinus's capital was Colchester (Camulodunum) and during the first half of the 1st century his tribe traded with the Romans for some time. He is thought to have died around 40 - 43 AD and was the subject of the Shakespeare play "Cymbeline".

So what did the Romans do for Silsoe? While they ruled the country for 300 - 400 years little evidence of them has been found within the parish area, and there is no sign of a typical Roman road nearby.[18] A fragment of a Roman roof tile was found in a field near to the Wrest Park cricket pitch, which implies some form of building nearby, whether farm house or other. In addition a Roman cremation urn was also found in the village, but unfortunately no location has been given for the find. This does however imply occupation somewhere, so there may have been a small villa nearby.

The nearest major area associated with the Romans is Ruxox some 2 miles to the west. The name Ruxox derives from Hroc's Oak; Hroc being the Saxon word for farmer. Flints have been found at the site that date from the Neolithic Period and earlier, and Belgic (Bronze Age) burial urns have also been found there. The earthworks at the present day farm may date from the Iron Age; but a great deal of evidence has been found there in archaeological digs of the Roman occupation, for a temple or a villa in the area.

Further proof of Roman occupation has also been found 2 miles to the east of Silsoe at Gravenhurst, where early Roman pottery and ashes were found in a ditch when a drainage trench was being dug.[19]

Also, there is a suggestion that some constructional sandstone in the Roman remains at Godmanchester, originated from quarries in Silsoe but evidence for this theory has not been proven.

The Saxons

Towards the end of the Roman occupation, the menace from the Saxons led to forts being constructed along the eastern and southern coasts of England. Then by the end of the 4th century the numbers of raids had increased such, that by the early 5th century, with the Roman strength gone, incursions into the East Midlands took place. The news of the new invaders would have spread quickly, leading to great fear amongst the residents of this area, but this was only the start of a series of invasions from the east!

In the 440's there was a permanent settlement by the Saxons in the Cambridge area, where the Roman villas had been destroyed and the towns emptied. Although at this distance the situation is not completely understood, it seems likely that the invaders slowly spread westwards along the Icknield Way and the Ouse Valley, fighting the British as they went.

Some parallel trenches found in excavations for work at the church, and associated with a possible early/middle Saxon boundary ditch, would indicate

---

[18] A group known as 'The Viatores' suggested that the straight road from Clophill towards Shefford may have been Roman but this has been proved to be an enclosure road of the 19th century.
[19] *Survey of Bedfordshire, The Roman Period*, Angela Simco, 1984.

settlement here at that time; although it is not possible to say who excavated them.

Other excavations north of West End Road and west of West End Farm found pits, a large sherd of sandstone tempered pottery and chewed bones which have been tentatively dated to the early/mid Saxon period, 450-850, and even though it may have been only a temporary settlement, it is the only evidence of this period.

Then in 493 a chieftain named Arthur, who subsequently became mythologised as King Arthur, beat the invaders at Badon Hill and for about 50 years the country was relatively peaceful.

However the pressure from the Saxons was relentless, and a new wave of invasions took place with the *Anglo Saxon Chronicle*[20] recording that "571 In this year Cuthwulf fought against the Britons (Bretwalas) at Biedcanford[21] and took four towns: Lygeanburh (now identified as Limbury), Aylesbury, Bensington (now Benson, Oxfordshire) and Eynsham, and in the same year he died." With fighting taking place at Limbury perhaps the early Silsonians became involved, either by supplying fighting men to help to resist the invaders, but then having to escape westwards with other Britons after the defeat, leaving the land to the Saxons.

The Tribal Hidage, an 8th century document gives a list of tribes with their lands[22] and this allocated to the 'Hicca' tribe in the Ivel Valley 300 hides, (approximately 56 square miles). Given that the Flit is a major tributary to the Ivel, and the better cultivatable soils between the two river systems, it is possible that Silsoe was within the 'Hicca' area.

From 731, until the consolidation of the country under Offa, there was an even more unstable time with regional Kings rising and falling. Offa died in 796, and was allegedly buried at Bedford, at which time his kingdom stretched from the Humber through to Kent in the south and from the North Sea, to his dyke in the west.

Then, towards the end of his reign, with other countries being more able to resist the Vikings, England became the obvious country to attack. Hence the Vikings, Danes and Norwegians, started raiding the country from which they took their booty and slaves back home. These raids increased until when in 850, they wintered in Kent.

---

[20] At present there are nine known versions or fragments of the "*Anglo-Saxon Chronicle*" in existence, all of which vary (sometimes greatly) in content and quality. They can be found at Corpus Christi Cambridge, The British Museum and The Bodleian.
[21] While 'Bedcanford' sounds like the present day Bedford, studies of name changes from this period suggest that it is not the same place
[22] *Tribal Hidage, "De numero hidarum Anglie in Britannia"*. British Library

The Danes

Fifteen years later, a great army landed in East Anglia, and using the Icknield Way and the Ouse valley spread westwards, no doubt terrorising the inhabitants of Silsoe. They initially concentrated their forces at Thetford, and then marched westwards down the Icknield Way reaching Reading in 870, passing close to Silsoe en route. Numerous incursions with battles between the existing inhabitants and the invaders took place but eventually Alfred, the most well known of a line of West Saxon Kings, was able to control them and around 878 he beat the Danes, who were led by Guthrum, decisively at Edington on Salisbury Plain.

Some eight years after that battle the Treaty of Wedmore was negotiated between King Alfred and Guthrum which was intended to lead to peace between the English nation, the Angles and Saxons, and the Danes. The first clause was intended to settle the boundary between them, and it defined the southern part as being "up the Thames, and then up the Lea and along the Lea to its source, then straight to Bedford, and then up the Ouse to Watling Street."[23] The "Danelaw", or land of the Danes, was to the east of this line and Arthur's kingdom to the west.

Plotting a straight line on a map from the source of the River Lea to Bedford, it would seem that Silsoe would lie at about 2.5km/1.5m to the East of this line, and thus within the Danelaw. However, it is unlikely that such a direct line would have been surveyed at that time, and the boundary would have utilised roads or have been between significant hills, or along natural or artificial lines. The boundary would have been near Silsoe and there is a field in Ion, just to the east of Fielden which has a Danish derived name 'The Holmes', meaning a damp meadow, which suggests that the Danes settled there[24].

Again this relatively peaceful situation did not last long, and in 893 the Danes from East Anglia, Northumberland and from Essex invaded westwards across the boundary, only to be defeated again by Alfred. The first two groups of these invaders may well have crossed from the Danelaw through the Silsoe area, to join with their army from Essex, near Oxford.

There followed in the next 150 years, further struggles between the Anglo-Saxon Kings and the Danes/Vikings although occasionally the relationship between the invaders and the local Danes was so strong, that the latter would not fight. With all the various invasions and internal battles for control listed above, this period would have been a dangerous time to have been alive in this area. It does seem unlikely that Silsoe would have been uninhabited however, as the soils were good, there was water around and plenty of trees to construct shelter.

---

[23] R,H. Hodgkin, A History of the Anglo-Saxons, Vol. 2, 3d ed., (Oxford, University Press, 1959) p578
[24] BLARS LJeayes 656, 1273

In some cases, as had been done in the past, the invading Danes were bought off by paying them with money levied through a tax called danegeld. *The Anglo-Saxon Chronicle* in 1006 was dismissive saying: "in spite of it all, the Danish army went about as it pleased". By 1012, 48,000 pounds of silver was being paid in danegeld to Danes camped in London.

In 1013 King Swein of Denmark (with his son Cnut), sailed up the Rivers Humber and Trent to be accepted as King in the Danelaw. King Ethelred the Unready fled to Normandy and by Christmas, all England had submitted to Swein. In 1014, Cnut became the leader of the Danes on his father's death, and eventually King of the whole country, consolidating his claim by marrying Ethelred's widow.

In 1042, Ethelred's son, Edward 'the Confessor', was invited to return from Normandy as King, (despite there being several other possible claimants to the throne). While in 1053 Harold Godwinson acceded to the Earldom of Wessex, to become the second most powerful man after the King. His status increased with a victory over the Welsh in 1063, and he became a strong candidate to become King of England, when Edward died. In 1065 Edward the Confessor became very ill, and Harold claimed that Edward promised him the throne just before he had died on 5th January 1066; even though he had also taken an oath that he would do his best to help William of Normandy, to become King when Edward the Confessor died.

As we know, William was not at all happy with this, and assembled an army to take the throne from Harold. Harold realised this and positioned his troops on the south coast of England to repel the invasion. After sending his men home in September to harvest their crops, some probably to Silsoe, he soon heard that King Harald Hardrada of Norway and his brother Tostig, had entered the Humber with the intentions of conquering England. He quickly re-assembled his army and headed north, and on 25th September routed the Norwegians at Stamford Bridge, killing both Hardrada and Tostig.

While celebrating his victory at a banquet in York on 1st October, Harold heard that William of Normandy had landed at Pevensey Bay and immediately collected together his army; probably most of the men suffering with headaches after celebrating, and marched south. He travelled at such a pace that he had to wait at London for them to catch up.

It seems probable that they travelled down what is now the A1 rather than the A6 line, but no doubt news of their recent success, and the reason for their southerly movement spread across the countryside and reached Silsoe.

The Normans

Harold's forced march from Stamford Bridge immediately after his battle with Hardrada and Tostig, further weakened his army and they were defeated at the Battle of Hastings in 1066 by William the Bastard (renamed the Conqueror after that event).

William was crowned on Christmas Day 1066 in Westminster Abbey, when he promised to uphold existing laws and customs. The Anglo-Saxon Shire Courts and the 'Hundred[25]' Courts (which administered defence and tax, as well as justice matters) remained intact, as did regional variations and private Anglo-Saxon jurisdictions.

However, the Danes were still not happy with William being in control, and there were uprisings in the Welsh Marches, Devon and Cornwall. Then a year later the Danes, in alliance with Prince Edgar the Aetheling, (Ethelred's great-grandson), and other English nobles, invaded the North, and took York.

William returned from France taking personal charge, and marched his army northwards, driving the Danes back to their ships on the Humber. Then, in a harsh campaign lasting into 1070, William systematically devastated Mercia and Northumbria, to deprive the Danes of their supplies and prevent recovery of English resistance. Churches and monasteries were burnt, and agricultural land was laid to waste, creating a famine for the unarmed and mostly peasant population, which lasted at least nine years. It is recorded that Clophill was hit by his army on their way north, with the value of the parish more than halved, and it seems more than likely that Silsoe also suffered, in the same way at that time.

William then proceeded to consolidate his power in the country by building castles. Originally these castles were wooden towers on earthen 'mottes' (mounds) with a bailey (defensive area) surrounded by earth ramparts, but many were later rebuilt in stone. By the end of William's reign over 80 castles had been built throughout his Kingdom, as a permanent reminder of the new Norman feudal order.

The castle at Cainhoe on the northern boundary of Silsoe was one of these fortifications of the motte and bailey type, although it does not appear to have been initially constructed in stone. Any stonework may have been used some time after, to improve the buildings.

The Domesday Book

Some 20 years after the Conquest, and in order to ascertain and confirm the extent of his Conquest, but perhaps more importantly, to see how much tax revenue he could raise, (either to pay off the Danes or fund his army), William commissioned the Domesday Book.

---

[25] A hundred was originally a division of a county which supported 100 families.

Every record in the Great Survey includes, for each settlement in England: its monetary value, any customary dues owed to the crown at the time of the survey, the value of each settlement recorded before Domesday, and their values from before 1066. It also listed lands held by the King and by his tenants, and the resources that went with those lands. It recorded which manors rightfully belonged to which estates, thus ending years of confusion resulting from the gradual and sometimes violent dispossession of the Anglo-Saxons by their Norman conquerors. It was moreover a 'feudal' statement, giving the identities of the tenants-in-chief (landholders) who held their lands directly from the crown, and of their tenants and under tenants.

A comparison of the value of many manors in the Silsoe area before and after the conquest based on the Great Survey, shows that there was a fall in value, with the exception of Silsoe/Wrest. As mentioned above, this may have been due to the result of William's army passing through the region to quell rebellion, and not worrying too much what damage they did, en route.

Habitations in most areas of late 11th century England followed a very ancient pattern of isolated farms, hamlets and tiny villages interspersed with fields, and scattered over most of the cultivable land, and over time settlements gradually shifted or were abandoned or even reclaimed. [26]

The Domesday Book records that in our area the bulk of the land holding was found to be with Nigel d'Aubigny, as the following extracts show:

Clophill (Clopelle)
Nigel of Aubigny
Nigel holds Clophill himself. It answers for 5 hides. Land for 8 ploughs. In lordship 3 hides 2 ploughs there.
5 villagers have 6 ploughs. 5 smallholders and one slave
Meadow for 4 ploughs; woodland, 200 pigs and 12d.
Value 60s; when acquired 30s; before 1066 £8
2 thanes held this manor; they were Earl Tosti's men.
Of these 5 hides , Nigel claims 1 virgate himself which his predecessor held before 1066. Nigel was put in possession himself after he came to the Honour, but Ralph Tallboys dispossessed him.

Cainhoe (Chainehou)
Nigel holds Cainhoe himself. It answers for 4 hides . Land for 6 ploughs .
3 villagers have 2 ploughs. 1 mill at 6s; meadow for 8 ploughs; woodland, 100 pigs and 2s too.
3 smallholders and 5 slaves .
Value 60s; when acquired 30s; before 1066 100s.
Aelric, a thane of King Edward's , held this manor; he could grant and sell without permission.

---

[26] The Domesday Book Online

Silsoe (Siwileffou) (Newbury Manor according to the Victoria County History.)

In Silsoe a concubine of Nigel's holds 2 hides.

Land for 4 ploughs. In lordship 1 plough .2 villagers have 2 ploughs; a third possible. 3 smallholders and 1 slave.

Aelfric Small, a thane of King Edward's held this land.

Pulloxhill (Polochessele)

Roger and Rhiwallon hold Pulloxhill from Nigel of Aubigny.

It answers for 10 hides . Land for 13 ploughs . In lordship 2 ploughs , another 2 possible.

11 villagers have 9 ploughs ; woodland, 100 pigs

Value £10; when acquired £8; before 1066 £13

8 freemen held this manor; they could grant and sell their land to whom they would.

Land of Robert (son of) Fafiton

Flitton (Flictha)

Robert Fafiton holds Flitton for the King. It answers for 5 hides. Land for 6 ploughs. In lordship 2 hides; 2 ploughs there.

3 villagers have 2 ploughs; another 2 possible. 3 smallholders and 4 slaves . Meadow for 6 ploughs; woodland 50 pigs.

In total, value 60s; as much as when acquired; before 1066, 100s.

Alwin Horn, a thane of King Edward's, held this manor.

Silsoe (Sewilessor) Land of Walter brother of Sihere.

(Wrest Manor according to the Victoria County History.)

In Silsoe Hugh holds 4 hides from Walter as one manor.

Land for 10 ploughs. In lordship 2 ploughs .6 villagers; 8 smallholders and 4 slaves with 7 ploughs. An eighth possible.

1 mill at 26d; meadow for 6 ploughs ; woodland, 100 pigs and 2s too.

In total, value £8; when acquired 100s; before 1066 £1

Leonorth, a thane of King Edward's, held this manor. 3 freemen held ½ hide; they could grant and sell to whom they would. Hugh holds this ½ hide from the King as his men state.

Cainhoe (Cainou)

Azelina is a wife of Ralph Tallboys.

In Cainhoe Thurston holds 1 hides from Azelina. Land for 2 ploughs. In lordship 1 hide.

1 villager has the other. 3 smallholders. Meadow for 1 plough; woodland 100 pigs.

Value 20s; when acquired 10s; before 1066 20s.

Wulfric, a freeman of King Edward's, held this land; he could grant and sell to whom he could.[27]

---

[27] *"History from the Sources"*, Domesday Book, Bedfordshire, Phillimore, 1977

So, according to the survey, the previous tenants of the two manors in Silsoe were Alfric Small and Leonorth, both Thanes of King Edward. A Thane was a man ranking above an ordinary freeman and below a noble in Anglo-Saxon England and was generally a man who gave military service in exchange for land. The two manors in Silsoe were thus run by men who, when the King called, would be expected to leave their manors, probably with some of his serfs and tenants, to fight for him. It may be that both Alfric and Leonorth were killed in the invasion or at least dispossessed when Aubigny took control.

Between them the two manors had 8 villagers, 11 smallholders and 5 slaves. These would have been the heads of families so with an average family size of, say 4 - 5 we have a population of between 100 – 150 people.

The approximate cultivated areas in the village, if it can be called a village then; totalled 14 ploughs for Wrest & Newbury, plus by the mill at Wrest, a meadow for 6 ploughs. The land ploughed by a team varies according to the soils, and from about 40 – 120 acres has been estimated: so if we allow 100 acres per team, then Newbury Manor would have had about 400 acres, and Wrest Manor 1,000 acres, plus 600 acres of meadow.

Nigel d'Aubigny's (alternatively d'Albini and eventually Daubeney) family came from, or near to, the Normandy village of Saint Martin d'Aubigny, (14 km. north of Coutances and 21 km. east of St Lo, Manche) and it is rumoured that his father William, accompanied William the Conqueror to England, on his invasion. Indeed, the family was favoured by King William after the Battle of Hastings, and the Aubignys obtained large possessions from William, including grants of land in Buckinghamshire, Bedfordshire, Warwickshire and Leicestershire.

If, after the conquest, Nigel d'Aubigny did not have his concubine installed at Newbury Manor; then at least she benefited from its income while Walter, brother of Sihere, held the Wrest Manor, leasing part to Hugh as a manor. Nigel held far more than this with several other manors including Flitton, Pulloxhill & Clophill, while probably having the seat of his Barony at Cainhoe Castle.

There were at this time more than one Nigel d' Aubigny, although both were related, and it seems that it was the other one that captured a castle in Normandy for King Henry I. For that he was given a Royal Grant of the forfeited lands of his maternal uncle, Robert de Montbray, Earl of Northumberland - lands both in England and Normandy, and ultimately became one of the most powerful men of his time.[28]

---

[28] Sir Bernard Burke, Dormant, Abeyant, Forfeited, and Extinct Peerages, Burke's Peerage, Ltd., London, 1883, p. 386, Mowbray, Earls of Nottingham, Dukes of Norfolk, Earls-Marshal, Earls of Warren and Surrey.

"Our" Nigel and his descendants remained at Cainhoe for many years, until in 1272, Simon de Albini's possessions were divided between his three sisters. The main residence was then described as "the hall of Kaynho with porch, chamber, cellar towards the east, with bakehouse, dovecote and garden westwards to the ditch of the marsh, the ditch which encloses the court…a ditch extends from the well to the bridge of Baybrugg, thence a ditch near the causeway…to the bottom of the old ditch…fishpond called Walebeck….houses of stone and lime…"[29]. By 1374 it seems the fortifications had become ruins with the Manor passing from the d'Aubigny family to the Lacys and the Nortons, and then to the Greys, Earls of Kent.

Cainhoe Castle nowadays is reduced to a series of grassy mounds, but has been dated to the late 11th or early 12th century through archaeological excavation[30]. It was not called a castle in the 1086 survey, only a manor, so the castle was probably thrown up quickly to convince the population that they were under new management. It is comprised of a motte and three baileys, well protected by ditches. The motte is approximately 8-9 meters high with a circular top. Some stonework was added, but as yet the nature of the castle in its final form is not known.

Other earthworks near the castle remains are what are left of associated dwellings, which were part of the small hamlet of Cainhoe, now within Clophill parish.

The Black Death 1349(ish)

There had been a fairly peaceful and prosperous interlude of a few hundred years for the inhabitants of the manors and farms, up until about 1349 when the Black Death, having worked its way up from southern England, arrived in Bedfordshire. It is probably due to this that Cainhoe disappeared as a village, and the Castle became uninhabited. In 1349 the Estate suffered severely from the Black Death, with the Lord of the Manor, Peter St Croix and all the inhabitants, dying of the pestilence.[31]

It is unlikely that the villagers of Silsoe did not similarly suffer, and it is estimated that about one third or even more of the country's population died from that plague. (Imagine the current village with one third of the houses empty, and for many weeks a constant procession to the graveyard, for the burial of people of all ages.)

With such a reduction in the population, naturally there were fewer labourers to work the land and so, in accordance with the law of supply and demand, wages and prices rose with the net effect that the standard of living for peasants greatly improved. Also, (and this would have been a totally new and

---

[29] CBC & BBC Community Archives, Clophill, Cainhoe
[30] Taylor A. and Woodward P. Cainho Castle excavations 1973. *Bedfordshire Archaeol. J. 10. 50-1*. England, Bedfordshire
[31] VCH Clophill

alarming concept for the land owners), if the farm workers did not like where they worked, or they considered their wages too low, they would move on to a more reasonable employer.

In addition the landscape changed, as land that had once been ploughed was given over to pasture for sheep or other beasts, because it was much less labour-intensive. It also helped in boosting the cloth and woollen industry. In addition, with the fall in population, most landowners were not receiving the rental they had been accustomed to, and were forced to lease their land, to maintain their income.

This short term economic prosperity for the poor did not last however, as there had not been any change to the underlying feudal structure of society. Therefore, by the mid-15th century the lords had re-imposed their controls, and standards of living had fallen again. However, for most levels of English society, the Black Death had represented a massive upheaval, one which had changed the face of English society, in a profound way.

Very little is known about the common people of Silsoe in the next few centuries, as it is generally only the major landowners, such as the Greys, who appear in sources such as land transfer documents, marriage settlements or court cases. In the case of the Greys, greater detail of their history can be found in the *Beds Historical Record Society* or the *Bedfordshire Magazine*. Briefly, the second Baron Grey de Ruthyn who was a favourite of Richard II, was captured by the Welsh in 1402, when fighting against them, and was then ransomed. He was also part of the Council that governed England during Henry V's absence in France. His eldest son fought at Agincourt, but died before his father and his grandson Edmund inherited the title, being created Earl of Kent, in 1465.

Even with their importance it seems that they visited Silsoe often, as even with their activities elsewhere such as fighting on behalf of the King or matters of governance, Silsoe was their primary residence. Their activities were not inexpensive and they found the necessary finance from rent and manorial taxes of their several manors, including those at Silsoe.

Moving on a century, there was no doubt much local consternation both with the villagers, and the clergy, when Henry VIII broke with Rome; and the habits and practices of a lifetime had to be changed, to fit with the new order. At the dissolution of the religious houses in the late 1530's, when their land and buildings passed to Henry, the nearest major site to Silsoe was Chicksands Priory. In 1538, the inhabitants of the priory were evicted and the property appropriated by the Crown. It is interesting that in 1541, the vicar of Flitton cum Silsoe resigned, with the new one, John Gale, having as patron, Henry VIII. Perhaps the old priest, Edward Philipe, could not agree with to the King's new status as head of the church.

The Civil War

In the mid-1640's the Civil War broke out, with Bedford coming down on the Parliamentary Side. In 1646, the army headquarters moved to Bedford for a year, being visited during that period several times by Cromwell. The VCH says that Cainhoe Castle was used for military purposes during the Civil War, so there would have been much coming and going of the Army through the village, with daughters being warned not to associate with the soldiers. Henry Grey, 10th Earl of Kent, presumably proved trustworthy, and overtly approved of the new regime as he was one of the six men entrusted with Parliament's Great Seal in 1643.

Anthony Grey had become the 11th Earl in 1651, when he was only 6 years old, which no doubt made it easier for the de Greys to revert to being Royalists by the time of Charles II's restoration, in 1660.

From the 18th century onwards, no doubt many national events had some impact on the inhabitants of the village, and where the results of these have been found, they are related elsewhere. The lives of the Grey family are more easily found from letters and other documents, but their life events are not those which generally impacted on most villagers, and have not been included in this book. For the average inhabitant life went on at a more prosaic, and unrecorded level.

Chapter 3 – Silsoe Manors

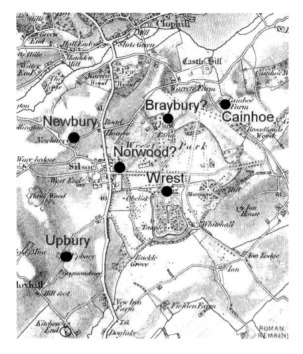

Plate 3/1 - Map of Silsoe with its Manors

Manors, what they were and what became of them

Although the present conception of a 'Manor' is of an imposing house nestling amongst woods and used as a residence or retirement home, their earlier existence was far more practical. Manors began as farming settlements grouped round the house of a local thane or leader, who was liable to provide fighting men, when the King required it.

After the Conquest of 1066, many manors were granted as estates to those of worth, who had supported William during his invasion. In many cases, they also grew over the years, to form the nucleus of a village, or at least a large farming complex. At their peak they were not only a central point for farming, but also where the power and laws of the King finally reached the common people.

Also, under the system called feudalism, land was granted on the understanding that the landholder had to provide a knight, or the cost of a knight (a knight's fee), or even a fraction of a knight's fee, when called upon to do so.

Manors performed several functions apart from being a farm. They were the seat of the local court, where the Lord of the Manor could fine the inhabitants for breaking the laws; and also as a centre from which the inhabitants could be controlled to ensure their allegiance to the Lord of the Manor, and through him, the King.

Later the functions and powers concerned with governance moved away from the manor, to become regional but still local power based, such as at the Assizes at Bedford. The farming function remained, and the farmer's financial power in being able to hire and fire, was still of great importance locally. The "Lord of the Manor" title has now become mainly a trophy title, with it being bought and sold like any other commodity, on the internet.

Thus in Silsoe, at the break up of the Wrest estate in the early 20th century, the manorial lordships which the de Greys had acquired over the centuries, Silsoe, Wrest, Brabury, Clophill along with Cainhoe and others, were sold off as a job lot, to the then deputy steward, William Frederick Ashby Fletcher of Biggleswade, the son and grandson of Cumberland coal mine owners, for £700[32]. However, there is no mention of Newbury, so maybe by then the title had lapsed. In 1931 the widow of Mr Fletcher, Mary Fletcher, was holding the lordships. As to their current worth, in 2006 the Lordship of the Manor of Cainhoe was on offer at £35,000!

Also, through the centuries with some manors being sold, broken up or joined to make bigger units, some manor houses became just a residence or they was demolished, and their locations lost. However, as a balance perhaps, small farms, whose landholdings grew substantially through the efforts of one man and his family, sometimes became known as a manor, with the farm taking the name of the owner.

The names of the manors which appear to be located within the parish are: Wrest, Norwood alias Silsoe, Brabury, Blundell and Newbury. There are other manors adjacent to Silsoe such as Cainhoe, Upbury, Kitchen and Higham Gobion which owned land within our parish, or had an impact on the parish, and these, with the exception of Higham Gobion, have also been commented on although not in detail.

The Manor Courts

At the time when the manors were the most important and powerful organisations in the village, most personal disputes were generally settled at the Manor Court, where everyone knew everyone, including the 'judge'; and justice could be dispensed in accordance with common practice.

Each manor belonged to a 'Lord of the Manor' and he organised and managed the life of the estate for his own profit, while acceding to the rights of the workers living there. From long before the 16th century private courts had been held at manors; but around the time of that century they had become more firmly established, meaning that if there was no manor, then a

---

[32] BLARS L23/397

court did not exist either. It was this right to hold a manor court that distinguished the manor from a large farm, a country house or a collection of properties in the hands of a wealthy individual. The manor courts were the lowest court of law in England, and governed those areas over which the Lord of the Manor had jurisdiction, and generally those people who resided in, or held lands within, the manor.

The Court Baron met regularly at approximately two to four weekly intervals, and it dealt with the tenants of manorial land by recording land transfers, managing the open fields, settling disputes between individuals, and other manorial offences.

The court took fees for the transference of land from one tenant to another, (even when a son took over from his father), rental charges, fines for minor offences and also for other matters. Apart from fines, other sentences were imposed such as placing the culprit in the stocks. No reference has been found for stocks in Silsoe, but if they were in use, the obvious location would have been in the road verge at the crossroads, by the church.

In addition to the Court Baron there was another court, the Court Leet, which was held after Michaelmas and after Easter, which all residents of the manor were obliged to attend. A record was kept of the homage sworn by tenants and if they were absent, a fine would be imposed. In addition, the Court Leet dealt with the election of constables and the presentment of offences, including those relating to matters of crown jurisdiction, franchised to the manorial lord (e.g., brewing and baking for sale).

However, there was often an overlap in the type of business conducted in the Court Baron and Court Leet, and to save time and expense, lords of the Manor generally applied to fuse their Court Baron and Court Leet into one court, meeting only twice annually.

The typical manor court records might include apologies for absence, a list of jurors, fines for absence, judgements on boundary disputes and petty crimes, fines for breaking the assizes of bread and ale, records of property transfers, the organisation of the common fields and meadows, the abatement of nuisances' (defective hedges, blocking of paths, straying beasts, etc) and anything concerning the occupations of the inhabitants, (which in most manors were agricultural), lists of stray animals taken into safekeeping, presentments for trespass by animals and sums of the money raised by the court. Most minor infringements up until about the 17th century, such as allowing cows to trespass, killing pigeons or failing to pay the manorial dues, were dealt with by the manorial courts, with more serious cases going to the Sessions Court or Kings Bench.

From at least the mid 17th century and certainly in 1757[33], when the manors were owned by the de Grey family, the courts for the Silsoe, Wrest &

---

[33] BLARS L26/390-392

Brabury Manors seem to have been held jointly at the same time and place. It would seem that from the 16th to the 17th centuries at least, the courts were held at what was probably the site of Norwood Manor. This is suggested later to have been where The Rowans is now. A lease of 1655 stated that the tenants must provide food for the steward and his men once a year[34]. Newbury Manor courts were presumably held at Newbury; although no records of these have been found, nor is there any indication of courts for that manor being held, after it was purchased by John, Lord Berkeley in about 1775.

The manorial administration was usually in the hands of a steward who kept the court records plus other documents such as rentals, terriers, extents and accounts. The local manorial laws were usually recorded in the court rolls under names such as 'pains', and in Silsoe there is one record, unfortunately written in a difficult script, which lists the pains of 1559-1562. In addition to the steward, there were other officers of the court such as the bailiff who was responsible for collecting fees, and other matters.

A 1467 account book gives the name of the collector of rents and bailiff as William Mile for Brobury and Wrest, with John Chappell then collecting the rents for Norwood.[35]

We can also find the names of several manor stewards in the records, such as Richard Carlisle, steward and receiver of Edmund de Grey, Earl of Kent in 1471. Edward Wingate had the job in 1633, followed by Thomas Hooper whose status as steward is recorded in the burial records for 1702. Joseph Pawsey was another long term steward, first found in the mid-1700's and being buried at Flitton in 1808.

No doubt the inhabitants of Silsoe were as lawless, or lawful, as those of any other part of the country, and a careful search of the old manorial records would probably throw light on the customs and by-laws then in operation, and incidentally, provide the names of the greatest offenders. However, until the 18th century at least most of the records were in Latin, and sometimes abbreviated Latin, with the handwriting not being particularly clear. We must therefore wait for someone to appear, who has the necessary skills to unravel these documents.

---

[34] BLARS L5/1091
[35] BLARS L26/4

The Manor of Newbury

Plate 3/2 - Newbury Manor

This manor appears to be the only manor in the parish which was identifiable from a very early time, and for which the location of the site of the manor house remained unchanged; with the latest manor building of the late 16th century, being visible to this day.

As stated above, after the Conquest, Nigel d'Albini became the main land owner in this area and made his main residence at Cainhoe. Obviously liking his home comforts, he also provided a manor for his concubine at Silsoe, not far from his castle and it is this which eventually became Newbury Manor.

Newbury Manor was held by the d'Albiny's or Daubeney Family, as the name eventually became, but by 1284 the family of Fitz Richard had possession of it. That family had held land in Silsoe from at least 1201, as Ralph Fitz Richard had in that year, leased a perch of land and 1½ acres of meadow to William Wiscard[36].

The Fitz Richards passed ¼ of a fee[37] to Ralph de Limbury and the Wiscards in 1302, but retained the manor. The manor must have prospered, as in 1323, Ralph Fitz Richard was granted permission to inclose a lane leading from the King's Highway below his dwelling, in order to enlarge his house. This

---

[36] The bulk of this early information is contained in the VCH p239.

[37] A Knights Fee was a land which provided sufficient revenue to equip and support one knight. This was about 30 marks (£20) and equated to about 1500 acres. The knight was required to attend his lord for 40 days per year in wars. Thus a quarter of a Knights fee would be 10 days per year.

diversion was conditional upon replacing the road with one on his own land.
[38]

The old road is believed to have been found during gardening work at No. 2, Newbury Close on the southern side of the moat, where a considerable amount of pottery dating from the 14th century has also been found. There were also other items including a quern, a buried stone slab and possibly home made glass, suggesting occupation of that site from the 1300's to the 18th century[39].

By 1346 the manor was in the possession of John & Margaret Morice, (through Margaret), and by 1428 one, John Wayte had it. After that it presumably was handed down in the Wayte Family as in 1524,(the sixteenth year of Henry VIII's reign), Henry Wayte sold the manor to Edward Danyell.
[40] There was a clause for Wayte to retain ownership if he repaid the purchase money within 7 years, but that didn't happen, and he relinquished ownership in 1528[41].

Edward Danyell's grandson, Stephen Daniel, was Lord of the Manor in 1573 & 1603, and when he died in 1631 aged 84, the lordship passed to Thomas Daniel, Stephen's brother as his natural son Richard, died shortly after Stephen's death.

Thomas died in 1664 and at the time of his interment, William Wheeler and John Webb of Silsoe, both threw the vicar out of the church refusing to allow the parson to bury him. Thomas's son William Daniel, obtained the manor as part of a marriage settlement, when he married Elizabeth Mulsoe of Finedon in 1658, and he was in possession in 1666.[42]

Perhaps William Daniel did not want to continuing farming at Silsoe, and presumably did not have a son and heir, as in 1685 he sold the manor and its lands for £6,500 to Robert Nicholls of St. Albans, gentleman. Daniel's Family had been at Newbury Manor for 160 years. However, for a rent of £24 per annum he retained for his life:

"the mansion house in which he dwells, with outhouses, gardens, courts, fishponds etc. ……. the Dairy Park, and New close; and loppings therefrom for a further £10 annually; to have rough timber for repairs; and also a free walk called Popler walk, and a free water - course from the springhead.[43]"

William Daniel was buried on 17 April 1706, at Flitton.

---

[38] ibid.
[39] Collection of pottery, clay pipes, samovar tap in the hands of Mr R Thurman.
[40] BLARS L5/345-347
[41] BLARS L5/347
[42] BLARS L5/372 & 380
[43] BLARS L5/394

It seems that Robert Nicholls left the estate to his son William Nicholls, who briefly appears in land exchange deeds up until 1722. He must have died without children, as his sisters Ann & Eleanor are said to be co-heiresses in the above conveyance. Ann Coghill nee Nicholls, also now being heir to Eleanor, left the whole property in 1736 to her daughter Sarah Hucks in trust, who then passed the land on to her son, Robert Hucks, in 1767.

Sarah had in 1757 drawn up a map, showing in detail the land holdings attached to Newbury Manor. Several years later she left the manor to her son Robert Hucks of Gt. Russell St., London, who presumably preferred a lump sum to annual rents, and so in 1775 the manor was conveyed to John, Lord Berkeley for £6,000. The money was lent by the Hon. John Yorke, probably the brother in law of Jemima, Marchioness Grey, thus increasing the family's holdings in Silsoe [44]. Later in 1796, the Manor passed to the Marchioness.

Unfortunately it seems that the manorial records for Newbury have not survived and furthermore, after Newbury's absorption into the Wrest estate, the name does not appear in those manorial court records that exist for that estate.

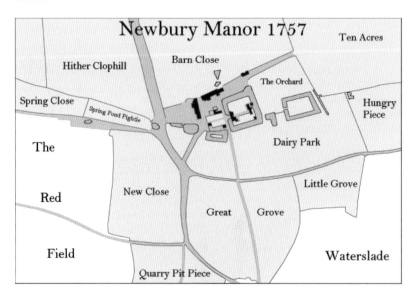

Plate 3/3 - Newbury Manor Layout in 1757

The conveyance for the sale helpfully describes the land in detail, giving field names and, apart from smaller rentals, shows the holding divided into three farms, Newbury, Englands and Warren. With the land and the manor absorbed into the Wrest Estate, there would have been over time, some land rationalisation, with the manor remaining as a farm and farming the

---

[44] BLARS L5/411

surrounding land, but with the other lands being merged into other farms, such as West End Farm.

There are a lack of Tenancy Agreements for the farm or manor after its absorption into the Wrest estate, but it seems that Joseph Squires may have been tenant there in 1834, as the burial record of Fanny Giggles in that year, states she was his servant at Newbury Farm.

From the censuses we can trace the tenants in the 19th century. William Peppercorn Squire, born at Stratton, Biggleswade, was the tenant at Newbury in 1841 and this is confirmed in 1845 by a map and schedule of West End Farm and Newbury, which shows the then tenant as W P Squire.[45] He remained there until his death in 1873, farming about 274 acres when it appears that his son Edward Frederick, who had been farming at Eaton Socon, came back to take over. Edward must have been a capable farmer as in 1851, aged 22, he had been at Cross Hall Farm farming 500 acres, and employing 19 men and 7 boys.

Edward's death is recorded at St Neots in 1897 before which time William Maddams, born at Flitton, had been installed. Presumably his father was Samuel Taylor Maddams, descended from Huguenots, as his tombstone at Silsoe reads:-

"In loving memory of Samuel Taylor Maddams
Whose ancestor came to England from
Normandy 1685 and settled at Clophill
He departed this life at Newbury
June 27th 1904 aged 71 years"

William was there only a short time, he was 67 years old in 1901 and perhaps older, as a death is recorded at Luton in 1903, of a William Maddams aged 76.

In 1918, when the Wrest Park Estate was being sold off, the manor farm was purchased, by the tenant Samuel Paterson, for £8,000 who remained there at least until 1936. The chapter on farming contains more information about activities at this manor in the 20th century.

The Manor of Norwood

This is another manor in the parish of Silsoe which was eventually absorbed into the de Grey Estates. The manor, sometimes known as the Manor of "Norwood alias Silsoe" may have originated with land held by Henry de Northwood who acquired 4 acres of land with 27 roods[46] of meadow in 1203

---

[45] BLARS L26/458
[46] The fourth part of an acre, or forty square rods, an area of 1 furlong long by 1 rod wide, or 1210 square yards.

and who also in 1206 leased half a virgate[47] to William the son of Henry de Ryde for 2d a year.[48]

Thomas of Norwode or Northwood plus others whose names were associated with the various Silsoe manors, appears in a grant of 1312 where witnesses included, Robert & John de Bray and Roger Blundel.[49]

It seems that this Thomas held half a knights fee in Flitton and Silsoe of John Peyvre but in 1360 Richard Peyve, presumably the son of John, passed the Manor to Reginald de Grey of Ruthyn and his wife Eleanor; and that family or their descendants held the lordship of the manor until 1919.

The overlordship was in the hands of the Wahull Family before 1388, and remained with that family until towards the end of the reign of Henry VII, when it was transferred to the Crown.

Although the lordship was in the hands of the de Greys, somewhere about 1445-1456, the manor was divided, with one third being then in the possession of a Thomas Boughton. In 1485 the Manor, then valued about 100s passed through Thomas's grandson William, to the father of Richard Decon. With Richard's decease in 1521, the Manor passed through the hands of Thomas and Elizabeth Warren[50] to their son Humphrey, who mortgaged the reversion of the property to Edmond Conquest and Thomas Palmer. In 1547, Elizabeth Warren agreed the conveyance to Thomas Palmer of the Manor of Silsoe alias Norwoods, by her son Humphrey,[51] and it was sold for 200 marks.

Thomas Warren is described as Lord of the Manor of Silsoe in a case of the 1530's, thus suggesting that Silsoe and Norwood Manors were one and the same.

There are several references in a lease of 1549[52] by Sir Henry Grey, Knight of Wrest, to Christopher Kynge, of 'Selvesho', to land abutting Norwood or Northwood; such as abutting an acre probably in Dodmere Furlong, and also very near Adamanyswell. However, this refers to land owned by the Manor of Norwood, and does not necessarily provide a clue as to the whereabouts of the manor house.

Only three years later in 1550, Thomas Palmer granted his Manor of "Sylso alias Sysho alias Norwood" to Joan Conquest, widow, for the sum of £78 13sh. 4d. It then included "..10 messuages, 3 cottages, a dovecote, orchards

---

[47] A virgate was one quarter of a hide which itself is estimated to be about 120 acres in Bedfordshire to 40 acres or much less in difficult arable country.
[48] VCH p 328 has the original sources for these and some subsequent transactions.
[49] BLARS I Jeayes 84
[50] At the time of the writing of the VCH there was a brass to Elizabeth 'Waren' in Flitton church dated 1544.
[51] BLARS LJeayes 794
[52] BLARS LJeayes 803

etc. in Sylso, Flytton, Malden Polloxhill, Yon, Ampthill and Barton on Cleye." It was said to be formerly called Warren's[53], which presumably relates back to the owners in 1547. Joan in 1556, leased the Manor of Norwood to Christopher Stele, baker, for 12 years, at a rent of £7 per annum[54].

Joan eventually sold the "Manor of Sylsho al. Sylso al. Norwood" in 1558 to Henry Grey, Knight of Wrest, for £170. This sale included ten messuages, three cottages, 120 acres of land, 20 acres of meadow and 40 acres of pasture although this acreage was in "Sylso, Flytton, Maldon, Polloxhill, Yon, Ampthill and Barton on claye" again formerly called Warrens[55]. Either this was very a profitable sale, being approximately double the price of 8 years earlier, or some land had been added to the holding.

There was evidently both land and buildings associated with it, as in 1567 Reginald Grey leased to a Robert Cheilde, the mansion house and site of the Manor of Norwoods, Silsoe, giving a possible acreage of 112. However, as early as 1544, a deed says that the Manor had appurtenances in "Gravenhurst, Flytton, Maldon, Ampthyll and Clophill"[56] and later other parishes are mentioned, so any description or acreage must bear this in mind.[57]

A later reference to the manor appears in the Inquisition Post Mortem taken at Ampthill, on the death of Charles, Earl of Kent, dated 1626, where we have the Manor of Norwood alias Silsoe, 1 messuage, 2 cottages and following, lands called Warrens in Silsoe, Flitton, Maulden, Pulloxhill, Ion, and Barton[58]. This latter gives a list of parishes similar to that in the 1558 sale document, and may be related to Norwood.

The last reference found to the manor house appears to be in the Earl of Kent's rental of 1658 where we have:

> "William Gamble & John Greene for the mannor or farm house in Silvesho called Norwoode with divers land pastures and meadowes in Silveshoo & Pulloxhill,
> £30 10 00"[59]

Now, in 1655, a few years earlier, there is a six year rental agreement between The Countess de Grey and William Gamble and John Green, for those two

---

[53] BLARS LJeayes 174
[54] BLARS LJeayes 805
[55] BLARS LJeayes 184
[56] BLARS LJeayes 163
[57] These descriptions are pre-enclosure when estates, and individual land ownerships, were comprised not only of fields but also of strips of land of a size starting at 1 rood, about one quarter of an acre. Allotments are to this day measured in poles where 40 square poles equals 1 rood.
[58] BLARS L22/17
[59] BLARS L26/1384

to rent the farmhouse anciently called Tabert "wherin the said William Gamble and John Greene do dwell together". The rent was £40 and the rental agreement also required that :

"...the said William Gamble and John Greene for themselves shall or will from tyme to tyme when and as often as the said Countess shall be pleased to summon and keep her court or courts within the Manor of Silsoe shall with sufficient warning suffer the court to be held in the said messuage herebye demised in the most convenient rooms for that purpose and shall suffer the Steward for the tyme being and all tenants and others and the stewards people to enter into and stay and abide in the said messuage or house until every such court shall be ended. And also at their cost shall at each court day provide and dress one competant dinner of whollsome meat for the Steward and his company soe as there be not above one court in any one year and the steward shall not bring above six persons with him."[60]

This latter agreement implies a house of some size and standing, and that it was being used as the location for manor court meetings. Also, the document says there was a dovehouse there, which is often an indication of a manor house. It is not unreasonable to suppose that this might be the location of the Silsoe alias Norwood Manor house, otherwise known as Tabert, especially given the earlier agreement.

So where was the Manor house situated? The references to the manor being "Silsoe alias Norwood" suggest perhaps a central location in Silsoe. It is unlikely that it was at the central crossroads where the Ragged Staff was; as this inn is referred to separately in the 1658 rental. Neither is it at West End Road farmhouse, as this was also mentioned in the same rental, as being farmed by Widow Caton.

Unfortunately the estate map of 1718 with its associated schedule, does not mention anywhere 'Norwood' or 'Tabert' and the only comparison that can be made is with the rentals of the various farms, assuming that the manor and associated lands had not been split up greatly over the years, since Gamble and Green.

On this basis there are two contenders, Edward Lawrence's farmstead at what is now The Maltings; and John Allen's farmstead opposite the Church in the grassed area fronting, what is now The Rowans. This is shown on the 1718 map as Home Farm and is a large complex of buildings together, where Allen was farming around 180 acres of land. The site with its buildings can be seen on the map in the Church & Chapel section. I suggest therefore that this is the best assumption for its location. It is unfortunate that when The Rowans was constructed there was very little archaeological work carried out there, to investigate the previous occupation of the site.

---

[60] BLARS L5/1108

The Manor of Wrest

In 1086 one of the entries in the Domesday Book for Silsoe had Leonorth, a thane of King Edward's, holding the manor in question, Wrest Manor according to the Victoria County History. A Leonorth, probably the same one as above, held Southill Manor in King Edward's time. The VCH suggests that Walter was related to Walter de Fleming, the ancestor of the barons of Wahull and indeed, by 1284 Wrest Manor was in the hands of the Barony of Wahull where it remained until 1623[61].

The Domesday survey indicates that there was a mill on the property. This would have been a water mill and was probably sited near the location of the old Wrest Park house or possibly adjacent to the site of the current 'Whitehall' cottage past which a stream flows. The manor itself would probably have been on the site of the old Wrest Park house, just east of the Orangery. After many extensions and modifications the house was deemed to be unsuitable, and demolished when the present mansion was built in the 1830's.

However, swiftly moving back to the 13th century, one Reginald de Grey, held one fee in Flitton and Silsoe of John de Wahull, (i.e. he could have the land as long as he provided one knight to de Wahull for 20 days a year, on request).

Other documents suggest that the de Greys became landowners in the area through marrying heiresses. If so, then they were very successful, as John de Grey became Sheriff of Bedfordshire in the reign of Henry III, 1216-1272; which would have required a certain degree of importance, land ownership or influence.

Reginald de Grey who was summoned to parliament in 1295, and died around 1307, seized of the manor when it was described as having a capital messuage, a dovecote, 100 acres of arable land, 6 acres of meadow, 3 acres of pasture and a wood although with no underwood,. It also had Rents of Assize, profits and perquisites of court. The total value was put at £4 per annum.[62]

The manor remained in the family through the succeeding centuries and in 1323 at the death of John de Grey when it passed to his son Roger it was described as having "1 team of 4 horses for ploughing, 4 farm horses, 8 oxen, 2 cows, 1 heifer, 2 calves, 28 wethers, 35 sheep, 12 lambs, 1 boar, 3 hogs, 35 sows, 6 little pigs, 5 geese, 36 quarters of corn, 10 quarters of rye, 40 quarters of beans & peas, 30 quarters of drag, 18 quarters of oats in the grange there with hay & forage, 1 pan, 1 shovel, 49 acres sown with corn, 7 with rye, 2

---

[61] VCH p 326 references.
[62] VCH p 327 refers to a post mortem which in those times was held to ascertain the value of the estate on death.

portions of cider, ½ quarter of salt and 1 iron plough"[63]. The numbers of labourers or farm workers required to control the farming is unfortunately not mentioned' but the figures imply quite an operation. At the death of Roger's son's in 1388 the rental was valued at £13 a year.

Throughout the following centuries the land, the manor and its rights and courts remained operational and with the de Greys and their descendants until, upon the death in action of Auberon Herbert, Baron Lucas in 1917, Mr Fletcher acquired the Manorial titles. The current Lord of the Manor of Wrest, is unknown.

The Stewards of the Wrest estate were very powerful men, and must have been people who today, would have held a high position in management. From his position, if not already wealthy, he could improve his lot and many of them became tenants of large farms.

Of the names that can be found are: Simon Fitz who in 1512 was granted the office of Seneschal, (another name for steward), and a terrier of 1519 shows he had many lands in Silsoe and beyond. His descendant, George Fitz, owned the Manors of Upbury and Beeches at the south of the parish.[64] A memorial to Thomas Hill in Flitton Church commemorating his death in 1628, at the age of 101 years, says he was the Receiver General to three Earls of Kent, Reginald, Henry & Charles[65]. One of his successors, Thomas Hooper, superintended the building of a new west wing at the old Wrest house, while another steward, John Allen, was in 1718 the tenant of the second biggest farm in Silsoe, (the one that was sited opposite the church, in The Rowans).

John Allen's job included, amongst other things, settling a right of way dispute at Newbury, finding tenants at Harrold, buying cows at Harrold Fair, ordering the felling of trees in the woods at Wrest as well as regularly reporting to the Earl or Countess and keeping the accounts.

The Manor of Braybury or Broybury

The earliest reference found to the name 'Broybury' is in a grant relating to land at Little Caynho dated 22 May 1295 by John de le Broybury of Little Caynho.[66] In this deed the rent appears to a be a sunflower, payable at Easter. This could be difficult as they do not flower until much later in the year, even in France! (Unless the 'sunflower' as they knew it then was a different flower.)

---

[63] Ibid.
[64] BLARS LJeayes 17, L26/804, L26/816
[65] Memorial Brasses in the Bedfordshire Churches by Grace Isherwood, London, 1906, pp.32-3
[66] BLARS LJeayes 280

A few years later in 1304, there is reference to a "William called le Broy son of Nicholas Russel of Great Caynho" in a document which relates to land in Little Caynho abutting Broybury Wood.[67] A further document dated 21 December, a Grant by Nicholas Russel of land in Little Caynho, is said to be dated at Broybury.[68]

No Manor of Broybury is listed in the Domesday Book so it seems likely that the de Broy family, or a branch of it, obtained manorial rights to their estate in Little Cainho and settled there.

The first record of the manor as such appears to be in a document dated 26 May 1340 at "Bletuesho" (Bletsoe) when Roger de Beauchamp (or "Roger de Bello Campo Lord of le Broybury" as his name is elsewhere written) gave Thomas Harlewyne of Checheley (probably Chicheley near North Crawley) power of attorney to receive the Manor of Broybury (except the wood) in Little Caynho on his behalf "from John Brian, attorney of John le filtz of John Pateshull"[69]. The wood in the Manor of Broybury was granted by John Pateshull to Dom[70] Roger de Bello Campo.

Roger Beauchamp was the first Lord of Bletsoe, with his wife Sibyl being the first of four sisters and co-heirs of Sir William Patshull, daughter of Sir John Patshull, of Bletsoe[71]. Roger was a descendant of Hugh de Beauchamp who was granted large areas of Bedfordshire at Domesday including Bletsoe, Gravenhurst and Haynes.

Broybury Wood in Little Cainho was leased by John Pateshull to Roger and his wife Sibilla on 1st June 1340, at "Shottelee"[72], when John, son of Dom. John de Pateshull, Knight, allowed Roger & Sibilla to make "waste and sale as they will."[73] On the same date, Roger granted a further power of attorney to Thomas Harlewyne to receive the seisin (ownership) of the wood; and another power of attorney was granted to John Bryan to deliver the seisin of the wood. In various leases and grants until at least 1345, Roger de Bello Campo is referred to as Lord of Broybury.

However, in 1351, Roger conveyed the Manor of Broybury, before witnesses at Westminster, to William de Risceby for 100 marks[74]; and on 12th May of that year he informed his tenants of this change in ownership. Then, three years later John Fyndal, of "Cyvelesho" and John Strete of Caddington, granted their rights in the Manor to William and his wife Alice in a grant signed at Little Cainhoe.

---

[67] BLARS LJeayes 283

[68] BLARS LJeayes 282

[69] BLARS LJeayes 301.

[70] Dom was a title of respect originally used for monks or priests.

[71] From the website www.medievalgenealogy.org.uk/cp/beauchampofbletsoe.shtml

[72] Possibly near Bromeswell, Suffolk

[73] BLARS LJeayes 340

[74] BLARS LJeayes 313

In addition to earlier documents, between 1354 & 1411 there are many documents relating to the sale or lease of land which are signed, or dated, at Broybury.

In the indenture of the will of John Russheby, Lord of Broybury, of 1416,[75] the Manor of Broybury was granted to his wife Alice " for life as long as she remain single & she may have it if she marries again as long as she has guided Thomas & William in all those necessities which befit such gentlemen". If her sons died, then the manor was to be sold to help the marriage of her daughter, and to pay for the good of the souls of John, Alice and her children.

Both John and Alice Russheby were still alive in 1425, but in 1428, a grant and quitclaim refers to Alice, widow of John Russheby, sometime lord of Broybury. That document also refers to the reversion of the manors of Broybury and La Hyde together with lands, which implies that Alice was selling, and that the two sons had pre-deceased her.

Three years later in 1431, all the houses and buildings with wood etc, adjacent to the Manor of Broybury (except a tiled barn, dovecot and sheepfold) were sold for £40; with permission for the purchasers to pull down the houses within 6 years, and the wood within 3 years.[76]

The manor and its lands had probably passed to Richard Grey, Earl of Kent around that time, if not earlier, as in 1506 there is a conveyance dated 1st October signed by Lord Daubeny Chamberlain to the King (Henry II), John Bourchier, Lord Fitzwaren, Lord Darcy and others granting to Richard, his wife Elizabeth, and their heirs the manors of "… Caynhowe, Brobury, Wrast and Flytte .."[77] The land was absorbed into the Wrest Park holdings, but the manorial court for that manor continued to be held.

Richard was forced to sell off most of his lands and manors to pay his debts(possibly gambling) to Sir Henry Wyatt but his heir Henry Grey managed to regain some of the land from Wyatt and Henry's son, Reginald Grey, regained more land and his title from Queen Elizabeth.

On the death of Charles 7th Earl of Kent in 1623, an enquiry found that he held the Manor of Brobury. In 1638 Ann Hale and her son-in-law, William Wheeler, rented several close from Henry, Earl of Kent, including one called Little Braybury. The final record of this manor is from the break up of the Wrest Estate in 1918, when, as previously mentioned, the Lordship of the Manor of Broybury was sold amongst the others, to Mr Fletcher.

---

[75] BLARS LJeayes 5
[76] BLARS LJeayes 335
[77] BLARS LJeayes 132

As to its location, the words "Broybury Wood" can be seen on a pre-Enclosure map of about 1814,[78] and the old northern entrance lodges to Wrest Park, north of Home Farm, are still called Brabury Lodges. This wood was sited in the north-east corner of the Wrest Park estate, just to the south-west of the Lodges. Some further clues are, firstly, that some early (14th century) documents are occasionally signed at "*Little Caynho*" and also at the "Manor of Broibury in Little Caynho",[79] and secondly, a lease of 1775, which refers to a farm house called "Cainhoe or the Park Farm situated in Silsoe"[80].

From the above, a reasonable assumption is that the present Home Farm farmhouse, which is shown on 19th century maps as Park Farm, is the most likely location for Broybury Manor. In its listing it is suggested to be of circa 15th century construction, and it is not unlikely that it may have been constructed on the site of the earlier manor.

The Manor of Blundells

This Manor is very elusive. According to the VCH it was held by the de Greys, as was their Manor of Wrest by "Knight Service" and in 1302 the de Greys held one twelfth of a knights fee, which required the provision of approximately 3-4 days service of a knight, per year.

In 1310 Robert Blundell acquired 4 messuages, 80 acres of land, 10 acres of meadow and 5 acres of wood in Flitton and Silsoe from John Blundell, although this land was probably held under the de Greys.

There are many other references to people in the 13th and 14th centuries with the surname of Blundel in or around Silsoe; and it seems probable that the land holding gradually acquired the title of the Manor of Blundells.

According to the book *The Blundells of Bedfordshire & Northants*,[81] Blundells Manor in Silsoe owned various rents, messuages, cottages & appurtenances in 8 parishes, but was centred on Silsoe. It further says that the manor was intact until 1420, when it was split up with part going to a branch of family, in 1512. On the death of John Blundell, lands in 8 counties with tenements (no manor house is mentioned) were passed to his childless son Thomas, who, then passed it on to his sister, Anne (or Agnes). The residue of his goods were left to John Wayte of Newberry, to distribute to charity. Anne/Agnes married Thomas White & then Hugo Swynnerton.[82]

In 1531 the manor was acquired by Richard & William Fermour from Anne & Hugo Swynnerton, although they retained a life interest. It was then said to

---

[78] BLARS L33/7
[79] BLARS LJeayes 305
[80] BLARS L4/335
[81] " *The Blundells of Bedfordshire & Northants*", Joseph Hight Blundell & Hight Blundel MD 1912, private subscription.
[82] Feet of Fines Beds 22 Hy VIII & will of JB dated 14/12/1512.

include 3 messuages, 3 cottages, 120 acres wood and 56 acres or meadow/pasture in all the surrounding parishes.

The manor was purchased by Simon Fitz of Aspley Guise, and at his death in 1544,[83] he left "..his manor of Blundelles in Flytton, Sevelysho, Pulloxhill and Maudon .." plus the Manor of Bellkemores in Pulloxhill, to his younger son, also Simon. In 1545, he alienated to his brother –in-law William Richardson, and to Thomas Fitz Hugh of Wavendon, but following Simon's death the alienation was taken to court as being illegal, and in 1547 it was split into sixths among the various claimants.

Some of these parts were amalgamated and bought by Francis Morgan, who had accumulated five sixths of the manor by the time he died in 1558; when in his will he left the Manor of "Bylkemore and Blundells" to his wife for life, and then to his second son, Anthony. There is unfortunately no further information on the location of this land in the will.

Then in 1559, there is a grant document by Anne Morgan and her son, to Sir Henry Grey and Dame Anne his wife, of the Manor of Blundells in Sevelysso and Flyton and other lands left to her by her late husband's will dated, 19th September 1558.[84] There followed a dispute over rents of the remaining sixth of the manor, when the tenants were said to be Richard Grey, Peter Richardson, Elizabeth Hill, Thomas Swayne, Roger Hill and John Weston, who rented it for £10.

The manor was last recorded in the Inquisition Post Mortem of Charles, Earl of Kent, on 23rd August 1626, where it was in the list of manors as Blundells in Silsoe.[85] It was presumably without any significance, or any manorial rights, as it appears to have been absorbed into the de Grey estates without further mention.

If there was a manor house then there may be a clue to its location in a record of a lease in 1682, of 1 acre of arable land at Buckle grove alias Bucklegrovegate, Flitton; " … abutting north on land late Goldstones, south on Blundells …" A meadow called Blundells also existed south of New Inn Farm. The name is also associated with the Manors of Upbury and Beeches, both adjacent to Silsoe but mainly in Pulloxhill, and more interestingly, the Manor of "Bilkemore or Kitchens" in Pulloxhill, is referred to several times in the 14th century.[86]

However, most of the indicators point to the centre of the manor lands being south of the village perhaps at West End, as Hugo Swynnerton can be traced there, Kitchen End or even more speculatively at New Inn.

---

[83] BLARS ABP/R11/57
[84] BLARS LJeayes 188
[85] BLARS L22/17
[86] VCH Pulloxhill

The Manor Of Upbury

Although the manor house site itself was sited just outside the South western edge of Silsoe in the parish of Pulloxhill, much of its land lay within the parish of Silsoe.

The VCH says that the Manor of Upbury or Beeches, first appeared after the dissolution, although the estate can be traced back to the Domesday Manor of Pulloxhill. At the dissolution it was probably granted to Simon Fitz, who also owned Kitchen Manor described below. A full description or terrier, of Simon's lands at Upbury appears in 1521, and there is another document said to be a terrier of Simon's lands in 1519, so his accession to the manor would have been before those dates.

Thomas Morgan acquired the manors of Bilkemore (Kitchen), Beeches (Upbury) and Blundells; and settled Upbury on George Fitz in 1567, on his marriage. George passed the manor to his niece Ann, the wife of Sir William Briers, at his death in 1608. He is buried in Pulloxhill Church.

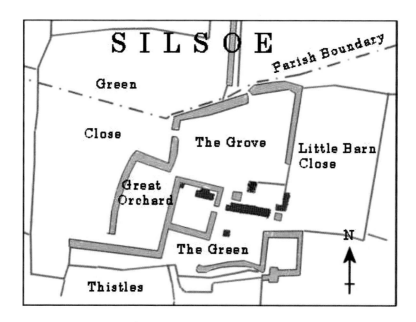

Plate 3/4 - Upbury Manor House Site 1768

William appears in documents of Upbury until about 1663[87] when he is exchanging land with Sir Henry Grey. He was the Deputy Lieutenant of Bedfordshire for many years, and was twice, High Sheriff. After his death in

---

[87] BLARS J5/1 NB This date is suspect as an inscription in Pulloxhill church gives his date of death as 1663.

1653 [88] aged 84, the property must have passed to Thomas Cheyne, as in 1676 Thomas conveyed the manor to John Coppins, with a detailed description of the associated land, split between Pulloxhill and Silsoe. John Coppins in 1699/1700, then sold on the mansion house, (built by himself), and lands, to William Boteler of Biddenham. At that time the house included two rooms, a necessarium and a toft which were occupied by Thomas Day,[89].

John Coppin probably sold the manor to the Duke of Kent, as by 1758 the Hon Philip Yorke is leasing the property, to John House.

The manor house together with farm buildings appear on an estate plan of 1768[90] and are much the same on a plan of 1826. They are not however, visible on a plan of 1868, so it appears that the old manor house with farm buildings, were sadly demolished between those dates.

Kechinge or Kitchen Manor

This manor, although in the South of Pulloxhill, is included as its name remained applied to land in Silsoe for many years, possibly due to the land having been part of the manor's land holdings.

According to the VCH this manor originated in land held in 1284, by Richard Wiscard of the abbot of St Albans. However, a 12th century document[91] William Wischard granted to John, son of Silvester de la Felde and Agnes, the daughter of Augustine de Kechinge, his wife, "the messuage and croft which the said Augustine formerly held in Kechinge". The manor thus goes back further in time than the 12th century.

In 1529, it was conveyed to Robert de Bilkemore, and through other owners, it eventually came to Simon Fitz who owned it on his death, in 1543. He would have been an important man as, in 1512, he held the office of seneschal[92] of the manors of Wrest, Broybury. Flitt, Silsoe, Nether Gravenhurst, Little Cainho & Pulloxhill, for a salary of 26s 8d.

The manor was split in the late 1500's, and later probably merged with the manors of Greenfield and Pulloxhill. The name remained, with Kitchen Common Field, half of which is in Silsoe, being shown adjacent to the Silsoe - Barton Road on the 1718 Estate map, and later in 1790. Kitchen End Farm off the Pulloxhill – Barton Road is marked on OS maps to this day.

---

[88] *The Beds Times* of February 1902 refers to an inscription in the church with details of his life and date of death.
[89] BLARS L12/1 & 2
[90] BLARS L33/
[91] BLARS LJeayes 630
[92] The seneschal administered estates on behalf of the lord, auditing, presiding at courts etc.

Cainhoe Manor

The manor house still exists just off the northern side of the Clophill to Gravenhurst road, where it is now a large house adjacent to farm buildings. It was originally linked with Clophill, and it was normally called the Manor of Clophill and Cainhoe. Several hundred years ago it seems that it was more important than the village of Clophill, having not only a large manor house or 'capital messuage', but also a warren (the ancestors of which remain in abundance today).

Cainhoe Manor lying only a few metres outside the North-eastern corner of Silsoe parish, came into the hands of the de Greys initially in 1415, although after being sold by them, it subsequently fell into the hands of King Henry VIII. However, after only a hundred years and after passing through several other hands, Amabella, the Dowager Duchess of Kent, reclaimed it into the Wrest estate in 1654, where it remained until the estate was sold off early in the 20th century.

This manor, or its lands, tended to be known as Great Cainhoe but there was another area called Little Cainhoe, which appears to have been south-westwards of the Gravenhurst Road, and which was closely associated with Broybury.

Chapter 4 - Wrest Park and its Owners

Wrest Park and its Owners

There is a huge amount of information in books, periodicals, county and national archives concerning the families which owned Wrest Park and established a major seat there, far too much for it all to be included here so what follows can only be a snapshot of the owners and events.

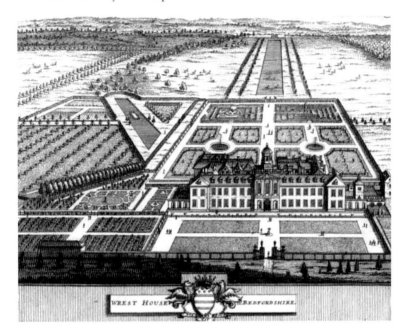

Plate 4/1 - Wrest Park Old House and Gardens
Kip & Knyff, Britannia Illustrata 1707

A Potted de Grey and Wrest Park Owners History[93]

Anciently the de Grey family is said to derive from Anchitel de Grey from Picardy who lived at the time of William the Conqueror. However, a John Grey, son of an Essex man & perhaps connected with the powerful Wahull Family, was at Silsoe very early on and his son Reginald de Grey seems to have risen in the King's service. He held Wrest in 1284 and on his death in 1308 it was valued at £4. At that time it would have been only one of several manors which he owned.

---

[93] Most of the following information and genealogy is taken from the thepeerage.com website and Wikipedia. I am aware of the inherent dangers here but they provided the most convenient source at the time. Also consulted are the VCH, Joyce Godber's The History of Bedfordshire, the Flitton memorials and William Treacher's account of the estate written in 1899.

On Reginald's death his son John, whose mother was Maud Fitzhugh, inherited the lands and titles. John married Maud Basset and became Justice of North Wales and Governor of Caernarfon Castle, a long way from Wrest.

His son, Sir Roger de Grey, married Elizabeth de Hastings and they had two sons John & Reynold or Reginald (born about 1323-7) and four daughters. By 1319 his manors included Brogborough, Thurleigh, Harrold, Puddington & Wrest plus land in other counties all of which provided a good income through fees and rents. His father also settled the Castle and Lordship of Ruthin on him in 1319. He was summoned to Parliament in 1325 where it seems he became Lord Grey. In 1328 there was a bit of a family upset when he complained that his older brother Henry, had entered his Ruthin castle without his permission. Henry eventually left conceding the place to Roger, and in addition, had to give some of his manors to him by way of compensation. Roger died in March 1352/3.

Roger's eldest son John had been present at the battle of Crécy in 1346 and the siege of Calais in 1347. He died in 1350 and so the heir became Reynold de Grey, the second Lord Grey of Ruthin, Wrest etc. In 1352 he was charged with abducting Margaret, the widow of Sir Ralph Fitz Richard. Around 1352 he married Eleanor le Strange and they had four sons, Reynold (b abt 1362), John, Edmund & Roger. He went to Parliament in 1353 and was part of the King's retinue on his trips to France in 1355 & 1359.

He died in 1388, at which time the value of Wrest was said to still be £4, presumably the annual rental income, and he was succeeded by his son, another Reynold born about 1362. This second Reynold's wife, whom he married in 1378, was Margaret Roos, a descendant of King Edward 1, and they had two sons Thomas & John and several daughters. He became Lord High Admiral of England and in 1389 assumed the style of Lord of Hastings, Wexford & Ruthin, and was in parliament from 1389. In 1399 he was one of those who assented to the secret imprisonment of King Richard II.

In Wales he seized land awarded to Owain Glyndwr and later tried to attack Glyndwr who went into hiding. This became a full scale rebellion and in one incident Reginald was captured and in 1402 he had to find 10,000 marks as a ransom and had to swear not to bear arms against Glyndwr. Reginald then turned his attention to France and fought in the Hundred Years War in 1420 eventually dying in 1440.

His son John, who married Constance Holand in 1410, succeeded him. She was the widow of the executed Thomas Mowbray, Earl of Norfolk, who was descended from Kings Edward I & Henry III. Their sons were Edmund born in October 1416, and Thomas. John travelled to France with the King in 1415 & 1417 and was nominated Knight of the Garter in 1436, he died in 1439.

The First Earls of Kent

Edmund inherited the land and titles becoming the 4th Lord Grey of Ruthin etc. His wife whom he married before 1440 was Katherine Percy, daughter of the 1st Earl of Northumberland. Their sons were Anthony, George & John plus two daughters Elizabeth & Anne. At the battle of Northampton in 1460 he changed sides to the Yorkists and is considered to have been one of the main causes of the Lancastrian defeat. He was created Earl of Kent in 1465. After attending King Richard III's Coronation in 1483 he died in 1490 aged 73, a good age in those days.

The second Earl of Kent was George, Edmund's second son who had two wives. The first was Anne Wydeville who died in 1489, but gave birth Richard in 1481 plus two daughters. He then married Katherine Herbert from who came Anthony, George and Henry.

Richard became the 3rd Earl when George died in 1503, but died himself in 1524 enabling his brother Henry to inherit the title. Richard wound up heavily in debt, probably through gambling, and was forced to alienate most of his property with a good part of it ending up in the hands of the Crown.

Richard died childless and was succeeded by his half-brother Henry, who became the 4th Earl. Henry tried, with little success, to reacquire the property Richard had sold, and had to live as a modest gentleman, never formally taking the title, Earl, as he was ashamed of his lack of property.

Sir Henry Wyatt, who had purchased Wrest house and manors, at one time considered pulling down Wrest Park and selling the timber in the estate but he felt pity for Sir Henry Grey and in 1560 he said:-

" as the said Grey had then no house of his own conveniant for him to dwell in, and also for pity he had that the said house wherein divers and many of his ancestors had dwelt should be so utterly destroyed, he offered to buy of Sir Henry the said manor and other lands in Beds. nigh unto it about the yearly value of 40; thereupon Sir Hen. sold the said manor of Wrest to him with other lands for 450 marks."[94]

Henry (1495-1562), married Anne Blennerhassett and they had two children, Henry Grey (1520-1545), who married Margaret St. John and then Katherine Grey. Although Henry failed to inherit, his three sons, Reginald, Henry and Charles each became Earl of Kent in turn.

Reginald Grey was the 5th Earl, the first of the three brothers to inherit the titles but little property along with it. His death was mentioned by William Camden in 1573 :-

---

[94] BLARS L24/16

"Not long after dyed also Reginald Grey Earle of Kent, whom the Queene a yeare before had raised from a private man to the honour of Earle of Kent, after that this title had lyen asleepe the space of fifty yeares from the death of Richard Grey Earle of Kent, who had set his Patrimony flying, and was elder Brother to this mans Grandfather. In this honour succeeded unto him Henry his Brother."

Henry Grey, 1541-1614, now came into the title as the 6th Earl. He was married to Mary Cotton, but there were no known children from this marriage. He served as Lord Lieutenant of Bedfordshire from 1586 to his death and the Flitton Mausoleum[95] contains a magnificent painted tomb, typical of its era, to Henry and his wife Mary. They are shown recumbent with their hands carved in prayer. Henry is said to have attended the trial of Mary, Queen of Scots, at which she was condemned to be beheaded.

Charles Grey became the 7th Earl on the death of his brother but as he died in 1623 could only enjoy the title for nine years. He had married Susan Cotton, daughter of Sir Richard Cotton, and they had two children, Henry Grey, who became the 8th Earl of Kent (c. 1583–1639) and Susan Grey. He served from 1615 to 1621 as Lord Lieutenant of Bedfordshire, and from 1621 to his death, shared the post jointly with his son Henry.

Before Henry inherited, he, on 16 November 1601, at St Martin's-in-the-Fields, had married Elizabeth Talbot, a daughter of Gilbert Talbot, 7th Earl of Shrewsbury and Mary Cavendish.[96] There were no known children from this marriage. He served as Lord Lieutenant of Bedfordshire from 1621 to 1627 and again from 1629 to his death. As he had died childless his primary title as Earl of Kent was inherited on his death in 1639, by his closest male relative, Anthony Grey, a second cousin of his father.

Anthony Grey, 9th Earl of Kent, 1557-1643, was a son of George Grey and Margery Salvaine. Anthony married Magdalene Purefoy, daughter of William Purefoy, and they had eleven children one of whom had the delightful Christian name of Faithmyjoy. His eldest son, Henry Grey, 1594–1651, became the 10th Earl of Kent in 1643.

Henry was married first to Mary Courteen and they had a son Henry who is believed to have died young. He then married Amabella Benn, daughter of Sir Anthony Benn and they had two children, Anthony and Elizabeth. Henry took the side of Parliament against the King but opposed the execution of Charles I and retired after that event into private life. He served as the Lord Lieutenant of Bedfordshire appointed by the Long Parliament, from 1646 to

---

[95] Flitton Mausoleum contains many monuments from 1545 to 1848 of members of the de Grey family and is well worth a visit. Note that the Henry's wife is down as Amabell on one monument and Amabella on one she had erected.

[96] In 1821, a note in the Gentleman's Magazine by J D Parry says that behind one of the pillars of Lady Elizabeth Talbot's monument is an old two-edged sword and a rusty iron gauntlet.

his death in 1651. His widow Amabella, described as the 'Good Countess', then took up residence at Wrest which she improved before she died there in 1698 aged 91. At this time Wrest was a rambling country mansion with many additions and amendments.

His son Anthony (1645–1702) was only 6 years old when his father died and he became the 11th Earl of Kent. Eventually he married an heiress, Mary Lucas, 1st Baroness Lucas of Crudwell, a title which could descend through the female line, and when her father, John Lucas, 1st Baron Lucas died, she inherited his property in Essex & Wiltshire. The family's finances were improving! Anthony improved the appearance of the old house at Wrest, adding a classical front portico in 1676 and started to formalise the garden layout. He also built a family house in St James' Square, London, which was to be the de Grey's London base for many generations. By Anthony, Mary had two children, Henry and Annabel Grey born 1671 and 1674. The 11th Earl died in 1702 at Tunbridge but was brought back for burial in the Flitton Mausoleum.

Henry First and only Duke of Kent

Anthony and Mary's son Henry had been on the Grand Tour of Europe and was evidently able to move in the highest circles with ease, as he became Lord Chamberlain and a Privy Counsellor in 1704, was created Marquess of Kent, Earl of Harold and Viscount Goderich in 1706, Duke of Kent in 1710, and was made a Knight of the Garter in 1712. He was succeeded as Lord Chamberlain by the Duke of Shrewsbury in 1710 but then served as Lord Steward from 1716 until 1718, and Lord Privy Seal from 1719 until 1720. At the age of 68, a year before his death, Grey took part, as a founding governor, in the creation of Britain's first home for abandoned children, the Foundling Hospital in London.

Henry married first Jemima Crewe, a daughter of Thomas Crewe and an heiress, and according to the memorial stone in the Mausoleum they had 4 sons and 7 daughters. These were Anthony Grey, the Earl of Harrold who died without children in 1723, Henry Grey who died after returning home from Europe in 1717, Amabell Grey who died in 1727 but produced two children with John Campbell, Jemima Grey 1699–1731, Anne Grey who had married Lord Charles Cavendish but died in 1733 and Mary Grey who married Mr. Gregory, the Dean of Christ Church. The others were George, Lucas, Henrietta, Jane and Carolina.

A year after Jemima's death Henry, at the age of 58, married Sophia Bentinck, aged 28, who was a daughter of the 1st Earl of Portland and Anne Villiers. He had two further children with Sophia, George Grey, Earl of Harold, 1732–1733, and Anne Sophia Grey who married John Egerton, the Bishop of Durham.

Left without a male heir, after his son Anthony choked on an ear of barley aged 28, he no doubt used his position at Court to provide for his succession. He was created Marquess Grey in 1740, with a special remainder to his granddaughter, Lady Jemima Campbell and her male heirs, to enable them to inherit the title with the properties, which included Wrest. She also succeeded to the Barony of Lucas. All Henry's other titles became extinct at his death. His and his wife's monument in Flitton Mausoleum is shown in Plate 4/2.

In addition to his public duties Henry was concerned with making the gardens at Wrest fit with the current thinking on landscaping. He had also intended building a new mansion at Wrest but lost so much money in the South Sea Bubble speculation of 1720 that he could not. He did however, lay out the formal woodland garden and added sculpture to the wooded circles, squares and oval.

In addition, about this time the Park was considerably changed being extended westwards up to the Barton Road, and northwards towards Clophill, together with new canals and avenues being laid out. Numerous garden buildings and structures on the principal axes were also constructed. These are notably Thomas Archer's Pavilion (or banqueting house) of around 1711 at the south end of the canal and a second pavilion located on the summit of the re-modelled Cain Hill to the east. This introduced a strong east-west axis, which was further emphasised by the erection of the obelisk on obelisk canal designed by William Kent although this was later re-erected on the west edge of Old Park around 1635. Much of the design appears to be the result of close collaboration between the Duke of Kent, his gardener John Duell, and the designer Thomas Ackres.

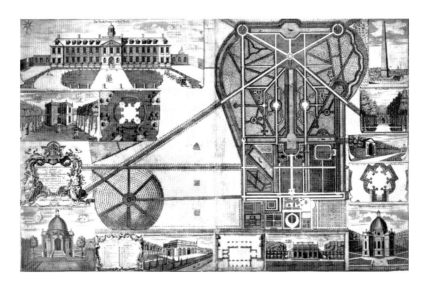

Plate 4/3 - A map of Wrest and Sketches, John Rocque, 1735

Henry's daughter Lady Amabell de Grey had married John Campbell in 1717/18, then styled Lord Glenorchy and who became the 3rd Earl of Breadalbane and Holland in 1752. Their two children were Henry Campbell who died in 1727 a few weeks after his mother, in Copenhagen where his father was Ambassador, and Jemima Campbell, 2nd Marchioness Grey, to whom the titles and land descended.

On 22 May 1740 Jemima, 2nd Marchioness Grey, married Hon. Philip Yorke (later Earl of Hardwicke) and they later had two daughters, Amabel 1751–1833 who married Alexander Hume-Campbell, Viscount Polwarth, but had no children and Mary Jemima, 1757–1830, who married the 2nd Baron Grantham and, luckily for the family, had issue.

Jemima succeeded as Marchioness Grey by a special remainder upon the death of her maternal grandfather, the Duke of Kent, but as she had no male heirs, the title became extinct upon her own death on 11th January 1797; with her eldest daughter Amabel later being created Countess de Grey in her own right. Jemima continued the Duke's interest in gardening and she employed Lancelot 'Capability' Brown to soften the edges of the gardens. However Brown was so impressed with the gardens that he declared that any dramatic alterations would only "unravel the mysteries of the garden". She was also a bit forgetful in old age, succeeding in falling asleep over a candle which set fire to her cap and badly burned her head.

However, she did introduce the then fashionable new elements into the gardens, including the Chinese Temple and Bridge, the Rustic Hermitage (Root House), the Mithraic Altar, the Bath House and a memorial to Lancelot 'Capability' Brown.

Amabel Hume-Campbell (1751–1833), 1st Countess de Grey and 5th Baroness Lucas, became a political writer of some stature and was also an accomplished amateur artist. She grew up in the political and intellectual atmosphere of her parents' homes at Wrest Park, Bedfordshire, and St. James's Square, Westminster. She was educated at home, and became an avid reader at an early age. She married Alexander Hume-Campbell, Viscount Polwarth in 1772.

Polwarth was interested in books but was a keen hunter too, and not only established a model farm on the Wrest estate, Warren Farm, but also built dog kennels there, just to the north of the parish. Sadly he died from consumption on 9 March 1781, and Amabel wrote that she had lost "the friend & protector I had hop'd for". She seems to have divided her time equally between Wrest and her house on Putney Heath. Then, on the death of her mother in 1797, she inherited the family houses at Wrest and at 4 St. James's Square, London, and the title Baroness Lucas. In 1816, she was created Countess de Grey of Wrest, her favourite estate, with a special remainder, failing to heirs male of her body, to her sister and the heirs male of her body.

Her diary reveals an intense interest in politics and it was a matter of lifelong frustration that, being a woman, she could not be elected to the Commons or, later, take her place in the House of Lords. In 1811, she wrote:

" I can only flutter & beat against the wires of my large gilded cage in St. James Square whilst I embody in my reveries an imaginary Marquis de Grey speaking in Parliament. But alas! when I wake from my day-dreams, I find out that my poor Marquis (with my soul in a manly form) would probably have had a bullet in the thorax...long ago for the vehemence of his speeches. "

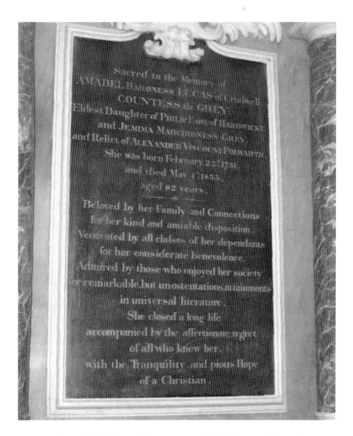

Plate 4/4 - Amabel's Memorial, Flitton Church

In 1792, she wrote An Historical Sketch of the French Revolution from its Commencement to the Year 1792, which she had anonymously published as John Debrett. In 1796, she wrote an historical essay on the ambition and conquests of France, with some remarks on the French Revolution, published in 1797.

She died on 4 May 1833[97] at St James's Square, aged 81, and is buried at the de Grey Mausoleum in Flitton, Bedfordshire. She was succeeded in her titles and estates by her nephew Thomas Philip Robinson/Weddell/de Grey (he changed his name twice), who had married her niece.

Thomas Philip Robinson (1781–1859), also Rector of Burbage, was the 2nd Earl de Grey and a British Tory politician and statesman of the 19th century. He was the eldest son of the 2nd Baron Grantham and inherited on 4 May 1833, the Wrest Park Estate and the titles 2nd Earl de Grey and Baron Lucas of Crudwell through Amabel's sister, Mary, who had married his father. He married Henrietta Frances Cole and they had two daughters, Anne Florence and Mary Gertrude

He was made a Privy Counsellor in December 1834 while holding office as first Lord of the Admiralty till April 1835, and was created a Knight of the Garter in 1844. He was also Lord Lieutenant of Ireland from September 1841 to July 1844. Thomas de Grey was nominated as Lord Lieutenant of Bedfordshire in 1818, an office which he held until his death.

On the founding of the Institute of British Architects in London in 1834, he was invited to become its first President and remained so until his death in 1859. The institute received its Royal Charter in 1837, becoming the Royal Institute of British Architects in London. Earl de Grey was also a fellow of the Royal Society, a fellow of the Society of Antiquaries, and served as one of the New Buckingham Palace Commissioners from 1848.

He also designed the new Wrest Park House, which was inspired by French architecture, between February 1833 and October 1839, being assisted by the architect, James Clephan. The works commenced on 12 Feb 1834, and when a trial on a new artificial stone failed there followed two years of waggons bringing Bath stone from Leighton, via the railway.

He added the new formal French and Italian gardens between the new house and where the old mediaeval house had been, and also added many statues to the Park.[98] . Plantations were created around the perimeter of the parkland, which tended to enclose the park thus concentrating on inward views rather than distant vistas.

Clephan also helped de Grey with the design of the new Orangery, which formed the western terminal of a new east-west axis located just to the north of the site of the old house, the other terminal being Cain Hill. The Cain Hill House was removed and replaced with an obelisk on a plinth as the house foundations were causing problems. The lodges at the Brabury and Silsoe

---

[97] Many internet sites record her death as on 4 March 1833, the May date is from her memorial in Flitton Church.
[98] James Clephan also in the 1850's designed the new Ampthill Workhouse at Dunstable Street.

entrances to the park, although similar in style to the new mansion, had been built in the 1820s.

In his History of Wrest House dated 1846, he wrote that the old house had cracked walls, long passages and unclosable windows all of which contributed to it needing to be replaced.

The old house was completely demolished upon completion of the new mansion with some materials being used in the village. There are beams in West End Farm and elsewhere which came from the old house and some items from the old chapel were moved to the new church.

Anne Florence de Grey, Baroness Lucas was born on 8 June 1806. She married Sir George Augustus Frederick Cowper, 6th Earl Cowper in 1833 and died in 1880, aged 74. She succeeded to the title of 6th Baroness Lucas in 1859 on the death of her father. She and George had six children, the second of whom was Francis Thomas de Grey, 1834–1905, who became the 7th Earl Cowper. Francis Thomas married Katrine Cecilia Compton, but he died without children in 1905, and thus the Earldom and Barony of Cowper became extinct. He was Lord Lieutenant of Bedfordshire in 1861, a Prince of the Holy Roman Empire and took on many other responsibilities, as befitted a landed earl.

His sister Florence Amabell Cowper had married Auberon Edward William Molyneux Herbert, the son of Henry John George Herbert, 3rd Earl of Carnarvon in 1871 and they had two children who survived into adulthood, Auberon Thomas Herbert, 9th Baron Lucas of Crudwell 1876-1916 and Nan Ino Herbert, Baroness Lucas of Crudwell 1880-1958.

Auberon Herbert gained the title of 9th Baron Lucas of Crudwell on 19 July 1905 and spent his life as a Liberal member of the House of Lords, a reporter for the Times and eventually as an airman; there is more about him in the Military chapter. He was killed in the first World War flying over enemy lines and being unmarried, the estates passed to his sister Nan Ino Herbert.

She succeeded to the titles of 6th Baroness Dingwall and 10th Baroness Lucas of Crudwell in 1916, on the death of her brother, and she decided to sell her estate at Wrest, her daughter eventually donated most of the family documents to the then Bedfordshire County Council archives.

Wrest Park after the Titled Families

Even before the commencement of the sale of the estate in 1917, Wrest Park had been leased out from August 1905 to Whitelaw Reid, the American Ambassador. He intended spending winters there as the fogs and other discomforts of London would seriously affect his health, but travel to London each day in his car. According to reports in the *New York Times* he held several parties at Wrest where other ambassadors and well known people attended.

In 1906 King Edward VII visited him at Wrest and stayed there, with the party attending the Sunday service at the Church. A bicycle service had to be specially installed between Silsoe and Ampthill so that His Majesty could use the telegraph service there.

Also, when in 1908, Reid's daughter married in London, the workers on the estate at Silsoe were given a party, paid for by Reid. The house then probably looked much like it is in Plate 4/5.

He rented the house until 1911 with his death taking place in London a year later. Two years later Lord Lucas had arranged a seven year tenancy of the estate with the Grand Duke Michael Alexandrovitch, the brother of the Tsar of Russia. Presumably this arrangement was cancelled with the outbreak of war as from 1914 onwards Wrest was allowed to be used as a military hospital. However, in 1916, two hundred wounded soldiers were rescued on stretchers from a fire in the house which caused serious damage to the attic storey of the east wing. Villagers helped police, firemen & nurses evacuate the wounded who were transferred to Woburn Abbey[99].

The sale and break up of the estate after the death of Auberon Herbert commenced in 1917 and resulted in the mansion, Wrest Park plus a good percentage of the estate, (and thus Silsoe), being bought by John George Murray; although some items in the house such as pictures had previously been sold at auction where they raised £11,758.

John George's father is listed in the 1891 census as a brewer, innkeeper, shipowner, builder and farmer, so no doubt John George had inherited a good deal of money with which to purchase the estate. He remained at Wrest for several years eventually becoming Sheriff of Bedfordshire in 1923.

However, in the 1930's and following financial difficulties caused by the Great Depression, some of the garden monuments and statuary were sold by Murray and it is known that items such as the Duke's Monument, the Duchess Column and the Park Obelisk are at Trent Park and Ditchling Park. Unfortunately a considerable amount of tree felling was also carried out, including specimen plantings and many of the mature trees in the park land. This had also happened just south of the Park where a timber company from Essex had purchased Fielden in 1918, taking out most of the useful timber, before selling it on as a farm.

John Murray also sold the Park and Wrest House to the Sun Insurance Company in the 1939 for their wartime headquarters, and they remained there until 1946 when the Ministry of Public Buildings and Works bought Wrest Park for the nation,. They then leased the house to the National

---

[99] New York Times & London Times.

Institute of Agricultural Engineering who moved there in 1947; and with a need to provide more accommodation for their research work, constructed many additional buildings towards the east end of the Mansion House - some of which were totally out of sympathy with the Mansion's style of architecture. In 1991 the NIAE changed its name to the more manageable Silsoe Research Institute but a few years later in 2006, following withdrawal of funds, the research was transferred to Rothamsted and other places.

English Heritage,[100] who had been managing the gardens since 1986, took over the house in 2006 and two years later in 2008, announced a 20 year Revitalisation Project costed at £3.8m. This would involve the restoration of the gardens and woodlands to earlier designs as they had been until then managed for minimal maintenance rather than respecting the original concepts.

In addition new visitor facilities would be provided, exhibitions of the history of the estate would be held and some rooms previously closed would be opened. Interestingly they will also be reinstating the Duchess' Column and the Duke's Obelisk which were integral to the original garden design, knitting together the spaces within the woodland garden. Some of the old research buildings had been erected with little sensitivity to the mansion's appearance, and some of these would be removed while others would be retained for use by English Heritage and its staff.

Wrest Park Gardens

The present gardens at Wrest are the result of some 300 years of changing ideas in landscaping and planting arrangements by the various owners, as each applied their own ideas while respecting the earlier layout and planting in the gardens.

The French gardens associated with the early old house, demolished in the 1830's, have been suggested to have been laid out by Le Nôtre (1613-1700) one the greatest geniuses in the history of the world's gardens, but it is more likely that Le Nôtre's designs, especially those at Versailles, were used to inspire the garden at Wrest.[101] Anthony, the 11th Earl constructed the formal gardens, parterres and the wilderness in the late 17th century and a glimpse of the original layout can be seen on the 1708 drawing above.

The gardens were subject to major modification by Henry, the Duke of Kent, who created in broad terms most of what can be seen today. He added the Banqueting House, designed by Thomas Archer, at the southern end of the Long Water in 1709-11 and Hill House on the summit of the adjacent Cain

---

[100] Much of the following information has been taken from English Heritage publications and its web site.
[101] A Book of English Gardens, M R Gloag, The Macmillan Company, New York, 1906

Hill at about the same time. Bowling Green House, which seems to have been built earlier, was modified in 1735.

An inscription on the " Rustic Column " (which itself was moved in 1828 from in front of the Bath House to near the Chinese Bridge) reads :-

" These Gardens, originally laid out by Henry, Duke of Kent, were altered and improved by Philip, Earl of Hardwicke, and Jemima, Marchioness Grey, with the professional assistance of Lancelot Brown, Esq., in the years 1758, 1759, 1760"

However, Lancelot Brown was unable to improve on much of what was already there and contented himself with 'serpentining' the canals on the east, south and west sides of the garden and opening out the edges of the Great Garden.

Jemima had the picturesque Bath House constructed in around 1770 and also added the Mithraic glade and the Chinese temple and bridge. The garden remained much as it was then until Thomas, Earl de Grey demolished the old mediaeval house in the 1830's. Although it had been subject to later alterations and modifications it was said to be draughty with uneven floors..

The demolition enabled him to construct his new mansion some 200 metres to the north thus providing him with more space in which to construct new formal gardens, including a parterre south of the new house, and extending over the site of the old house where he later built the marble fountain, and to the west, the Orangery in 1836. Subsequent generations replaced the Chinese Bridge originally constructed by Jemima.

Chapter 5 - Church, Chantry and Chapel

Introduction

Having no imposing hill or plateau, Silsoe has no henge or similar monument to pre-Christian religions, but no doubt the inhabitants in the pre-Roman times continued with the tribal customs and worshipped whatever local god had been instituted. Springs, being the magic source of life-giving water, were particularly venerated and as there is a named spring in the valley up from Newbury Manor, that may have been a location for such practices.

The Romans brought their own gods, but were happy to accommodate the local gods where necessary. Although with the continued occupation, there was some transference from the local god to the gods that the Romans imported, and who were presumably seen as more effective.

Also through the Romans came Christianity. Christianity became the official state religion of the Roman Empire in the early 4th century A.D. when the Emperor Constantine became convinced of the power of the Christian God and with that change, persecution stopped and Christianity became a favoured religion. In the early days Christianity found most of its followers in the towns and cities of the Roman Empire, but it was not long before wealthy landowners were establishing small churches at their private houses on their country estates throughout the Empire. However, despite official recognition there was no mass conversion to Christianity and the worship of the pagan gods and goddesses was not formally banned until late in the 4th century.

After the fall of the Roman Empire it is believed that some pockets of Christianity survived, but then came the Saxons with their pantheon of gods. With Silsoe being right on the boundary between them and the Britons, no doubt there was some instant conversions to the Anglo-Saxon gods and vice versa, if only to avoid death or worse.

It was not until 597 A.D. when a mission was sent out from Rome under St Augustine, that serious conversion took place in this country. With the assistance of evangelising missions from Ireland, England became primarily a Christian land over the following centuries even allowing for setbacks due to Viking invasions when many monasteries were destroyed.

It is worthwhile remembering that until Henry VIII's Reformation started in 1534 and the birth of the Church of England took place, the country was entirely Roman Catholic. This change would have been incomprehensible and shocking to the common man. Monasteries were suppressed and the buildings sold as stone quarries, some priests were thrown out, worshipping practices were changed and he would have been told to alter his beliefs to agree with the new articles of faith or else…. After a short reversion to

Catholicism with Queen Mary, Protestantism became the predominant religion with Elizabeth I, and has continued so since then.

Flitton parish was held by the nuns of the Abbey of Elstow from earlier than 1159, (when there was a dispute recorded with Dunstable Priory), until the Reformation by Henry VIII in 1536.[1]

However, while there was at any one time the authorised religion as a background, there was a continuation of previous pagan practices, with a tradition of witchcraft in the form of village healers, 'Wise Women' and 'Cunning Men', which persisted through the Middle Ages to at least the 19th century. In addition, pagan celebrations such as harvest festivals or the winter solstice were incorporated into the Christian tradition.

A story from the Northants Mercury of 1788, shows that such practices or beliefs existed in Silsoe even as late as then[2] The article says that around 8 years ago before in 1780, the daughter of Mr Capon, a local farmer, (probably West End Farm) discharged from her stomach 52 brass pins, a pin cushion, scissors and other things. This was attributed by the locals to witchcraft (and not discouraged by the farmer?) and Saunders, a gardener at Silsoe was accused of being a 'wizzard'. (Why, we wonder? Was he too good at making things grow, a bit simple or just ugly?)

He and his wife were then ducked at Silsoe in the village pond, probably the pond opposite West End Farm, until nearly drowned. Capon's daughter then recovered and the local peasants reasoned that this proved that Saunders was a 'wizzard'.

In October 1780 Hadley Cox, the local vicar and a Justice of the Peace, said he had been "engaged in a very troublesome and disagreeable employment suppressing riotous assemblies", when people had been trying people suspected of sorcery, by ducking them in the mill dam at Flitton. "A poor woman of Maulden had been so severely treated in undergoing the experience as to be very ill the day after". Then, following that a fellow had requested that he should be ducked at his own desire, for entertainment or for gambling purpose. Mr Cox managed to stop that.

Burning people in effigy is also not particularly Christian, even though we do it every year with Guy Fawkes. In the latter years of the 18th century, Thomas Paine wrote pamphlets and books promoting America's independence from Britain, and championing rights for the excluded majority. In his most well known book, The Age of Reason, he also attacked state subsidised religion. All of this was total anathema to the ruling classes; and they started smear campaigns with the result that not only were the books banned, but they provoked 'Church and King' mobs all over England, to burn him in effigy. This ceremony took place in Silsoe 1795.

---

[1] VCH p332 et seq gives sources where not otherwise noted.
[2] BLARS AD4000/1

Then there is the story of the Beaumont Tree sited on the Maulden Road on the parish boundary near Beaumont Farm

In the Folklore magazine of 1923, a contributor from McGill's University, Montreal, provided the information that in his boyhood (around 1880-1890), persons wanting to be cured of an unspecified disease would nail some of their hair or a nail clipping, to an old elm in Beaumont Tree Lane which was said to have grown from a murderer's gallows.[3]

A subsequent edition of that magazine quoted someone else in Silsoe (un-named) as saying that he had been told that Beaumont's Tree was an elm that had grown from a stake stuck through the body of a murderer buried at that spot; and that until about 1890 people suffering from ague (malaria) would nail clippings and hair to the tree. The person hearing this, had in 1932, gone to the site and had found two elms, one old and rotting from which he had cut a section containing nails with hair attached, (that he had subsequently given to the Cambridge University Museum of Archaeology); and another healthy tree containing one or two nails evidently knocked in fairly recently.

Interest in this tree was aroused more recently, and as the old elm had died some time ago in 1970, a new tree was planted in 2004, near the original spot. A commemorative plaque on a post was also erected there. At the time of that planting, it was suggested that the original tree had developed from an elm stake thrust through the heart of a highwayman who was shot on the road nearby in 1751, and that locals nailed hair, fingernails etc. to it, to ward off malaria or the ague as it was then known [4] . Now the Flitton parish records note the burial in the churchyard in April 1751, of a highwayman shot in Silsoe Lane, but no name is given. Thus, as he was buried at Flitton and not by the side of the road, it seems improbable that the tree sprouted from an impaling stake. Also, as the name of the highwayman is unknown, why call the tree Beaumont's? There was a land owning family by the name of Beaumont in the area from the 1600's, so the name may have derived from them.

In addition, field names tend to remain for many years and thus as the field was called Beaumont Tree Piece in 1757, only 6 years after the shooting, it is unlikely not to have been called that for many years before. The track from the site of the tree eastwards was called Lady Ash Road in the 1500's, (another tree association), and it could be that the tree at earlier times was an ash, which had magical associations back to Druidic times. Hence perhaps the continuation of quasi-religious practices of nailing hair etc. to it. (If you have ever said "Touch wood" then you have been using, inadvertently, a very old practice.)

---

[3] Folklore Vol 34 No2 (June 30 1923) p 157 & Vol 56 No 3 (Sept 1945) p307. Arthur Steward Eve, 1862 – 1948, was Professor of Physics at McGill and so was probably the informant.
[4] See MBDC Horizon magazine, Jan 2005 and Bedford Today, 11 Nov 2004.

Or, more prosaically, as the parish boundary turns through 180 degrees at this point, the tree may have originally just have been a marker post!

General Church & Parochial History

In the 7th and 8th centuries regional churches or 'minsters' were founded in England staffed by teams of priests who served large 'parochiae' covering the area of perhaps five to about fifteen parishes.

The 'parochiae' were broken up during the 10th to 12th centuries as large landowners founded local churches for themselves and their tenants. It was probably only in the 12th century that the territories which these served crystallised into a formal parochial system and in that century, following the Lateran Council at Rome, the Bishops were given greater control over the parishes. parishes were sized so that they were big enough to support a priest and church through the tithe system, yet not too large so that all could get to the church on a Sunday.

parishes became units of civil administration in the 16th century, when they were made responsible for the highways and for administering the poor law and eventually even appointed a constable. Through the passage of time the boundaries of civil and ecclesiastical parishes, at first corresponding, increasingly diverged with the growing complexity of local government, especially in the 19th century.

Nowadays with population changes, such as new towns or cities, new parishes are created in response to population changes by the Church Commissioners.

Tithes and Church Finances

From Genesis onwards, the Bible required the giving of tithes, generally 1/10th of your annual earnings or property, as a means of providing support for a priest or vicar and the provision of a place of worship. The tithes were eventually calculated on the produce of a man's labour or on things grown or sustained by the soil, being payable to the rector or vicar and would have been paid in kind, such as one in ten sheep, or in cash. However, following the Dissolution of the Monasteries and the sale of church land, it happened that tithes were transferred with the land and could then be bought and sold outside of the church.

The great tithes[5] in Silsoe Parsonage, Vicarage and Glebe lands were owned by Christ Church of Oxford and eventually the de Greys became their tenants. They then, possibly to avoid having to collect the many dues themselves, sub-leased the tithes, church lands and other buildings to others. One of the leases dated 1638, had Ann Hale and William Wheeler (her son-

---

[5] Great Tithes included tithes of from corn, other grains, hay and wood.

in-law) paying £140 a year for most of the Flitton parsonage, plus the "… tithes of grain, pease, pulse, hay and all manner of other tythes…" and "…. the psonage house and the outhouses wh the tythe barne and the yarde and orchard and close thereto adjoining in Silsoe ….". They also had to agree to pay the Earl's rent to Christ Church from the £140 above, and also to provide 'dyet' for family and servants of the Earl at Wrest when the Earl was absent.[6]

The Glebe land was owned by Christ Church and so when the Duke of Kent wanted to extend his parkland in the early 1700's, he needed to get the Dean & Chapter's consent to moving some of the church land out of the area he wanted for the park. This he did by giving 2 acres alongside the Barton Road in exchange for the 1½ acres of church land in the extended park site.[7]

With payment in kind, most parishes needed somewhere to store the produce and so tithe barns were constructed for this purpose. Many of these quite substantial structures still exist in the country but unfortunately Silsoe's has gone.

Silsoe's barn was mentioned in the lease quoted from above and it also appears in an unexecuted lease of 1676 when Amabella was proposing to let to Thomas & Philip Allen of Silsoe, yeomen, for £140 pa the parsonage of Silsoe, and also the tithes within the hamlet, with the tithe barn, yard & close adjacent but excepting the glebe lands.[8]

The location of the glebe lands can also be picked out on the estate plans but a schedule, or terrier, of lands in Silsoe belonging to Christ Church, Oxford, held by lease by the Earl of Hardwicke and Marchioness Grey dated 1771/2[9] exists. This shows the following:-

> Parsonage Close in Silsoe wherein the tithe barn stands, Wrest Park east, The Vicarage west, Park Way north, The George Close south, 1ac.
> A close of arable land called Park Field, the Park east, Long Close west & north, Butchers Close south. 3ac 2r 10p
> A pightle of pasture behind Mr Milwards House in Fielden, Braid Close east, Mr Milward west and north, Brook south 1ac 2r 10p
> In Fielden West field, Watlong Furlong, 2 great leys late Duke of Kent east, late George Fitz west 1ac 0r 24p
> In north field, Watlong Furlong, 3 lands late Duke of Kent east, late Geo Fitz west, 33p
> In south field Fan Furlong, 2 headlands the hedge north, Fan Furlong south, 1ac 1r 0p

---

[6] BLARS L5/1082

[7] Christ Church Oxford records.

[8] BLARS L5/1087 Glebe Lands are lands which provide income through rent etc. to the incumbent. They still exist in some parishes today.

[9] BLARS L26/450

In south field 2 lands more , the hedge east, late Duke of Kent west, 0ac 3r 33p.

This totals 9 acres 2 roods 30 poles

There is a receipt of 1774 for £4 10s[10] from the George for entertainment of the Silsoe tithe renters and that would have bought a lot of ale and food in those days. Presumably this was an annual event to smooth relationships.

The Silsoe 'great tithes' were until 1775 let for £50 per annum but by 1793 they had risen to £98 9s 6d. According to the Jemima's steward, Joseph Pawsey, he paid Land Tax plus Poor Rates out of that which amounted to £26 6s. Tithes were still collected in kind. The titheable lands included 378 acres in the park and Park Farm of which 1/3 was mown for hay with the rest being grazed by deer, oxen & cows.[11]

At the enclosure of land in Silsoe in the early 1800's the associated schedule shows that the church made sure that the land belonging to the vicarage was consolidated.

The tithing system, being based on an agrarian way of life, became unworkable with major population movement from the countryside to towns, and in addition the poor harvests and food shortages of the late 1820's led to resentment and even riots, when tithes were taken from near-starving labourers with vicars being attacked in their own parishes. The opposition to tithes continued until the clergy realised that reform had to be made and they dropped their long-standing opposition to all tithes being commuted to monetary payments.

The Wrest Park agent, George Trethewy spoke at The Farmers Club meeting in London in 1890, on the effect of the 1836 Tithe Commutation Act, whose intent was to convert tithes to a rent charge, but also that land should be let tithe free. He had decided not to speak on ending tithes as no doubt this was too contentious.

They, or their substitute, rent charges, were only finally abolished through the Tithe Act of 1936.

Apart from tithes, the church gained through bequests of land or money, although in some cases not much. For example, John Hill of "Sevellshoo"[12] in the parish of Flytton, in his will made 9th October 1546 left the sum of 4d to Sevellyshoo chapel after allocating his manors, lands and larger monetary bequests.

---

[10] BLARS L27/18
[11] Christ Church Oxford records.
[12] BLARS ABP/R11/240

The Parish of Flitton cum Silsoe

From the start of the parish of Flitton until the break away in 1846, Silsoe was perceived of as a hamlet within the parish of Flitton even though it probably was always the larger part of that parish. There may have been some reason why the main church was not built in Silsoe, perhaps there was no suitably imposing site, or the Flitton church, as has been suggested, was erected upon an earlier religious site. In any event the existing church of St John the Baptist was built where it is in Flitton in the mid 15th century by Edmund de Grey probably after an earlier church was demolished.

The main evidence for the earlier Flitton church are the references to the parish from the 12th century, and of course the list of Vicars which commences with Henry de Hattele, prior to Robert in 1261. The latter construction date is deduced from the heraldry on the south porch. It is also probable that the local red sandstone stone from which most of it, and other buildings in Flitton are constructed, came from the quarry in Silsoe.

The de Greys owned much of Flitton parish and built their mausoleum as an extension to the church in 1614, although it was enlarged in 1705. Unfortunately its rendered appearance is out of sympathy with the main church, having the appearance of a castellated air raid shelter.

Silsoe Chapel, Chantry and Church

However, the parishioners living in Silsoe did not have to make the 1½ mile trek every Sunday to attend church at Flitton as, apart from minor chapels at the manors including a chapel at Wrest from the 13th century, there was from early times, a Free Chapel[13] or a chapel of easel[14] in Silsoe dedicated to St Leonard. This seems to be first mentioned in the Liber Antiquus, 1209-1235, of Bishop Hugh Wells of Lincoln where it was stated that it was held by the Abbey of Elstow. To support the chapel and the priest, the church owned more than 86 acres in the following fields of Silsoe; Kennelfurlong, Waterslade, Redfield, Goshill, Parkfield, Darrelfield, Beechfield at 'Suthend', and Feldonfield.[15]

Why the Silsoe Chapel was dedicated to St Leonard is a mystery. He had served in the army in 6th century Gaul, before he heard the voice of God calling him to lead the life of a hermit. Leonard became a popular holy-man in his own day, as he brought healing to lepers and others who sought his prayers. St Leonard soon became a popular patron of churches and of

---

[13] Free Chapel: A chapel not subject to the jurisdiction of the ordinary, having been founded by the King or by a subject specially authorised.

[14] Chapel of ease: a chapel or dependent church built for the ease or accommodation of an increasing parish, or for parishioners who live at a distance from the principal church.

[15] Mary Phillips in the Bedfordshire Magazine, Vol 7, No. 54.

hospitals and he is also remembered as the patron saint of prisoners. His feast day is on 6 November.

When the chapel changed its saint is not known, but it was before 1821, as an article on Flitton & Silsoe of that year, said that the chapel of easel was dedicated to St James.

Other mentions of the chapel occur in the early 13th century when there is a reference in a grant to '4 sellions'[16] of land lying between Wrest and the chapel of Silsoe; and in 1312 it is recorded that Thomas de Bray, the father of the first party to the deed of grant, had established a chantry in the chapel. This is confirmed by ecclesiastical references in the VCH where the date of foundation is given as 1275; with the endowment being increased in 1290 by Thomas de Bray with the grant of a messuage (a house with outbuildings and land) and land to the Chaplain. The right of alternative presentation (the approval of every other priest) to the chantry was evidently held by the de Bray family.

A further chantry was established by Ralph Fitz Richard who owned Newbury Manor and who in 1327 endowed the chantry with a messuage, plus rent. There are several documents of around this date, where the de Brays and Fitz Richards exchange or witness land deals and if, as is suggested elsewhere, the de Brays founded Broybury Manor, then we have perhaps two of the main land owners in the parish establishing chantries in Silsoe. While a chantry can be a part of an existing religious building, a chapel extension, it was more likely in this case to be a payment to provide for masses to be said or sung for the soul of the donors.

In 1311 John de Grey bestowed a messuage and 5 marks rent upon Ralph Fitz Richard's chantry.

A year later Thomas de Bray granted to his brother Rode, his lands etc in Silsoe but excepted his right to presentation alternately to the chantry in the chapel of Silsoe.[17]

Then Ralph Fitz Richard in 1327 was granted the right by Peter Sancta Cruce to assign his perpetual alms for a chaplain to perform divine service for the repose of the dead in Silsoe chapel in the form of one toft, three acres of land, three acres of meadow on an annual rent of 16s 4d. The property was held by Peter by military service[18]. Perhaps the first to benefit was a chaplain called Henry (his surname is missing) as he bought an acre of land in 1336 in the parish[19].

---

[16] Selion is a mediaeval open strip of land or small field used for growing crops, usually owned or rented to peasants. There could often be several selions to the acre.

[17] BLARS LJeayes84

[18] BLARS LJeayes690

[19] BLARS LJeayes702

It has been estimated that 40% of England's priests died in the Black Death epidemic of 1348, and Silsoe was not exempt, losing its chantry priest.[20] Nationally this left a huge gap, which was hastily filled with underqualified and poorly trained applicants, accelerating the decline in church power and influence, that culminated in the English Reformation. Many survivors of the plague were also disillusioned by the church's inability to explain, or deal with the outbreak.

Thomas Prest of Silsoe escaped death then but his will of 1359, a few years after, is interesting in that he left, in addition to one penny to the priest of Silsoe, "to lights of the Holy Cross & St Mary & St Leonard & St Nicholas of Silsoe 4 bushells of dredge" (a mixture of oats & barley) thus providing two more names of dedication of Silsoe chapel.[21]

It seems that Dom Robert Merston was chaplain for several years in the 15th century as in 1412, he was granted for the term of his life all lands belonging to the chantry of Newburie for 6 pence a year and in 1431, still described as chaplain of the chantry of Syvelesho, he granted power of attorney to William Jacob.

A dispute arose between the priest Richard Hyneman and Thomas Eymewe in the years 1486 – 1493. Richard had agreed to resign upon payment of an annuity by Thomas of 100s. It appears that while Richard had resigned Thomas refused to pay up and in addition brought an action of trespass against Richard.[22] A further name to conjure with is that of Symgwyn who at that time, was the master of the free chapel.

In the early 1500's, the priest of Silsoe chantry, Hugh Massey, was complained against by Thomas Warren, Lord of the Manor of Silsoe, for neglecting his chantry and wasting the chantry lands. Thomas was the patron of the chantry and he said that Massey had not visited the chantry for some 30 years. He was still there in 1535 when he was not only rector of Maulden but also minister of the chapel, and at that time he put its value as £3 10s while the vicar of Flitton, Edward Philips, stated that £3 9s 2d was paid annually as a salary from his vicarage to the Minister of the chapel.

Four years later in 1539, Humphrey Warren the son of Thomas & Elizabeth Warren, sold the reversion of his right to appoint a new priest, together with the chapel of Norwood Manor to Edmund Conquest. This is probably to do with tidying up the details of the ownership of the manor, as it was later sold in 1544. However, it does show that Norwood Manor was substantial enough to have had a chapel attached to it.

The Dissolution began in 1536 and during Edward VI's reign in 1544, Hugh Massey was still the "clerk, chaplin or 'cantarista' of the chantry of Syvelshoo

---

[20] History of Bedfordshire, Joyce Godber.
[21] BLARS LJeayes 2
[22] VCH

in the parish of Flytton" when he surrendered to Henry Grey and Edward Daniell for 'certain considerations' the chantry with all rights and land[23.] According to the VCH he lived in Cheshire and had apparently not visited Silsoe for some 30 years! Services were carried out by another priest found by the vicar of Flitton and paid for by Elstow Abbey. At the dissolution it was said that the chantry was of no use, and that it had no goods or ornaments.

After the dissolution the chantry was granted to Sir Edward Warner and John Goswood by King Edward VI, but in 1549 the "late chantry of Silsoe with all its possessions", which would have included the associated land, was granted to Sir Henry Grey and Dame Anne his wife[24] by Edward and John.

There may also have been a problem with the existing priest, Edward Philipe, who was installed in 1532, as in 1541 a new priest, John Gale, whose patron was Henry VIII, was installed. A priest at Silsoe in 1595, John Gleeston, (although not on the list of Vicars), was described as being recusant, in other words he was continuing the practices of the Roman Catholic Church.[25]

During the time of the Commonweath in 1645, when William Ramsey had been the Vicar of Flitton cum Silsoe for 17 years, he was summoned to appear before The Committee for Plundered Ministers on a charge of drunkenness. This committee had been instituted in 1643, as a means of replacing those ministers who were still loyal to Charles I, and as a result they were described as 'scandalous', which meant that their political and theological attitudes were Roman Catholic. Ramsey did not turn up for his hearing and in his absence in May 1647, and perhaps on the evidence of dissatisfied parishioners, he was declared a common drunkard. The vicarage was ordered to be taken from him and given to " some godley and orthodox divine". This was possibly John Gardner, a minister, whose son Samuel was born in Flitton in 1649.

Ramsey put up a fight however, and it was not until 1655 that he was ejected for refusing to conform to the standards of Presbyterianism.[26] A note by Joseph Barbor, JP of that year stating that Thomas Hill was appointed to record births, marriages and burials particularly infuriated him and he added the following:-

> "A furious zeal, blind understanding. – Fye uppon such hereticall dunces. – By this note of regestring, by births, mariages and burialls and not by baptising, doth plainely show that the authors thereof were anabaptisticall.[27]"

---

[23] Bro LJeayes 791

[24] BLARS LJeayes 801

[25] Mary Phillips etc etc

[26] VCH

[27] An Anabaptist believes that you should be baptised as an adult, when you understand what you are doing.

He maintained a stubborn resistance even after being ejected, and for a long time remained in the parsonage until the restoration of the monarchy officially restored the living and the parsonage to him, in 1660. His wife died in May 1665, with him following in September that year, and he was succeeded by William Harris who, for some reason, was unable to get the registry book given to him for nearly seven months.

An interesting event occurred in October 1664 when the minister, and according to the dates this must have been Ramsey, was thrown out of the church at the burial of Thomas Daniel. The vicar recorded :-

> "Thomas Daniel of Newburie was buried with great contention against me being the minister of the parish church; by Wm Wheeler of Silsoe, Jn Webb, Ric Wheeler of Flitton and Jn Greene the ygr of Flitton, who did cast me out of the church by force and would not suffer me to bury him."

Presumably Thomas was eventually buried.

Wrest Park old house had an early chapel within it which was mentioned in a schedule of 1573, in which also many rooms were described as being adjacent to the chapel; and no doubt there was a chaplain there when the family was in residence. The chantry was mentioned in the Inquisition Post Mortem[28] taken at Ampthill on the death of Charles, Earl of Kent in 1626, although this probably related only to the land holding of the old chantry, which was perhaps now being used to provide money for upkeep of the chapel of easel. A further Wrest inventory of 1667 also mentions the chapel and chapel chamber and also the Chaplains room [29]. Also, in 1671 when there were major works being carried out to the old house at Wrest, a schedule of works says that the "chapel chamber to be raised to 13', 2 new windows, old window to be arched and put in maids' chapel", there may therefore have been a secondary chapel.[30] In 1701 more works were being carried out to the house, this time outside, and several times reference is made to a chapel garden.[31]

Despite having their own chapel, the family had some regard for the spiritual needs of the Silsoe residents and at some time the chapel of easel mentioned above, was founded on the old chantry site for use of Wrest Park tenants and others[32]. Perhaps the old chantry building had remained and this procedure formalised its use.

---

[28] An Inquisition Post Mortem was an inquiry taken after the death of a major landowner to establish what lands were owned and who should succeed to them. BLARS L22/17.
[29] Bro L31/170-178
[30] BLARS L31/228
[31] BLARS L31/289
[32] VCH p333

An account of 1653 includes a payment made by the Countess Dowager of Kent to Mr Garner, the curate of Silsoe.[33]

We have no record of how the common people were involved with the church. Sunday attendance was virtually compulsory with names being reported to the local Assizes if someone did not attend for two weeks or more. For example[34] in 1683 William Fowler presented Elizabeth Godfrey of Silsoe "widdow for not comeing to her parish church or chapell for the space of three weeks last". She held to her beliefs probably until her death in 1707 as in 1685, she committed the same "offence" and was accordingly reported again.

As a more literate group, the de Grey family and their friends regularly wrote in their diaries so that, for example, we have from Catherine Talbot writing on 2 June 1745 that "All went to the parish church at 11. Home at 2. Chapel in the Afternoon". Two days later she wrote that she, having visited the chapel she was much pleased with Dr Calamy's sermons which she had read. Then on 9 June (Tuesday) she wrote "…went with her (Jemima) to church, where the Service was very long, but not at all tedious, for Mr. 2.19 [35] reads Prayers better than most people I know, the Sermon was well enough, we had a churching & two christenings." It seems improbable that the villagers had enough time off from work to indulge themselves in such continuous churchgoing.

In 1821, the interior was described in the Gentleman's Magazine as being 'very neat, a handsome gallery has been erected parallel with the whole west end, the pews have been painted. The altar piece is well wainscoted and has a painting of the adoration of the shepherds, the production of Mrs Mary Lloyd[36] and presented by her to the chapel. Over the west end is a small and ugly steeple and spire, containing two prayer-bells and a clock'.

Unfortunately during later renovations the altarpiece disappeared.

By 1828, the chapel was further in need of repair, and this together with a population increase in the village, and perhaps because his Lordship wanted a pleasant church at the start of the drive to his new mansion, led Lord Grantham, later Earl de Grey, to whom the Prince Consort turned for architectural advice, to have drawings made and a report of the work needed, drawn up by the architect Thomas Smith of Hertford. Smith wrote that the timber in the spire and tower was split and rotten, the west wall was fractured and the timber to the nave roof was decaying. However, the chancel only

---

[33] BLARS L26/16

[34] BLARS HSA1685/W/20-23 & HSA1683/S/16

[35] She put personal names in code. The Vicar of Flitton at that time was John Robinson, however, Mr 2.19 might be the private Chaplain.

[36] Mrs Lloyd was Mary Moser (1744-1819), the first woman member of the Royal Academy, and probably a friend of the family.

needed re-tiling. The cost for the reconstruction, re-roofing and repair work was estimated at £1,185 [37].

Plate 5/1 - Silsoe Chapel, early 19th century, from the North West

Plate 5/2 - Silsoe Chapel, early 19th century, from the South East

The plans and elevations drawn at this time enable us to see that the chapel was in two different styles and presumably of different ages. The chancel to the east was narrower, with a steeper tiled roof, and may well have been the location, if not the building of the earlier chapel. The nave was wider with side aisles and had a flatter, possibly leaded roof, and had more regularly spaced windows. This latter part supported the small tower and spire, which

---

[37] BLARS L33/244

was by then propped up by timbers from each corner running down to the roof [38].

In 1821 the steeple contained two prayer-bells plus a clock.

The architect also drew up plans for the improvement to the chapel and it seems that approval was given to go ahead with the works, as an article in the Bedford Gazette records that in 1829 the parishioners entered into a contract for the erection of a steeple on the old chapel[39]. Work proceeded until the second window when the foundation was found to be insecure - presumably some cracks opened up.

The work carried out was taken down, and piles were driven into the ground to support the structure. Feeling now more safe the workers recommenced, and reached the same height as it had been previously before the earlier instability became apparent. Then, while the workers were away having some refreshment, presumably some ale, the whole fell down with a tremendous crash so that 'scarcely one stone was left upon another'. Thomas, Earl de Grey wrote that

> ' 1 day after I left Wrest in March 1829 the steeple was up to 30 – 40 feet when the workmen had left for lunch at the inn. Some quarrel occurred and only one man returned. He sat with his back to wall when he thought he felt it tremble and moved out of way when down it all came. The walls were thick but constructed of two skins with rubble fill and no connecting blocks.'

Richard Eve of West End Farm, the churchwarden from 1811 to 1885, was also apparently fond of telling the story of the collapse.[40]

Following this disaster it was then decided to rebuild the whole chapel some feet further from the road and all of it was pulled down and altered. This, together with a few modern additions, is what we have today. The first service was held in the new chapel on Sunday 20th February 1831, when no doubt it was overflowing.

In 1830, the then vicar, the Rev. H Wellesley (related to the Duke of Wellington), applied to the Dean of Christ Church asking for financial help. He said that the Countess was supplying timber & stone from her estate but that the cost would be around £2,000. They offered all of £50.

An account of the expense in rebuilding the chapel shows that William Jeeves, bricklayer, slater and mason, received £1,489 with two masons William and John Warren, receiving £144. The carpenter Joshua Watson, was paid £608 (after arbitration) with the local blacksmith, John Lowings

---

[38] BLARS L33/245 & 246 drawings
[39] BLARS AD4000/1
[40] Bedfordshire Standard 14 Nov 1885.

receiving £61. The cost of the collapse was reflected in John Stevens, the original builder, being paid £158 for materials left after that event, plus £55 for the loss of labour and materials. The implication of those costs is that Mr Stevens was not allowed to continue with the new construction, and perhaps was held partially to blame for the collapse. It appears that the final construction work was carried out using direct and where possible, local labour. The architect's fees were £212 with the final cost in the region of £5,000.

It seems likely that around the time that the old chapel became a church, it was decided that the ground in which it sat was insufficient to provide sufficient use as a graveyard, as plans show the chapel land ending a few metres beyond the east wall; and so the old vicarage plus another building, perhaps the old workhouse, were demolished and the graveyard extended[41].

During the time that the church was being built, the Earl had been erecting his brand new mansion at Wrest Park and presumably, with the new chapel being so close to the mansion, he decided not to incorporate a chapel in his new house. He subsequently, in 1845, pressed both Christ Church and the Bishop of Lincoln, for Silsoe to become a separate parish from Flitton, and for the chapel to be re-consecrated as a church.

The Vicar of Flitton at the time of the division of the parish, the Rev. Alfred Bourne, acquiesced with this and it was progressed by Earl de Grey We learn from the queries made by the bishop that baptisms and churchings had previously been carried out in the chapel, that there was a churchyard suitable for burials and that chapelwardens had been elected by the inhabitants of Silsoe. The glebe lands would be retained by Flitton church and it was stated that the inhabitants of Silsoe had never contributed to the upkeep of Flitton church. The Earl agreed to endow £150 pa to the new church, and to provide suitable accommodation for the clergyman, which had already been built. This included the provisos that he was given the patronage of the new church[42], (previously with Christ Church, Oxford) and that the allocation of pews remained as before[43].

(The advowson or presentation[44] of Flitton parish was held by the Abbey of Elstow until the dissolution when it was bestowed upon the Dean & Chapter of Christ Church College, Oxford[45] who owned the right of presentation of a new vicar even though this right had been leased to the de Greys.)

---

[41] That the Old Vicarage was there is indicated in the deed referred to above (BLARS L26/450).

[42] The right to appoint the Vicar, subject to the Bishops approval

[43] BLARS L27/52, 59

[44] Advowson, The right of presentation to a benefice by a bishop or layman. Lay patronage dates from the 8th century, when laymen began to build churches on their land. Advowsons still exist as property rights tenable by British citizens who are not Roman Catholics.

[45] VCH

The new vicar, the Rev. Stephen Hastings Atkins, who started his incumbency in 1846, was installed in a new vicarage built at the junction of Ampthill Road with Vicarage Road. Eventually in the late 1990's this large Victorian building with its extensive gardens was sold by the Church Commissioners, and a modern vicarage built in Fir Tree Road within the land of the old vicarage.

On the matter of pews; a Miss Bishop wrote on an important matter" regarding her pew to the de Grey's agent, John Allen, now managing the estates at Crudwell in Wiltshire and he responded thus;-

> Crudwells, 26 April 1741
> Miss Bishop,
> I am sorry to hear you are disturb'd in the enjoyment of the seat I made up in Silsoe Chapel. You have the same right to that and the small piece of ground taken from The George Close unto the garden as I have had and suer none at Silsoe can question my having so quietly enjoy'd them so long. I should never if have had nor also we expected to have heard any dispute could have arose about so clear and so trifling a matter. My kind respects to all your famely and all that asks after me
> I am your friend and humble servt
> John Allen[46].

As implied above, pews were important as a status symbol both then and earlier, and this continued well into the 20th century. The Earl and his family sat in their allocated pews close to the altar in the chancel, and important village people, reducing in importance with distance from the Earl, had their own allocated pews. Woe betide anyone who sat in another's pew! No doubt, (and may still happen in the country) on the Earl's entrance, all those in the church stood and at the end of the service they stood again until he had left.

Also, in 1828 when the "new built" mansion house (now the Red House) was leased, the particulars included a pew in the church or chapel of Silsoe. The pew arrangement for 1831 for the old chapel is still extant and is shown in Plate 5/3 below giving a good indication of the 'pecking order' at that time.

---

[46] BLARS L5/428

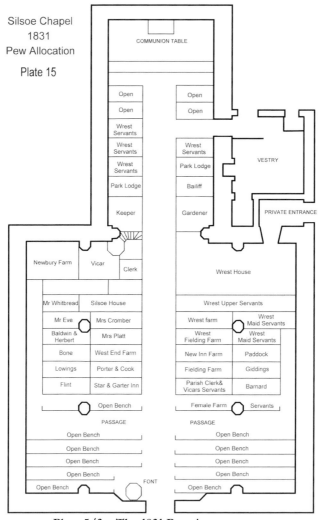

Plate 5/3 – The 1831 Pew Arrangement

A plan of the chapelyard of 1845 shows that its extent at that time was only as far as to include the first row of graves beyond the path on the east of the chapel[47] and with this area becoming insufficient an extension of the burial land took place with this land being consecrated in 1891.[48] The eastern boundary was extended a further 65 ft or so between 1896 and 1901 and then, in association with the construction of 'The Beeches' development which started in about 1997, the developers provided a 40 ft addition to the east side together with an oak lytch gate over a new eastern entrance.

---

[47] BLARS L27/49
[48] BLARS P54/2/3/1

Major alterations were made to the interior of the church in 1884 when new flooring was laid and the existing pews were replaced. The old pews were presumably box pews, as there was sufficient timber from them for it to be used to construct the wooden panelling in the nave. At the same time the organ was installed, although originally it was at the east end of the north aisle, before being moved at a later date to its present position.

For many years in the latter part of the 20th century the profits from Silsoe village fair were used for the maintenance and improvement of the church; and works have taken place recently to make the church more in line with the comfort expected in these times with toilets and washrooms being added in 2003, and in 2006 the entrance porch was improved.

A Short Description of the Church

The new church was constructed in the local sandstone excavated from the old quarry in Ampthill Road where The Maples now lies. The internal layout closely followed that of the old chapel but with the tower providing a more imposing aspect than the old squat spire.

The author of the 'Round the County' pieces in the Bedfordshire Times, Arthur Ransom, wrote in 1902 that " the style was perpendicular and that the building has a charm that many more pretentious structures lack being constructed in the local re-brown stone. There are a western tower with octagonal newel-turret at its south east angle, a clerestoried nave, two aisles, a chancel and a small vestry on the south side of the chancel". He considered that the lack of south and north doors to be unusual as were the wooden newel stairs, as opposed to stone, leading to the turret. He admired the moulding around the main door and the embattlemented roofs.

The clock in the tower was erected in 1910 to commemorate the visit by King Edward VII to Wrest Park in July 1909, when he also attended a service in the church and made a donation to the clock fund.

Nikolaus Pevsner in his book "The Buildings of England: Bedfordshire, Huntingdon and Peterborough" expressed his admiration for it as "an astonishing job for its day" and he thought that the architect had achieved "an antiquarian accuracy here extremely rare ten years before Pugin".

As the building is listed, the extension at the west end to provide modern toilet facilities had to be constructed using matching sandstone; but as the local Silsoe quarry had shut down years ago, a similar stone had to be sourced from outside the village to satisfy English Heritage.

There are several items of interest inside the church such as, the reredos and oak altar given by Mrs Murray of Wrest Park, the credence table[49] made from

---

[49] A reredos is a screen behind the altar and a credence table was used to hold the bread and wine.

the oak beams of an old house, and the oak altar rails which were constructed of 17th century timber from the old house at Wrest when it was demolished.

There is also a Royal Coat of Arms hanging from the west gallery which is said to be of George I vintage, 1714 – 1727, and which presumably came originally from the old chapel. This is there because Queen Elizabeth I required that all churches should have a royal coat of arms to symbolise the fact that the monarch was the head of the Church of England.

There are also in existence altar vessels brought from Wrest Park chapel, but which are now sadly held in a security vault. They are a flagon of 1686, and a chalice and paten of 1667 the gift of Amabella, Dowager Countess of Kent.

The stained glass windows are also of interest, with many having the coats of arms of the Wrest Park families such as Robinson, Campbell, Crewe, Weddell, Perrefoy, Ben, Grey & Lucas as well as the arms of the Bishop of Lincoln and Christ Church College, Oxford.

Bellringing

The earliest mention of bells at Silsoe is in 1640, when Philip Haynes in his will gave 5s to the ringers of Flitton and 2s to the ringers of Silsoe [50]. This does not necessarily mean that there was a peal of bells, but more likely the existence of only one bell that was to be rung by ringers in turn, at his funeral. This bell would also have been used to signal a death in the village, one toll for each year of age; times when gleaning could start and finish and perhaps as an alarm.

There is no mention of bells at the reconstruction of the church in 1830, but it seems likely that the small tower was built with the intention to hang one or more bells there. The list of bells below shows that 3 bells hung, were cast in 1857 and presumably hung there that, or the next year. This number is stated in Kelly's directories from 1890 up until 1928, then in 1931 5 bells are mentioned.

Ransom's description of the church of 1902 records three bells which were the 4th, 5th and the tenor in the following list.

The bells currently in the tower are:-

> Treble, G#, cast by John Taylor & Co. of Loughborough, installed 1951, weight 3.0.7. Inscribed " With my song I will praise him. Restoration of the peal 1951. This Treble Bell was added through the zeal and energy of the Bell Fund Restoration Committee and many friends. A J Woodward, Chairman, T P Harris, Secretary, E J Baigent, Treasurer, J Adams, Vicar."

---

[50] Will of Phillip Haynes, Nat Archives Prob/11/184, Probate in BLARS L5/68

2[nd,] F#, cast by Alfred Bowell of Ipswich, hung in 1926, weight 4.0.14. Inscribed "To the Glory of God and in memory of Richard and Mary Eve."

3[rd,] E, cast by Alfred Bowell, hung in 1926, weight 4.3.8. Inscribed "To the Glory of God and in memory of William and Caroline Eve."

4[th,] D#, cast by John Warner & Sons of London, hung in 1857, weight 4.2.25. Royal Crest only.

5[th,] C#, cast by John Warner & Sons, hung in 1857, weight 6.1.3. Royal Crest only.

Tenor, B, cast by John Warner & Son , hung in 1887, weight 6.1.9. Inscribed "Pro Jubilaes Victoria R.I LAVS." [51]

This peal of six bells enables several combinations to be rung. The maximum of changes for this number of bells is 720, which would take about half an hour of concentrated effort.

The Parsonage and other Buildings Associated with the Chapel

In 1717 the Vicar of Flitton, William Cauldwell together with a group which included Charles Millward, the church or chapel Warden of Silsoe, and John Gwyn, the church or chapel Clerk, sold a cottage in Silsoe called the Town House, to the east of the chapel to the Duke of Kent[52]. This may have been the parsonage and what became, and is referred to elsewhere, as the 'poor house'. It was the place to which the poor of the parish could go when totally skint and which the Duke was possibly taking over to keep it maintained or so he could use the land for his park extension.

In 1708 a terrier says it had timber walls, was roofed with tiles and had three lower rooms, a parlour, and a kitchen and wash-house all with earthen floors, with only the parlour being ceiled. The three upper rooms were floored but not ceiled and there was a thatched barn which may also have originally been the tithe barn. In 1762 the vicar, Phillip Birt, wrote in the Flitton register that he had greatly improved the building by converting it into two dwellings and providing a new chimney.[53]
A terrier of 1771/1772 includes the comment "Parsonage Close in Silsoe wherein the tithe barn stands, Wrest Park east, the Vicarage west, Park Way north, the George Close south, 1 acre." while a draft lease of 1676 between Amabella, Dowager Countess of Kent and Thomas & Philip Allen of Silsoe, yeo. refers to "…the parsonage of Silsoe, and tithes within the hamlet, with the tithe barn, yard & close adjacent, except the parsonage house and the

---

[51] From sheet giving bell details from Simon Stranks, current Tower Captain (2009).

[52] BLARS L5/101

[53] M Phillips etc etc

glebe lands…"[54] These documents locate the parsonage and the tithe barn fairly accurately if the 'Parsonage close' is, as seems probable, the 'Parsonage pikle' which is shown on the 1718 map in Plate 15/5

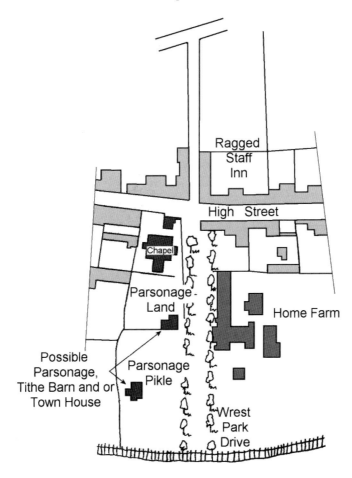

Plate 5/5 – The Church and its Environs in 1718

Also appearing on this map is the chapel, at the approximate location of the current church, but with a building in front, at the corner of the cross roads. This may have been a small barn in which to store the bier, the cart used to collect coffins; but as there was also from early times, a 'poor house' in the churchyard it may have been this. Repeated attempts were made in the 18th century to have the miserable building removed and rebuilt, and early in the 19th century both the vicarage and the poor house were pulled down. The poor house was rebuilt on a new site in West End.

---

[54] BLARS L26/450 & L5/1076

The chapel itself was probably deteriorating even in the 18th century and in 1774 on 28th November Amabel at Wrest wrote in one of her letters to say that "Silsoe Church is full of Workmen yet, so Mr Cox read Prayers in our chapel". Mr Cox was the Rev. Hadley Cox, the then Vicar of Flitton.

The Chapel House was still in existence in 1808 when a valuation of Flitton & Silsoe Vicarage, includes a tenement called the Chapel House which was divided into two dwellings, occupied by William Arnold and Robert Upton the parish Clerk and rented for £6 per annum.

Until about 1845 when the chapel became a church, there was no need for a house for a parson as such, but the chapel curate, if resident in the village, would have had to live somewhere. In 1841 there is a clergyman by the name of Edward Sayer aged 30, living in "Silsoe Town" and he was not the incumbent of Flitton so he was either the curate, just living there or the Wrest Park private chaplain.[55] The status of vicars in the mid 19th century required them to have a suitably large vicarage, and so in 1846 Earl de Grey conveyed a house and garden which he had bought from George Henry Whitbread, to Queen Anne's Bounty to be used as such.

There were three vicars within the space of a few years, but in the census of 1851 the third incumbent, Thomas Ferguson aged 35, is found at the new vicarage described as the Perpetual Curate of Silsoe[56]. The old vicarage is still in existence although, like two of the pubs in the village, it is now being used as housing with a new vicarage having been built in Fir Tree Road.

Chaplains and Vicars

Although there are mentions of chaplains in early documents relating to Wrest Park they may have been associated with other chapels and not necessarily Silsoe.

There are several references to Hamo(ne) le Clerk in documents from 1334 - 1351 who is of "Eyen" (Ion) but as it seems unlikely that there was a chapel there so he may have officiated at Silsoe. Others chaplains are mentioned in that century such as "Henry ------ the chaplain" who in 1336 was granted an acre of land by Thomas le Webbe of La Felde[57]. Then in 1334 & 1335 John Fyndal, chaplain, witnesses documents[58]. He is also in the list of vicars for Flitton erected in the Silsoe Church for the period 1350 – 1390, and was presumably promoted as a replacement for the previous incumbent who probably succumbed to the great plague of 1349.

---

[55] There was also William Whitbread, a minister, living near Edward Sayer and William Dawson, a clergyman living at Fielden at this time.
[56] A Perpetual Curate was the vicar of a parish which had been created out of an existing parish.
[57] BLARS LJeayes 702
[58] BLARS LJeayes 713 & 714

Then in 1393[59] Stephen Carpenter, chaplain, is selling 1½ acres of land, probably in Fielden, and in 1404[60], Richard Parchemenere, chaplain, is jointly selling 7 acres of land with a messuage and croft. The 1408 grant of the Manor of Broybury, probably in the north east of Silsoe, has William Tappe, vicar of the church of Silsoe, and, John Doncesson, chaplain, as parties to the grant.

In 1416[61] John atte Lye, Chaplain, is referred to, and in 1410 and 1431 documents have Dom / Master Robert Merston as chaplain, and also as the chaplain of the chantry of Syvelesho[62]. However, he is also recorded as the Vicar for Flitton from 1414 - 1418, so there may not have been a separate chaplain at that time. Indeed in one document of 1354 he is said to be the *"Vicar of Cyvelesho"*[63] so perhaps the titles were not as fixed as they are now. This is shown by Thomas Prest's will of 1359 where he gives " ... half a mark to chaplain of parish of Fliton for celebrating masses for my soul 1d to priest of Silsoe…"[64]. He also gave "…1 bushell of wheat to lights of the Holy Cross & St Mary & St Leonard & St Nicholas of Silsoe…" which suggests that the chapel was dedicated to two saints. As only Robert Merston is directly connected to Silsoe chapel, it is possible that the other chaplains were connected to other chapels.

In 1437 Richard Milward of *"Feelde in Flitt"* covenanted that if William his son should wish to buy (land in the deed) he should pay (two trustees) " for one year the rent of one messuage with 3 acres of land to find a priest in the chapel of St. Leonard of Sevyllyshoo to celebrate divine service for one year for the said Richard's soul"[65].

By 1535 Hugh Massey, rector of Maulden was also minister of the chapel and put its value as £3 10s while the vicar of Flitton, Edward Philips, stated that £3 9s 2d was paid annually as a salary to the minister of the chapel.

Hugh Massey, mentioned above as *the "clerk, chaplin or 'cantarista' of the chantry of Syvelshoo"* in 1544 also appears earlier in 1541, as "Hugh Massy chantry Priest"[66] when he gives a receipt for 54s to the Duke of Kent for the rent of the chantry.

After that date no mentions of named chaplains have been found in documents outside the lists of incumbents, with the following exception, (although a search of the Diocesan records may result in further names). The exception is William Henry Lambert whose memorial in the churchyard says

---

[59] BLARS LJeayes 717
[60] BLARS LJeayes 736
[61] BLARS LJeayes 739
[62] BLARS LJeayes 743 & 739
[63] BLARS LJeayes 317
[64] BLARS LJeayes 2
[65] BLARS LJeayes 750
[66] BLARS L26/1422

he was sometime curate of this parish who died March 19th 1871 aged 31, he had married Eliza Eve on 31st December 1869.

Letters to and from the owners of Wrest in the 18th century give some indication of the men who became the vicar for Flitton cum Silsoe. John Birt and Hadley Cox appear very energetic men, being Justices, with all that entails in sitting on the bench and signing warrants etc, as well as men of the cloth and spent much time corresponding with the owners of Wrest Park. Mr Cox's successor, Mr Drummond who had "very much the behaviour and manners of a gentleman" appears to have been very conscious of his status, perceiving rudeness when, what he saw was just " general rusticity and neglect of religious worship." (according to his Lordship). Once on the way to London, seeing the postboy heading northwards, he opened the mailbags to search for letters addressed to him - an offence punishable by death. He eventually found a better appointment in Northumberland and left.

Following him came the Rev. John Robinson, vicar from 1784 to 1817, who was described in 1786 by Joseph Pawsey, the Wrest steward, as follows "On the whole Mr Robinson does his duty as well as he can, but he a man of very mean appearance very low voice and a bad delivery, and reads and preaches without energy". In fact a petition was started in 1811 calling for his removal which was signed by all the parishioners except his tenants and Tryphosa Box, lately Amabel's maid.

(The 1831 census has under the somewhat unfortunate grouping of "Wholesale, Capitalists & Clergy" one un-named person listed which could have been a Chaplain/Vicar.)

With the creation of Silsoe parish in the early 1840's the new vicarage and its land was conveyed in 1845 to the "Bounty of Queen Anne", the predecessors of the Church Commissioners, with the Earl de Grey retaining patronage of Silsoe, the right to appoint the vicar[67].

Schedules of the various vicars and priests of Flitton church, Silsoe chapel and church are appended at the end of this chapter.

---

[67] BLARS L27/62

Churchwardens

There are few early references to chapel or church wardens which directly relate to Silsoe. The first is of 1717 when Charles Milward, gentleman of Fielden is said to be the church or chapel warden of Silsoe with Thomas Bishop, a carpenter and also chapel warden of Silsoe. Also, Russell Finney who tenanted Newbury was a church warden in 1771.

Richard Eve who commenced as churchwarden in Flitton in 1811 with the new church opening in Silsoe in 1846, transferred there, only leaving that post in 1885.

George Frederick Ford who died in 1905, a gardener at Wrest, is mentioned on his churchyard memorial as having been for many years a churchwarden and Charles Ireson Robinson who died in 1908, was a sometime churchwarden also according to his memorial.

A further more recent memorial records Kenneth William Scott born in 1925 and died in 2002, as having been churchwarden of this parish for 29 years.

The churchwardens in 2009 were Michael Olney & Gillian Liddle.

Churchyard Memorials

Following the 'split' from Flitton and the consecration of Silsoe church and grounds, baptisms, marriages and burials could then be carried out here. Although it is possible that baptisms had taken place before parish records for Silsoe recording these events were commenced in 1846. Before that year, the Flitton parish registers record these important events but for Silsoe, while the early books are in the Bedfordshire archives, the current book remains with the present vicar.

The earliest date remaining on a memorial in the churchyard is of January 1850, the tombstone is to John Arnold of New Inn Farm who died of consumption (tuberculosis) and is located to the south of the church, presumably the area where burials commenced. Earlier memorials may have been of timber or of a poor quality stone which have eroded and so no longer can be found. In some areas the old memorials were removed for ease of maintenance.

As might be expected, the remaining older inscriptions have a Victorian flavour, but some give an insight into the 19th century attitudes to death and the hereafter. Other Silsonians died away from their village such as Annie Elizabeth Walker, the daughter of William and Susannah Walker of Ampthill Street, whose internment in the Protestant Cemetery in Rome is commemorated on a memorial in Silsoe. A schedule of the Rome cemetery records "Annie Elizabeth Walker of Silsoe, Ampthill, England, Died January 6 1916 in her 46th year. Faithful servant to Sir Henry Howard, British

Minister to the Holy See." She is in good company as both Shelley and Keats were buried there.

There are several references to Wrest; one to the 13 year old Arthur Walker who was killed in an accident in October 1854 in Wrest Park and others such as that to the Snow and Ford families who lived and worked for many years in the gardens :-

> "Sacred to the memory of Seward Snow (son of William Snow of Handley in the County of Dorset Yeoman and Ann his wife) who died on the 10th March 1869 in the 75th year of his age
> also In loving memory of George Frederick Ford Nephew of the above who died November 12th 1905 aged 85 years. He succeeded his uncle as head gardener to the Countess Cowper and Earl Cowper KG and was for many years churchwarden of this parish beloved and respected by all who knew him.
> In the year 1835 he laid out the new gardens at Wrest Park and to the year 1839 continued to improve the pleasure grounds under the direction of his noble employers Earl de Grey KC and Countess Cowper."

And we also have associated with Wrest, Charles Ireson Robinson originally from Harrold, who lived at Wrest Park Farm and was "Clerk of the Works to the Wrest Estate for 31 years and sometime churchwarden of this parish", he died in 1908 aged 63.

Then there is a memorial to William Treacher, teacher at the school, which commemorates his 39 years as headmaster of Silsoe School from 1883 to 1922. He wrote a pamphlet on the village of Silsoe, which can be found in the Bedfordshire archives. Nearby lies Charlotte Mann who died in 1914 aged 81 and who was for 50 years teacher in the Infants School and a member of the church choir.

Also commemorated is Benjamin Carter who was 35 years at the George Inn, and who died in 1856 aged 63, the memorial says that he was respected by all who knew him.

On the north side of the churchyard are the memorials to the Eve family from the earliest member who came to Silsoe to run West End Farm, Richard Eve, who was for 70 years churchwarden of Silsoe and who died in 1885 in his 98th year, to his grandson Malcolm Trustram Eve, 1st Baronet & 1st Baron Silsoe who died in 1976.

The War Memorial, recently restored in 2000 contains the names of 18 men of, or associated with the village, who died in the two World Wars. It includes the name of Auberon Thomas Herbert, 9th Baron Lucas, who was shot down whilst flying over the German lines, and whose death caused the break up of the Wrest Park estate.

Non-Conformism

With the families at Wrest virtually controlling the village and being strongly supportive of the Church of England, there would have been great difficulty early on for new faiths such as Quakers, Baptists and Methodists in finding somewhere to worship within Silsoe.

However there must have been a good Quaker representation in this area as there was a field used as a Quaker cemetery in Flitton, presumably not owned by Wrest. A "burying place" is mentioned in 1675[68] and in 1674 Nicholas & Susannah Crouch who died of smallpox were "layd in ye corner of Broom close as Quakers". Nicholas and his wife who lived in Pulloxhill, had been given the close as part of a marriage settlement in 1648, and perhaps those from Silsoe reported as not attending the official church were members of that faith. Other burials "in a field" and "with Quakers in a field" in 1684, of people from Barton, Ampthill and Gravenhurst shows that the burial ground attracted members of that faith from elsewhere.

The parish records also have the mother of Eleezers Hawkins who "being an infidell, and also her son Eleeser and her daughter (were infidels) she was buried in her orchard at home", this was in 1664. In 1682 widow Ann Carter was buried in Hawkins garden and later that year Eleagar, the son of widow Hawkins, was buried in a garden, presumably the same one. The word infidel is nowadays taken to mean a non-Christian but as there was a "professed atheist" being buried around the same time, the term probably meant not being a member of the Church of England, or being a Non-Conformist.

As to Baptists, there is no evidence that John Bunyan preached here, although he did nearby, but William Daniel, who was at Newbury Manor from 1666 to 1685 was only too aware of him; as he was one of the 13 Justices who signed a warrant for his arrest in 1674: only two years after Bunyan's 12 year stint in Bedford Gaol for not complying with the Anglican authorities.[69]

In 1754 John Wesley spent some hours visiting the gardens at Wrest, which he thought were better than Lord Cobham's Park.[70] No record has been found that John Wesley preached near Silsoe although he did preach in St Pauls at Bedford in 1758, in 1766 at Cople and at other locations in the county.

Early in the 19th century there are several mentions in Wrest Park correspondence about the encroachment of Non-Conformism. One written in 1812, objects to the proposal for a Methodist chapel and a later one states that, in the opinion of the writer, there was no need for a new place of

---

[68] BLARS L5/1078
[69] John Bunyan, His Life and Times, John Brown, Archan, 1967
[70] BLARS CRT 170/6/18

worship in the area. A year later they complained that preaching had taken place at Roadhouses, how dare they![71]

Continuing with Methodism, there still remains on the east side of a remaining section of the old A6, near the River Flitt, and a few yards outside Silsoe parish, a building which was once a small Methodist chapel belonging to the Primitive Methodists. This was built on land owned by Francis Read of Maulden, bought in 1814 by a minister of the Gospel and six others, presumably trustees, using money partly provided by the Society of Methodists[72]. By this time the chapel had already been built which no doubt served Maulden, Clophill and Silsoe being at the junction of all three parishes. It became redundant in 1937 with the opening of a new Methodist chapel in Clophill, and was subsequently sold and until 2005 was used by 'Chapel Feeds' who supplied pet and animal food and requirements. It has since been sold again for conversion to a private house.

In the *Bedfordshire Times* of April 1934, it was reported that a new Mission Hall (or a Tin Tabernacle as they were commonly known) had been opened in Vicarage Road on the previous Saturday. A special workers meeting had been arranged for the afternoon with also a series of preachings from the Rev. E J Willis and Mr F R Andrews. An organ, presented by Mrs Martin, was played and on the Sunday it was used again with Miss Ena Upton playing.

The newspaper reported many anniversary meetings through the war up to 1948, but after that it seems that there was no more use for it and it closed down. It is said to have been a building typical of the period, having a corrugated iron roof with a wooden floor, and no doubt freezing in the winter. No record of what denomination used this building has been found, but local sources suggest it may have been Methodist.

There was at least one other location in the village where worship took place, and that was in West End Road where the house of James Chapman was registered as a meeting place in 1802, and in 1808. A letter dated 1816 from Sarah Harrison, the schoolteacher's wife, written to Tryphosa Box may refer to it:-

> "A Methodist preacher has taken a large room in the only house that has one at West End to preach in once, some say twice, a week. He is an elderley man and was an intimate of Wesley's and had been a (?) to propagate the Gospel and means to give up the room in the summer and preach from the Green"

There was another manifestation of non-conformity in Silsoe, in 1813, when Lewis Harrison, the steward of Wrest Park, wrote that:-

---

[71] BLARS L30/11/132/108,124 & 141
[72] BLARS Z210/143 & 144

> " I am sorry to mention that a New Meeting House has reared its head at Clophill and Mr Nethersole (the Vicar) tells me that your tenant and dependant Stormer of Road Houses at Silsoe is going to erect one or at least promote it near the parsonage on a more permanent footing. Your Ladyship may very readilly put a stop to their proceedings ……. Stormer is the man who has built the white house on your Ladyship's land at the Road Houses."

Nothing apparently came of this proposal, William Stormer presumably having been "leant on".

The census of 1841 has a family of Chapmans in West End, and given the several mentions of meeting houses in West End it seems that this is where the dissenters met, and where they may even have met earlier.

An 1861 schedule of meeting houses & chapels records that the dwelling house of Jacob Swannell was used and licensed as a meeting house for the Primitive Methodists, with the licence being cancelled in 1894.[73] From the censuses it seems as though Jacob lived with his wife Hannah at what is now 18 West End Road.

There is further evidence of this 'Chapel' in a sale document of about 1883 of the Alma beerhouse together with adjacent cottages includes the following which was behind the Alma,

> "Lot 3, two freehold thatched cottages, one with sitting room and one bedroom, another with sitting room kitchen and two bedrooms and a Messuage or Building of the same size let as a chapel on a 10 years lease from 1881"[74].

Jacob Swannell had died in 1880 and as it is unlikely that there were two meeting houses in West End Road it may be that at some time the meeting place moved down the road from No. 18 to the house behind what is now No. 17 West End Road.

---

[73] BHRS 89/6
[74] BLARS WE 1288

Appendix i. Vicars and Priests of Flitton & Silsoe[75]

There is also a list of incumbents on the wall of Silsoe church which differs slightly from and has less detail than the above.

The Chapel of St. Leonard, Silsoe

- Richard [de Ybestock?] [to chantry in church of Silsoe; patron Thomas Gray];

❖ Hugh de Blunham - 2 May 1297 [capellanus; on death of Richard; patron Thomas de Bray];

❖ John de Huthe - 6 Jul 1298 [capellanus; on resignation of Hugh de Blunham; patron Sir Thomas de Bray];

❖ Richard de Parva Lynford - 20 Jan 1317 [capellanus; to chantry chapel; patron John de Grey, Lord of Deffreneloyt];

❖ Adam de Wolde - 12 Dec 1334 [priest; to chantry in honour of St. Leonard at altar of SS.Katherine & Margaret; on death of D.Richard de Lynford; patron Sir Roger de Grey];

❖ Henry Wale of East Haddon - 22 Nov 1335 [priest; on resignation of Adam de Wolde; patron Thomas, son of Roger de Gray];

❖ ordination of chantry - 1337;

❖ John Fyndell;

❖ Thomas Umfrey of Southyeuell - 16 Aug 1349 [priest; on death of John Fyndell; to chantry of Blessed Virgin Mary, SS.Katherine & Mary Magdalene, in chapel of Silsoe; patron D. Roger de Grey, Lord of Deffrencloyt];

❖ John de Hoo of Upwell - 13 Jul 1355 [priest; to chantry of St.Leonard's chapel; on resignation of Thomas Umfrey; patron D.Reginald de Grey];

❖ John de Podyngton - 6 Jul 1358 [priest; on resignation of John de Hoo; patron Reginald de Grey];

❖ Roger Spicer of Cicestr.- 17 Jul 1362 [priest; on resignation of John Podyngton; patron Reginald de Grey];

❖ Robert de Asschewell - 1364 [deacon; on resignation of D.Roger Spicer to chantry of SS.Katherine & Margaret; found by inquest that the presentation belonged to the Bishop, by lapse];

❖ John Tournour of Biggleswade - 3 Jul 1379 [priest; patron the Bishop by lapse];

❖ D.John Russell - 17 Mar 1395 [Vicar of Shepreth; on exchange with D.John Tornour; patron Lady Alienora Grey de Ruthyn];

❖ John Taillour of Flatton - 31 Jan 1398 [priest; on resignation of John Russell; patron Sir Gerard Braybrok senior, Sir Gerard Braybrok junior, Reginald Ragonn, John Hervy, John Lee and William Goff];

---

[75] Unless stated otherwise, the lists of vicars, chaplains etc are taken from the BLARS Fasti lists of Parish Incumbents which was compiled by the BCC Records Office in 1950-1960.

- ❖ D.Richard Pavenham - 13 May 1405 [priest; on resignation of D.John Tayllour; patron Reginald Grey, Lord de Ruthin];
- ❖ John Stubbyng - 9 Aug 1410 [capellanus; on resignation of D.Richard Pavenham; patron Reginald Grey, Lord de Ruthin][76]

Vicars of Flitton cum Silsoe
(St. John the Baptist)

- ❖ Henry de Hattell - 1235 [capellanus]
- ❖ Robert - 1260 [deacon; on death of Henry last vicar
- ❖ Reginald
- ❖ Robert de Hicch - 15 Jan 1278 [priest; on death of Reginald]
- ❖ John Maurieij - 16 May 1308 [capellanus; on death of Robert de Hoggele]
- ❖ John Ghissop
- ❖ John le Deister - 31 Mar 1341 [Rector of Childecomb Diocese, Wynton by exchange with John of Ghissop]
- ❖ William le Messuag - 28 Jul 1346 [of Stamford, priest, on resignation of John Deystere]
- ❖ Henry de Shrynton - 4 Jul 1349 [priest; on death of D. William – probably the Black death]
- ❖ John Fyndel - 27 Apr 1350 [priest; on resignation of D. Henry]
  Dom, William Lynfeld, 1362, Vicar of Flitte – party to a grant of land[77]
- ❖ William Tappe - 11 Sep 1394 [priest]
- ❖ D. Robert Merston - 10 Apr 1409 [priest; on exchange with D. William Tappe]
- ❖ William Skynnere - 9 Oct 1409 [priest; on resignation of D. Robert Merston, exchanged with Corby vicarage]
- ❖ Robert Merston - 15 Feb 1409 [capellanus; on resignation of D. William Skynnere, exchanged to Corby vicarage]
- ❖ D. Nicholas Throndeston
- ❖ D. Robert Merston - 31 Jan 1418 [Vicar of Middleton; Ely diocese, on exchange with D. Nicholas Throndeston]
- ❖ D. John Kyrkeby - 2 Aug 1419 [capellanus]
- ❖ John Aldham - 29 Oct 1420 [priest; on resignation of D. Robert Kyrkeby]
- ❖ William Edenham - 24 Sep 1422 [late monk of Vawey, on resignation of D. John Aldham]
- ❖ D. William Launder
- ❖ Richard Michell - 10 Oct 1443 [priest; on death of D. William Launder]
- ❖ William Lyngfeld - 22 Jul 1443
- ❖ Henry Byllok - 6 May 1444 [priest; on death of D. Richard Mechell]
- ❖ Edmond Bryon - 20 Mar 1444 [priest; on resignation of D. Henry Byllock]

---

[76] D means Dominus or Lord
[77] BLARS LJeayes 414

- ❖ William atte Fenne - 5 Nov 1445 [priest; on resignation of D. Edmund Byron]
- ❖ D. Robert Drury - 31 Jul 1457 [priest; on death of D. William Fenne]
- ❖ D. Robert Drury - 6 Feb 1472 [vacant]
- ❖ D. Richard Bysshop - 22 Apr 1477 [on death of Robert Drury]
- ❖ D. Richard Purser - 8 May 1484 [priest; on death of D. Richard Bisshop]
- ❖ D. Richard Kyrke - 10 Sep 1492 [priest; on resignation of D. Ri Purser]
- ❖ D. Roger Bullock - 8 Nov 1504 [priest; on death of Richard Kyrke]
- ❖ D. Henry Richardes - 30 Sep 1517 [on death of D. Roger Bulloke]
- ❖ D. Edward Philipe - 11 Jan 1532 [B.A.; to Flitton cum Silsoe vicarage, on resignation of D. Henry Richardes]
- ❖ D. John Gale - 1 Sep 1541 [capellanus; on resignation of Edward Philipe; Patron, King Henry VIII]
- ❖ D. Richard Wilson - 14 May 1551 [clerk, on resignation of D. John Gale; Patron, the Bishop]
- ❖ William Broke - 4 Jul 1554 [clerk; Patron, Dean & Chapter of Christ Church, Oxon][78]
- ❖ Henry Coleman - 28 Mar 1555
- ❖ Ludovic Price - 1555 [clerk; on death of last rector; Patron, Richard Marshall, S.T.P., DCCC]
- ❖ Thomas Falle - 12 Nov 1580 [B.A.; He married Judith Hill & was buried 2 Oct 1600; will dated 2 Apr 1599 and proved 2 May 1601]
- ❖ Richard Wood - 9 Feb 1600 [B.A.; on death of last incumbent. Patron, DCCC]
- ❖ Reynold Burden
- ❖ Thomas Paxton - 4 Jul 1622 [Patron, DCCC]
- ❖ William Ramsey - 16 May 1629 [Patron, DCCC]
- ❖ William Harris - 20 Sep 1665 [deacon; M.A. on death of last vicar. Patron, DCCC]
- ❖ William Cauldwell - 17 Aug 1686 [B.A.; on death of William Harris; Patron the Bishop, by lapse. Married Mrs Sanderson at Pulloxhill on 17 Nov 1709 and was buried 21 Jul 1722]
- ❖ John Birt - 20 Sep 1722 [B.A.; on death of William Cauldwell; patron, DCCC]
- ❖ Philip Birt
- ❖ Hadley Cox - 20 Jan 1763 [M.A.; on death of Philip Birt]
- ❖ Edward Auriol Drummond - 30 Jul 1782 [M.A.; on death of Hadley Cox]
- ❖ John Robinson - 12 May 1784 [M.A.; on cessation of Edward A. Drummond. Died 12 Oct 1817]
- ❖ John Thomas James - 9 Mar 1818 [M.A.; on death of John Robinson]
- ❖ Henry Wellesley - 5 Sep 1827 [M.A.; on resignation of John Thomas James][H W was the illegitimate nephew of the Duke of Wellington.]
- ❖ Alfred Browne - 18 Mar 1834 [M.A.; on cessation of Henry Wellesley]

---

[78] From now on the "Dean & Chapter of Christ Church, Oxon is referred to as DCCC

Vicars of Silsoe (St. James)

❖ D.Henry - 1336 [Chaplain];

❖ Stephen Hastings Atkins MA - 13 May 1846 [licenced to parish church; vacant on separation from vicarage of Flitton; patron Earl de Grey; resigned 16 Mar 1847];

❖ William Pennefather MA - 6 Aug 1847 [on resignation of Stephen Hastings Atkins; resigned 30 Oct 1847];

❖ Thomas Pattinson Ferguson MA - 7 Dec 1847 [on resignation of William Pennefather; presented to Rectory of Shenfield [Essex] 1863; died 28 Jan 1892 at Shenfield, aged 76];

❖ George Renaud [resigned 4 May 1870];

❖ Richard James Mooyaart MA - 30 May 1870

❖ Robert Lang MA - 8 Jan 1873 [on cess. of James Mooyaart];

❖ Charles Henry Farmer - Nov 1887;

❖ Henry Amhurst Orlebar- 1893 [patron Lord Lucas]

❖ Thomas Francis Ford Williams - Jul 1905;

❖ Allured Elliot Black - Oct 1916;

❖ Sydney Meade MA [Patron Bishop of St Albans]- Mar 1931;

❖ John Humphrey Burn BA - Feb 1947;

❖ James Adams AKC - Sep 1950;

❖ Geoffrey Morris Oakeshott - 1953;

❖ John Anthony Benton MA - 1956; [held with Gravenhurst]

❖ Robert Leslie d'Esterre Archdale Byrn - 1962;

❖ Bernard Lawrence Nixon BA Dip Th- 1967;

Vicars of Silsoe, Flitton and Pulloxhill

❖ Canon Bernard Lawrence Nixon BA Dip Th- 1967;

❖ Stephen C. Holroyd MA LTh – 1997

Stipendiary Curates found in the village in the 19th century[79]

William Alfred Hamilton, as stipendiary curate (£100 p.a) 1849
Alexander Taylor, as stip. curate (£50 p.a.) P54/0/2 1854
Hammond Roberson Bailey, as stip. curate (£50p.a) 1857
Arthur Henry Sanxay Barwell, as stip. curate (£60 p.a) 1860
William Henry Lambert, as assistant stip. curate (£90p.a) 1864
Alfred Menzies, as assistant stip. curate at Flitton (£126 p. a.) 1864
George Edward William Norman, as stip. curate in the place of Wm Hen Lambert (£110 p. a.) 1867
John Storr, as assistant stip. curate, in place of G W E Norman (£100 p.a) 1867
William Henry Sharp, as assistant stip. curate, in place of Jn Storr (£105 p.a.) 1869

---

[79] BLARS Silsoe parish records P54/0

Chapter 6 – The Governance of Silsoe

Manorial and Vestry

The history of governing a parish seems for many centuries to be one of power slowly being sucked away from the local arena to the central authorities.

As mentioned elsewhere, the various Lords of the Manor were initially the local representative of the King, and they governed their manors and the people in them as required, under the law. They ran the estate and the people in their manors, administering justice through their local courts.

Alongside this, the church tended to concentrate on the well-being of the individual, both spiritual and practical. Aid was provided through monasteries, charities and other sources of help, with assistance during illness and in hard times. From about the 16th century however, the church started to become more organised with the 'Vestry', which was what we now call, the Parochial Church Council. It became responsible not only for the ecclesiastical affairs of the parish, but also for some items of lay business, which nowadays would be supervised by the parish or other councils.

Before 1834, this business included, administrating the Poor Laws through the Overseers of the Poor; such as making payments to poor people and also distributing bread etc from charities. They also maintained the roads and bridges in the parish through Surveyors of the Highways, organised lighting and watching of the streets and thoroughfares of the parish. They even ensured the maintenance of law and order by the provision of the parish constables, and were responsible for selecting men to serve in the militia.

While the villagers would have elected the unpaid officials, such as, churchwardens and constables, the local Justice of the Peace was in charge of the whole parish, and he, in his turn, was appointed and controlled by the Lord Lieutenant of the County, the King's representative.

The Justice was required to be a land owner and thus he tended to be the local squire, a Lord of the Manor, or the vicar. He had many powers and as well as judicial and peace-keeping duties, he administered the Poor Law, (deciding which poor people should receive parish relief), or be punished as vagrants. After the first Jacobite Rebellion of 1715, he was given power to 'Read the Riot Act'. This Act warned people to stop behaving in a rowdy manner, and if they continued after the Act had been read, the Justice could order their arrest.

Small matters were dealt with in a Justice's own house, while more important cases came before a court called Petty Sessions, where two Justices sat together to decide the case. All the County Justices met four times a year at Quarter Sessions, when national as well as local affairs, (like the selection of parliamentary candidates), were discussed. This system, with justice being dispensed locally by a known figure may have had an advantage, in that it might dissuade the locals from excess; but on the other hand, there was the possibility that the local man might come down very hard, especially if his neighbours and possibly his property were being threatened.

For Flitton and Silsoe the names of several local Justices can be found, and there may well have been more whose names might be found, from a more detailed study of the Assizes and Sessions records. William Daniel from Newbury Manor was one who appears in 1681, in the case of the rustled chickens when "an oath was take … before me William Daniel Esq. (one of his Majesties Justices of Peace)".[1]

As noted above, one of the parish concerns was the highway, and in 1685 William Daniel and another Justice, John Ventris of Campton, certified that:-

"Wee whose names are here underwritten Twoe of his Majesties of the peace for the said County of Bedford doe hereby humbly certifye that on the seaventeenth day of June last wee viewed the highway called Tagg lake lyeinge in the parish of Higham Gobion in the said County of Bedford and leadinge from Silvesthoe in the said County to Luton in the said County and wee doe hereby Certifye that the said way is well repaired and amended and is in good and sufficient repaire

In Witnes whereof Wee have hereunto sett our hands and seales this sixteenthe day of July in the first yeare of the raigne of our Soveraigne Lord Kinge James the Second Annoque Dni 1685. Wm Daniel John Ventris "

At a time when the church and state was more closely entwined, there were two consecutive vicars of Flitton cum Silsoe, Philip Birt (1741–1762) and Hadley Cox (1762–1782), both of whom were Justices of the Peace. In those days the village constable took the names of those who did not attend the church regularly, so there was no doubt a great deal of forelock touching to the vicar cum local magistrate.

Both would also have been away from their parish[2] much of the time attending to JP business and in March 1774, Hadley Cox wrote that he "..had been in court trying twenty people of which four were to be hung and four transported." Apparently the four to be hung were reprieved, but it is a strange conscience that can sentence people to be hung, and then preach forgiveness on a Sunday.

Cox was also presumably unpopular in Maulden when in 1772, there was a disturbance about rumours that the common pasture and moor would be divided, so as to exclude use of it by the peasants. About 200 assembled there

---

[1] BLARS HSA/1681 S/33
[2] Both were also vicars of Blunham at the same time as being vicar of Flitton cum Silsoe.

suspecting they were about to be deprived of its use but he managed to disperse them. Later he apparently harangued the parishioners in the church and then in reporting on the event in a letter to the Earl of Hardwicke, said he "..had even considered using the light horse to ride the objectors down."

Ten years later the poor were again getting too uppity and the estate steward, Joseph Pawsey, reported to the Earl in 1782 that "…the lower order is most depraved, did not attend church as well as they should and showed a lack of respect to the vicar even though he, the Rev. Drummond, had reduced the length of his sermons."[3] A year later Pawsey also said that " I have had a great deal of trouble in the ordering and management of the poor of Silsoe, and in keeping the farmers up to their duty, the lower class of farmers are about as deficient in good manners as the labouring men."[4]

With the increasing complexity of society, the administration of the Poor Law no longer remained the direct responsibility of the Silsoe vestry, and eventually came under the elected Boards of Guardians of, in Silsoe's case, the Ampthill Poor Law Union.

The archives for Silsoe parish until the end of the 19th century, are taken up mainly by the records for the Overseers relating to the settlement of individuals, (which have been referred to in the Health and Safety chapter), but there is also much detail on the maintenance of the church and the graveyard extensions. Thus we know that in 1891 the Rt. Hon. Francis Thomas de Grey, Earl Cowper, granted an area of 1 rood and 12 poles of land adjoining the Churchyard as a graveyard extension, and that a licence was obtained to inter in this land in July of that year.

Parochial Church Councils (PCC) were set up in 1919, as a successor to the Vestries which had had their civil functions removed in 1894, with the establishment of civil parishes.

Currently, in the 21st century, the Silsoe Parochial Church Council consists of the vicar and churchwardens of the parish, together with a number of representatives of the laity elected by the annual parochial church council meeting of the parish. Its powers and duties are nowadays limited and defined by law;[5] but principally it has the responsibility of co-operating with the vicar in promoting the mission of the church in the parish.

It is also still responsible for the financial affairs of the church and the care and maintenance of the church fabric and its contents, although these latter responsibilities are executed by churchwardens. It also has a voice in the forms of service used by the church and may make representations to the bishop on matters affecting the welfare of the parish.

---

[3] Rev Edward Auriol Drummond, 1782 to 1784.
[4] BLARS CRT 100 27 4 II
[5] *Parochial Church Councils (Powers) Measure 1956* and others

Silsoe Parish Council

On the lay side, parish Councils were created through the 1894 Local Government Act, to take over local oversight of social welfare and civic duties, in towns and villages for which previously the PCC had had responsibility. They are elected bodies, usually on a four year cycle with the number of councillors varying, according to the population of the parish.

parish Councils have the power to tax their residents to support their operations, and to carry out local projects. Although there is no limit to the amount that can be precepted, the money can only be raised for a limited number of purposes, defined in the 1894 Act. Although there are wide variations, parish councils tend to be responsible for the provision of such facilities as village halls, allotments, recreation grounds and children's play areas. In Silsoe the parish Council is in charge of the Waterslade Allotments, and instigated the provision of the Millennium Green. They also have a legal right to be consulted, and to comment, on all planning applications in their areas which are initially submitted to the District Council.[6]

Recently in 2009 another re-organisation of the local administration scene by central government has taken place, with the result that the smaller District Councils have been amalgamated in the name of efficiency. What were the Mid-Bedfordshire District Council, parts of the functions of Bedfordshire County Council and South Bedfordshire District Councils have now become the Central Bedfordshire Council.

National Elections

In 1832 only men over the age of 21, who owned property worth at least £2 a year, could vote. However, an Act of 1867 extended the vote to men owning or renting property worth at least £5 per year, which included skilled workers and craftsmen, and some tenant farmers. Then in 1884 a further Act enabled men who owned, rented or lodged in property worth at least £10 a year to vote, thus enfranchising rural labourers.

But while most people were disenfranchised before 1832, there was still some benefit to the local populace, as at election times the candidates could be generous with their hospitality at the local inns. It was also a good move to support the party that the current earl supported. In May 1785, there was an upset in the village when John Field of New Inn rang the church bells, to celebrate the defeat of Lord Ongley, someone supported by the Earl of Hardwicke. Thomas Gostelow, hearing the sound, raced out of Wrest down to the chapel where he assaulted Mr Field, cut the bell ropes and grabbed hold of Field's collar and threw him out of the church, saying he would put him in the kennel. It was suggested that the parishioners objected to the bell-

---

[6] Perhaps because of its greater size France still manages to devolve to the parishes or communes planning and building control, highway maintenance plus a local police force.

ringing and supported the Earl of Hardwicke's candidate – even though they had no vote?. His Lordship said that only the minister, the churchwardens or the Lord of the Manor were entitled to ring the bells!

Eventually it was all sorted out with Field apologising to his Lordship, and Gostelow apologising to Field.

Chapter 7 – Crime and Punishment

In the chapter on Manors it was described how minor misdemeanours in the village were dealt with by the Manorial Courts while they were in operation; although more important cases were dealt with at the Assizes in Bedford, or even higher courts. Later, after the Middle Ages when local power had slowly been eroded, most cases were dealt with elsewhere, resulting in the Manor Court ceasing to be more than a rent collection service.

Pounds and Lockups

One way of dealing with offenders, or their animals, was to incarcerate them; and in Silsoe there was a pound for the animals and, a lockup or mini-prison to hold the local drunk, or someone on the way to a court elsewhere. From early times these small enclosures or buildings, had been constructed in many villages in the county and they performed much the same function: the first was for lost or straying animals, and the latter for straying (in a moral sense) villagers.

Pounds or pinfolds were initially built when the fields were divided into strips; and the consequences of an animal straying into neighbouring strips and devouring crops that were essential to the life of the tenant, were severe. The errant beast would have been rounded up by the 'pinder' or 'pounder', locked in the pound and only released upon payment of a fine. The owner could enter the pound to feed the animal, but it was an offence to release it as William Stormer found out in 1830, at the Epiphany Sessions, when he was fined 1 shilling for breaking open the pound to release his sow and three pigs which James Bone's bailiff, William Bailey had found damaging potatoes [7].

The earliest reference found to a Silsoe pound appears in a 1567 lease of Norwood Manor,[8] where an 8 acre plot in Town Field is said to be next to the pinfold. No other reference to Town Field has been found, so the location of this early pound is undecided. The next mentions of the pound are in documents of the 17th and 18th Centuries which use the pound as a location; for example a plot is said to be "in Waterslade and abutting south on the highway near the pound". In addition, in a conveyance of 1747[9] the implication is that the pound then, was located west of the High Street, near to where Ampthill Road now is. The document says:-

"…a messuage or tenement at Silsoe with outhouses, barns, stables warehouses yards gardens orchards etc, ….. also 1 ac. in a field called Waterslade in which messuage is situated, abutting west on the highway near the pound formerly belonging to a farm called Raworths; also 2 roods with

---

[7] BLARS QSR/27/1826/641
[8] BLARS L5/1091
[9] BLARS L5/935

warehouses stables outhouses abutting south on said highway near the pound
….. "

It seems to have been rebuilt at least once, as a survey of pounds in Bedfordshire carried out in 1936 by the Bedfordshire Historical Record Society, refers to a description dated 1902,[10] of the Silsoe pound as a quadrangle enclosed by a moss covered stone wall with the possible remains of an earlier one nearby. This survey said that it was situated on the south verge of the road by the stone quarry. The 1901 OS map actually shows a small square by the old entrance to the quarry with 'Pound' inscribed nearby. Clophill pound still remains by The Green and Silsoe's, would probably have been about the same size.

Although the pound has disappeared, Silsoe still retains its lockup, which is situated in a lane off the south of Church Road. Until the early 19th century the lockup would have been on the north side of Church Road; but when that road was moved to the north the lockup found itself isolated. It is perhaps fortunate that it did stay away from the road as it may well have otherwise been demolished; indeed, in 1902 it was being used as a store for fuel for the street lamps.

Village lockups were intended to serve as temporary gaols and were generally built from `county funds' after approval of a scheme at the Quarter Sessions. The Silsoe lockup, shown in Plate 7/1, is built from local sandstone and is octagonal with a conical roof, the door is oak with strong strap hinges. There is a plaque on it which says it was built in 1796.

Higher Courts

In early times when the local Lord's sense of propriety was threatened, they tended to take the law into their own hands. Sir John Cornwall, who in the Battle of Agincourt in 1415, was one of the chosen officers who had the post of honour with the Duke of York in the vanguard, had "builded the castle of Antehill of such spoils as it is said he won in France."[11] He was later created Lord Fanhope with his new castle attracting some people to transfer their allegiance to him, thus causing the elderly Lord Reynold Grey some resentment.

In 1437 four judges, appointed to make some special enquiries, proposed meeting at Silsoe Church and Lord Fanhope and Sir John Wenloch turned up accompanied by some 60 armed men. Lord Grey didn't like this going on his own turf so promptly came out of his house with 50-60 men, supported by Sir John Enderby, and asked why the Commission couldn't have found a place other than his village of Silsoe to meet in. During the ensuing argument the numbers of Lord Grey's men grew to 300, so getting a bit outnumbered, Lord Fanhope sent to Ampthill for his armour and reinforcements

---

[10] *A Ransom 'Round the County'* Beds Times & Ind, 24 Jan 1902
[11] *Magna Britannia*, Rev Daniel Lysons, 1806

However, Sir Thomas Wauton managed to cool down the various lords' tempers and they withdrew to opposite ends of the village, during which the enquiries were postponed.[12]

Apart from the above extreme event, there were higher courts which dealt with more serious offences and much later, the Magistrate Courts evolved, which dealt with the misdemeanours originally considered by the Manor Courts.

There is a lack of continuity in the High Sheriff Assizes records relating to the Silsoe area, and the earliest that do exist cover the period 1653-1688. The cases reported are very much of their age: there is the crime of uttering dangerous and treasonable words, of being Quakers or Non–Conformist, or not attending the village Church. Plus there are several cases of witchcraft, where the details of the examination of suspected witches make frightening reading. No witches seem to have been found in Silsoe. Punishments, where listed, were also much of that age, including physical torture such as whipping for stealing small items, and branding for stealing a few sheep.

There are some cases from about that time relating to Silsoe village, which provide an indication of life there and what crimes were taken to court.

The Chicken Rustler and Bottle Thief [13]

Agnes Pearles, a spinster of Flitton, swore on 23 June 1681 before William Daniel, a Justice of the Peace who lived at Newbury Manor, that "about 7 weekes before Easter was a twelvemonth, on a Monday about 3 of the clocke in the morning she heard her fathers hens cry in the Henhouse, and rising to the chamber window she saw the said Henry Johnson come from the Henhouse doore and runne through the yard." When it was day "she went that way (she saw him run) and found feathers scattered and severall of her fathers hens coming out of an hedge about halfe a furlong from her fathers house which she verily believes the said Johnson stole and dropt thereabouts because of her discovery of him in the Yard."

Her father was William Pearles of Flitton, yeoman and farmer, added to the story by swearing that in the morning he went the way she said Henry had run, "and found (as he believed) the track of the said Henry Johnson's "foote, and severall of this Informts Hens creeping out of the hedges and bushes about 20 pole from his house which he verily thinkes the said Johnson fearing to be pursued dropt out of some sack or bag because the said Informt hath a long time knowne him by report to be notorious for stealing poultrey and other misdemeanours."

On the same date John Allen, Silsoe, innholder of the Ragged Staff at Silsoe, swore that "about the 7th of Aprill was a twelvemonth he saw the said Henry

Johnson goeing out of this Informts ground with his breeches stufft with glass bottles of which this Informt had severall dozen standing in hampers in his barne, and this Informt was going after him with a cudgell to have beat him but that his wife for feare of mischeife persuaded him to the contrary, Upon which he sent his servant Thomas Else after him who brought backe 5 or 7 of above 3 dozen bottles he had lost out of his said barne. And this Informt further saith that about the same time he lost out of his house 5 or 6 case knives two of which he found at an house in Flitton which the said Johnson did usually frequent and upon his asking Johnson where he had them he confessed he stole them out of this Informts house, and severall other things this Informt hath had stollen from him which he verily believes this Johnson stole because he hath found some of them in houses where he usually frequents and because he hath knowne him to be a notorious rogue for severall yeares."

Thomas Else confirmed this by saying "that about the 7th of Aprill was a twelvemonth he saw the said Johnson take severall glasse bottles of his Master John Allens that stood in hampers in the said barne and put them through an hole of the wall into a ditch, and then came out of the barne and went round about and filled his breeches with as many as he could gett in, and was gone with them above a furlong when this Informt overtooke the said Henry Johnson and made him deliver the said bottles out of his breeches which were about 6 or 7 as neare as he can remember, and this Informt went back and found 5 or 6 more in the said ditch ..."

Henry was committed to gaol on 23 June for the thefts of hens, 18 ducks and some glass bottles. Whether he was found guilty, is not known, but he is probably the same Henry Johnson who was baptised in 1650 at Flitton, and buried at the same place in 1685.

The Case of the Missing Cheeses

On 19th April in 1675 Richard Hopkins swore on oath before George Wayn, one of His Majesties Justices of the Peace, that the house of his father William in Silsoe had been broken into at night on the 16th and two cheeses belonging to his father had been stolen[14]. He went on to say "that in search after theese goods hee did finde parte of the cheeses in the house of John Savill of Mogerhanger in the county of Bedford aforesaid."
How he came to search at Moggerhanger, which is a fair distance from Silsoe is not stated, but on the same day John Savill, a labourer, denied ever having been in William's house. The cheeses found in his house had been brought there by someone who he did not know. (Where have we heard that story before?)

William Hopkins was buried at Flitton in January of 1677 as being from "*Caino Bayley at Wrast*" so was presumably quite old at the time of the theft,

---

[14] BLARS HSA1675/S/63, 64 &

and was living just in the parish at the north end, possibly near the remnants of Cainhoe castle.

Hung at the Old Bailey

A sad case comes from the records of "The Ordinary of Newgate his account of The Behaviour, Confessions, and Last Speeches of the Malefactors that were Executed at Tyburn on Wednesday the 26th of June, 1717." He spoke to

"George Mortice, alias Fashion, alias Savil, alias Saven (which last, he said, was his right Name)" who was condemned for breaking into the house of Mrs. Ann and Margaret Moise at Chelsea where he stole 34 pair of Men's Gloves, and other Millenery-Ware … on the 7th of May last."

"He said, he was 30 years of age, born at Silvisho in Bedfordshire.[15] That when but young, his Friends brought him up to London, and put him to a Shoomaker, whom he was not bound to, nor staid long with, but soon left him and went to Sea ; where he serv'd several Years off and on, in diverse Men of War. He at first deny'd the Fact he was condemn'd for, saying, That he never did it, nor was in the least concern'd in it, neither had done any thing of that nature in his whole Life:

"But upon my telling him, That I believ'd him not, for I knew him to be an old Offender, who once (viz. the 12th of August, 1713) pleaded the late Queen's Free Pardon at the Old-baily, under the Name of George Savil; and, that I was afraid he had done many ill things since; he own'd, it was true, and wish'd now he had been wiser, and (as I then advis'd him) had improv'd that Mercy better.

"Here also he confess'd the Fact he was to suffer for, which before he had very strongly deny'd; and now said, That if he could, he would be very glad to help the Persons to their Goods, whom he had wrong'd; but all he was now able to do, was to beg GOD's Pardon and theirs, as he did, praying GOD to bless them, and make up their Losses."

The Ordinary was with them to the end when:

" ….I pray'd again, and having recommended their departing Souls to GOD, I withdrew, and left them to their private Devotions, for which they had some time allotted them; which when expir'd, the Cart drew away, and they were turn'd off; all the while praying for that Mercy which some of them especially had so little regarded before; and GOD only knows whether it was not now too late for them to find it."

---

[15] This event has not been found in the parish records.

Don't hide your money in packs of butter

In 1737 on 13 June Ann Best of Silsoe packed 38 guineas and 2s under a lump of butter in the middle of a 'flat' of butter[16] 'tied fast with two strings' that she was sending to her sister White, in London. She saw it loaded so that it could not be accessed until the butter had been off-loaded and a note about the money was inside the lid. The driver George Lee said that he drove it that day to South Mimms, (was there a service station there even then?) with about 40 other flats, and then Thomas Whitehead took the load on overnight, to Newgate Market.

William Best in the market at four in the morning opened the letter in the flat, as allowed by Daniel White, but when Daniel arrived later and found no money awaiting him, William said that the money had been taken by William Harvey who had been seen opening packages. William Best went to Mrs White's and found that the butter had been delivered but there was no money. Daniel then 'ran out of the market to Mrs White's, and said to the Maid, shew me where this Rascal lives; so the Wench and I, went to the Prisoner's House, and I look'd in an old Chest of Drawers.' Neither the money nor any greasy package was found.

Further evidence relating to Harvey's job at the market which involved delivering goods, was given at the trial at the Old Bailey in July. However, as the money had not been found in the search of Harvey's lodgings and following several good character references, he was acquitted.

Now £40 in 1737, is worth about £5,400 today, which is an enormous amount to be sending in a slab of butter, but Ann said she had sent money this way before. John Best, Ann's husband, was a yeoman of Silsoe tenanting land at Lady Ash Meadow in 1739, and in 1757 a dairyman at Kitchen End (which shows that there was a very good living to be had then as a dairyman). Also that the banking system was either not trusted to transfer money, or was too expensive. (Nothing much has changed since then!)

Burglary involving Silsoe 1754

The Rev Philip Birt wrote to Philip Yorke Earl of Hardwicke in February that year, to inform him of a burglary that had been carried out by two men at James Poulton's, the Park Keeper's house. He was quick to suggest that the offenders may "…have come from the 20-30 tinkers, chair-bottomers, brook-makers and sailors, who from time to time congregate in William Burleigh's old barn, 'sturdy, dangerous and revengeful fellows." But said that rewards had been offered for the perpetrator's arrest.

---

[16] A flat of butter was about 30 to 45 pounds in weight.

One man, Lawrence Cripps, was quickly arrested and statements were taken from, amongst others, Cripps' wife and mother; and also James Poulton on why he suspected both Lawrence and William Cripps of the crime.

Lawrence was examined in Bedford Gaol and quickly confessed that he, with his brother William, had decided to break into the house of James Poulton in Upper Gravenhurst while he was asleep. They knew that there were ladders at Mr Beaumont's malting and Mr Cooper's ground at Silsoe; and to carry out the burglary stole the ladders and carried them to Poulton's house, a distance of at least 2 miles, with the direct route taking them past Wrest Park house.

One ladder was too short and the other was too long, so his brother William shortened the longer one. Then, at about 12am on 12 February they broke in, but Poulson woke up, and they threatened to kill him if he got up. They then rifled the house and stole "4 gold Portuguese coins, other money, a silver watch, 2 waistcoats, 3 shirts, silver shoe buckles and a girdle buckle, a gold ring, spoons, a tea canister with green tea, 2 pairs of worsted stockings, bread and cold pork". They escaped through the street door and made off to London, where they sold their booty.

In addition to this confession the Justices also hoped to use Mr Birt's clergyman nephew (who attended prisoners), to get what information he could from Lawrence.

Lawrence was convicted on 19th March at Bedford and duly executed. At the Bedford Summer Assizes, William was also tried for felony and burglary on the basis of his brother's confession. It transpired that they had sold the valuables to a goldsmith in St. Martin-in-the-Fields, but the tea canister was given to William Cripps' father-in-law, William Oddy. On hearing of Lawrence's arrest William started calling himself William Yarrow, and said that if anyone "offered to take him he would 'rip them up' before he would be taken". He was eventually arrested at Southwark

The various rewards were shared out to several including his father-in-law, but only after Poulton had been reimbursed the cost of his stolen goods. [17]

Some 18th and 19th century cases

There are many minor cases reported in the Quarter Sessions records for these centuries, where Silsoe inhabitants were accused.

Thus Wm. Peacock, a labourer of Silsoe, was indicted in 1763 for stealing a brass kettle from Thomas Giddings, a wheelwright of Silsoe; and in 1764 for stealing a large Common Prayer book from John Payne. Then John Lowings aged about 20, a Blacksmith was in 1772 arraigned for producing a bastard with Sarah Harley.

---

[17] BLARS L29/6 to 21

In 1802 George Butterfield a waggoner of Silsoe, and Vincent Field a labourer, gave evidence against Jonathan Hicks for theft of grain from John Edwards. He later confessed that he was guilty but said that he did not take it for himself but for his master's horses, he being the horse-keeper of Jos. Pawsey, Silsoe, "his Master often imposed such a Hard Time upon his Horses that they were not able to perform their work with their usual allowance of corn." This Joseph Pawsey was the steward to Wrest Park, and perhaps treated his employees in the same manner.

Silsoe inhabitants appear regularly in the 1834 to 1840 Petty Sessions books. [18] So Francis White of Roadhouses was fined 2/6 plus costs in 1835 for trespass in pursuit of game. In the same year James White a butcher of West End, offered game for sale without a licence, and was fined £2 plus costs (or alternatively 3 weeks in jail). The next year Samuel Sturgeon was ordered to pay 1s a week to support his father John, yet in the year 1841 both John aged 70, and his sons, were listed as paupers, so how could Samuel pay for his father's support? Others were fined for stealing turnips, part of a tree, or for assault.

There are also several cases of poaching, such as when in 1821, John Simpson who was watching the game in Thrift Wood, Silsoe, with several others, repeatedly heard the report of a gun. Eventually John Arnold, William Lincoln and Thomas Lincoln came out of the wood and were taken into custody.

The attitude of Lord Grantham to poachers is well described in an article in the Times of 1832, this says:-

"Lord Grantham has adopted a new and most successful way of preserving his game at Wrest-park, in Bedfordshire. He has allotted to every labourer a portion of land at a fair rent, sufficient to employ all his leisure time, with this condition annexed - that any one of them who shall be convicted of an offence against the Game Laws shall forfeit his land. The old keeper, Hills, declares that from the time that these allotments have been got into crop, and the men have tasted the fruits of the labour of their own hands, his office has been pretty near a sinecure. "If it were not for them Lununners what come down in gigs in September," he says, "I could easier preserve my Lord's manors with one helper or two than I used to do with a score. There cannot be a snare set in the parish but there is a race amongst the men who shall be the first to come and tell me, and then the lucky fellow knows he is sure of my good word when he wants any favour from our good steward, Mr Brown."

Lord Grantham having a great dislike to shutting up active young fellows in prison like felons, for following the natural bent of their minds in the pursuit of the wild animals of the field, has another plan for keeping away loose fellows from the neighbouring parishes, who are out of the reach of the

---

[18] BLARS *Petty Sessions Book* PSA 1/1

former and more excellent plan, which may be worth consideration. His keepers are chosen for their strength and activity, well paid, and well fed. Fire-arms are strictly forbidden them but they are furnished with long sticks, one size less than a bludgeon. So armed , he calculates them to be more than a match for a half-starved poacher, and he authorises them to give all such a good drubbing, and then let them go."

Violence also took place in the village in 1829 when two cases were reported. Firstly, the Silsoe constable was warranted to arrest George Ashwell of Silsoe, to appear at the Quarter Sessions, for riotous conduct in the house of John Haytred, the Star and Garter; and secondly Richard Cook was arrested for assaulting Wm. Pearce, the Silsoe constable.

At that time it was also an offence to leave your family to be cared for by the parish, as the 64 year old Edward Wilson found out in 1850. He was charged with absconding, and leaving his wife Ann Wilson at Silsoe, chargeable to the common fund of the Ampthill Union. He received 1 months hard labour but evidently preferred this to going back to his wife, as a year later he was back again in Court where he received 2 months hard labour, for the same offence.

The innkeeper of The George, Benjamin Carter, once had a case taken as far as the Old Bailey, when in 1750, he had James Collins indicted for stealing a 20 year old gelding valued at £1, from a paddock 100 yards from his house. In court Carter said:-

"I keep the George Inn, at Silso, in Bedfordshire . On the 19th of June. I had a bay gelding pony; at nine o'clock that evening I gave it to the boy to take to the paddock near my house; I did not see it in the paddock; I saw the boy take it, and he brought the halter back; there is a gate and a lock to the paddock; I made some inquiry for the pony, and a little boy said he could not find it; in consequence of some communication, I came to Hampstead on the following Monday, and found my pony in possession of John Hinton, who keeps ponies and gigs; I have got it since - it is not worth more than £5. in the market."

Other evidence as to sale of the horse at Kensington was given, but eventually Collins was found not guilty.

Bedfordshire Gaol Registers, 19th century

The Bedford Gaol Registers[19] give a great amount of detail about those who were locked up in the gaol, what their offences were, and for what period they were behind bars. Between 1802 and 1856, there are 84 records for those living in Silsoe, or giving Silsoe as a birthplace, and there are among these, several serial offenders.

---

[19] BLARS QGV10 *Bedfordshire Gaol Registers*

In the latter category are John Newell and Thomas Taylor. John was convicted in 1820 for receiving money under false pretences, for which he received 12 months; but for the second similar offence ten years later, he was sentenced to be transported for 7 years.

Thomas had received three months in 1829 for stealing clothes. The crime was committed on the road between New Inn and Silsoe, when he and a friend both on horseback, got into conversation with a waggon driver. The owner of the clothing had put it on the back of the waggon, and while Taylor's friend chatted at the front, Taylor dropped back to the end of the waggon and took the parcel. After the theft was discovered, his lodgings in Silsoe were searched and the bundle was found. A year later, he was sentenced by the Rev G Cardale to be transported for 7 years for house breaking. He was 22, of fresh complexion, 5 ft 4 inches tall and was destined for the prison ship Retribution, at Sheerness Dockyard. Thomas's cousin Samuel was also a bit wild, having 5 convictions by the age of 21. At 13 he was sentenced by Rev T B Whitehouse (many magistrates appear to have been vicars) to be whipped, and to spend one month in gaol for stealing from shops in Ampthill; and a year later, again whipped for larceny. For his final offence of stealing chickens in 1851, he received 6 months hard labour.

Poaching was rife in the village, as was stealing food such as plums, and taking wood for heating. So George Mann, 5 ft 4 ins tall, with a small head, received 3 months hard labour for stealing chickens; and the 14 year old William Odell, was given one month's hard labour, for stealing part of an oak tree.

Most peoples' conduct in gaol was 'orderly' but there were exceptions: such as the 21 year old Elizabeth Adams, a turnip thief, whose conduct was bad. Elizabeth Adams was arrested for a second time in 1850, when she was sentenced to 7 days or a fine of 4s 9d, for assaulting and beating Mary Ann Seymour, at Shefford. We have a description of her; 5 ft 1 ins tall, brown hair, blue eyes, a fair complexion, a bold face and could read and write imperfectly.

During these 55 years, most offences might be attributed to poverty, as out of the 84 offences some 30 were for poaching (game law offences), or stealing food or wood. Of the rest, there were 15 assault cases ranging from manslaughter, to breach of the peace, with the remainder being larceny of some type, with a scattering, of what nowadays would not be an offence, such as bastardy, being idle and disorderly, neglect of his family or misbehaviour in service.

Not all of the Gaol Registers have been searched for Silsoe offenders and no doubt there are other cases yet to surface. In addition, the 20th century would have had several interesting cases, but further searching in newspapers and Court records would be needed, to dig out these other cases.

However, one recent case of murder in Silsoe was in August 1998, when a field to the north of Newbury Manor was used to murder, and dump the body of Amjad Farooq, in a so-called honour killing. He had been having an affair with his 21-year-old niece, and members of the woman's family dragged him from his bedsit in Bedford, beat him and drove him to Silsoe, where he was hacked to death with an axe, meat cleaver or sword. Two of the murderers were jailed for life in 2000, and the third participant, who had fled to Pakistan, was arrested on his return in 2005, and subsequently jailed for 6 years.

The Village Constable

The word 'Constable' is of Norman origin, coming from the Latin 'Comes Stabuli' meaning Count of the Stables, or Master of the Horse. Where the Anglo-Saxons used the term 'Tithingman' or 'Head Borough', the Normans would use the word 'Constable' and the names gradually became interchangeable. The constable acted for his parish and a place was not regarded as a parish, unless it had a constable. They were appointed to their office by ballot carried out by the Manorial Courts, and later by the parish.

The constables became the hands and eyes of the justices. Early on they maintained the village armour, organised the assembly and training of the militia, collected some taxes and supervised local alehouses. They enquired into offences, served summonses, executed warrants, organised the 'Hue and Cry', took charge of prisoners and prosecuted them, and in general, obeyed the orders of the Justices.

The Hue and Cry existed as the method of pursuit of suspected offenders. The constable had authority to raise this, and all who heard it were expected to take part in apprehending the person suspected, armed with pitchforks or knives, or whatever came to hand. He was also in charge of the village lockup, and would put people in it who were to be moved to Bedford, or another court.

It seems that in early times one of the other jobs of the parish constable was to sit at the church door checking the villagers as they entered, and reporting those who did not attend regularly. As it was a temporary job, no doubt some did not want to get too much on the wrong side of their friends in the village, and some were perhaps less diligent that others at this job. However, failure by the local constable to carry out his duties could result in him appearing before the Justices, so it is not surprising that men tried to avoid this post. In 1682, the Pulloxhill constable was presented to the Sessions for not being honest about how many, had failed to appear at church.

There were, however, several cases where the constable reported those who did not attend church regularly[20]. In 1680, the 'Silsveshoe' constables William Worrell and Nicholas Payne presented at the court John Sellars and Thomas

---

[20] BLARS HSA1685/W/20-23, 15

Hill senior for not coming to their parish church for two weeks. In addition, the widow Elizabeth Godfrey of Silsoe was reported in 1683, 1684 and 1685 for not going to her church regularly while in March 1665, Richard Astin of Silsoe, a yeoman, was similarly accused. Unless they had good reason for not going to church the offenders were liable to pay a fine.

In the 17th century there is regular mention of the Silsoe Petty Sessions, and this would have been an important event in the south of the county, when constables and others from all over the Flit Hundred, from Caddington to Clophill, attended to report on the situation in their parish. At this and other sessions in the Hundred, Silsoe's constable also reported on church attendance and other matters.

Many Silsoe constables are named in that period such as:-

1677	John Godfrey,
1678	George Paternoster and Thomas Crouch, the Petty Sessions at 'Ligrave'
1679	Willm Wretchford, Silveshoe
1680	Nicholas Payne, the Silsoe Petty Sessions
1681, March	Silsoe constable Nicholas Payne
1681, July	John Allen, Petty sessions at the Ragged Staff, Silsoe
1683, July	Silsoe, William Fowler

Many others are mentioned in the old parish records[21] for the 18th century, and in the 19th century, the Quarter Sessions Rolls and Petty Session papers give the names of the Silsoe constables acting then. It is also worthy of note, that when a local gang (see Chapter 16, People and Families) was operating from New Inn, that the police at Silsoe were considered not to be powerful enough, and the Bow Street Runners were sent for. The 19th century constabulary were:-

1829	William Pearce, Silsoe, constable. (a carpenter, b 1787, d 1872)
1830	William Henry Haytread of Silsoe, the High Constable of Flitt Hundred[22] (the son of John Haytread of the Star and Garter, Innkeeper)
1834/5	James Kitchener
1836	William Mason and John Lowings
1837	William Mann and Samuel Taylor
1839	Richard Eve farmer at West End, William Mann
1840	Samuel Taylor and James Rich

Like the 'specials' of today, the parish constable was unpaid, (apart from small allowances), and he had to carry out his normal work in addition to his police work. He was answerable to the Chief or High Constable of the Hundred of Flitt, (the post of High or Chief Constable originated in the

---

[21] BLARS For list of constables 1718-1777, see P54/5/1
[22] BLARS for constable References at Sessions and Assizes see QSR and HSA documents plus jury lists.

Statute of Winchester of 1285). Apart from controlling the constabulary, he was responsible for suppressing riots and violent crimes, and for arming the militia, to enable him to do so. Apart from William H Haytread mentioned above, there was at least one other High Constable from Silsoe. This was in the 1770's when John Sharpe, a gentleman of Silsoe was buried and the Vicar recorded that he was "Chief Constable of ye Hundd of Flitton"

There were pleasurable parts of being high constable, such as when in 1815 John Partridge was appointed the high constable of the Flitt Hundred, he proceeded to the front of Wrest mansion and fired a gun to assert the rights of the Lord of the Manor of Luton, and the Flitt Hundred, to the sporting rights over the Hundred.[23]

With an increasing population, it was felt that the parish constable system was not sufficient; and so following the County Police Act of 1839, a professional police force was established for Bedfordshire in 1840, replacing the old system of locally elected parish constables. It initially had a Chief Constable based in Ampthill with 6 superintendents and 40 constables. Constables were paid 19 shillings a week, which was nearly twice the typical wage of an agricultural labourer in the County, at that time.[24]

After the reorganisation, it is possible that Silsoe had no resident constable, as it is not until the 1881 and 1891 censuses that a constable is found. He was John Barnes, who lived in Wrest House Lodge, next to the mansion. An 1898 Directory[25] has Joseph Lovall as the constable, so Silsoe may have had several policemen at this period, as in 1901, John Barnes was still a police constable, aged 57, and living near the almshouses. In addition constable Alfred Baldwin and he, his wife and four children were then living at 9 High Street with Arnold Sylvanus, another police constable living in the Wrest Park police accommodation.

Alfred Baldwin was still constable in 1903 while in 1910, it was Ernest Frederick Carter. In 1914, acting-sergeant Ralph Tingey, was resident for the county police and in the 1920's, Herbert Robinson was Silsoe's PC.

Until 1968 Bedfordshire Police had three divisions with C Division being based at Biggleswade and with a Sub-Division at Ampthill. Silsoe was a Rural Section under Ampthill which covered 11 villages, including Silsoe. The Silsoe constable initially lived at 9 High Street until in 1952 a police house with an office was built in the High Street just north of Juniper Close. This is still there at 70 High Street, now known as 'The Old Police House'.

A few years later in 1957 a house was bought in Bedford Avenue to accommodate the Silsoe sergeant. This housed three sergeants before 1968, Sergeant Vaughan who later became Assistant Chief Constable for Mid

---

[23] William Austin, *History of Luton*, 1928. P114
[24] *The Bedfordshire Police 1840-1856*, C Emsley, Open University
[25] *Kelly's Directories*

Wales, Sergeant Absolom who became Chief Superintendent at Bedford and Sergeant Dereck Lett who became Operations Superintendent at Luton and who still lives in the village.

The constables worked four hours during the daytime and four hours at night between 6pm and 6am and had 'night points', usually telephone kiosks, where they could receive messages from Ampthill by phone.

The constable's wife was expected to take messages when the constable was out and pass them on as necessary but they were discouraged from fraternising with local families which made them seem aloof and not friendly.

Then, in 1968 the old system of policing was changed by the Home Office with Panda Cars being introduced and the local police houses being sold. This had a disastrous effect on local policing in rural areas as policemen were posted to these areas who had no local knowledge and no contacts and were thus completely out of touch.

Plate 1/4 Aerial view of Silsoe 1953

Plate 1/5 Walnut Tree Lane from Wrest Park Drive

Plate 4/2 - Monument to Henry & Mary de Grey in Flitton Mausoleum

WREST PARK SILSOE (NORTH FRONT)

Plate 4/5 - Wrest Park Early in the 19th Century

Plate 5/4 – Silsoe Church from South East 2008

Plate 5/6 Silsoe War Memorial

Plate 5/7 Silsoe Bells 7 November 1951 with Sam Stapleton, Tom Harris, Cliff White, Norman Stevens, John Scott, Frank Bunker.

Plate 7/1 Silsoe Lock-up

Plate 9/2 - Silsoe Old School with the bell still in its Bellcote

Plate 9/4 - The Village School 1905, possibly with Mr Treacher on the right.

Plate 10/ 8 The Co-op staff in the early 1900s.

Plate 10/9   The Co-op staff in their shop, taken about 1950.

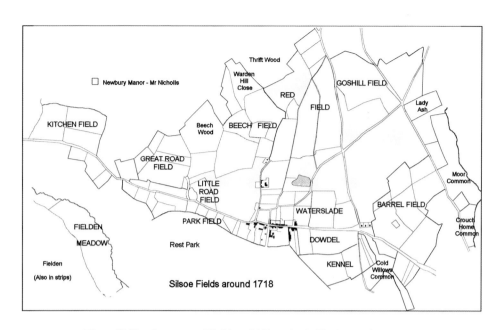

Plate 11/3 - Common Fields of Silsoe in 1718 shown in yellow

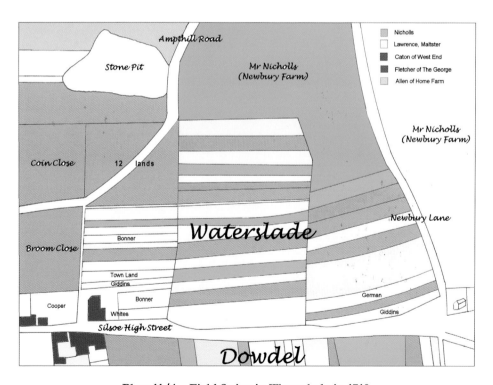

Plate 11/4 – Field Strips in Waterslade in 1718

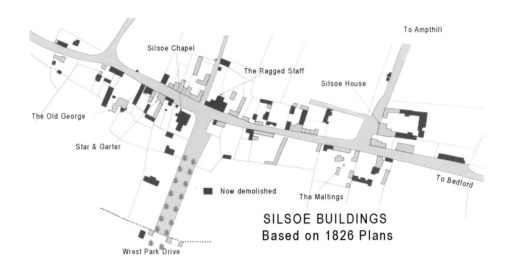

Plate 12/1

The buildings coloured purple are those that have since been demolished and those in green the ones which substantially remain today:.

Plate 13/3   Road Houses from the east, this road was stopped up
when the by-pass was built.

Chapter 8 – Silsoe and the Military

Silsoe at War.

For centuries before and after the Romans, it was absolutely essential for communal survival that able-bodied men lay their hands on weapons of some sort and join up with others, when called upon to defend their territory. Bedfordshire generally, because of the river systems, suffered attacks from the marauding invasions of the Danes or Vikings. It is unknown how many Bedfordshire men joined the battles of 1066, the first in September with King Harold when the King of Norway invaded in the north; and then turned back south to meet William, Duke of Normandy, at the Battle of Hastings on 14th October. Likewise there are no records to tell how many men, if any, from Silsoe fought in the following centuries.

Later, in the 15th century however, as mentioned elsewhere, the Earl of Kent could apparently call up 40-50 armed men within several hours to help assert himself against upstart minor nobility; but in the ensuing years and with the formation of established armies it became less necessary for the average peasant to be able to pick up his sword or spear and go to war. However, the kings did ensure a certain level of proficiency in the long bow, and required men to practice their archery.

The kings were still concerned about protecting their realms though, and they established the militia whereby local men were trained in the art of war. The history of the militia and the volunteers goes back several hundred years, before the creation of the regular army by Oliver Cromwell, when they provided armed forces for the defence of the country as well as men for overseas campaigns. Once the regular army had come into being they provided a reserve and were, from time to time, called upon to aid the government during civil unrest or when rioting broke out; and when invasion was threatened by Napoleon they came out in their thousands to support the nation.

The Bedfordshire Muster Lists 1539-1831 from the Bedfordshire Historical Record Society Vol. 17 1992 written by Nigel Lutt, lists several men from Silsoe serving in the County Militia. Silsoe, along with the surrounding villages belonged within the Flitt Hundred[26]. It should be noted that there are substantial gaps in the dates of the Muster Lists, and some may have been destroyed whilst not being considered important enough to retain. In the first list of 1539 no Silsoe men appear, although there are some from Flitton, Maulden and Clophill. However by 1591 – 1602 two men from Silsoe were impressed for service in Ireland. Edward Gellis armed with a halberd, which was a staff combining a spear and axe for thrusting and cutting. (The halberd had become obsolete by the late 16th century, by which time the wide blade had given way to a crescent shape accompanied by a very long spike.) The other unfortunate man was William Brown who was armed with a caliver,

---

[26] A hundred was originally a land measurement that could sustain a hundred families.

which was an infantry firearm, about 3½ feet long that fired without a rest, which was later rendered obsolete by the musket.

After the restoration of the monarchy in 1660, a new series of Militia Acts were passed to strengthen the authority of the Crown. The parish constables of Flitton and Silsoe were directed in October 1660 to levy £1.10s. on the parish and to require:

All Gent. within yr. Precincts to meete the Lord Lieutenants at the Signe of the White-hart in Ampthill upon Munday the 29th inst. in order to the raising of Volunteers.

The rates of pay were 1s. per day for a foot soldier (the same pay a soldier was given in WWI), and 2s. rising to 2s.6d. in 1663 for a horseman, and the rates were laid down by statute.

In the circa 1683 list four men from Silsoe were drawn: Joseph Bland, William Whittamore, Thomas Godfrey and Thomas Layton who served in the Flitt Hundred Militia Foote in Captain Palmer's Company. Also in 1683, Mr Daniel was in Sir William Gostwicke's 'Troope' (presumably mounted).

The Militia Act of 1757 re-established local part-time forces of one or more regiments for each county where men were chosen by ballot from among the inhabitants of each parish. There was a way out though, and if someone who had drawn the short straw could get another man to replace him, he did not need to serve. The militia were linked to regular army regiments in the 19th century as the third and sometimes fourth battalions of county regiments.

In the County Enrolments of 1763, the following men were selected by lot: Step Browning, William Bolton, Joseph How, William Worker and Thomas Freeman.

The Napoleonic Wars created a gap in the Muster Lists and judging by the dates there were four Silsonians who joined up to serve and possibly remained in the army afterwards.

(It is interesting to note that the army was not considered to be an honourable place of employment until after the Great War of 1914-18. Up until then, army service was an alternative to serving a gaol sentence for offences such as theft, affray or even GBH. It is fair to say that the standing army in Napoleonic times, and beyond was full of 'rum uns'. There is no evidence to suggest that the following belonged to that category however.) They were Henry Mclean, who served in the 14th Foot Regiment, 95th Foot Regiment and 2nd Foot Guards from, 1807-1821, and was discharged aged 33. John Lowings, the son of Henry and Sarah, who served in the 30th Foot Regiment from 1803-1827, and was discharged aged 43. (John Lowings came back to the village and in the 1851 and 1861 censuses is listed as a Chelsea Pensioner living with his deaf and dumb sister Mary, at 25 High Street.)

Samuel Sturgeon, who served in the 40th Foot Regiment from 1811-1833 and was discharged aged 39, and finally, Joseph Field, the son of Robert and Mary, who served in the Rifle Brigade between 1812-1840, probably in Spain and Waterloo, and was discharged aged 42. [27] In 1809, during a lull in the Napoleonic Wars, the various volunteer corps became local Militia Regiments, where substitution in the ballot was prohibited.

By 1831 the Bedfordshire Militia list includes the recruiting of, James Porter, Class1, age 20. A Class 1 militiaman was under 30 years of age with no children living, and had to undertake four weeks annual training at Bedford.

There are records dated 1863 of the Ampthill and Silsoe Volunteer Force, with the regulations book, letters and purchase invoices, but unfortunately no names of the volunteers are included. [28]

MID-DAY STABLES. Bed's Imperial Yoemanry Camp, Silsoe. 1905.
PHOTO, ANDERSON, *Luton & Leighton Buzzard.*

Plate 8/1 – Yeomanry Camp at Wrest Park 1905

The Bedfordshire Imperial Yeomanry enjoyed the facilities at Wrest Park for their annual camp according to the above postcard. The Bedfordshire Yeomanry formed in 1797 as an independent body of mounted troops, but was disbanded after the Napoleonic Wars. In 1901 it reformed as the Bedfordshire Imperial Yeomanry for service in the Boer War, and from 1908 became part of the Territorial Force training as lancers with headquarters at Bedford and squadrons and divisions scattered across Bedfordshire. The nearest squadron to Silsoe was based at Shefford.

---

[27] National Archives WO 97/190/22, WO 97/489/80, WO 97/566/76 & WO 97/1078/23
[28] BLARS 1863 SFM3/219 – 221

The Great War

The Great War began rather unexpectedly on 4th August 1914. Three days later the Silsoe Reservists had left the village, followed a little later by the Territorials, the volunteers of Kitchener's Army and then the conscripts from early 1915. The war was expected to be over by Christmas that year. Many wealthy Bedfordshire landowners offered properties to be used as convalescent homes for wounded soldiers returning from the front, possibly believing it would be a short-term loan.

Samuel Whitbread was one of the first to loan, in his case Howard Villa, in Cardington to the Red Cross for use as a hospital and convalescent home; whilst Cecil Polhill offered Howbury Hall. Other properties soon followed in Mid and North Bedfordshire: Old Warden Park, Hinwick House, Tempsford Hall, Melchbourne Priory, Bromham House (owned by WH Allen), Aspley House, and Bourne End Farm, Wootton. The Duchess of Bedford pledged 25 beds in the Cottage Hospital and a wing of the Abbey to be used as a gymnasium or temporary hospital, if required (which it most definitely was, as the war progressed). Other well-to-do people (mainly elderly spinsters) offered rooms within their properties.

Wrest Park Hospital

On 28th August 1914 the following report was printed in the Bedfordshire Standard (a Tory newspaper)

'Lord Lucas has generously fitted up Wrest House as a convalescent home for those who may be injured in the present European war. All the portable furniture in the dining and drawing room and library has been removed and over 100 beds erected while the bedrooms have been given up to the nursing staff; and the electric light is being temporarily installed. Wrest House with its spacious terrace facing south. and beautiful pleasure grounds, is an ideal spot for the purpose. The Hon Nan Herbert, sister of Lord Lucas, is supervising the arrangements. A committee of ladies is busily engaged in making garments for the soldiers. Some of the scouts are acting as messengers, and assisting the police in guarding bridges and railway tunnels. The sum of £15 has been sent to the Prince of Wales National Relief Fund.'

The Hon N Herbert, a rather formidable lady by all accounts, took on the management of the hospital. The first resident surgeon was Dr Beauchamp who arrived on 6th September 1914 along with a matron and Red Cross nurses. According to the newspaper, 66 wounded soldiers arrived on 7th September 1914. They were sent from the General Hospital Whitechapel, after being in action at the Battle of Mons, and arrived by motor cars and omnibuses. However, the motor buses, due to their height were unable to pass through the lodge gates, and the majority of the soldiers had to walk the length of the avenue. Crowds of women and children (the mentolk being at work) awaited their arrival. They waved Union Jacks and cheered and brought a smile to the faces of the dust-stained, khaki clad visitors. Apart from 3 or 4, they were all walking-wounded, and felt better after a cup of tea and a wash. It was reported that all were eager to get back to the front.

During this early part of the war, censorship had not begun; and the soldiers readily told of the secret landing, the journey by train, the road to Mons, the hasty digging of trenches by the canal on 25th August, the sudden German onslaught and the partial annihilation during the next 36 hours. They said they had been outnumbered by 10 to 1, and very few were injured by bullets; most had suffered shrapnel wounds. They said that the Belgian and French people had been very kind to them and they had given their regimental insignia to them as souvenirs. They also spoke of German atrocities.

Games were organised within the pleasure grounds for those fit enough to join in, but the soldiers were confined within the Park. The villagers would have liked a church parade on the first Sunday, but a chaplain had been provided and a service took place at the park. The number of beds expanded to 220, as more wounded were expected. The newspaper reported that: "'The sanitary arrangements are perfect as Lord Lucas had spent a considerable sum after the late Mr Whitelaw Reid left." (Whitelaw Reid was the United States Ambassador, who rented Wrest as his country house, until his death in 1912.) The following Sunday there was a church parade and St James's was packed. The hymns sung included Fight the Good Fight and Onward Christian Soldiers. The Vicar's sermon was 'God is our refuge and strength', and he said that the present war was a grand opportunity for bringing out the patriotism of British subjects, and the noble response that had been made to Lord Kitchener's appeal. Turning to the men, he said he heartily welcomed their presence at worship. They had been wounded in an honourable and uneven conflict, and he trusted that after a short stay and rest in Bedfordshire, they would be able to return to fight for their God, their King, and their Country. Those that were able did their best to stand for the National Anthem.

Football, quoits and fishing were the soldiers' daytime activities and they played billiards in the evening. Books were made available and the morning and evening papers were delivered. A smoking concert was arranged one Saturday evening and Lord Lucas attended. By 9th October 1914, only 16 of the original 66 remained at Wrest House, and a week later it was empty.

After the first batch of wounded soldiers left, Wrest Hospital became a very much more important place. It was no longer used as a convalescent home but as a base hospital with soldiers being taken straight there from the Front. It was not long until the hospital became busy again. By the end of November, 140 wounded soldiers had arrived from the trenches of the First Battle of Ypres. They had been taken by motor ambulances to Boulogne, shipped to Southampton, and sent by train to Ampthill Station, where they were met by the ladies of the local Red Cross Society under the command of the Hon Constance Russell. Despite being exhausted and in much pain and discomfort, they thanked the ladies for the tea they had provided, and one remarked that they were going to have a happy Christmas and a rest.

There were about sixty stretcher cases, most being maimed for life by an amputation or serious shrapnel wounds. They were given cigarettes and chocolates before getting into motorised Red Cross vans, ambulances and motor carriages for the journey to Wrest Park. Some of the regiments they belonged to were the Munster Fusiliers, Welsh Fusiliers, Lancasters, Norfolks and Seaforth Highlanders. (Despite the 2nd Battalion Bedfordshire Regiment being very much involved in that battle, none of their wounded seemed to end up at Wrest.) X-ray apparatus had been installed before their arrival, and Army experts spoke very highly of the equipment at Wrest House. The vicar of Silsoe, as chaplain, was in daily attendance. Certainly in December, some very seriously wounded soldiers were being treated there, and reports stated that their wives had been sent for at the expense of the National Relief Fund.

Wrest Park Hospital. took in wounded from all the major battles, and in the 19th March 1915 edition of the *Bedfordshire Times & Independent* the following was reported:

'On Friday evening 73 wounded soldiers were brought to Wrest Park hospital from Flanders, and 37 were sent on from Ampthill station to Woburn. Most of these were wounded at Neuve Chapelle the previous Wednesday, when the Allied forces drove back the enemy with such precision and dash. As one poor fellow remarked, "The Commanding Officer said, There must be no retreat." They were in a sad plight on arrival - and there were more stretcher cases than ever - but now they are very comfortable and all on the road to recovery. At present 42 sick and 90 wounded are receiving attention at Wrest, and when sufficiently recovered they are transferred to one of the convalescent homes in connection with the base hospital. Reveille is sounded at 6.30 every morning, breakfast is served at 7.30, dinner at noon, tea at 4.30, and supper at 9.30. Lights are out at 10p.m. Every Sunday morning those who are able, attend the service in the parish Church under the charge of Sergt-Major Kingsley.[29]

Inevitably, soldiers died in the hospital, and the first was on 7th December 1914. He was Pte John Dalton, aged 29 of the Somerset Light Infantry. John's cause of death is listed as pneumonia and chronic rheumatism. A Union Jack covered his coffin as he was conveyed by trolley accompanied by other soldiers. Boy Scouts from Silsoe and Shefford formed a guard of honour. Lord Lucas sent a wreath; and the doctors, matron and nurses attended his funeral. John was a Roman Catholic, and the Rev. Father Youens of Shefford conducted his burial service. His grave is in Silsoe churchyard near the large holly tree.

---

[29] *Bedfordshire Times & Citizen* for extracts from *Bedfordshire Times & Independent and the Bedfordshire Standard (1914,15 & 16) The Luton News, for extracts from the Luton* News & Bedfordshire Advertiser (1916)

Some soldiers were taken home for their burial, but there are four more soldiers from Wrest Park Hospital buried at Silsoe. Their graves form a line, as soldiers on parade, and have the standard Imperial (now Commonwealth) War Graves Commission headstone. They are:

Pte J Cunningham, Seaforth Highlanders died 2nd February 1915

L/Cpl L F Foster, Royal Lancaster Regiment died 9th May 1915 (the only stone with an inscription 'Thy Will Be Done R.I.P.')[30]

Gunner E Hand, Royal Field Artillery died 14th July 1915

Pte G E Dorman, 3rd Batt Australian Infantry died 14th July 1916.
George Dorman was wounded in the leg on 26th June 1916, in the lead up to the Battle of the Somme that began on 1st July 1916. He, like all the Australians, was a volunteer, and before joining up, George was a coal lumper (meaning carrier) from Paddington, Sydney. He had a wife, Minnie, and a small daughter. He was 26 years old and had been at the Front since late 1915. When his condition deteriorated, his wife was informed and his leg was amputated at Wrest House, where he subsequently died. George was also buried according to the rites of the Roman Catholic Church.

There are two other CWGC headstones in Silsoe churchyard, one from the Great War - Pte G C Petty, Royal Army Service Corps died 13th March 1918 - this soldier did not die at the hospital, and the other to F/Lieut. J Craig, Royal Air Force died 23rd April 1946.

It is worthy of note, that every year, on Armistice Sunday, the Silsoe Branch of the Royal British Legion places a cross on the graves of the seven servicemen buried in the churchyard.

Wrest Park Hospital played a vital role in the treatment of the Great War wounded until 14th September 1916, when at. 5.30pm that day, the East Wing caught fire. The official Fire Brigade report says that sparks from a defective flue caught the old timber in the roof. Wrest Park Fire Brigade arrived within 10 minutes, followed by Shefford, Luton, Ampthill, Letchworth, Hitchin, Kings Walden, Woburn Abbey and eventually Bedford. Luton and Letchworth had motorised transport and after the Wrest fire it was thought that Bedford should be modernised. They had left with 1,000 feet of hose and a Victoria steamer, pulled by horses. They had to change their horses at Haynes Park for a motor tractor, but then the towing rope broke and had to be spliced before they could continue. However, they stayed at the scene of the fire until 4.30am. Luton arrived after the estate brigade, and their journey of almost eleven miles took 22 minutes, during which several times they touched 40 miles per hour. One Luton fireman almost lost his life, from smoke inhalation. A steamer, belonging to the London Fire Brigade was sent

---

[30] (Initially, the families of the deceased were expected to pay for any inscription at 3½d per letter, and many simply could not afford the expense.)

from Holloway and that arrived at 10pm. The fire was initially fought with rainwater stored in tanks, but that soon ran out, and water was pumped from the lake, canal and ornamental gardens.

The hospital had 160 patients at the time. Most, fortunately, were convalescing, but there had been some recent operations and many of the wounded were amputees. It was a fine evening but cold, and beds were made up on the lawn. The Duchess of Bedford then arrived with motor ambulances and took 50 of them to the Abbey Hospital and Ampthill Camp. The remainder were housed in the Orangery until accommodation at other hospitals and convalescent homes could be found. There was an apparently unfounded rumour that although all the patients got out safely, two then died of shock. The resident surgeon, Dr Kirkwood, was most emphatic in his denial of any such happening! Able-bodied soldiers in training arrived from Ampthill Camp and Haynes Park to remove the valuable furniture and paintings. The fire did £20,000 worth of damage (an enormous figure at that time).

From then on, Wrest. Park, having made a most valuable contribution to the Great War, ceased to be used as a Military Hospital.

It was also, however, used for training purposes and Archibald Gordon Macgregor's War Diary[31] written for his Grandchildren Alison and Kathryn, read :-

"After final (embarkation) leave and inoculation I was at Wrest Park, Silsoe, Beds. from 5th to 11th April 1917. Wrest Park was a large English country seat which had belonged to Lord Lucas. He seems to have been a very fine chap, for after he was killed in the Royal Flying Corps in 1916, a long poem was written about him by Maurice Baring ("In Memoriam A. H." - Auberon Herbert, Captain Lord Lucas).

The house, of which the army occupied one wing, was in extensive grounds, with many magnificent trees, statues, monuments, a horse-shoe shaped lake and a swimming pool surrounded by high yew hedges.

At Wrest Park reinforcement drafts for R.E. Signals of the British Expeditionary Force were assembled. The men and most of the officers were under canvas. I was in the house for most of the time. The weather was frightful - constant showers of rain, sleet and snow, and the ground in the camp area was ankle-deep in mud and slush when we left to entrain at Flitwick."

Lord Lucas

On 13-08-1914, nine days after the declaration of the Great War, a report was printed in the *Bedfordshire Times* regarding Lord Lucas. It stated that he

---

[31] http://www.annawelti.com/archie.asp

had been appointed the President of the Board of Agriculture, upon the promotion of the previous holder to President of the Board of Trade, after a resignation due to views with regard to Great Britain's participation in the war not coinciding with those of the Government.

Lucas's full title was Lord Lucas and Dingwall. The Lucas baronetcy dated back to 1663 and Dingwall to 1600. He was born as Auberon Thomas Herbert, in 1876, and was the only surviving son of the Hon Auberon Herbert and Lady Florence Amabell, a daughter of the sixth Earl Cowper. Lord Lucas was under-secretary of State for War from 1908 to 1911. In 1911 he was appointed under-secretary for the Colonies, and in the same year became Parliamentary Secretary to the Board of Agriculture.

He only very occasionally visited Wrest Park, and had his country residence at Pickett Post, Ringwood, Hampshire. He succeeded to his title in 1905 and was unmarried. According to the Silsoe *Roll of Honour,* Lord Lucas was educated at Bedford Grammar School and at Balliol College, Oxford, where he was a successful rower, but only gained a Third in Modern History. He was very interested in fauna, poetry and music.

At the outbreak of the Boer War, he took the first chance he could to go to South Africa, as a *Times* correspondent. He loved the adventure and the beautiful South African countryside, but was not especially interested in military matters. However, one day he advanced too far forward whilst covering an action, and stopped a rifle bullet with his foot. The wound was poorly treated and upon returning to England, he had his leg amputated below the knee. Reports say that the loss of his leg made little difference to his lifestyle.

He was drawn into politics by Raymond Asquith, an old university chum, and became a Liberal Parliamentary candidate. When the Liberal Government came into power his political career took off, and he was a Cabinet Minister at the age of 38.

He left the Cabinet when the Coalition Government was formed in May 1915, and although many years over age, managed to join the Royal Flying Corps, where he became a very competent and well-respected pilot. He first went to Egypt, and then in the spring of 1916 was back in England instructing recruits. He was offered the command of a squadron, but refused until he had gained experience on the Western Front. He was posted to France in October 1916, and was reported missing in stormy weather, over the German lines, on 3rd November. Early in December news came from the Germans that he had died. In the autumn of 1918, advancing British troops found his grave. His memorial in the Commonwealth War Graves Cemetery at Ecoust-Saint-Mein, Pas de Calais, north-east of the town of Albert states simply "Captain Auberon Thomas Herbert / 8th Baron Lucas/ and 11th

Baron Dingwall / Hants Carabiniers Yeomanry / and Royal Flying Corps / 3rd November 1916".[32]

The Great War of 1914-18 had a profound effect on the village of Silsoe along with many other 'estate villages' throughout England; as after the death of Baron Lucas, Wrest Park estate was sold, and along with it went a way of life that had been followed for centuries.

The Bedfordshire and Essex estates were sold as just before leaving for the Front, Lord Lucas had left instructions for the breaking up of the estates in the event of his death. It was the express wish of his Lordship, that so far as possible the tenants should not be disturbed, but that an offer to purchase the more extensive Bedfordshire estate, including the mansion would be entertained.

Following the Great War, as was common throughout the country, a War Memorial was built at the front of the churchyard. Of the names on the memorial for the First World War only the following can be traced as Silsoe born :-

Gunner Ernest J Ambridge of the Royal Garrison Artillery, died on 13th September 1918 aged 31, commemorated on the Hersin Communal Cemetery Extension,

Ernest William Dunham of the Canadian Infantry, died between 4th and 7th September 1916 aged 22, the son of James and Sophia Dunham, of 19 High St, commemorated on the Vimy Memorial

Eustace Charles Martin from West End Road who was killed on 2nd December 1917 aged 20, buried at the Rocquigny-Equancourt Road British Cemetery, Manancourt in France,

Herbert Henry Fennemore son of Francis and Eliza Fennemore and whose wife May was living in Christchurch, Hants, killed in action in France 31st August 1918 aged 41, buried at Eterpigny British Cemetery.

Walter Chase (Edward on memorial) Upton of the South Wales Borderers, died 1st July 1916 aged 26 from 5 Church Road, buried at Y Ravine Cemetery, Beaumont-Hamel, Somme, France.

---

[32] Bedfordshire Times & Citizen *extracts from Bedfordshire Times & Independent Silsoe Roll of Honour*

There are a total of fifteen names for the War Dead of The Great War, they are inscribed as follows:

Ambridge	Ernest John	31	13/9/1918	B Silsoe, registered as John Ernest 1884
Bangs	Leonard	21	5/7/1916	From Tottenham, birth not found but there is an Arthur Leonard b Greenwich 1895.
Baron Lucas and Dingwall	Auberon	40	03/11/1916	B Lymington, Hants, Captain, RFC
Clayson	John William	22	24/4/1917	B Ulverston, Cumbria 1874. Parents gardeners at Wrest 1901
Cornwall	Jack	22	09/08/1915	B Hitchin, parents at Wrest Park 1901
Dunham	Ernest William	22	between 04 & 07/09/1916	B Silsoe but a Canadian national in 1916.
Fahey	Albert	?	31/03/1916	B Chorlton or Barnet, on Menin Gate memorial.
Fennemore	Herbert Henry	41	31/8/1918	B Silsoe 1877
Gudgion	William Henry	39	04/05/1917	B Islington, son of William Gudgion, of Rose Cottage, Silsoe; husband of Charlotte Harding (formerly Gudgion), of Cheam, Surrey.
Jones	Lumley Owen Williams	41	14/09/1918	Brig Gen. Parents and land in Wales, no Silsoe connection yet found
Laird	Frederick Harry	28	10/12/1914	Husband of Julia Laird, of High St., Silsoe
Mann	Cyril	18	01/08/1917	Family probably from Silsoe, on Menin Gate memorial.
Martin	Eustace Charles	20	2/12/1917	1901 census family at W E Rd, says b Silsoe but not in records. Brother of May Cooper.
Pratt	Charles Henry	25	14/10/1918	Born Maulden, commemorated at Damascus Commonwealth War Cemetery
Upton	Walter (Chase) Edward	26	01/07/1916	B Silsoe 1889 to Mrs Emily Upton. Buried Y Ravine CWG Cemetery, Somme, France

The Second World War

The following names are inscribed on the Silsoe War Memorial for 1939-1945:

Brown	Donald Arthur	24	18/11/1943	Of the Royal Air Force Volunteer Reserve, Son of Frank William and Annie Margaret Brown, of Silsoe. Commemorated on the Runnymede Memorial
Shirley	R C			Lt RCS IA Not found in Commonwealth War Roll of Honour
Squires	Albert Henry	59	06/11/1944	Husband of Ellen E. Squires, of 20 Newbury Lane, Silsoe. Died at Commer Car Works, Biscot Road, Luton

Although Silsoe was some way away from the areas where bombing was carried out regularly by the Luftwaffe it was not totally exempt from the danger. A V1 flying bomb, (a 'doodlebug'), exploded on 18th December 1944,

20 yards east of the A6 and 800 yards from the Clophill roundabout, approximately where the old A6 joins the bypass, causing some damage to the Lord Nelson. Even more recently, in 1989, an unexploded incendiary bomb was found adjacent to the High Street in the village.

Silsoe, being an agricultural community in the war had to maintain and even improve its production of food. Consequently, as in the first war, the farms were inspected and the farmers were instructed how much pasture they needed to plough up for cereals.

To help the farmers and to replace those young men sent to fight, the Women's Land Army was formed with girls sent from towns to live in hostels in the countryside and to work during the day. In Silsoe, Wrest Park Lodge, located where The Beeches now is, was used as the hostel and up to 32 land girls were accommodated there from 1943 onwards, in five rooms containing six girls each. They were under the eye of a warden, Mrs Stone was the first, followed by Mrs Futter in 1946.

The girls were paid but the regime was strict with girls being fined if they were late or caught climbing in after hours. They did go out though, using the George as their pub and attending dances in the Village Hall. They had to wear green jerseys, brown breeches and brown felt hats and worked hard, having to do all the usual farm jobs, Mrs B Brandon said:-

"We went out daily to various farms at 7.30 a.m. doing a variety of jobs, cleaning out cattle sheds, spreading fertiliser, fruit picking, vegetable picking, haymaking, working late in the summer months, also threshing which was back breaking and dirty work, then having to queue up for a bath when we returned to the hostel, no showers in those days."

Plate 8/2 - Wrest Park Lodge Hostel

Sun Insurance

In April 1939, as 'the storm clouds' were gathering over Europe, the Sun Insurance Company bought Wrest Park along with 260 acres of the park and woodlands from Mr John G Murray for £25,000, with the idea that when the inevitable war broke out, they would operate from the safety of the countryside. It was reported that at the end of Murray's time at Wrest Park, the grounds had become somewhat neglected. Initially Sun Insurance transferred the departments whose presence in London was not essential, those being: Accounts, Foreign, Marine and Reinsurance and at the outbreak of war in September, the Head Office relocated to Silsoe.

Plans were drawn up to house the relocated employees and those to follow later. The stable block had to be altered and huts were to be erected as sleeping quarters, washing facilities and air-raid shelters. There was to be twelve huts as sleeping quarters and four air-raid shelters on either side of the Avenue behind the stable block.

The construction work was given to a Stanley L Mighell from Sutton, Surrey, and the man in charge was Frederick G Worker, who had relatives in the village and lodged with his family at Silsoe Post Office (then in the High Street). (In 1763 William Worker was enrolled to serve in the County Militia, so the family had obviously been in Silsoe for quite a while.) Men were brought from Surrey to complete the work, but also some were recruited from Silsoe, and they were: P Ansell, R G Cole, A H Cooper, B Jenkins, D R Payne, D Twydell, whose job titles were unknown; and also J Scott a carpenter from 22 West End Road, and three labourers, W R S Dickens of West End Road, H Albinson of Cane Hill Lodge and A J Mann of 82 West End. (The addresses are recorded as they were written.) The work was completed in 1940, after a very severe winter.

Very little work was done in the mansion, apart from the fitting of two Aga cookers in order to feed the 300 staff in two sittings, with food of the highest order. A local dairy delivered excellent milk daily, and it was much enjoyed at elevenses apparently. The existing drains leading to a cesspit near the Chinese Bridge were inadequate for the number of extra people, so new ones had to be dug. It was reported that the sediment cleared from the old cesspit and when spread over adjoining land, produced lush new bushes from the tomato seeds in it.

Sun Insurance began to move back to London at the end of 1945 and was completely reinstated by early 1946. [33]

---

[33] Information taken from *Bedfordshire Magazine Vol 19 No 148,* Spring 1984, written by Leslie Worker, son of F G Worker.

Evacuees

Many of the more senior residents of Silsoe remember evacuees coming to the village during WWII. It would appear that they arrived in two batches, firstly a few 'normal evacuees', as we know them, who went on to attend the village school and generally did their best to wreak havoc. Then a girls' school from Walthamstow in London was evacuated to Silsoe. The girls did not attend the village school but brought their schoolmistresses with them, and from reports seemed to have set up their own school at Silsoe House. Many of the girls were billeted with local families, and in the interview with Dora Brazier she recalls her parents taking in three of them.

Through a series of coincidences one of those girl evacuees has been tracked down and she very kindly told of her, very pleasant days at Silsoe.

Life as an evacuee in Silsoe

In 1939, at the age of 13 years, Doreen Soane-Sands (now Lloyd-White) was evacuated to Silsoe. She was a pupil at the William Morris Girls Central School in Walthamstow, London, and arrived by train (most likely to Ampthill Station), along with the other girls from her school and three schoolteachers. Although Doreen has no recollection of the journey, she remembers being quite composed and really thought of her evacuation from London as a great adventure.

The girls were taken to the Village Hall for inspection by their prospective hosts. A man went up to Doreen, and said he thought his sister would like to have her stay with her. He happened to be the local taxi driver and she was taken in style to her new home; which turned out to be a lovely thatched cottage (Doreen's words) at the very end of the village, near the Lord Nelson public house. It was at no. 5 Newbury Lane, which has the front door facing the High Street. Mr and Mrs Upton, their 18 year old daughter, Ena, and King Charles spaniel, Bonnie, became her new temporary family. She was made immediately welcome, and after changing out of her school uniform, she thinks Mrs Upton (Ella), realised that she was older than she first thought.

Doreen has very fond memories of the family that made her so welcome, and she was told that should anything happen to her parents, they would gladly adopt her. Ena and Doreen became great friends, which as Doreen says, was just as well as they shared a cosy goose feather bed. Ena worked as a manageress in a cake shop and was engaged to a young farmer. Ena and her fiancée took her under their wing, and often took her with them to the cinema in Bedford or Luton. After being brought up with three older brothers, Doreen says that Ena being very tidy set her a good example.

Mrs Upton was a superb cook and regularly made Bedfordshire Clangers (a suet dumpling with meat, onion and potato at one end and jam at the other, separated by a thick piece of suet crust; which is peculiar to Bedfordshire and now almost disappeared in our health-conscious society). Doreen regularly accompanied her on visits to her father in Clophill, where she cleaned his cottage and generally looked after him. He had been a schoolmaster at Clophill School until his retirement. Every weekend Mr Upton gave her a bar of chocolate and taught her how to handle his pet ferrets. Much of their socialising was with the brother of Mr Upton and his large family who lived further up in the village.

Although Doreen has no recollection of writing or receiving letters from home, she is sure she must have done; but she remembers her mother coming to visit and also her brother, Bryan when he was home on leave, because apparently she was a little moody when he left. (Bryan, although only 18, was a Territorial and was called up as soon as the war started. Thankfully he, along with her other two brothers survived.)

The cottage had no bathroom facilities, and the toilet was at the bottom of the garden. Every week the girls went to a large house in Silsoe where they could enjoy the luxury of a bath and dry themselves on large fluffy bath towels.

However, after what she thinks to be about a year, Doreen's mother wanted her to go home. Their school lessons were generally inadequate, and she was learning little. The situation was not helped by one of their accompanying teachers breaking a leg. She cannot remember any real structured classes, and the girls certainly did not attend the village school. She should have stayed in Silsoe until she was 16 years, but after perseverance by her mother, Doreen went back to London and commercial college and worked in an insurance office in Moorgate, London, travelling during the air raids. (She is still adept with a typewriter, as the letter she wrote to me proved.) When 18, she joined the Civil Nursing Reserve, and worked at Black Notley Hospital, caring for wounded airmen and soldiers of the Egyptian Campaign, known as the Desert Rats.

After leaving Silsoe, Doreen kept in touch with the Uptons and had two summer holidays there, taking along her friends Margaret and Iris. When she was married in 1948, Mrs Upton, Ena and her baby attended the wedding. Doreen has very fond memories of Silsoe and especially of the Upton family.

Holidays in Silsoe during WWII

The Margaret Litchfield (mentioned above) who visited Silsoe for summer holidays with Iris Deppe (another friend) along with Doreen also has fond memories of the Upton family. She remembers them as being very welcoming. Margaret lived close to Doreen in London, but being a little younger did not attend the same school. She and her sister were sent to live with their aunt in Wales during the War.

Margaret thought all the green fields around Silsoe were lovely, and the girls used to walk to Ampthill to visit a relative of Mrs Upton who told their fortunes from teacups. Margaret also remembers travelling to Bedford to see *The Desert Song*, and recalls enjoying the performance so much that they almost missed the last bus back to Silsoe. Margaret notes that thinking of Silsoe brings back very happy memories of their time spent there with the Uptons, but also the many sad and traumatic experiences of the war.

Chapter 9 - Education

Education

There is little evidence of any general literacy prior to the 10th century and indeed King Alfred complained of this in the 9th century. Illuminated manuscripts were produced in monasteries by literate monks, but it is possible that the average monk could not actually read or write but was purely copying originals, with no understanding of their contents.

However the church did have a requirement for learning, especially in Latin, and this eventually gave rise to the formation of the Cathedral Schools. Many of these schools had choirs, as this was thought to assist in the enunciation of the Latin. However, at the same time it is thought that nearly half of the ecclesiastical benefices could have been filled with clerics who were unable to read or write.

There were many different kinds of schools in mediaeval England but these were small, informal schools held in the parish church, song schools at cathedrals, almonry schools attached to monasteries, chantry schools, guild schools, preparatory grammar schools, and full grammar schools. The curriculum of these schools was limited to basics such as learning the alphabet, psalters, and religious rites and lessons, such as the Ten Commandments and the Seven Deadly Sins.

Before Henry VIII's break from the Roman Catholic Church in 1534, efforts to provide learning remained associated in some way with the church. cathedrals, large churches, chantry chapels, Benedictine monasteries, colleges of priests, town burgesses, religious hospitals and religious guilds all supported grammar and song schools. Wealthy benefactors – for example, members of the Royal Family, those linked to the church, like bishops, and wealthy London-based merchants also founded schools. Winchester School founded by Bishop William of Wykeham in 1394, was an example, and also Eton, founded by Henry VI in 1441.

Many of the schools founded in the Middle Ages were designed to educate boys and young men employed by the various religious foundations themselves, but the sons of noblemen, gentry, merchants etc., could also often attend these schools as private, fee-paying pupils. They were intended for the university, the priesthood, or for indentured apprenticeships which required a knowledge of Latin and of reading and writing – e.g. scriveners, stationers, copyists, apothecaries etc. On a smaller scale, some parish priests boarded boys and hired a teacher for them, and private schoolmasters in towns rented rooms and taught a group of boys. Noblemen and gentry sometimes hired a chaplain or tutor for their sons at home.

During the upheavals of the 1640s and 1650s when the monarchy, the House of Lords and the established church hierarchy were swept away, educational ideas such as 'education for all' were debated, and ideas of radical reform circulated. However under the Commonwealth, action lagged far behind reformers' plans and ideas, and in the disruption of the Civil War and the new government, the proposed education ideas lost out.

Between 1660 and 1689 some dissenting preachers and schoolmasters defied the law, and opened schools to train theological candidates and Non-Conformist schoolchildren. The Declaration of Indulgence in 1672, followed by the Act of Toleration in 1689, granted Protestant Non-Conformists greater freedom of worship, and the penalties against illegal teaching became unworkable. The chief enemies of dissent remained the anglican clergy and the 'squirearchy', but non-licensed dissenting schools and academies operated more openly, and more of them were founded. Finally in 1779 the Dissenting Schoolmasters Relief Act legalised the existing situation.

Large numbers of endowed parish schools to educate the poor opened in this period, under the supervision of the parish vestry or trustees/feoffees. The village schoolteacher was often also the parish clerk, or a husbandman with a holding in the parish. Charity schools financed by subscription and managed by committees of anglican or dissenting subscribers opened in London from 1685. After 1699, the Society for Promoting Christian Knowledge (SPCK) took up this idea to spread charity schools throughout England. They started adult reading classes in 1700.

Silsoe Schools

The earliest mention found of schooling in Silsoe, although it was probably very elementary and based on biblical studies, is in the Bishop of Lincoln's Visitation of 1717, where it was stated that there was a school established at the chapel of Silsoe and that the Duchess of Kent had made a contribution of £63 towards the support of a National Day School at Silsoe.

The Duke of Kent paid out money in 1730 towards Silsoe school, and ten years later there is a note that the Duke had retained the £100 left by his grandmother, Amabella, for Silsoe school, but paid 6% interest to the Vicar, Mr Birt, Mr Fletcher, Mr Towersley and the minister at Gravenhurst. Presumably this went towards education and perhaps either Mr Fletcher or Mr Towersley was the Master at Silsoe school.[34] The same document notes that there used to be 6d per week paid for two scholars at Silsoe Girls School.

Both Flitton and Silsoe had schools in the 18th century with Silsoe's being held in part of the old chapel. Ezekial and William Rouse, who both became rectors at Clophill, had put down Silsoe as the school they attended, in their records at Cambridge.[35]

---

[34] BLARS L26/1393
[35] *Bedfordshire Magazine Vol. 7, No 54* Autumn 1960 *Silsoe Village* by Mary Phillips.

The schoolmaster, at least around the mid 18th century, was Richard Harrison, and the Rev. Hadley Cox, in one of his letters to the Earl of Hardwicke, said that there was need for better accommodation for the increasing seminary,

"He has already filled his small accommodation with a set of very decent well-behaved young scholars, the sons of clergymen, and reputable tradesmen and has been obliged to refuse several boarders for want of room. and
A good school and comfortable workhouse are principal subjects of my vicarial attention. I should say of my wishes, as those objects appear at present so remote."

There were about 40 pupils, boarder and day and lessons were held in the Chapel and from the above description of the pupil's origins, there was probably not much education on offer in that school to the children of the common man. There was for them however, a charity school which had been set up by the Good Countess. Richard Harrison died in August 1758 and what became of his school is not known.[36]

Amabel, later Countess de Grey, had, it seems, been asking about the history of the Silsoe schools as when on 10th December 1800, Joseph Pawsey, the estate agent, is reporting to her, he says:-

......."I have made what enquiry I could about the School, that is how it was carried out on formerly & before Mr & Mrs Harrison kept it. Another person of the same name kept the school in the Chapel at Silsoe, and when Master Harrison died his Widow kept the school in the house in which Mr Reed now lives, and in former times none of the Charity Children were taught to Write, the boys were taught Reading and the Girls Reading & Working- it is thought by some that in the Duke of Kent's time, the extent of the Charity School was what I call the Earl of Kent's Charity, which was then £5.2.0 .p. annum but now £6.13.0. p. Annum. Old G. Wilmer says he remembers it so. I presume all above that sum was My Lady Greys generous and free gift, and I am inclined to believe established by her Ladyship when this Mr & Mrs Harrison came to live at Silsoe, but I will not positively say so. The Book in which the persons names are set down who receive the Cloaths &c. at Xmas, and many other memorandums I left with Mr Harrison a year since, and as he is yet in London I cannot come at it, and in that Book I think there was some Memorandums about the School, but its having been kept in several Cottages in the Village convinces me that formerly it only Extended to the Earl of Kent's Charity.""

Although Sunday schools may date back as far as the 16th century, the Sunday schools movement is often associated with Robert Raikes, a

---

[36] There is a further complication in that there may have been another Mr & Mrs Harrison working as teachers in Silsoe at the same time. See Joseph Pawsey's letters to Amabel, Contess de Grey about this time.

newspaper publisher, who popularised the idea. His interest led to the opening of a church-based Sunday school in Gloucester, in 1780. With support from the Bishops of Chester and Salisbury, a London Society for the Establishment of Sunday Schools was established in 1785. By 1787, it was reckoned that there were 250,000 Sunday school pupils. By 1831, this had risen in England to over 1.25 million and by the mid 19th century around two-thirds of all working-class children, aged between 5 and 15, were attending Sunday school.

In the early 19th century, there emerged indications of new thinking in the field of education, and of particular interest is the Bill introduced in 1807 into the House of Commons, by Samuel Whitbread, the son of the brewer Samuel Whitbread, from Cardington.

He proposed the introduction of a Bill in the House of Commons which in the first part dealt specifically with education, intending that the parish should become responsible for education; and that each child should have two years of education, between the ages of 7 and 14. He thought this would reduce crime and pauperism.

However he was unable to persuade Parliament to accept his ideas as most of the Members considered that, apart from being expensive, the introduction of such a scheme would take the people away from manual work, and make them dissatisfied with their social situation. (We were not so far away from the French Revolution at this time and fear that the workers would rise up was prevalent in the ruling classes.)

The Greys at Wrest also did not care for such an idea, and in a letter of February 1811 to Amabel, Countess de Grey, her nephew Lord Grantham wrote that Whitbread should be defeated.

However, maybe some of the new ideas filtered through, as in 1813 plans were drawn up to convert most of the buildings on the left hand side, of what is now The Maltings, into a schoolhouse with housing for the master[37]. This may have been intended to kill two birds with one stone, as The Maltings was occupied by John Field, and in a letter a year later, Lord Grantham wrote that he expected to soon interview a man he had engaged for Silsoe school, which he hoped to open soon. He thought he would be able to put Field out of The Maltings, and so save time and money in finishing and opening the new school; which he was anxious to do, "as the only chance, considering how the church is served, of counteracting the Dissenters." [38]

---

[37] BLARS L26/459 & 460
[38] BLARS L30/11/243/30

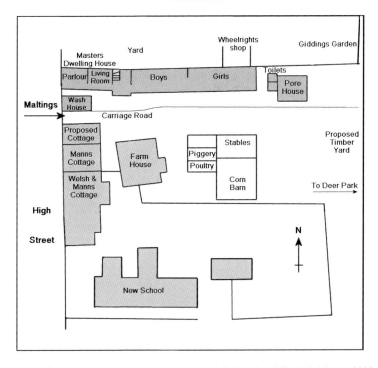

**Plate 9/1 - Map Showing the Proposed School at The Maltings 1813
and the School which was built nearby later.**

This scheme for the new school in the Maltings does not appear to have been carried out, but a new school was constructed about 1813, alongside the present entrance to the village hall, and a letter from Mary Yorke dated September 1816 mentions the new school at Silsoe having been opened at Silsoe with Amabel, Countess de Grey, and her sister, Mary Jemima, as patrons. By 1818 the '*National Day School*', was well established and maintained by the Countess de Grey, with 70 boys and 30 girls being instructed there. It attracted children from elsewhere and in 1820 the new Vicar of Flitton, the Rev James, wrote that "The number of girls at day school are thirty nine including six from Clophill".

In 1821 J D Parry writing in the *Gentleman's Magazine* said that a National School had been established in Silsoe, and was in "a good school house erected by the Countess de Grey and received into the connection of the Bedfordshire National Society". The educational purpose of the National Society, founded in 1811, was that:

"… the National Religion should be made the foundation of National Education, and should be the first and chief thing taught to the poor, according to the excellent Liturgy and Catechism provided by our Church."

The Education Return of 1833, a national survey, says that the Infant School, which commenced in 1828, contained 77 children and was supported by the Earl de Grey. There was "One daily school (commenced 1831) containing 2 males and 16 females, instructed at the expense of their parents." There were also two Day and Sunday "Lancasterian"[39] Schools which "98 males and 87 females attended daily, and 73 males and 87 females on Sunday." The day scholars were paid for by the Earl de Grey and the Sunday scholars were funded by the parish. There was also a Library for the use of all the schools".

The report further says that there were "Active and intelligent teachers. Good disciplinarians." but that "Perhaps the most important, ends of education might be more kept in view. The Children were "trained in some measure in Horticulture" and the building was satisfactory. One school, presumably the infants, was headed by a mistress, the "Teacher a motherly dame".

In 1836, the Earl de Grey proposed moving the right of way from Silsoe to Gravenhurst, from in front of his nice new mansion, so as to run further to the north and to emerge onto the High Street, opposite Ampthill Road alongside "the Old School House".[40] The implication is thus that by then a new school had been in operation for some time, and it was probably the one described by Parry in 1821.

In addition to the ruling classes not being able to understand why a farm labourer should want to be able to read and write, the average labourer probably did not have any real interest in education. Child labour was common practice in this period, and working-class families were very reluctant to give up the earnings of their children for the benefit of education. Indeed, the employment of children continued to increase, even after 1850.

Religious conflict also delayed the establishment of a national system of education. One example of this can be seen in the reaction to the clauses regarding education in the 1843 Factory Bill. There was violent opposition on the part of Non-Conformists and Catholics alike because, according to the Bill, headmasters had to be of the Church of England. Furthermore, the children were to be taught the catechism and be present at liturgical celebrations, as well as service on Sundays. The Bill failed.

A Church Enquiry of 1846/47 found that the Sunday School consisted of 61 boys and 67 girls with the Daily School having 69 boys and 81 girls. The Infant Daily School had 39 boys and 38 girls attending and the schools were "supported solely by the Countess de Grey, and are under the

---

[39] The Quaker Joseph Lancaster, backed by King George 3rd, pioneered the monitorial system whereby pupils, coached by teachers, also taught. This is reflected in the census returns of the 19th century for Silsoe where many older children are described as teachers.
[40] BLARS L33/211

superintendence of the Clergyman of the parish." These figures are considerably less than the 1833 Return.

The 1882, 1901 and 1924 Ordnance Survey maps still have the label 'School, Boys and Girls' over the old school house by the Village Hall and the words 'Infant School' are imposed over the house and probably school rooms to the rear, which used to stand where the village newsagent now is, in the High Street. Tom Harris recalled that the boys and girls playgrounds near the Village Hall were separate and that each had a horse chestnut tree in it. The last tree was retained in the Village Hall car park until 2008 when it was felled due to disease.

The Countess Cowper introduced red cloaks for the girls in the 1860's and there are records of them being issued in the early winters from 1866 until about 1916, it is also said that the girls visited Wrest Park for tea wearing these.[41] One of these cloaks was donated to a museum by Mr and Mrs Lilley of Elm Cottage in West End Road in 1983 and it was said to have probably belonged to her great aunt Ivy Case.

It was with the Education Act of 1870 that the real birth of the modern system of education in England came about. This not only gave rise to a national system of state education but also assured the existence of a dual system, voluntary denominational schools and non-denominational state schools.

In that year a report for the 1870 Act says that Silsoe had a Church of England School for 97 boys and 72 girls with an Infant School which had accommodation for 80 children.

Elementary education became effectively free with the passing of the 1891 Education Act, and by the early 20th century, education for all, including farm workers, was beginning to become acceptable. In Silsoe evening classes were established with reading, composition, arithmetic, drawing and elementary rural science being taught. This was at a time when at the commencement of the school term in September, many boys were kept away from school so that they could work in the fields to help with the harvest, or other work, and of course to augment the family income. [42]

More radical events were underfoot and in 1896 the Boys and Girls Schools were amalgamated becoming Silsoe Church Mixed School. There was more to come in the next century.

---

[41] BLARS Silsoe School Handbook 1985
[42] *Beds Times* 26 September 1902

The 20th century

In 1933 Silsoe Infants merged with the Boys and Girls school to become a Public Elementary mixed school and the next year, in 1934, a new school for infants was built on the southern edge of the Waterslade allotments. The old school near the village hall, was then closed and eventually sold to the Co-op. The new 'huts' were not of a permanent construction and in 1972 a brick built school was constructed on the same site but further back from the road with another extension being built in 1981. In 2001 even more accommodation was added on the already restricted site.

Older children had to travel further afield and nowadays, with the availability of 'choice', middle school pupils tend to go to Barton while older pupils go to Harlington Upper School.

The village school is a Church of England Voluntary Controlled Lower School and in 2009, had an establishment of one Headteacher plus six teaching staff with six classrooms. There are 106 children enrolled, although it has space for up to 130 pupils between the ages of 4 and 9. It also has a large hall, and the school is equipped with modern ICT (Information and Communication Technology) equipment. A temporary classroom is used by the Before and After School Care Club and the Pre-School unit. Following an Ofsted inspection in 2009 it was classified as outstanding

There is a strong possibility that as part of the village extension at the south end of the village, the developers will construct a new, larger school to accommodate the increase in numbers, to which the existing school will migrate.

There was another educational establishment which was in the village from the 1930's to the 1940's which was run by Mrs Eva Harris. She had been the Headmistress of the Infant School, located at the Newsagent's site, which had two school rooms, toilets and a small playground. Mrs Harris was assisted by Mrs Elsie Olney and they taught children from a young as 3½ years up to 7 when they left for the other school. When Mrs Harris retired in 1930 she started a private school in Yellow House Farm, 26 High Street, which was renamed Yellow House School. It started with only 3 pupils but the number increased to 36 when children from London were evacuated to the village. This school closed just after the war.

The Teachers of the 19th century

The 19th century censuses provide a more detailed insight into how many teachers were employed and sometimes which older children were used as monitors.

Thus, in 1841 and living in West End was Thomas Humberstone aged 60, a schoolmaster, with at 24 the High Street, Jane Baldwin a schoolmistress, aged

40. There was then also at 40 High Street, Francis Walker, a schoolmaster aged 33. No 40 was next door to the school buildings that still stand alongside the path leading to the Village Hall, so it may be assumed that he was the headmaster.[43]

It appears that around 1851 the Vicar of Silsoe, Thomas Ferguson, was making good use of his contacts, and through these he had started a school at the Vicarage, for young members of the aristocracy. At the census there were three young pupil Viscounts, all from London being taught there: Valetort aged 18, Bogle aged 17 and Fordwych aged 16. They had to manage however with only one valet between them; John Vaughan aged 22, although there was a cook, a laundry maid and three other servants there to help.

At a more prosaic level, William Ross, aged 36, is described as an infant school teacher, aged 36, and from Yorkshire. Martha Studman aged 16, was an assistant school teacher living in the High Street. Jane Baldwin has moved on to become a midwife, although is described as "late a school mistress". Francis Walker is now getting his whole family involved, as not only is he a schoolmaster, but his wife Ann is a schoolmistress, and their daughter Ann aged 15, is also a school teacher. This time Francis's place of birth is given as Hanover Square, London, so he was probably selected by the Earl or his wife, who had a house near there.

Now the survey of 1856 has Jane Baldwin at the infant school which was situated where the Village Newsagents is now.[44] The Boys and Girls School and yards, are shown as the building on the left of the entrance to the village hall together with the land surrounding it. The main evidence which remains today to prove the use of the buildings as a school, is the school bell still contained in its small tower.

The schoolmaster's house continued to be next door, and consisted of about half the length of the ancient row, which is now numbered as 40 - 44. The boys gardens were a large area between the School and the Wrest Park boundary wall, indicating that learning how to grow crops was an essential part of their education, and implying to them that their future life would be as their fathers, working in the fields.

Ten years later in 1861 William Ross was still an infant school master, but then living at 37 High Street. James Chamberlain from Oxford, was at 40 High Street, aged 21, a national schoolmaster, while at 42 High Street two daughters of Thomas Lavender, Emily and Sarah Ann, 19 and 16, were school teachers. There was also Charlotte Mann living in 48 The Maltings, an infant school teacher. Jane Baldwin, who was to die in 1865, had by then turned her hand to millinery.

---

[43] The information for 1841 to 1901 is from the censuses carried out every ten years, copies can be found in public libraries.
[44] BLARS L33/12b

Education

In 1871 William Ross has become a superannuated school master (aged only 55), Charlotte Mann and Rosina Armstrong, probably at Pear Tree Cottage in Church Street, were governesses, Charlotte at the Infant School. Governess was presumably a better title than teacher. Power has devolved downwards as there was also Jane Worker, 13, Emily Worker, 15, Mary Wheeler 17 and William Clark, 16, all described in the census as monitors at the infant school.

In what seems to be confirmed as the teachers residences there are Ellen Chandler, 22, from Battersea, a schoolmistress, and next door at 40 is William Quelch, schoolmaster, aged 25 of Stratford, Middlesex.

William Quelch was still there at the next census, now described as the master of the Boys Elementary School and Charlotte Mann, now living with Elizabeth Mann in The Maltings, were mistress and teacher at the Infant School. Alfred White at 56 High Street aged 15, was a teacher at the National School.

1891 had Charlotte Mann 58 along with Elizabeth Mann 46, living in The Maltings at No 48, and are noted as schoolmistress and assistant schoolmistress respectively. Two other Manns, Catherine from 13 High Street and Emily 31 at Brabury Lodge were respectively assistant school teacher and school teacher. Jane Worker living in West End aged 30, was also a school teacher.

The head teacher at the school has again changed, and William Treacher aged 30, from Chesham, was installed at 40 High Street, together with his wife Clara and his two daughters, Ethel and Minnie. Mr Treacher would be Headmaster at Silsoe for nearly 40 years, and wrote a small booklet on Wrest Park and the village.[45] Miss Phoebe Cuff, a schoolmistress, aged 46 and from Gloucestershire, was living next door.

The school caretaker who lived at No 7 Church Road was the widowed Alice Wilson aged 40. The census return says that she had been born in India.

In 1901 the new vicar, Henry Amhurst Orlebar, has a governess for his children, Constance Poore, 22, from Birkenhead. (Obviously well brought up children did not mix with the peasantry then.) Annie Upton, then aged 68 and from 5 Church Road, had taken over the school caretakers job and Jane Worker is now described as a school monitor. Also unchanged were Charlotte Mann and Elizabeth Mann at The Maltings, schoolmistress and assistant schoolmistress.

At 42 High Street, Emily and May Brightman, 31 and 26, were both schoolmistresses. William Treacher, schoolmaster, and Phoebe Cuff, schoolmistress were in what is described as the School House, but this is probably still number 40 High Street. The numbers given are current day but it can be seen from the outside that two doors at least, have been closed up

---

[45] *Wrest and its Surroundings*, William Treacher, 1899

showing that the building would have contained more separate dwelling spaces than now. Emily Mann living at Brabury Lodge, was still teaching in 1901.

Charlotte Mann died aged 81 in 1914, and is recorded on her memorial as being for 50 years in the choir and a teacher at the Infants School. William Treacher is buried nearby and his headstone proudly records that he was for 39 years Headmaster of Silsoe School, 1883 – 1922.

Plate 9/3 - To the right of the car is the building then used as a School, now the site of the Newsagents.

Many teachers have come and gone since then and the school log books show the head teachers since the Second World War to have been :-

1945	Miss Foulerton
1945	Mrs B.M. Bishop
1946	Mrs E.G. Barber
1960	Miss D.M.P.Wisson
1965	Mrs W. Ramage
1969	Mrs Lister
1979	Mr Shufflebottom
1983	Mrs May
1997	Mrs H Cook
1998	Mrs Taylor
1998	Mr B. Storey
2004	Mrs S Purdue

Chapter 10 - The Silsoe Economy

Mills, Wind and Water

In the past, mills were essential to the local farming community to ensure that grain could be milled for flour, and bread could then be baked using that flour. For many hundreds of years only watermills could be constructed as the technology for windmills had not been invented. Therefore, manors or other settlements tended to be near streams which could not only supply water for everyday purposes, but also provide the power to turn the mill wheels.

At the time of the Great Survey in 1089, only one mill was recorded at Silsoe, and according to the Domesday Book, it was worth 26d. Surprisingly no mills were recorded at Flitton, Cainhoe or at Clophill, even though the Flitt would have provided more water power than any stream in Silsoe.

The Silsoe mill was situated at Wrest, but the precise location of the mill is no longer obvious, because along with the original manor site, the various landscaping operations that have taken place have obliterated all surface traces of its location. In addition, water flows in streams have changed radically over the centuries. For example, before water abstraction started near Pulloxhill in 1952 the flow from the spring at the bath house in the park was reputed to be very strong[46]. If you allow for the flow from the small stream coming from the north east and the numerous references in the early 18th century account books[47] to the 'millpond' being sited south east of the old mediaeval house, then it seems probable that the mill was sited near that pond.

Windmills were probably first erected in England in the late 12th century, with their use rapidly spreading, and in a Land Grant dated 28th November 1360[48], where Thomas de Bray of Stagsden granted to Ralph Fitz Richard of Silsoe, a "reversion of 2 acres lying in 4 buts in Donworth in the parishes of Pulloxhill and Silsoe one with a windmill built on it". Ralph, who was Lord of Newbury Manor at the time, had to pay Joan de Bray, Thomas's mother, 12d a year during her life for the lease of the mill. No location of the mill is given but as it seems to be on, or near, the boundary of Pulloxhill and Silsoe the high point of Thrift Wood could have been the site.

Two hundred years later in 1540, there is another mention of a windmill in Silsoe where some land is said to be on "Winmill furlong abutting the Kings Highway to Newbury"[49]. This locates it at the ridge of land between Wardhedges and Silsoe, where later plans show a windmill hill.

---

[46] The History of the Development of the Waterways at Wrest Park, M J B Turner, 1991, Ampthill & District Archaeological & Local History Society
[47] BLARS L31/289 & 290
[48] BLARS LJeayes90
[49] BLARS L5/1182

There is in addition, a lease of West End Farm land dated 1549, which refers to land abutting the way to "Wynmill Hill"[50].

The next found reference to a windmill is in 1560, where one which had been built by Henry Samwell (described as a miller in another document of the same year), is located in an acre of land which was being rented from Sir Henry and Lady Anne Grey[51] at 'Grenefyeld' in Flitton in a field called Westworthyng. This field does not appear again in documents, so the location of that mill site is a mystery.

Thirty six years later in 1596, John Morgan of Little Park, Ampthill, settled on his son Francis Morgan on his marriage to Judith Duncombe, some land in Flitton plus Hollington Mills and a Windmill in the same parish. Presumably Hollington was now a primary site in the parish for milling by water, with competition, or back up, provided by the windmill.

That the windmill continued to operate is proved by its mention in another marriage settlement this time relating to Newbury Manor[52]. In 1658 William Daniel, the son of the owner of Newbury, Thomas Daniel, was getting married to Elizabeth Mulsoe and his father settled on him the manor with all its lands plus The Windmill in half an acre occupied by Richard Draper, presumably the miller.

It is not known when the windmill closed down. There is a squiggle on the 1718 map which may be it, and the 1757 Newbury Manor map has a circle of trees at the right location. In addition, a map of about 1826 relating to enclosures[53] shows a plot of land of area 0acres 02rods 20poles on the south east corner of Wardhedges entitled "Windmill in exchange from de Grey". Maps of the late 19th century[54] have the legend "Windmill Hill" written to the left of the track from West End Farm at the top of the hill, just before it turns right to connect to the old road from Silsoe, which then descends to Ward Hedges.

A BHRS publication of 1931 on windmills in the county[55], contains a photograph taken at about the turn of the century with people on what was then, a large mound. The mound was said to be 72 ft across and 8-9 ft tall. In the text it is said that it is the remnants of an early post mill and that nothing is traceable on it. Nowadays the whole site is flat and planted with trees, with no indication of even the mound.

---

[50] BLARS LJeayes803
[51] BLARS LJeayes368 & 370
[52] BLARS L5/372
[53] BLAL MA/56/01
[54] OS map of 1894
[55] Beds Historical Records Society X14 p34 1920

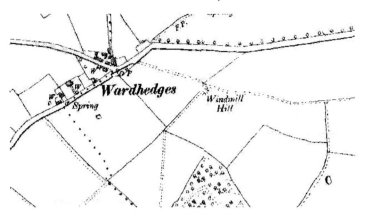

Plate 10/1 - 1902 OS Map showing Windmill Hill

Population Growth in Silsoe

It is impossible to know accurately the population of the village before the 19th century censuses came about, and even with those aids, the accuracy of those processes is down to the accuracy of the enumerators, and the truthfulness (or knowledge) of the villagers answering the questions. Avoidance of being recorded through fear of additional taxation or the perceived possibility of being forced into the army or militia, perhaps forgetting one of the ten or eleven children plus lack of knowledge of a true age are not unknown, and all led to errors. However, there are available from this source, the records of the numbers of villagers from 1801 to, at the moment, 1911.

Prior to the 1800's, the sources for estimating population include the Domesday Survey of 1086 and one method of estimating a village's population at Domesday was by multiplying the number of freeholders, slaves etc. by 5. This gives a conservative total of 120 for the parish, as there may have been others who are recorded as being of Cainhoe or Fielden, but who may have been living within the current parish boundary.

Other early sources for population are the 14th century Poll Tax records, and the 17th century Hearth Tax records. There are vast gaps in between these, and not all are available for the village of Silsoe. The Hearth Tax did what it says, the more firehearths or stoves you had the more tax you paid, and that of 1670/71 lists 58 households in the village. From this Lydia M Marshall[56] estimates that the population of Silsoe was then about 246.

Other sources for estimating the population are the parish registers which recorded baptisms, marriages and burials from the late 1500's until the present date. It has been suggested that an approximate assessment of numbers of people in a parish can be made by counting the average number

---

[56] BHRS Vol xvi *The Rural Population of Bedfordshire 1671-1921.*

of baptisms over a ten year period, and multiplying by 30, and this is what has been done.

A further complication in Silsoe's case is that until 1843, the parish registers are for Flitton with Silsoe, and so the proportion of Silsoe baptisms in the totals of the 1801 to 1861 censuses for Silsoe and Flitton, has been used to calculate Silsoe baptisms for earlier dates. And of course the registers do not include Non-Conformists nor Roman Catholics and thus under-records the true numbers of births. There was for example a relatively strong Quaker presence in Silsoe during the 1700's. On top of that, not all people had their children baptised either because they had to pay, or they were forgetful.

So, the stated methods are not accurate, for example: an estimation made from the Hearth Tax results in a greater number than that based on parish records, but they are all we have to work with. The resulting graph of population growth for Silsoe since the 16th century is as shown.

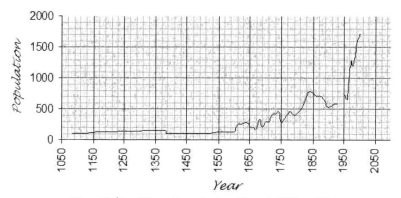

Plate 10/2 – Silsoe Population Trend 1050 to 2001

The graph below shows a relatively stable population for hundreds of years, although there would, of course, have been significant variations due to outbreaks of diseases, such as smallpox and plague devastating the population, plus the effects of bad weather on crops, resulting in starvation and famine. Then, after the 1600's the population of Silsoe started to grow, as it did throughout England, more than doubling every 100 years when, until in the mid 19th century people started to leave the village due to the attractions of urban living such as higher wages and better prospects.

While for England as a whole the population rose at a relatively uniform rate in the 20th century, for Silsoe, that century saw a steep rise in numbers from 528 in 1901, to 1729 in 2001. This was mainly due to better communications and transport allowing people to live in Silsoe while working elsewhere, plus the development of Silsoe Institute and the College of Agricultural Engineering at West End providing local employment. There was of course a concomitant release of land for house building to accommodate the desire to live in the village.

It is now suggested, as a result of the housing developments south of West End Road, that there will be further increases. The Bedfordshire County Council 2007 and 2008[57] reports, Population Estimates and Forecasts shows a radical upgrading in estimated figures from 1730 in 2001 to 2130 in 2012.

Earning a crust

Finding Jobs before the 19th century

Prior to the 19th century censuses, the best source for finding a man's employment is the parish burial records, and after 1813 the baptism records. Parish records commenced in the mid to late 1500's, but not every vicar decided to enter the occupation - most only appear in the 17th and 18th centuries - and then inconsistently. Only very rarely is a woman's occupation mentioned, even though it was more than likely that they would help their husbands, or find another paid job when they had any spare time.

Before the parish records, the occupations of the common man are difficult to ascertain, although quite probably in a rural economy like Silsoe, most worked as agricultural labourers. Most legal documents and wills were created by the landed classes and, apart from rare references to the occupations of tenants, the jobs of the common person are not detailed. Generally most would have been employed on the farms or manors but with larger settlements appearing, someone would be able to start selling products from his house, which could eventually be described as what we now call a shop. There would still have been the itinerant peddler selling dress items or pots and pans, but these would become rarer over the centuries until nowadays, we even have laws forbidding such trading or 'Cold Calling'.

Some mention of occupations are found in the records of cases reported at the Sessions, but these would not necessarily be representative of the village as a whole; and as Silsoe appears to have been more law abiding than other areas in Bedfordshire, relevant cases are rare.

In addition to the problems the local man had in finding work there was, even in those days, itinerant families or gypsies[58] who travelled around, and who apparently received the same 'welcome' then as now. So, in 1765 the Rev. Rouse wrote about them that "A file of musquetiers seems necessary to convey them to their proper place, and keep them under government and discipline when there." He suggested that Louisiana and Florida might be suitable for them!

---

[57] *Bedfordshire County Council & Luton Borough Council, Population Forecasts and Estimation,* 2007.
[58] In 1724 the parish records have the burial of "a travelling woman commonly called a gypsy".

Jobs in the Censuses of the 19th century

It is not until the 19th century with its decennial censuses that the complexity of village life, the jobs available and the need to work until it was impossible to carry on, is evident. However, while there is a great amount of detail in the later censuses (the early ones before 1841 were basically just numbers), we are to some extent at the mercy of what the enumerator was allowed to put down, and also what the inhabitants considered their main job to be.

So, for example, in some years almost every child that was not working and was older than 2 or less than about 14, is noted as a 'scholar'; whereas in other years, very few children of schooling age are shown as such. Also, later in the century, more people put down double occupations such as 'mole catcher and clock cleaner', whereas it is known that, whatever their stated job was, at different times of the year, such as harvest, almost everyone available was out in the fields helping or later garnering the un-harvested corn to ward off starvation later in the year. (No one put down 'poacher' as an occupation even though that may have kept the family alive!)

Other occupations, with many being carried out by women, were those which took place at home. This included washerwomen, dressmakers, tailors and, as Silsoe is near Luton, the jobs associated with the hat or bonnet trade.

By far the major job recorded is that of 'agricultural labourer' although this term was used to include cowmen, ploughmen and other agricultural specialists. The work was hard, seasonal, and they were laid off if the weather precluded their working. With the increased use of mechanisation leading to fewer jobs, poor pay and other reasons, many left the land and this trend for Silsoe this can be seen in the following chart.

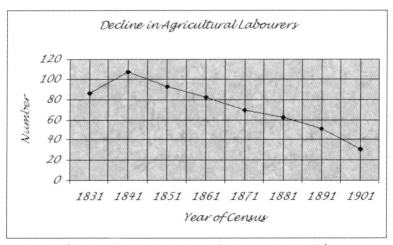

Plate 10/3 – Decline in Agricultural Labourers in the 19th century

In order to keep the landowners and the wealthy in the state to which they were accustomed, a great number of servants, either living in or working from home, were required. It can be seen that when Anne Florence, dowager Countess Cowper was in Wrest Park for the census in 1871, the number of servants radically increased, showing how there must have been a waggon train of carriages etc bringing them all from residence to residence.

Further up the social scale wheelwrights, blacksmiths, shopkeepers and other trades are shown, and from these it can be seen that the village was virtually self-sufficient. Again however, the presence of Wrest Park skews the job types, with many gardeners working in the park and gardens, and many others in other occupations such as brickmakers, being employed at the great house in maintenance or improvements.

Then there were the employers, farmers who either owned land, or were tenants or bailiffs for the major land owners.

The next grouping used are the professional classes; land agents, vicars or chaplains, land owners, accountants or surveyors and of course the Wrest Park family. Included also here are people living off annuities or pensions.

The Professionals.

Jobs which did not involve manual work, such as a schoolmaster or mistress, also appear in the records. The first teacher who surfaces is John Hale, schoolmaster of Silsoe who was christening his son John, in 1667. He no doubt worked in a school probably founded by Amabel, the Good Countess, and funded by the 11th Earl of Kent, Anthony Grey and his wife Mary, which was designed to improve the local children's religious knowledge.

There was probably a continuity of teachers in the village, but only a few after John Hale appear until the 19th century, and these together with the rest in that century are dealt with in the Education chapter.

Similarly the chaplains and vicars of Silsoe are listed in the Church chapter and the innkeepers are in the Pubs and Inns chapter.

Other white-collar workers are not mentioned until the 19th century when, in 1851, an accountant from St. Neots, Henry Joyce, is in the village as is also Henry Trethewy, the Wrest Park land agent at Silsoe House. In 1861 Henry Joyce was in Ruthyns and his profession is then described as auctioneer and surveyor. William Eve was at West End Farm, a land agent, and there was also a surveyor's clerk in the village, and a messenger of the House of Commons staying at The George.

It seems as though the Ordnance Survey was re-surveying the area in 1881 as one of their surveyors was lodging in No 3 High Street, with John Eddy from the Vicarage Cottages working as his assistant.

From 1881 the village was blessed with a permanent police constable. Initially it was John Barnes who lived with his family at Wrest House Lodge; and then in 1901, Sylvanus Arnold was at Wrest Park Police Lodge with his wife. Also in the village (had it become more lawless?) was PC Alfred Baldwin at 9 High Street, with PC John Barnes now in Holly Walk.

Yeomen, Farmers and Husbandmen.

The title yeoman generally described a farmer who was more prosperous than the average and husbandman described a lower status farmer with less land. By the 19th century nearly all those who owned land or tenanted a farm had become 'farmers'.

A study of the marriage records from the 17th century show that there was much intermarriage between the farming community, thus keeping what land they owned within that class and family. Thus the Millward (or Milward) family, who farmed at Fielding, can be found at that place and in Silsoe, at least from the 15th century, when Richard Millward, of "Feelde in Flitte" was buying land there, until at least 1717. In that year Charles Milward was Chapel Warden at Silsoe and renting a large house approximately where No 26 High Street is (then called the White Horse or White House), plus 113 acres mainly in Fielding.

Much land originally owned by the Millwards had passed into the ownership of the Abdy family, when in 1681 the Rev Dr Richard Milward, Rector of Great Braxted, Essex, evidently an absentee landlord, left his lands and main house in Fielden, to his only child, Mary, who married Sir Anthony Abdy a year later.

As the de Greys owned most of the land in the parish, most farmers mentioned in the records were probably those who were able to rent a larger landholding than most, and managed to make a living from that land. Their farms are described in the Farming chapter elsewhere.

However it seems that starting from the 19th century more were able to obtain land for themselves, and make a living as market gardeners or small farmers.

Agricultural Labourers and Land Workers

In the parish records, occasionally a man might be described as 'labourer' and at that time and in Silsoe, the job would have been almost universally that of an agricultural labourer. However, there were many specialised and expert jobs carried out which were encompassed by the general term "agricultural labourer". Being able to control a team of horses or oxen so as to plough a straight furrow is not simple; and knowledge of pruning and other work was not easily available in books then – even if you could read.

Occasionally some specialist jobs emerge from the parish records or other sources, in the early centuries. It is thanks to a case at Bedford in 1589, regarding alleged trespass by Thomas Power of Cainhoe on Stephen Danyell's land of Newbury, that we know that Richard Gells of Silsoe, then aged 59, a labourer existed. He gave evidence, and said that as a boy he had been servant to Edward Danyell, and that he had heard him say that the extent of his land was up to the hollow way road from Clophill to Silsoe.

Henry Gellys, probably Richard's descendant, was the warrener to Mr Daniel of Newbury Manor in 1666, and as he was having children in the parish for 28 years from 1650 to 1678, he probably had the job for life. This implies his family had been working at Newbury Manor for at least 150 years. Being a warrener was an important job, as he would have supplied meat for the family at the manor throughout the year, and no doubt he ate well himself. It seems likely that he lived at the north end of the village, possibly at Simpsonhill Farm as his burial record says he is from near Clophill Bridge. The warren was on the sandy hill on what is now Simpsonhill Plantation.

We also find references to shepherds with 'Old Tringe', a shepherd, being buried in 1618 and John Wheeler, "an old shepherd" a year later. Other shepherds appear up to 1789 and later, showing that sheep farming was continuing over those centuries. This occupation re-surfaces in 1861, probably when acknowledgement was given to differing types of agricultural labouring jobs, with four shepherds being found. One, John Kemp was at the bailiff's cottage in Wrest Park, a foreman shepherd. He had moved on ten years after but two of the others, William Stapleton and Joseph Ashby were still shepherding together with Henry Porter. By 1881 there were four again, but in 1891 there were only two, and in another ten years James Pratt was the remaining shepherd in the village.

A more specialist agricultural skill is found in 1841 when John Wheatley, probably living at No. 2 High Street, was a mole catcher. By 1851 he had enlarged his job description, being a clock cleaner as well as being able to catch moles.

The influence of mechanisation in agriculture and other factors can be seen from the graph of those described as agricultural labourers shown above. Yet the population did not decline in the same proportion and even grew slightly, indicating that other jobs had been created in the village or that they had started the trend of living there and working elsewhere.

Henry Trethewy, the Wrest Park estate steward living in Silsoe House, seems to have had some concern for the agricultural labourers in his writings. He said that he considered cottages should be available for men living on a farm as the cowman or shepherd who should not be in a worse situation than the groom or domestic servant. This seems a fairly modern approach, but by way of contrast he also said that he had never known any evil result of the labourer being more under control of the farmer![59]

He also spoke to the London Central Farmers Club (not many farms in London, surely) in 1858, saying that he thought that the labourers should have allotments as they improve diet and social stability. At that time there were 24 acres of allotments available for them in Silsoe, with Earl de Grey giving prizes for exhibits at the Silsoe and Ampthill Labourers Friendly Society annual show.

However, perhaps his ideas did not work so well in practice, as in 1876 the *Beds Times* said that there had been a Silsoe Labourers Union strike at the farms of Mr Eve and Mr Squire, West End Farm and Newbury Farm. This was due to an imposed wage reduction as a result of the agricultural depression, and a meeting had been held near the Almshouses when they were told not to succumb to their oppressors, and should consider the advantages of emigration.

The Times article proposed that the workers should confer with the farmers, and then go to arbitration and also suggested that conditions in Canada and New Zealand were worse than here.

Gardeners and Woodsmen

With its huge acreage of parkland, Wrest Park required its upkeep to be well managed and there was also, and still is, a need for gardeners to be employed there. The early records have many gardeners mentioned, and the work was not without its dangers even early on, as Thomas Gurnett was killed in levelling the great court at Wrest, in 1681.

There are several gardeners mentioned in the parish records for the 18th century, such as John Adams and Thomas Thorpe and also John Duell senior, the Duke of Kent's gardener, buried in 1740, and his son John buried four years later. In the next century there is in 1851, Humphrey Fletcher who was the park-keeper, in charge of all the gardeners. Many other records of gardeners are in the censuses throughout the 19th century and they were mostly employed at Wrest. In 1841 nine gardeners or under gardeners are mentioned, some definitely working at Wrest and some said to be of the village.

From early on in that century the term 'gardener' could refer to market gardeners and so the number of people described as gardeners had increased enormously ten years later in 1851. For example the family of Richard Simpson living near Simpsonhill Plantation listed his wife Ann plus five sons down to Joel aged 11, as gardener's labourers, with Richard himself as a market gardener. There were also two gardeners, John Eddy in the village and Seward Snow at Wrest, plus 18 gardener's labourers scattered around the

[59] BHRS No. 60, *The Farm Worker*.

village including, such village names as Swannell, Upton, Giddings, Squire and Mann.

Seward, when he died in 1869, was head gardener at Wrest and was replaced by his nephew, George Frederick Ford.

The work was considered as hard as the agricultural labourer's lot, and the 82 year old William Swannell living at Road Houses, described himself to the census enumerator in 1881 as a "worn out gardeners labourer"

Even early on into the 20th century, many inhabitants regarded themselves as gardeners or gardener's labourers, with a total of 25 being listed in 1901.

The countryside was far more heavily wooded than it is today up until the middle of the 20th century, as can be seen by photographs from the start of that century. Several men were employed in both maintaining the woods and cropping them such as William Millward, woodcutter to the Duke of Kent. One hundred years later in 1841 and living at Wrest Park Lodge was Hamlet Ashford, a woodranger, and two sawyers lived at number 42 High Street. Hamlet was a wood bailiff ten years later, and there were then in addition four wood labourers and a woodman as well as George and Thomas Whittamore, both sawyers.

Home Occupations

Servants.

While in earlier centuries a typical rural village would have had a number of living-in and living-out servants who worked for the major farmers, landowners, local notables and others; the existence of Wrest Park has resulted in the number of servants required in Silsoe being proportionally more than in other villages. As an example, in the 18th century, 23 servants can be identified as being from Wrest are recorded in the burial records, and that excludes gardeners and other types of servant who lived in the village.

The earliest servant mentioned was John Boulton who died in 1602, not long after records started in 1581, closely followed by Robert Purcell who died in 1604. At about the same time Anthony was a porter in 1606 when he died. Elizabeth Harris, a servant at Wrest, seems to have had an illegitimate child, John Lawrell, in 1674.

Other more specific servant jobs included are, William Burton who was a coachman to the Earl in 1666, then there was "James" dying in 1611 as "the cooke" at Wrest and Mr Kent the "cooke att Wrest" before 1672. John Whitehead was an undercook there in 1669 and Anthony Peacock a groom to Lord Polworth, in 1779.

One of the most important jobs at the big house was that of the steward who ran the household, and whose responsibilities included ensuring provisions were obtained, organising the maintenance and hiring and paying the servants. Thomas Hill was the receiver general, or steward, to three Earls of Kent. In Flitton Church there is a brass of him and an inscription includes:-

> Here lyeth Interred the body of Thomas Hill gent.
> Receiver generall to three worthy Earles of Kent, viz.
> Reginald, Henry and Charles: he departed this life
> Aprill ye second 1628, being aged a hundred and one year"

Many of the family of John Allen, steward early in the 18th century, are buried in Flitton Church and two others are mentioned in the parish records, Thomas Hooper who died in 1702, steward to Amabel, the Good Countess, who supervised the re-fronting of the house in the 1670's, and Joseph Pawsey who was interred in 1808.

A gentleman of the horse was required, amongst other things, to help his Lordship mount his horse and Thomas Bigcliffe was in this post in 1676. There were other 'gentlemen' referred to such as Mr Bonofos, who was gentleman to the Duke of Kent in 1736. He may have been a 'gentleman usher' whose responsibility under the steward was to be in charge of the wardrobes.

In the 19th century there was even more of a need for servants, as anyone with a reasonable income could afford to employ one or two. So in 1851 there are five cooks mentioned in the village (none at Wrest), eight house maids, eight house servants, two nursemaids, a still room maid, two general servants and a valet staying at the vicar's school, where several junior viscounts were being educated.

The schedules for Silsoe House, which was occupied through the end part of that century by the Wrest Park land agent, Henry Trethewy and his family, indicate what a man in that position needed to maintain his household. So, in 1851, with only himself and his wife there, he needed a cook and a groom but ten years later with four young children, he needed a nursemaid, a cook, two housemaids and a page boy, the 9 year old Thomas Porter.

In 1861, and now with four different young children (the first set were probably being educated away from Silsoe), he had a head nursemaid, another nursemaid, a cook, a housemaid and a new page boy John Bowden, aged 13 from Ampthill. In 1881, now aged 67 with his wife dead and five children in the house aged from 16 to 19 years old, they only had a cook and two housemaids to support them. This number remained the same for the next 20 years, although their names changed. Over 6 censuses 22 different servants can be counted with only two being from Silsoe. At that time servants were generally hired through advertisements or at hiring fairs.

The 1871 census shows that when Wrest mansion was occupied, at that time by the Countess Cowper, the number of servants required by that household filled both the mansion and also the ancillary buildings. She and her daughters required 3 ladies maids or attendants, a butler and house steward, 4 footmen, a cook and 3 kitchen maids, 10 other maids plus coachmen and grooms.

Thirty years later the numbers of servants in the village had decreased and continued to diminish in the 20th century when a job description containing 'servant' became considered to be demeaning.

Tailors, Dressmakers and Lace Makers

There seems to have been no problem in getting clothed in the village. In the 18th century over ten tailors are mentioned for Flitton and Silsoe. Dressmakers are not mentioned but then very few women's occupations were.

William Peacock in 1724 was a tailor who also owned and rented some farming land in the village. A few years earlier in 1718, he seems to be living opposite Ruthyn Cottage and in one document is described as a chapman, a merchant or dealer.

Continuing into the next century, there were 5 tailors recorded in 1831, but only three are to be found in 1841: William Cook and his son working from what became the Alma in West End Road, and David Scott, a Scot, staying in the High Street. At last the dressmakers get a mention and six appear in that census. One of the daughters of James Flint, the village grocer was one, with Elizabeth Cherry and Frances Leader, both from West End Road, along with Mary Cooke from Church Street.

David Scott continued his tailoring for at least another ten years, but Isaac Cooke had taken over in West End Road and continued in that occupation for longer. By 1901 there were no tailors mentioned, and 10 years earlier there was only a tailoress, Mary Worker.

The names of the dressmakers tended to change from census to census, probably when they married they gave up their work, but the numbers remained high. In 1861 there were eight, in 1871 ten, in 1881 ten plus three apprentices, eight in 1891 but only four in 1901: Elizabeth Goodall at 7 High Street, the 14 year old Catherine Mann at No 11, Sarah Eddy in the Almshouses, and the tailoress Mary Worker at 23 High Street. The women of the Eddy family had been dressmaking since 1871 when Ann, Mary and Sarah were sewing away.

Apart from dressmaking, one of the other jobs which a woman could do from home was lace making and there was a tradition of this skill in Bedfordshire. For several centuries this was taught to poor children and women in the workhouse, together with chants or 'tells' to prevent total boredom.[60]

Although the earnings of Bedfordshire lacemaking fell during the 19th century due to machine -made lace there was still some carrying on the craft, and in 1841 there are nine lacemakers mentioned with only two remaining ten years later, five in 1861 and the 89 year old Ann Fennemore in 1871. Some others took up the work later that century but by 1901 no-one said it was their occupation.

Straw Plaiting and the Hat Trade

The straw hat making industry began in the 17th century, and by the 18th century it was one of the main industries of Luton and Dunstable. Plaiting and straw hat making were very well suited as a cottage industry and was usually carried out by women and children, whose fingers were more nimble than the men. There was also a huge age range of those able to earn from this business. The youngest found is Jane Taylor aged 7, while the oldest seems to have been Elizabeth Studman aged 79. Plaiting tended to be confined to the rural areas, while the better paid sewing or trimming of the hats, was concentrated in the towns.

Plaiting, in particular, was a good way of supplementing an agricultural wage, and in fact the plaiters could earn more than their labouring husbands at the height of the plaiting season, which was December to May. This led to farmers complaining that they were unable to find labour when they wanted it and, more relevantly, at a price they wanted to pay.

This home industry boomed during the middle of the 19th century, but had dwindled away towards its end, due to cheap imported plait becoming available at around the middle of the century.

Dealers supplied the straw either to households, or to a village middleman, and the finished plait or hats were collected when ready. With Silsoe being so close to Luton the work was very popular, and was no doubt carried out before the census enumerators started to record the numbers of people working in the trade in the village.

Some central supplying and collecting took place in the village, and in 1851 Elizabeth King from West End Road, was a straw factor and in 1861 Ann Simpson of Wardhedges was a straw plait dealer.

While the decline may well be as accurately shown in the chart, it is possible that there were more involved in the industry at the start of the century than that shown, as many women may have been reluctant to say that they were working. The 1831 census only collected the jobs of males, and this attitude may have been retained for the next one.

---

[60] Bedford Borough Council website '*Aragon lacemakers*'.

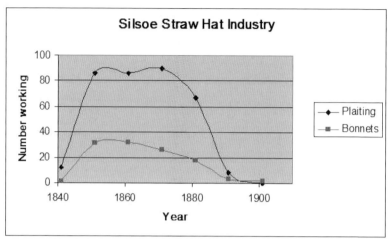

Plate 10/4 – The Rise and Fall of Straw Hat Workers in Silsoe.

Laundresses and Charwomen.

These were other jobs that the ladies of the village could do, and while they first appear in the 19th century censuses, no doubt this work was carried on before then. In 1841 there were five charwomen and two laundresses, while by 1881 the numbers had risen to nine charwomen and five laundresses. The women doing these jobs tended to be above middle age and from poorer families or widowed, so no doubt the money they earned helped to keep themselves alive. By 1901 there were only four laundresses but no charwomen listed, perhaps they preferred to use a different job title such as housemaid.

In the 20th century such work continued, with charwomen being known late in that century, but with the advent of the cleaning of clothes being carried out more centrally and of washing machines, laundresses tended to disappear.

General Shops, Grocers

The first record of a shop in Silsoe seems to be in October 1636 when John Godfrey, yeoman, entered into a 21 year lease with the Earl of Kent, paying £5 down and 16s a year for a tenement and a shop etc., and with two cow gates upon the common. John died in 1655, but his widow Ann took over a few years later, with a new 6 year lease at the same annual rate, from the Countess Amabella. [61] Their son Henry was also a shopkeeper in 1675 and 1681, carrying on the family business.[62] What their shop sold or where it was is not known, but it was probably a general shop selling food and other items.

---

[61] BLARS LJeayes820 & LJeayes821
[62] BLARS L5/789 & PR

By the early 1700's the Joyce family, Thomas and Ann, had a shop although they passed away in 1727 and 1728 respectively. Following this there appear to have been two shops, one run by William and later Richard Lee, and another by the Gwyns. The Gwyn family had been in the village for some time, at least since the mid 17th century and John Gwyn had been the chapel clerk in 1717. However, his son Henry although initially a carpenter, was described as a grocer and a carpenter at his death in 1745, even though it was probably his wife who ran the shop while he was out carpentering. Their son Henry was a shopkeeper in the 1760's, probably taking over from his father, whilst in 1812 John Porter had a shop in the village.

In 1841 there were two grocers mentioned. One shop was run by James Flint and his son William, and the other by William Mann. Now there was a James Flint in the village in 1831, aged about 49, so with only one shopkeeper recorded for that year, it is probable that the shop had been running from at least that year. James was still there until after 1861 following which the shop, a grocers and drapers, was run by two Charlottes, one James's daughter and the other his daughter-in-law. This shop was run by the Flints until after 1891 when Charlotte was aged 79, and her daughter Selina 45, but then Isaac Cook from Grundisburgh, near Woodbridge in Suffolk, took it over.

I. J. COOK,
HIGH STREET, SILSOE.

Family Grocer and Provision Merchant,
General and Fancy Draper.

Try our NOTED TEAS, from 1s. to 2s. 6d. per lb.

Packham's Celebrated Mineral Waters in Syphons & Bottles.

HUNTLEY AND PALMER'S BISCUITS.

HILL & SON'S SLAB AND FANCY CAKES.

Plain and Fancy Chocolates, &c.

A GOOD ASSORTMENT OF FANCY ARTICLES SUITABLE FOR PRESENTS.

Oils, Ironmongery, China and Glass Ware.

Plate 10/5 – Isaac Cook's Advertisement in William Treacher's Booklet

In 1910 Isaac was also running the Post Office, and in 1918 the Post Office and Shop was bought by James Cook from Wrest for £400. After 1928 and before 1931, it seems that Frank Batt had taken over as the village grocer and he was still there in 1940. This shop, situated at 31 High Street, opposite Church Cottage, only closed down recently when it was converted into a house, but it may have been used as a shop for 200 years, and possibly even longer.

Prior to the Post Office moving to 31 High Street it had, in 1851, been at the George where Benjamin Carter had managed to be an innkeeper, postmaster and farmer. Then in 1861 William Rich at 51 High Street was the postmaster, assisted by a post messenger, John Worker from 22 West End Road, and a post boy, John Bunker aged 45 at 33 High Street. Elizabeth Rich, William's widow, had taken over as post mistress ten years later with John Worker being the postman.

Plate 10/6 - Isaac Cook's Shop in the 1900s

Elizabeth Rich was still a post mistress at 31 High Street, aged 77, in 1881, with her daughter Mary being her deputy; and in 1891 Mary was the sub-post mistress. At the same house lived her niece Elizabeth Rich a telegraph operator, and Frank Eddy, her nephew, a messenger. The 20 year old Samuel Rich from West End was a rural postman while John Worker described himself as a superannuated postman.

William Mann had a grocer's shop which he ran from his house at what is now 34 High Street. After he became a jobbing gardener, his son Arthur took over the shop until he too in 1881, was also gardening. Also around this time Mary Huckle, who seems to have lived in the row of cottages that existed just to the north of the George, was for a few years a grocer and shopkeeper.

In West End Road in the old houses (if that word does not over emphasise their size) that used to be situated in a courtyard just to the east of the thatched cottages Nos. 31-37, there were several dwelling houses which housed about 10 people, but also a grocer's shop together with, in 1856, a recently erected oven. Joshua Croxford is described in 1851 as a shopkeeper and farmer but although there were still people living in the tenements in 1861 but none of their occupations was shopkeeping.

However, around that time William and Isaac Cooke, at what became the Battle of Alma beerhouse in West End Road, were expanding their business from being a tailors in 1841; to a tailor and drapers in 1851; to a tailor, draper and grocers in 1861, and by 1871 a tailor, draper, publican and grocers. No doubt most of the customers from the other shop changed over to his.

THE SILSOE CO-OPERATIVE SOCIETY, LTD.

LOOK FORWARD—CO-OPERATION IS COMING.

The above Society } done a trade of £47,754,
in Twenty-two { and returned to
years has } Members and Purchasers, £5327.

The Co-Operative Wholesale Society's
Yearly Trade is £12,000,000.
In Tea alone, £506,045.

WE HAVE SHARES IN THE ABOVE.
WE BUY THEIR GOODS.
TRY THEIR CELEBRATED TEAS.

FOR PARTICULARS APPLY TO THE SECRETARY,

P. BRIGHTMAN.

Plate 10/7 – The Co-op's Advertisement in William Treacher's Booklet

In 1854 William was also described as a baker, and in a sale document for the Alma of about 1883, one of the cottages adjacent included a bakehouse and an oven. William's wife was still there in 1901 aged 79, although assisted by her son George and daughter Louisa.

Louisa bought the Alma Inn and grocers, plus the use of James Case's well at No 8 in 1919 for £350; and the Cooke's grocers and alehouse lasted until the 1970's, with George Cooke still being in charge in 1940[63]. He lived with his bachelor brother Charles, and a newspaper report of about 1939 said that " … he only gave up an active role in running the pub and shop three years ago when he was 87 ".[64]

---

[63] *Kelly's Directory*
[64] *Luton News and Hertfordshire Advertiser, 'An A to Z Tour of the Villages – Silsoe'.* Abt 1939.

The Co-op's advertisement in William Treacher's notes on Silsoe published about 1903, says that the Silsoe Co-operative Society started about 22 years before, which makes the starting date around 1880. It was said in the Silsoe News of June 1985 that it was formed by disgruntled Wrest Park gardeners who objected to the high prices being charged for food. They constructed a building in The Maltings for the purpose but as two cottages which could easily be sold in case it failed. Eventually what was called The Silsoe Co-operative Society was situated in the large house on the left hand side, which was the shop, with the bakery being to the left of the house. Philip Brightman was the secretary in 1914, and in 1925 the enterprise was taken over by The Luton Co-operative Society. Then in 1928 Frank Harris had taken over as manager, with James Harris being there in 1931.

In 1932 the Co-op purchased the old school buildings on the left of the entrance to the Village Hall and, after initially using them as a warehouse, moved the shop in the 1950's. The Co-op eventually closed in the early 1970's.

Meanwhile at the other end of the village, Cornelius Kinns, a stone mason in the 1881 census and probably living adjacent to the Lord Nelson, is said to have been a shopkeeper in 1854. There is a document of 1859[65] which says that the cottage/tenement now a beer house had a shop which was formerly a blacksmiths shop, and since then a shoemakers shop. Now, Cornelius's son Charles, is also described as a shopkeeper in 1862 when he was 17 years old, having been a "labourer in nobleman's garden" in the previous census. There may thus have been two shops at Roadhouses at that time.

Specialist Shops, Butchers, Bakers ...

If you wanted fresh meat or bread, and as there were no fridges, only cool larders in those days, then you went to the local butcher or baker.

Many people would bake their own bread, and the first mention of a baker is of Nathaniel Poulton in 1752. This may have been a family concern as James Poulton, baker of Silsoe, is mentioned in 1807.[66] One baker is mentioned in the 1831 census although his/her name is not given. There are no Poultons left in that year but Charlotte Bone, who was baking in 1841, aged about 50, may well have been the 1831 baker. Her business operated from No. 26 High Street, and this may well have been the location of the Poulton's bakery. She was still baking until her death in 1868 and was assisted by her daughters, Charlotte and Elizabeth, who never married; and by a journeyman baker named Abraham Robinson, who lived with the family from at least 1841, until both he and Charlotte died in the same year in 1893. The older Charlotte's eldest son James, also learned the trade, and by 1881 he was employing three men in the family business. However, he died in 1882 and

---

[65] BLARS L23/285
[66] BLARS L5/948

follow the death of Charlotte in 1893 the Bone family disappeared from the village.

However, it seems that the business survived at the same address, as in 1901 John Harris, baker and farmer from Southill was there, probably being helped by John Rich from 47 High Street. In 1903 he was advertising himself as baker and confectioner, noted for sponge cakes, and had good accommodation for cyclists. When the estate was sold off in 1919, he was still there, but competition had sprung up with the Co-op in The Maltings having an attached bakehouse. Various directories have him as a baker up until the mid 1920's.

Many farmers and tenants in the early years would slaughter their own animals as and when it was required either for their own use, or to sell some of the meat for cash. In addition to the farmers there are several names of butchers who were recorded in the church records. The earliest was John Wright who died in 1663. It seems likely that Nicholas Bonner who was a butcher from at least 1700 to 1718 was in Silsoe, probably operating from a building just south of the old George.[67] William Worrall was a butcher of Silsoe in 1679, and there are others, such as William Brooks who was in the village around 1770, Nicholas Egram in 1777, Robert Osborn in 1796 until 1804, and Edward Newell in 1805.

The 1831 census has three butchers listed for Silsoe, but they are not named.

In 1841, Charles Brightman was a butcher living in the village, possibly at Holly Walk, and there was another butcher, William Herbert, who probably lived at No.8 West End Road. By 1851 Charles had moved to William's house in West End Road where he remained farming and butchering with the help of his son Leonard, until he died late in 1871.

Meanwhile, since before 1851, Joseph Olney had been building up a butchery business from the house at the old George, No. 10 High Street. His son Frank and nephew Valentine from Hexton, were helping as butchers in 1881, with Joseph doing some farming. Joseph and Valentine were still butchering in 1901, but Joseph died in 1904 and in 1914, his daughter Bessie was recorded as the butcher. Valentine may have been serving in the First World War as he is listed as a butcher from 1924, right the way through to 1940. Now there are neither bakers nor butchers in the village.

---

[67] BLARS L5/433

Practical Professions: Shoemakers, Carpenters, Bricklayers, Wheelwrights.

Although many of these jobs were found in small communities from early times, it is unusual for them to be recorded, as people of this status were unlikely to be connected with land transactions. However, there is in a list of 'fines' (land disputes), and in the following example, which is dated to the 13th century and which concerns land in Cainhoe and 'Civelesho' there is a carpenter mentioned viz.;

"land abttg Wateresslade & in Riecroft & in Fennifurlong. Wm de Bray, Agnes Cok, Adam le Carpenter, Hugh le Parmenter, Hy son of Romay, Jn de la Rode, Hy de Norwde, Nigel de Smittescroft …."[68]

So, probably the first mention of occupations in Silsoe (apart from farming) has Adam who was a carpenter and Hugh whose occupation as a parmenter, concerning the processing of cloth.

Boot and Shoemakers

Another useful and continuing job was that of shoe or bootmaker. A conveyance of 1674 which includes a "shop or house sometime a shoomaker" is the first reference to this job but unfortunately gives no occupier's name, or where the shop was.[69] Thomas Hill of Silsoe shoemaker, whose death was in 1669, is the first definite shoemaker of this village. His son Thomas was also a shoemaker, and he died in 1677.

In the next century there are many shoemakers mentioned in the parish records, (upwards of seven), although it is not certain whether they are from Silsoe or Flitton, except for William Crouch who was of Silsoe. However, the 1831 census counted a total of five shoemakers in Silsoe, of whom two, George Swannell from Church Street aged about 60 and John Doggett aged about 45 were still plying their trade in 1841.

John Doggett had probably been a village shoemaker for some time as in 1839 he made a declaration saying he was 53 years old, and had known various Silsonians for many years. He probably lived in the house which stood on the plot occupied by what is now number 41 High Street (Barnards). However, he died in 1848 with his wife staying on in the same house until she died, in 1863.

David Dunham was in the village in 1841 as a shoemaker, initially in the High Street and possibly assisting John Doggett. By 1851 he had moved away, and George Ansell Dunham from Shillington was in Silsoe making boots and shoes and employing three men, probably his sons, William, Henry and Abraham. He lived, possibly, at number 11 Church Street, but ten years later

---

[68] BHRS vii
[69] BLARS L5/85-86

in 1861 he was at 23 West End Road and still employing Henry and Abraham, but probably also George Edwards who lived in 'Flitton Road' and was the town clerk. (He was probably living in the cottages in Holly Walk.)

There was also another shoemaking David Dunham in the village in 1861, living at Wardhedges but originally from Barton, who was possibly another son of George Abraham. He had left the village by the next census.

George Abraham was still at age 82 in 1881, making boots and shoes two employees. James Dunham, his son, who was still at 23 West End Road, was possibly one of them and the other George Edwards. James was there in 1891 but by 1901 seems to have moved to his father's place at 39 High Street. He was still shoemaking in 1924 by which time he was 75. His son Harold took over boot and shoemaking until he died in 1946 aged 61.

Blacksmiths

There are records of at least 200 years showing that the Lowings family were the main blacksmiths for the village. Henry Lowins was a blacksmith who lived from 1678 to 1748 with his descendants, son Francis, grandsons John and Henry, great grandson Henry, great great great grandsons Francis and William, and finally Alfred, Williams son, each working at that trade. There were at least two Lowings or Lowens generations in the village prior to the first Henry, and it seems probable that they worked at the same trade, repairing ironwork, creating new work and shoeing the numerous horses working on the farms or carrying the wealthier families around.

When the need for smiths work from the big house and farms dried up, Alfred had to diversify and in 1901, he was listed as a blacksmith and cycle repairer in 1901. He finally gave in smithing and had become a market gardener by 1928.

In 1718 there was a smiths shop run by William Crawley, which cost only 10s a year rent, and was sited on an island, in the middle of the road, at the junction of West End Road with the High Street. It was well situated for passing trade.

The 1718 schedule of the estate plan of the village had another smith's house for which Henry Lowings was paying £1 a year to the estate. This appears to have been in the north west corner of the chapel yard just in front of where the war memorial is now. By 1731 Henry Lowins had a 21 year lease for 10s a year for a blacksmiths shop and shed, which he had erected on ground where an old cottage had once stood.[70]

Where this was is not known, as a letter of June 1807 reports that the blacksmith's forge had been removed to "the end of Lowing's own garden ... a most convenient situation for it as there is a good entrance to it from the

---

[70] BLARS L5/1126

land at the back of Mr Harrison's." Subsequent plans from 1809 onwards show what was until recently the village blacksmiths shop, on a short lane off Church Road.

By the 1760's Francis Lowing was paying £1 10s rent for his smithy.

In 1844 there are bills presented to Earl de Grey by John Lowings, for work to the mausoleum at Flitton, for smith's work at the farm and the mansion, and for shoeing farm and carriage horses. There are also bills presented in the 1820's which have Mary Lowings as the blacksmith.[71] Throughout that century there were about 4/5 blacksmiths working in the village, probably at the main shop off Church Street, but they would also go out to farms and Wrest Park, when called.

William Lowings lived at number 19 High Street opposite the church from which he could walk out of his back door and be in the smithy in two shakes of a lamb's tail. He retired before 1901, but even then he remained at No 19 while his son Alfred moved to live at what is now 11 Church Street, also bang next door to his work. William's father Henry, was living in the row of cottages just north of The George, but whether he had a shop there is not known. Alfred bought the blacksmith's shop together with the house in the High Street, at the break up of the Wrest estate.

Prior to its conversion to a house in the 1990's, the interior of the old blacksmith's shop near the village lock up, still had evidence of its previous use with the location of the furnaces still obvious on the floor.

Finally, another smithy was located on the corner of West End Rd and Vicarage Road, No 10, which in 1918 land that William Brightman was buying is described as running from the Alms Houses down to the smithy on the corner. This house had also been used as a dairy, supplying milk through a window giving onto Vicarage Road as well as being the Wrest Park estate workshop and smithy.[72]

Carpenters and Wheelwrights

With houses, barns and outhouses mainly constructed of wood until recently, there had been a need for centuries for carpenters who could construct and repair such buildings, and make rough furniture. Similarly, there was a need for someone whose expertise enabled him to make and repair wheels and carriages, for farming and other uses.

After the Adam le Carpenter mentioned above as being in Silsoe in the 13th century, the next carpenter found to be recorded in Silsoe is in 1655, when Thomas Hill was given a cottage and a little barn near the highway probably from which to carry on his trade. Then a few years after in 1696 Thomas

---

[71] BLARS L26/896 1844 & L26/1454 1820/21
[72] BLARS L23/327 & BLARS L23/249

Burrows, also a carpenter, rented an acre from the Countess of Kent on the north side of Ampthill Road, near the pound. He was to build a good cottage with outhouses, presumably for his work, and had to plant hedges, tress and had to maintain everything in good order.

Early in the next century Thomas Bishop, also the chapel warden, was carpentering in the village and was also building up a small farmstead. In 1718 he owned the field bounded by Vicarage Road, West End Road, the High Street and Church Street, and in addition to other fields also rented a tenement with a yard, presumably the location of his business, near where The Maltings is now. Later on, in the 1770's, Richard Bunker, William Stevens, John Pierce and John Wilmore were all hammering out a living in the village.

The 19th century had on average three to four carpenters, and a similar number of wheelwrights working in the village of Silsoe. They included William Pearce and his son John in the 1841 census, probably descendants of the John Pierce of the 1770's, with William still working at age 72, twenty years later.

The Giddings family produced many wheelwrights, Thomas Giddins was wheelwrighting in the 17th century in Silsoe until his death in 1718, by which time his son Thomas had taken up that work; and then in their turn his two sons, Thomas and John, were operating in that trade until the early 1800's. In 1718 they may have worked from what is now nos. 45-47 High Street. William the son of John carried on the trade while in the next century Charles Giddings, William's son, was recorded as working at that trade from 1841 until at least 1868 when he died. They appear to have worked as wheelwrights from 56 High Street but in addition they farmed several acres in the village.

The Fennemore family also produced wheelwrights, with James Fennemore working at that trade in the middle of the 19th century, possibly for the Giddings as he lived at 28 High Street, where there was no space for such an occupation.

Robert Upton who had been a wheelwright in 1851 aged 21, had become a carpenter ten years later and continued in that trade until 1890. He had evidently trained his sons Charles and Albert, in the art of carpentry and wheelwrighting, as Charles was a carpenter in 1891 and a wheelwright in 1901, with Albert was a wheelwright in 1881.

Charles Upton continued as a wheelwright, being mentioned in trade directories, probably until the 1920's by which time the need for such skills had died out.

Bricklayers

Bricklayers are recorded back to the early 18th century when they were probably employed in extending or renovating buildings in the Park. In the 1830's there was the great rebuilding of Wrest Park, and with most bricks being made locally, there was a need for brickmakers. One, George Plowman, is at West End Road in 1841. Bricklayers remained in the village until at least 1901 and beyond, as the village was being developed and extended. In that year there are two bricklayers with one apprentice and three brickies labourers. They were James Cox, Alexander Bottoms whose son Herbert was the apprentice, and the labourers were William Bunker, John Mann and George Downing of Wardhedges.

Barbers and Dairymen

If you wanted a haircut in the 18th century then there seemed to be plenty to choose from, with five being recorded. Of those, however, we do not know who worked from Silsoe, but there would probably have been at least one of them at any time. However, they seem to be omitted from the 19th century censuses so either people went to the nearby towns, it was cut by someone in the family, or the occupation was part-time and so was not recorded.

If you wanted milk then you would have gone to the local farmer or his wife, who sold it straight from the cow. Some men are recorded as dairy men such as Ralph Shaw in 1716, John Hill and William Partridge in 1742; and in 1757 John Best, a yeoman of Silsoe, was said to be a dairyman from Kitchen End.

The dairy needs of Wrest were probably supplied from the park dairy which in 1774 was rented by John Porter of Silsoe for £85, for which he got a dairy house with appliances and land, which seems to have been in Fielden meadows and in the Old Park area.[73]

However, in the next century we have only dairy maids such as Mary Gudgin and Lucy Lowe being mentioned in 1841, and no doubt it was more prestigious to be called a farmer than a dairy man.

When parts of the Wrest estate were still being sold in 1918, Christopher Harris was at the Dairy Farm, (now 56 High Street), which, from its name, no doubt supplied some of the village with milk. The farm included about 64 acres which were to be found all over the village, and he bought the farmhouse plus the land, for £1440.[74]

In the early 21st century some older residents remembered getting their milk in pails from Mr Olney, who lived at the Victorian house built in front of the old George building. Some time in that century milk delivery became popular

---

[73] BLARS L5/1142
[74] BLARS L23/384

in bottles to individual houses by the milkman,[75] and this has continued until the present day.

Carriers

Carriers were a form of early post office, and they were used for centuries to collect and deliver items to villages and towns whether nearby, or to London and other major towns. The earliest carrier found in the village is John Steppin in 1678, but after him it seems that William White took over by 1700, and he is again recorded as such, in a conveyance of 1717.[76] He seems to have had an entrepreneurial streak, as two years later he is renting a malting house in Silsoe. The 1718 map shows him probably operating his business from the house that is now number 53 High Street, Ruthyn Cottage. This corner of Ampthill Road became the village centre for carriers, and after he died in 1739, his son John apparently took over the business. However, it seems that Henry Sharpe, a carrier from Bedford, obtained the business in 1764 together with land and the house which was known as the Waggon House.

John Edwards inherited the business from his father-in-law Henry Sharp, and he also continued to develop the business which his son, another John Edwards, took over after 1820 after John 1st died. However, he was far too keen on hunting and this led to his demise in December 1823. As *The Times* had it:-

"It appears that Mr Edwards was out with the Oakley hounds, when in attempting to cross a ford at a place called Newton, in Buckinghamshire …. he, along with several other gentlemen …… took a wrong direction, when all of them flounced headlong into deep water, Mr Edwards, who was on a very spirited horse, unhappily lost his seat, but still kept fast hold of the bridle, and it is supposed in his exertions to save himself, that the animal whilst struggling and plunging in the water, struck him on the head with its fore feet, which stunned him, through which accident he sank, and was drowned. …. Mr Edwards was a most respectable man, and possessed very considerable property in the county – he has left a widow and eight children to deplore his lamentable fate and Mrs Edwards is now fast advanced in a state of pregnancy."

Others took over the carrier business in Silsoe, with George Whitbread doing it early in the 19th century followed by John Whittemore until 1861; then Daniel Harris with the last found reference being, Arthur Wheeler in 1901.

---

[75] And milk bottle tops changed from cardboard inserts which blue tits learned to open to metal foil tops which they also learned to peck open.
[76] BLARS L5/102/103

Unusual Jobs such as Collar Making, Cricketer, Toll collector etc

Robert Barnard of the village was a 'collar maker' in 1769 and trained his son, William, in that trade. This involved making the large leather collars which fitted round the necks of the working horses of the day, but he would also have been involved in making all kinds of harness for horses. The trade must have been a good one, as when William died in 1825 he had a house and two closes to pass on, probably the same house that the first Robert had left in his will.[77] William's brother, Robert, was also a harness maker and in 1851 aged 82, he was still making harnesses. William's son James also followed on with the trade. The memorial to Robert in the churchyard says:-

In memory / of / Robert Barnard / of this parish / bachelor / who died in the same house / wherein he was born / more than / one hundred and one years / he died December 1? 1865.

This house was probably what is now known as Old Village Farm, 43 High Street, as Robert was farming 30 acres in the 1851 census, as well as making saddles.

In the early 19th century the road from Gravenhurst through to the A6 south of New Inn Farm was turnpiked; and the only toll gate within the village, called The Wheel House, was sited at that junction. In 1851 Ann, the 17 year old daughter of Alfred Wheeler (agricultural labourer) was the toll collector. Ten years later at Fielden Bar, Henry Burley is letting his wife Mary do the toll collecting, and in 1871, (the last mention of this job), he is not only the turnpike gatekeeper but also a farm labourer.

As for more unusual jobs, for this century, there are also recorded in various places: waggoners, weavers, a thatcher, rake makers and a cricketer, as well as a travelling chimney sweep.

The professional cricketer was Harry White aged 23 who was staying in 1891 at West End Road with his father, William White.

Finally, a good mixture of occupations were ascribed to Soloman Wright of 49 High Street, who in 1881, described himself as a bill poster and rat catcher.

Changes since the 19th Century

With the growth of public transport such as buses, and also with private vehicles becoming available and affordable, it slowly became possible for those living in Silsoe to work away from the village and away from the agricultural sphere, without moving home. Thus in the 20th century many would find work in Luton, Bedford or the other smaller towns nearby, and even later on in London and other places further afield. In addition, with

---

[77] BLARS L5/852

Wrest Park being used as a centre for agricultural engineering research and with the Cranfield University developing its campus south of West End Road, work of a more intellectual nature became available, leading to a change in the nature of the village.

As to facilities, in 2009 there was the Silsoe newsagents shop in the centre of the village which also has a range of grocery items available. Next to it was Urban and Rural estate agents. The Post Office, which had been threatened with closure under a cost cutting exercise, was at the northern end of the village in Newbury Lane, as was Aspects Hair Design and an estate agent, Village Homes. Off the Clophill Road and just behind Road Farm, was the Apples and Pears farm shop while right at the northern tip of the parish on the A6, was the Jet service station and convenience store.

The 2007 survey associated with the Village parish Plan found that more than one third of those responding and living in the village worked away from it, with about one quarter being retired. A century earlier there was no option other than to carry on working, probably in the village, until you were unable due to sickness or extreme old age when, if your family could not support you, you went into the workhouse. Thankfully things have changed.

Chapter 11 - Farms, Farming and Agriculture

General

No doubt the first farming in Silsoe occurred very early on when the nomadic life of hunting and gathering gave way to the new ideas of clearing ground, planting crops and keeping animals. The soils of Silsoe are very varied, from a good sandy loam to the sticky clay in the land to the south, and it is expected that the very early settlements, of which no trace has been yet found, took place where it was easier to work the soil.

The first records of settlement are the Anglo Saxon ditches found near the Church and bits of pottery near West End Farm, which probably indicate where the first farming took place. However, until the Domesday Book we do not know where the centres of farming were, the sizes of them, or what form of agriculture was going on.

Over the centuries the localised settlements grew until there were discrete communities clustered around the main manor buildings. This settlement pattern is what William the Conqueror found in 1066 and which his army pillaged on their march northwards through, or very close to Silsoe. Then, having overcome most resistance, and in order to see what he had won, he carried out the 1086 Survey which enables us also to see what the agricultural set up was in this area.

The entry which probably relates to Wrest says it has 4 hides of land as one manor, which equates to about 480 acres. However, at that time an acre was not a precise measurement of land but a unit of assessment, so care should be taken with this statement[78]. A further land area, although again not precise, can be obtained from the number of ploughs measured or said to possible in the Great Survey. Each plough team could operate about 100 acres per year so, as Domesday lists land for 10 ploughs plus another 6 as meadow , we have another area of 1600 acres. There is thus about 2100 acres included for Wrest in total. In addition there was a mill and woodland sufficient to keep 100 pigs. Now each plough needed 10 oxen (depending on the type of soil) to pull it, and so fodder or grazing had to be provided for a total of 160 oxen plus presumably some breeding stock throughout the year. The survey states that there was meadow land for 6 ploughs, about 600 acres.

Two hundred years after the Conquest, when King Edward I needed more money, he decided to tax crops and stock, and accordingly a taxation survey was carried out which included Flitton with Silsoe.[79] This only applied to people with taxable items greater that 9s but even so there are some 39 persons, of which three were women, ranging from the Abbott of Woburn and Lord Reginald de Grei to John Est, who only just made it onto the list.

---

[78] Bede suggests that one hide is sufficient for one family and its dependants
[79] BHRS xxxix *1297 taxation survey*

The total numbers of farm animals for the parish of Flitton cum Silsoe in that survey were:-

Bullock	Heifers	Cows	Calves	Pigs	Sows	Ewes	Lambs
30	12	34	4	14	6	124	39

Oxen	Affers[80]	Horses	Foals	Mares
12	14	2	3	12

The crops were in quarters (64 gallons in volume) :-

Wheat	Maslin	Oats	Barley	Rye	Beans & peas	Drage
33.75	0.6	2.25	1	3.875	14.53	19

Plate 11/1 – Schedule of Animals and Crops 1297

The owner with the highest value of stock and crops was the Abbott, then came Walter de Teie who had oxen and horses, then Lord Reginald, then Robert de Wardhegges, then John de Bray etc. However, this is not quite a rich list as the value of land holdings is not taken into account.

It does though indicate some changes in farming practice since the Great Survey. There are fewer oxen for ploughs, with an increase in horses for general and plough work. In addition the sheep population is now quite high, showing that there may have been a move from arable to pasture. There is also a good variation of crop types, with beans and peas showing well.

Moving on 400 years the de Grey archives give an indication of the numbers of people having small holdings of land by the amount they paid in rental. Thus, in 1658 a rental book[81] includes the following:-

"William Gamble and John Greene for the mannor or farm
house in Silvesho called Norwoode with divers land pastures
and meadowes in Silveshoo and Pulloxhill   £30 10s
Katheryne Hill widdow for two closes and certen arable lands
in the common fields   £7 00
John Allen for the inn called the Ragged Staff in Silveshoo and
6 acres of land and one acre of meadow   £7 00
Ditto John for the toll and profits of the fayre   5s
Henery Millward for one messuage in Silveshoo and wherein
Gaby? now dwells and divers land pastures and meadowes
hereunto belonging lying in Flitton Silsoe Pulloxhill Gravenhurst
 and Maulden and for 40 acres of land and leys in the field of
Fielding   £34 00

[80] Affers are work a day horses and Drage is a mixture of wheat and barley. Maslin is a mixture of wheat and rye
[81] BLARS L26/1384

Widdow Caton for the farm house in Silveshoo called Westend farm with divers land pasture and meadows hereunto belonging lying in Flitton Silsoe and Maulden	£50 00
Widow Barnett for a tenement and two pightles in Silveshoo and one acre of meadow and about 4 acres of land	£6 00
Robt Cooze? for one cottage with pightle in Silveshoo and 1 acre of arrable land	£1 10s
Richard Cawne for a cott. in Silsoe being the sign of the wayfer and ragged staff and a pightle adjoining being about 4 acres of arable land	£2 00
Widow Raworth for part of Parsonage house	£2 00
Henry Bird for the other end of the house	£1 00
Thos Pigott … on the back side of the farm	£1 6s
Widdow Godrey for her house by the year being a small cottage	£1 6s
Willm Wilson the towne clerk for his habitation being two rooms and nos? yard	4s
John Lowens for the Smythes shop yearley	£1 00
Nocholas Gosse for one cottage wich stande upon the waste built at his own charge	5s
Wm. Harris for one cottage built upon 2 or 3 poals of my Ladys ground at his own charge	2s
Edward Hunter for one cottage built upon the waste at my Ladys charge	6s "

There were hundreds of other small strips at this time in the common fields which were not mentioned, with individual owners perhaps farming strips all over the parish.

The farming system prior to the conquest, had for many centuries used the principle of leaving land fallow or uncultivated for a period. Half the area would be in crop with the other half fallow for a year, being grazed and fertilised by the beasts' droppings. In addition, the strip farming system was in operation with families having one or more strips of about one furlong in length, (about 201m), with a width of about 20m giving between ¼ acre to 1 acre or more[82], with each scattered over the open fields, so that the members of the community shared the good and bad soils. There was also common land where the villagers could graze cattle, or collect wood. The manorial lands were generally held by the Lord locally around the manor or farm buildings, although he also probably held land in strips in the common fields. This system, which is described simplistically, was retained after the conquest, and lasted in some areas until the early 1800's.

The advantage to the villagers of this system was that it could be said to have been fair, with peasants being able to have strips both in good and in bad land. In addition, the system encouraged local democracy with what to sow and when, being decided communally and with fencing and foraging by animals being allowed, only when all had reaped their harvest.

---

[82] *A review of Balks as Strip Boundaries in the Open Fields*, H A Beecham, British Agricultural History Society

As to the common land, there were three fields in Silsoe parish which had the appendage 'common' attached. There was Moor Common on the southern edge of the River Flit, Crouch Home Common, further to the east near the A6, and Cold Willows Common in the north eastern corner of the junction of the High Street, and the old road that used to be the Shefford Road.

When this system changed with the enclosures, it was generally due to the perceived need for agricultural efficiency, which would result from combining the strips into fields. These could be more economically run being closer to the main farms. As the more powerful would be able to enforce such a change, they could also arrange that they obtained the better land resulting in the poorer section of the community becoming worse off, when the enclosures took place.

There is evidence that some enclosure took place in Silsoe very early on, as the 1468 Valor of Grey of Ruthyn (a schedule of his property, rents etc) mentions the enclosure of parks at Broybury and Norwood manors.[83] However, it seems probable that strip farming remained over much of Silsoe, until the final enclosure took place in 1826.

Agricultural Labourers' Protests

Throughout the centuries the life of both small farmers and their agricultural labourers has been hard, the hours were long, the work strenuous and in times of bad weather there was a lack of work, when the labourers could not have been paid. Mostly they were unorganised and could not easily express their discontent, and it was not considered a good thing for the lower classes to be 'above themselves'. Mr. Bishton, who wrote a Report on the enclosures in Shropshire in 1794, repeated the view that if labourers could support themselves from access to common land they would not work hard for farmers:-

" When the commons are enclosed 'the labourers will work every day in the year, their children will be put out to labour early,' and 'that subordination of the lower ranks of society which in the present times is so much wanted, would be thereby considerably secured."[84]

A year later when the price of bread rose dramatically due to the stopping of grain imports, there was a series of food riots throughout the land, when people demanded that food be sold to them at affordable prices. At Aylesbury, for example, a mob comprising mainly of women, took all the wheat that came to market, and paid the farmers the prices that they thought reasonable.

---

[83] BHRS xlvi *Grey of Ruthyn Valor , 1468*
[84] This and the following is taken from *The Village Labourer 1760-1832: A Study in the Government of England before the Reform Bill* by J.L. and Barbara Hammond. Originally published 1911, New Edition, 1920.

Also in 1795 Samuel Whitbread, the Member of Parliament for Bedford, attempted to introduce a bill in the House of Commons for a minimum wage to alleviate the conditions of the agricultural poor, but it met with opposition mainly from those who considered that the poor were not in so desperate a plight as Whitbread supposed. He tried again in 1800 but it met with the same opposition, and failed.

Further disturbances occurred in 1816 when labourers were suffering both from a lack of work and from high prices. In 1815, a bitterly cold summer had been followed by so poor a harvest that the price of corn rose, with the prices for bread and meat rapidly following.

The riots broke out in May of that year, and the counties affected were Norfolk, Suffolk, Huntingdon and Cambridgeshire. Apparently Bedfordshire was not greatly affected by riots so perhaps here there was enough affordable food for the workers. Elsewhere night meetings were held, threatening letters were sent, and houses, barns and ricks were set on fire.

There was even a serious disturbance at Littleport in the Isle of Ely, which began with a clergyman magistrate of the name of Vachel being driven from his house, after which several houses were attacked and money extorted. This state of anarchy ended in a battle in which two rioters were killed, and seventy-five prisoners taken. The prisoners were tried the next month and then twenty-four were capitally convicted of which five were hung, nine were transported and ten were imprisoned for twelve months in Ely gaol. There was no sympathy from the judges and one opined that " the rioters were receiving 'great wages' and that 'any change in the price of provisions could only lessen that superfluity, which, I fear, they too frequently wasted in drunkenness."

Further risings took place in 1830 with the so called Captain Swing Riots, which resulted from the combination of poor harvests, and the introduction of farming machinery considerably reducing the need for farm workers. This uprising was, however, far more general and serious with some counties in the south of England being in a state bordering on insurrection. London was in a panic and the fright of the landowners during those weeks is reflected in such language as that of the Duke of Buckingham, who talked of the country being in the hands of the rebels. Soldiers were called out and in one case even artillery was called for.

The riots spread northwards from Kent and Sussex reaching Buckinghamshire and with Bedfordshire being one of the last counties to become embroiled.[85] No threshing machines were broken but one or two stacks were set alight and there were two riots. The more alarming one was at Stotfold on the 1st and 2nd December, and the other at Flitwick four days later.

---

[85] Most information on the Stotfold event taken from BCC Libraries *The Stotfold Riot* by Mr Bert Hyde

The Stotfold riot may have been sparked by the previous conduct of the overseer, a Mr Smith, who was one of the first to be confronted by the mob. However, after further rioting on the Saturday the Rev. John Lafont, a Hertfordshire Magistrate, who at the time of the riot was doing the services of a curate at Stotfold, wrote to Lord Grantham at Wrest Park, Silsoe.

He said that " upon hearing of the "revolutionary proceedings" at Stotfold on the Thursday it struck him at once as essential for the general good that a blow should be struck at Stotfold before dark on Saturday as he was fearful of an uprising of up to 2000 men across the North Hertfordshire border if nothing was done about the situation at Stotfold."

He decided to ride to Silsoe and inform Lord Grantham, who was Lord Lieutenant of Bedfordshire, of the state of affairs at Stotfold; and was on his horse before daylight and had travelled the 13 miles from Hinxworth to Silsoe by 8.30 a.m. Lord Grantham was absent, and so he rode on to Henlow and met Mr Edwards, a Bedfordshire magistrate, and also Mr Whitbread and it was agreed that he should immediately gallop back to Silsoe, muster 50 of Lord Grantham's men and join up with the force of Mr Whitbread and Mr Edwards at a prearranged spot, near Stotfold in the afternoon.

He arrived at the rendezvous with Mr Whitbread and Mr Edwards at 3 o'clock, together with 120 of Lord Grantham's men, some of whom were mounted. The men on foot had done the 10 miles from Silsoe to Stotfold in less than two hours. Lord Grantham's mounted tenants first surrounded the village and then dashed in. Ten of the ringleaders were taken, only one escaped. Lafont wrote afterwards that the result was that "instead of being in positive revolt on Sunday, men are touching their hats to their masters who never did so in their lives before." What they were thinking may not have been so charitable.

It is evident that if Lord Grantham could muster 120 local men to fight people of their own class, then there may have been an unspoken threat that their jobs or farms might not be available at the next hiring or lease renewal.

The Field Names of Silsoe

Field names can be of great significance because in some cases they have remained unchanged for hundreds of years dating back to Anglo-Saxon times, and can indicate what the state of the land was then, to what use it was put, or even the name of the owner. Although some fields have names derived from that age, others would be newer due to change of ownership, sub-division or being newly won from forests. Conversely other names have probably been lost due to amalgamation of smaller fields, the names being forgotten or new names being introduced.

As most fields had been sub-divided into strips for some time, probably prior to the Norman invasion, and remained so until either being thrown into Wrest or other manorial parks, or being merged in enclosures, the earlier documents relate to small portions of land of ½ acre or 1 acre, within the major fields.

Thanks to the Wrest Park archives there are enough records with field names on them for a PhD thesis, so although some detail is given here, there is more information available to those who want to take the subject further.

Fields in Fielden

South of the parish and Wrest Park is the area known as Fielden, Fielding or earlier la Felde, which seems to have been almost a separate adjunct to the parish by its land ownership; and also by it being virtually separated from the main village area by Wrest Park and Buckle Grove Wood. It is low lying and was probably won over time from fens and wet areas.

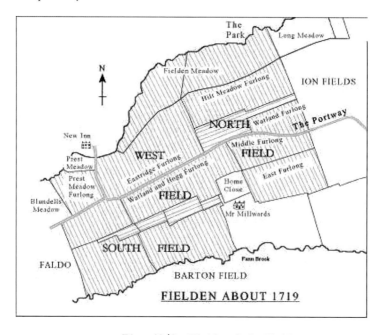

Plate 11/2 – Fielden Strip Fields

The meandering division shown on older maps between the field known as Fielden Meadow to the north, and the remaining area to the south, may well have been an earlier alignment of the New Inn stream route. While now ploughed out, this boundary persisted on OS maps into the late 19th century. There is also a difference in land ownership shown in the early 18th century with the Duke of Kent owning a substantial area of land in the meadow, and little in Fielden to the south, thus confirming an old boundary of some sort.

Early documents not only refer to the South Field of Silsoe (1273) but also to the East Field or 'del Est' (1276). Both of these seem to be in Fielden as the names of the buyer or seller are usually of 'la Felde'. No East Field is shown on the later maps so it is possible that any East Field may have been transferred to the parish of what is now, Gravenhurst.

A late 12th century document which refers to fields in the south of Silsoe (and which may refer to the sale of the old 'Manor of Kechinge' or Kitchen, as the area is now called) included single acres in 'Loddocksmerefurlong' and 'Watelonde' and two acres in 'Langefurlong'. These seem to be in Fielden as two other acres abutting on 'Portweye', the road from the present A6 towards Gravenhurst, are also included.

It is evident therefore that the name Watelonde has persisted in this area for at least 500 years and perhaps 650 years, being gently changed to Watland. The Watland name appears three times alongside the Portway and may well derive from wheatland, indicating the drier ridge along which the road runs.

'Ludocksmere furlong' reappears once more in 1202 that then disappears. The Langmede furlong mentioned in 1410 as of Eyen is perhaps the last reference to Langefurlong.[86]

One of the more interesting names is in the field 'del suth in 'le Holmes'[87]. The latter name derives from the Old Norse 'holmr' which means a water meadow, or more probably a field beside a wet area or stream. This provides some evidence that the Danes settled and farmed the area.

Proof of the wet nature of the area is also found in the 'fan' in Suthfan furlong (1322), the 'Van' in Le Vanfurlong abutting on Barthon Hul (1324) and both Fann Brook (1439), the stream between Barton and Silsoe, and Fann furlong (1533 and 1774) south of Fielden House, all meaning a fen or marshy area.

Prest meadow south of New Inn Farm and shown on an 18th century map probably indicates that it was at one time owned or associated with a priest. There is a Prestmadefurlong (prest meadow furlong) in a document of the 13th century where it is said to abut the Kings Highway.

Hogg furlong on the southern side of the Gravenhurst Road was probably used as an enclosure for pigs; while the Long and Short Honey Pots north of the road suggest a sticky clay area. Hilt (1563) sometimes Hill (1712) Meadow may be a facetious reference to a small rise in the land, although this is not now visible and there may be some other source for the name.

---

[86] BLARS Ljeayes 104, BHRS vii Fines
[87] BLARS LJeayes 656, 1273

Most of these names were still used in the late 18th century and are shown on a map dated 1784. They probably only became redundant with the inclosure of field strips into larger fields.

South East of the parish and North of Fielden

While fields in Fielden had been identified using the compass points, in the rest of the village to the north of Fielden, the names of the common fields were more usually used. These are shown on the plan in the Inclosure chapter which also shows some of the further sub-divisions used.

Heading north from New Inn Farm and not missing the small field called Cherry Orchard bisected by the parish boundary which lies behind it, Kitchen End Road is crossed, and just beyond that lays Kitchen End Field. These names have nothing to do with any food preparation but are nearly all that remains of an old manor called Kitchen or Ketchynge, which was probably sited at the far end of the lane.

To the north of Kitchen End Field lies another field called Bray Close, which was farmed by the families at New Inn Farm.

On the east side of the road are three fields called Thatchy, Bushey and Crab Tree Closes. Thatchy may have derived from a damp area where reeds could be cut for thatching; Bushey perhaps because it had scrub growing on it; and Crab Tree because of a large crab apple tree. Bushey still remains to this day as a separate field, but Thatchy and Crab Tree have been absorbed into adjacent fields. The word close tended to refer to old enclosures, usually for pasture.

Staying on the east side of the A6 there is a run of small fields right up to the village. In 1718 these were only about 150m deep but the park side boundary is shown as curved, and has a symbol for a fence. This was the Wrest Park boundary at that time, and there is an annotation "Part of Rest Park" to the east of it. Further to the east and shown on the 1814 map is a field, half wooded and abutting the canal, which was called in 1814 'The Old Park'. This was probably an old deer park attached to the old mediaeval house but was separated from it when the canal was built.

To the south of the Old Park and on the north side of Southill Ford Brook, lies the ancient wood called Buckle Grove. 'Bokulgrove' is found in 1521 and 'Bockyll' Grove appears in documents of 1525, when it is being sold to Edward Daniell of Newbury Manor by Henry Waite. In the mid 1400's there appears William Bockell who was involved in land transactions in that area, and it is possible that the grove was named after him. However, it is also possible that the name predates William as two documents of the 13th century have Bogildegrave and Buggildegrave, which when said fast after a glass of wine sound quite like Buckle Grove!

Going back to the fields alongside the A6, opposite Buckle Grove are Plough'd Wicks, Dry Wicks and on the west side Water Wicks. Water Wicks with Oate Wicks appear in 1670, and in 1682 they are written as Wickesse which gives an indication as to how the word was pronounced. It is suggested that field names such as 'Wickres' indicate their use in wicker production for baskets etc, but as the fields lie on top of a hill, this seems an unlikely place for willow cultivation.

After the Wicks is Butchers Close, which becomes Mile Stone Close in 1814, and then Long Close, which it was (long, that is). Then on the east of Long Close was the first of two park fields. The schedule attached to the 1718 plan comments on several fields in this area such as Long Stocking, New Close and Park Field that were recently inclosed or taken into the park. Long Stocking and New Close are said to be in Park Field in 1674. This inclosure was carried out when the park was remodelled in about 1717, which is confirmed in a document which says whereas the Duke of Kent "...is desirous to inclose for pasture 32 acres 1r. 6p. in Park Field, Flitton, which time out of mind has been used for arable and sown with corn"[88]. Lands in Park Field are mentioned as early as 1521 with New Close in 1641, so presumably after 1717 the tenants with their small strips were thrown out, and the land turned into parkland for deer.

Just south of the village are Towns End Closes which describes them perfectly, and then Bonners Close which surrounded what is now No 2 High Street, and which was at one time farmed by Nicholas Bonner.

East of the George Inn were the George Closes first noted in 1628 and which were probably used to stable horses or drover's cattle. North of the church was the Home Close of the large farm which was sited there, and then after several dwellings and commencing opposite where lies the new George came Dowdell alongside the High Street, with Kennel Field just west of Dowdell.

These fields are obviously truncated in 1718 by the park fence so must have been much larger with the chopped off land thrown into the park, at the same time as fields to the south of the village. The schedule to the 1718 map says nearly 10 acres had recently been so absorbed and more was to be taken before 1814.

Kennel field was said in 1677 to abut 'Caynomore' or 'Kaynoe More' on the east and also had a wood in it. Kennell in 1649 had been Kenehul in 1345 and may have come from the Cain of Cainhoe; we also have Keyno elsewhere.

Deudene is found in 1329 and is in the "Est field of Syvelesho" "in the furlong called Deudene" in 1339 and 1342. Both references have participants to the deed coming from Cainhoe which implies a location in that area, even

---

[88] BLARS L5/1024

though most other references to an East Field relate to Fielden. This name probably evolved into Dowdale or Dowdell through the name Deweden in 1530, Dewden in 1539, and Dewdale in 1633. It may derive from the dew of a damp area.

North of the Shefford Road lies Cold Willows, part of which is Cold Willows Common. The name transmogrifies from Colewell in about 1202, to Colwellowes in 1530 and 1549 and Cold wellowes in 1563. If the first name is correct, then it may have indicated a well that gave cold water.

The next and final field before Clophill is where Warren Wood is now, evidently the location of the Wrest Park warren mentioned in 1579, but which was called 'New Wood' in 1814.

Little Cainhoe and North of the parish

By the mid to late 1600's and certainly by 1718, when the first map is available, all the land within the extreme north east end of the parish seems to have been thrown into the park, but a consideration of early documents provides field names which appear to have been within the parish limits, as they were at that time.

Cainhoe, just outside the northern edge of Silsoe, was mentioned in the Domesday Book and the castle was built there in the early 12th century. A village grew up there, but when the plague ripped through in about 1348 or afterwards, it seems that the village was abandoned. In 1340[89] Broybury Manor is said to be in Little Cainhoe, and later William Risceby is in 1373 the Lord of Little Cainhoe and in 1375[90] Lord of the Manor of Breyberi. Evidently, Little Cainhoe is Broybury.

Fennifurlong, (probably a damp place), in a 13th century grant is said to be of Little Cainho, and extended to land owned by Walter Pateshull called Wrast. Little Cainhoe is also the probable location of fields such as Witteride (possibly Whitteridge Mead in 1579), Musemereshale and Blakestokking (13thC), Shortcroft abutting on Braybury Wood (1307 et alia), Bonecroft (1310), Berehullys (Barley Hills, 1342) or Berrehull (1459) (barley hill), Walewort (1342), Fremanhul (Free mans hill) (1345) and Netherfield which abuts Scallards Way and the old Shefford Road (1358 and 1375).

Also, in 1533 William Caryngton of Gravenhurst was selling to Henry Grey a 'close called Boynons in Le Newe Parke, Flytton', probably situated in the extreme north east and possibly already thrown into the park.

A wood called 'le Hydewode' was used to locate land called 'le Hydehegge' in 1341 which was owned by Ralph Boynon of Little Caynho, and which came complete with a hedge ditch and 'francbord'. If the name is derived from the

---

[89] BLARS LJeayes 302
[90] BLARS LJeayes 332& 333

area known as a hyde then this was a very large wood of up to 120 acres, and may have been an earlier name for Cainhoe Wood.

Other fields associated with land owners of that area are included in a Fine[91] of 1202 and are Porcheria, Hadure (or Haddon), Bem, Norhfen (*a northern fen*), Aluithebrigg *(norse brigg = bridge)*, Murielesheg (*Muriel's fence or enclosure*) and Fardales. A half acre in Haddonecroft in a 1308 grant may be another reference to the Hadure or Haddon above, as could Le Northhill in the same document be derived from Norhfen.

None of these field names have been found on the 18th century maps, suggesting that they may have been absorbed into the parkland, north of Wrest house in the 1670's.

The field names associated with Home Farm are The Great Close, Home Close by the farm, Gravel Pit Field, Bean Close and the Sheepwalk; all of which are descriptive of either their use, or of a feature. Hogg Moor, a place where pigs were kept at one time, lies on the south of the old Shefford Road and west of the present track to the farm house.

South West and West of the Village

Returning to the south of the village, and now the west side of the A6, the Manor of Upbury, which lies just outside the parish in Pulloxhill had fields within Silsoe along most of the south western border. All along here the parish boundary crosses through fields following what were probably ancient field divisions. From the south and after Kitchen Field, the boundary first crosses Bray Field, owned by John Field of New Inn in 1768, but still with Upbury in 1676. It then cuts through Clover Hill before entering Wolves Field or Close (1676 and 1675). This sounds as though it might be a throw back to the time when wolves roamed England, but it seems more likely to have been named after a family called Wolf.

The parish boundary then crosses Green Close, Hither Beech Field and Warden Hill (1676). Warden Hill appears elsewhere in the country and in Bedfordshire notably to the north east of Luton. The name Warden, can be derived from the Old English "weard dun" meaning 'watch hill'. Research has been carried out on the Anglo-Saxon system of beacons which was in existence over the south of England, where fires were lit when an invading force was seen. There is a good view to the east from Thrift Wood from where the invaders might come, and as there is a clear line of sight over the scarp at Barton to the Luton Warden Hill, it is possible that the village was at the front line of communication in those days.

The division called Warden Hill Close next to the Thrift in 1718 is shown as planted with trees and with an avenue of trees, which line up with the distant

---

[91] A 'Fine' in the 12th century was an agree payment to the King for a grant or privilege.

Wrest Park mansion. The other division, Warden Hill Corner is south of this, and of 5 acres.

Thrift Wood (1717, Frith 1666) was part of the Newbury Manor Estate in 1757, and on the map of that date it is shown with an open field in the centre of a ring of woods. However, the whole area was probably wooded in early times, as a field on the Flitton side is called Rideing Corner, or earlier in 1670 Redding Corner; the word 'ryding' indicating a clearing in a wood. Frith probably comes from the Old English or Saxon for a wooded enclosure.

On the west side of Thrift Wood is Wardhedges, which was separate from Flitton and partly included in Silsoe, until a boundary change in the 20th century moved it to Flitton. The name is applied to several fields or closes, and is probably derived from the old English word for a wood; suggesting that the wood has been there for a considerable time. On the south side of the Greenfield Road and reaching down to Thrift Wood and Reding Corner, was Wardhedges Close, mentioned in 1687 and again early in the 18th century.

North of the wood was Frith Piece, a field of some 25 acres, which earlier was split into Frith Furlong on the east and Windmill Hill Furlong (1540) on the west, where the 16th century windmill was sited.

Returning to the A6 the next area up the road to the village on the west side is Great Road Field (1634) (sometimes Rode or Rood field); and on the north of the track to Upbury, Little Road Field whose names are probably taken from their proximity to the 'Kings Highway'. More than half of Little 'Rode' Field was in 1676, called Bode Piece. Around the track in 1853[92] were several pightels or small fields, Elm Pightle, Crane Pightle and Road Pightle, a narrow strip running approximately on the western side of what was the Cranfield University playing field.

Then, between Little Road Field and West End Road, lies what was called "Inlondise" in 1524, 'Endlands' in 1666 and 'England's' from 1674. This was part of Newbury Manor land until the sale to Wrest in 1775. The older name suggests that the field was an old enclosure relating to a particular house rather than it being at the end of the village, or named as a patriotic gesture.

England's was a large area, up to 40 acres and had been split into Ploughed, Middle and Hither England's by 1757, the whole area was called Englandsoms in 1812 when it was farmed from West End Farm.

Between Endlands and Thrift Wood was one of the larger common fields called Beech Field (1549). In 1675 Beech Piece which was a 20 acre area in Beech Field, was north of 'Beach Wood'. This wood was still shown there in 1718 although possibly reduced in area by the forming of Beech Wood Close, but the remaining woodland had been reduced to a copse on the southern edge by 1809. It may have been the last wooded area in the parish to be

---

[92] BLARS L5/844

converted to farmland due to its clayey and damp nature. Beeches prefer a dry soil so it seems unlikely that the name derived from the tree.

Within Beech Field a furlong called Dodmers is referred to several times from 1543 to 1563, while also near there is Dodmers Field, and in 1524 a six acre piece in "walden ffeelde callid dodissmere". In 1717 a land exchange has 1 acre of land abutting north on Thrift Way and south on 'The Hades'. This name probably comes from the old English word for a headland, but it is strange that it only occurs this late and not much earlier.

Between the track that runs from the end of West End Road to Wardhedges and the footpath that follows the bottom of the valley from Newbury Farm to Wardhedges is the Red Field (1554). This is almost certainly named after the colour of the soil there, which is derived from the underlying greensand. This field was probably larger extending more into the village at one time including Saffron Piece, and, like other fields was sub-divided into furlongs. There were Lower and Middle Furlongs, Poule (or Pule in 1679) Furlong next to Silsoe Road, Popler Furlong which ran down to the spring head, Broad Plot and also Waywynnyng (1549) with its Balk[93]. Broad Plot, courtesy of a 1675 grant appears to lie half way along the part of Red Field which is between the valley and what is now, The Avenue. Somewhere also was 'Pye Bushe' (1567), perhaps named from a large bush which was used by Magpies as a perch.

Between the bottom of the valley to the other footpath that follows the parish boundary from Beaumont Oak to Wardhedges is another large common field, Gosshill or Gosehyll (1521), much of which was strip farmed. This being a sandy area is where gorse would have grown and hence the name.

In the same field but abutting the Maulden Road on the west, in 1524 is an area known as Clapperhills which belonged to Newbury Manor. This name indicates that there was probably once a warren there for the production of rabbits for meat. However, at that date the warren was at Simpsonhill Plantation by the A6, which is described as 'The Hethe' (heath) and was full of 'conys' (rabbits). Clapperhills eventually became Hither, Lower and Further Clophill fields and by 1845 Kiln Field, Clophill Hill and part of Gose Hill Field.

In the valley bottom, the narrow strip from the road to the spring source was called 'The Valey' but later by 1757, it was split into Pond Spring Pightle, as there was a pond half way up, Long Close and Well Head, (all descriptive names). Long Mead mentioned in 1644 as a locating plot, may have been an alternative name.

Further down the road towards Maulden between Lower Clophill and the parish Boundary, the 1757 Newbury Manor Estate map has Beamont Tree

---

[93] A balk is the uncultivated strip between adjacent strips.

Piece, a field of about 8 acres. However, the map of 1718 shows Lady Ash Close of 4 acres and Lady Ash Meadow of 3½ acres, both owned by the de Greys. Earlier deeds of 1524 have a field called Lady Ashe Pece of 8 acres and in 1666, Lady Ash of 10 acres but the location is not shown. In 1739 a lease of part of Lady Ash mead, late in the tenure of Thomas Beaumont gent., had Silsoe moor on the east.

Oddly, the 1814 map shows Lady Ash where Beaumont Tree Piece was in 1718, and Beaumont Tree Piece written where Lady Ash Meadow was.

Crossing the Maulden Road and heading eastwards are more Newbury Manor land holdings with Barrel Field, another great common field to the east of these lands.

Surrounding or near the Manor in 1524 were Little Inynge, Great Inynge a piece called the Dowers and The Grove. The former two names come from the Middle English "inning", a piece of land taken in or enclosed, and although not clear, the above named fields probably became Ten Acres, Barn Close and Lower and Middle Pastures. The Grove may have originally applied to the fields to the south of Newbury Lane where Great and Little Grove fields existed in the 18th century and where the name 'Grove' has been preserved in the name of the road now there. The name probably came from dower land, the old tradition of giving land in dowry when a woman married. Between Newbury Lane, Newbury Manor and the stream running from the old ponds, Dairy Park existed from the 1650's to at least 1918; Newbury Close was built on part of it. From halfway down Newbury Lane to Appletree Close was Hunger or Hungry Piece. This denoted the need to apply lots of fertiliser as the ground was poor quality.

East of Middle Pasture in 1524 was Sheppcotte Leys and Foxhollis. In the early part of the 16th century the keeping of sheep increased rapidly due to the need for more wool and this was a major factor leading to the inclosure of land to allow for more efficient farming, this may have been the impetus for the early enclosure at Newbury and hence the name of Sheppcotte or later Sheepcote, a pen to keep sheep. Sheepcote was split into Broom Close and Sheepcote Close by 1757, and then became part of Horns Close together with Foxhollis. Foxhollis, from fox holes, first changed to another Shepcote Leys and then was Gravel Close. In 1814 it is called Pond Close although no trace of a pond can now be seen.

Back in 1524 Newbury Manor owned the 12 acre Quarry Piece, probably where The Maples now is, but also somewhere in the Manor was an 11 acre field called Rie Close which first appears in 1666. In no document do Rie Close and Quarry Piece appear together so they may be one and the same. (Rie croft does show up in a 13th century document but may not be the same place and Rie close, a close generally being much larger than a croft.)

Now we return to Barrel Field (1549). The only obvious reason for this name is its shape in that it is rounded similar to a barrel shape and it is unlikely to have been a burial site. However, Berrehull has been mentioned above and perhaps this is its derivation. In the middle of it was the Barrel Bush which was mentioned in 1524 and also in 1757, a very old bush evidently. Nearby was Rushy Plat, a damp place enabling rushes to be grown and adjacent a gravel pit.

To enable the position of strips to be located some areas were called 'furlongs', this was not a precise area but more a descriptive device. Thus in 1757 we have Road Furlong alongside the A6, Moor Furlong down towards Silsoe Moor, Middle Furlong to the west and Barrel Bush and Gravel Pit Furlongs in the centre. Two hundred years earlier there were Longlasthmere and Colwey Furlongs, now lost as are their meanings. Also there was a 'gret stone', probably a large sandstone rock dug up, and nearby the 'foule slowe', an old term for a marshy area, probably down by the Flit.

Between the track called Lady Ash and the Flit near Beaumont Farm was a sliver of land called Pynatt Mead early on, which by 1757 had become Penny Mead. This may have been named after magpies. Next towards the west was Smiths Close later divided and called Dry Close, which was possibly land assigned to the village smith. A 1591 document[94] refers to 'the road leading from Warde Hegge to Smythescroft' which substantiates its location.

Then came Silsoe Moor later called Silsoe Common first mentioned in 1449, which was a field freely available for the parishioners use until the inclosure in the 19th century. There is a reference in 1657 to Anne Godfrey having two cow-gates on the common, (meaning two pastures suitable for a cow on each). Somewhere to the west of the common was in 1499 Long Lechmore, possibly the Longlasthmere mentioned above.

East of the Barrel Field the land rises up and is very sandy so it was natural to have a warren there. In 1524 this 40 acre area was called 'The Hethe' or heath and was occupied by 'conys' or rabbits. In 1667 it was The Warren or Cunnigree, another rabbit name, and later in the 19th century Warren Wood and afterwards and still on OS maps Simpsonhill Plantation, named after Mr Richard Simpson who lived and farmed from Warren House.

Adjacent to that house or farm was in 1775 Sand Close, and Great and Little Ruine or Rimie Closes. The former named from the sandy soil and the others possibly as they ruined farmers who tried to farm them. In 1687 these fields were called Bottom, Upper and Sand closes in a lease so the ruination must have occurred between those dates!

Between The Warren and the River Flit the low lying area was called Growte Holmes in 1525 when Edward Daniel of Newbury Manor bought it, and this name continued becoming Crouch Home Common by 1718. Growte may be

---

[94] BLARS LJeayes 812

from great and Holmes from an old name for holly so there may have been a
'Great Holly' tree there. Although the first mention of this name is 1525
there is also the possibility that it could be derived from the Old Norse for a
wet area (which it is) thus suggesting that the Danes were there, as well as in
Fielden.

Back towards the village on the west side of the A6 is the ancient common
field of Waterslade whose name is retained in the Waterslade Allotments
which occupy the bulk of this ancient field. It is named as 'Waterisslade' in a
document of the 13th century and this name indicates that it was once very
wet, doubly wet; the water part is obvious and 'slade' is from the Anglo
-Saxon for a shallow damp place.

Fields in the Village

Near to the village centre most land or field names relate to their location,
use or to their past owners. However, there are a few larger plots such as
those between West End Road, Church Road and Vicarage Road. Firstly, to
the west of Vicarage Road was the Home Close of what is now 8 West End
Road and to the west of that Russels Close, which was recorded between
1549 and 1747 and which was farmed by West End Farm. Saffron Close was
behind and around the farm. Russels Close was probably named after
someone but Saffuren (1531), Safforn or Saffron Close indicated a place
where the saffron crocus was at one time grown.

At the end of West End Road in West End Green, the small house was in
1717 said to lie north of Bleak Hall Close and west of the Beech Common.
This is the only mention of Bleak Hall Close, and it is not shown on the 1718
Wrest estate map presumably being owned by someone other than the de
Grey family.

East of West End Farm in 1521 was the 'Church Closse', land owned by the
church which only 28 years later was called 'Town Close'. This was possibly a
consequence of the Dissolution of Henry VIII with the land claimed by him
eventually being owned by the town. It retained this name for several
centuries being in the 1700's 'Town Land' and was the plot on which the
village workhouse would be built.

North of, and from Vicarage Road to Fir Tree Red was in 1718 a field called
Corn Close which presumably grew corn which on the enclosure map of
1826 was called Cow Close.

Between the High Street, Vicarage Road, West End Road and Church Street
was in 1718 a close called Bishops of about 2 acres. This, one of the few
fields not controlled by the de Greys but probably bought by that family in
1775, was probably owned by Thomas Bishop, carpenter and Chapel
Warden.

Behind the house on the west side of the High Street were other closes, between West End Road and Church Street the land was owned by Thomas Bishop in 1718 but north of Church St was Cox's Close, Chandlers Close and Broom Close. Broom Close became Barnards Close in 1826 named after its owner at that time. Cox's close was named after Thomas Cox of the Ragged Staff, Innholder, Chandler's Close after John Godfrey of Silsoe, a tallow-chandler but Broom Close over which is now Poplar Close, has no amanuensis. Opposite Broom Close where Fir Tree Road now is, was Corn Close where presumably corn grew well.

On the south side of West End Road and running from the High Street up to Vicarage Road was Cooper's Pikle with an area of about ½ acre. There were families called Cooper in the village at that period who may have rented the pikle for some time.

Several documents[95] from the 1630's, group Parsonage, Dovehouse and Beeches Closes together, and it appears that they were adjacent to the village rather that in outlying areas. They total 12, 10 or 8 acres, depending on the source, and were associated with a 'capital messuage'[96] , possibly the large building shown north of the Church where The Rowans now is. They were also leased together so they were probably adjacent but there is insufficient evidence to locate them all. Parsonage Pikle or Close, approximately 1 acre, is shown in 1676 to be just east of the Church and south of the road to Wrest and contained the Parsonage. A small portion of it was absorbed into the Park in 1717 when that was expanded. Dovehouse Close is not mentioned after 1674. Beeches Close also disappears at that time.

Somewhere also in the village in the 16th century was a farmhouse called The Tabert which had a close called Stocking, (fields were usually called this from their shape) next to its back yard.

Also probably near to the village was a 2 or 3 acre field called Gibb or Gibbs Close. It first appears in William Hill's will of 1622 being then associated with Coldwillows and after passing through several owners, is bought by the Dowager Countess Amabella, in 1679. It is on the east of the highway and with such a large area cannot easily be placed in the centre of the village. It was probably in Dowdell Field opposite Waterslade where in 1718 there were several large plots belonging to Wrest. No villager named Gibb has been found in the parish records, so the source may possibly originate from the Middle English 'gibbe' for a hump.

Other Lost Fields

A few other field names appear in old documents which cannot easily be located.

---

[95] *Will of Reginald Hill ABP/W 1622-3/18,* L5/65, 67, 70, 73, 74, 85
[96] A Capital Messuage at this time was a large farmhouse or manor house.

In the 12th century there is 'an acre of land abutting on Doyt towards Donwothe and the fields of Sewelesho'. This perhaps reappears in 1202 as Parva (little) Dunesworth, and in 1270 Doneworthe which has "one head abutting on the King's road which leads thro' the village of Silsoe as far as Barton" in 1270. A few years later in 1314 a 'culture called Dunworth' in 'Sivelesho' and in 1360, '2 acs lying in 4 buts in Donworth, in parishes of Pulloxhill and Silsoe, one with a windmill built on it".

The context of the first reference to this field places it in the Kitchen End area, so it was probably near to the New Inn and on the west side of the A6.

Also gone is Astillesmade originally found in 1202 but which emerges again in 1270 when "a meadow lying in Astillemede" is referred to, and again in 1342 there is also "a piece of meadow in Astildusmede in Syvelesho", it then quietly evaporates. It does however seem to be in the Cainhoe area.

Lost also is an area known as Bromdichforlong which is in "le Northfeld of Syvelesho" in 1384 and which is more precisely located by being said to be abutting on "Waterslud". An earlier reference of 1308 has "le Brondich", probably this is the same place. Brompytte is found in 1530 as is Birifield Furlong, both were probably taken into Newbury Manor and absorbed into other fields upon inclosure there.

Inclosures

For centuries most parishes, and Silsoe was no exception, contained large areas or fields which were subdivided into narrow strips which were leased out to tenant farmers. Inclosure was the means by which the strips were aggregated into enclosed plots to provide areas which could be farmed in one piece, while at the same time any rights over the land were extinguished.

The complexity of the common open field system can be seen on the 1718 Wrest estate maps. The first map, Plate 11/3, shows the fields in the village which were sub-divided while the second, Plate 11/4, gives more detail of Waterslade common field.

Although the motives for enclosing are not agreed,[97] and may have varied from county to county and over the centuries, there was a general move at that time towards enclosure. The net effect was, once enclosure had occurred, that the landowners then had sole control over the land and could lease it or farm it at a more efficient level.

Enclosure took place either formally or informally. In the latter case the landowner slowly obtained the land and common rights in a manor after which he could enclose the land as he wanted. In the former case the major land owners could use the Enclosure Acts to speed up the process.

---

[97] See "*The Enclosure Maps of England and Wales 1595–1918*", Kain, Chapman & Oliver for a summary of the arguments.

Newbury Manor Inclosure

While we do not have many documents relating to the history of Newbury Manor before it was sold to the de Greys in 1775, it seems that the fields in nearly all of that estate were informally enclosed much earlier. The map of 1757 shows that most of the field surrounding the manor were without strips, and the schedule on the map suggests that three quarters of the estate was enclosed.

That enclosure took place at Newbury much earlier is backed up by a document of 1634[98] in which a plot is said to be next to the inclosed land of Thomas Daniel called Clapperhills; and also a reference to inclosed land of William Bryers at Roade Field lately purchased of Thomas Daniel.

Other earlier enclosed areas relating to Newbury are Growte Holmes which was mentioned in a grant of 1525, and the wood called Bockill or nowadays Buckle Grove, which had also been enclosed before 1525[99]. In addition, England's, the large area south of West End Road and east of the old A66 was also said to be enclosed in a document dated 1740[100].

Wrest Park Inclosures

The owners of Wrest were continually extending their ownership of land in the village when possible, and this led to their owning large areas of land, together with many strips in the common fields with varying numbers of tenants. So, for example, in 1682 John Sparkes of Peterborough sold to Amabella, Dowager Countess of Kent, a house with 5 adjacent cottages and about 48 acres of land including six closes, Townsend Close, Roade Close, Dry Wickesse, Water Wickesse, Long Stockinge Close and New Close all on the west side of the A6 on the Barton Road.[101] With land purchases such as these they were able to extend their parkland by enclosing some of the land.

Some fields north of Wrest Park mansion were probably enclosed quite early on, as in 1638[102] a lease refers to enclosed land in Wrest or Cainhoe excepting High Field and Broadlands. Both the latter fields are shown on the 1718 maps as lying in this area around Home Farm. Again in 1672[103] enclosed lands in Flitton (which must also lie in Silsoe) called Middle Ground and Cainhoe Hill are mentioned.

At Wrest, in the early 1700's, the Duke of Kent was intending to build a new mansion further to the north, and in order to provide more land for his park

---

[98] BLARS L5/368a
[99] BLARS L5/346
[100] BLARS L5/960
[101] BLARS L5/48
[102] BLARS L5/1082
[103] BLARS L5/1117

in front of the house enclosed 10 acres from the common field lands of Dowdell and Kennel. At about the same time he also enclosed land by exchange, to the south in Ion for improving his park there.[104]

Also, around 1717, he enclosed much of Park Field to the west of the existing house. This is a large area and probably relates to the bulk of the land between the Old Park, west of the present parkland and the old A6. The 1718 map shows only a narrow strip of fields remaining between the A6 and the parkland and a lease of 1721[105] refers the lands being purchased by the Duke in Park Field (south of Barton Road and East of the old A6) "the greatest part of which are now inclosed in the Duke's park called Wrest Park".

The above lands were enclosed into the park but others appear to have been enclosed so that large field undivided into strips were created, to enable more 'modern' farming to be carried out. Thus a further enclosure which took place just before 1762 is suggested in a conveyance[106] of that year, when an adjoining close called Beech Wood belonging to Viscount Royston is said to be lately enclosed. Beech Wood Field, 22 acres, and Beech Wood Close of 8 acres both appear in the 1718 map to be without sub-division into strips, showing that the enclosure had been carried out.

The 1826 Formal Inclosure

The main inclosure of fields in Silsoe followed the national trend by taking place at around the beginning of the 19th century. It was started by obtaining a Private Act of Parliament, dated 1809, for enclosing land in Flitton cum Silsoe and Pulloxhill and in it two commissioners were appointed, Thomas Thorpe of Great Barford and Richard Davis of Aston Rowant with a third, John Maugham of Hitchin as arbiter in case of disagreement. It was their job to measure the areas of the land, to determine ownership and rights and to apportion the land in accordance with the act.

Following meetings and discussions and consideration of the various claims, a final layout and agreement was arrived at which was set down in the inclosure awards document with the new field layout being shown on a map.[107]

---

[104] BLARS L25/6, 19
[105] BLARS L5/139
[106] BLARS L5/821
[107] BLARS Flitton with Silsoe and Pulloxhill award; text:- A Book N; A56/2 , map:- MA56; MA56/2 & L25/57/2

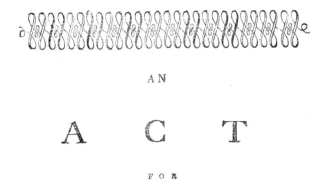

A N

A C T

F O R

Inclofing Lands in the Parifhes of *Flitton cum Silsoe* and *Pulloxhill,* in the County of *Bedford.*

WHEREAS there are within the Parifhes of *Flitton* Preamble. *cum Silfoe* and *Pulloxhill,* in the County of *Bedford,* feveral Open and Common Fields, Common Meadows, Common Paftures, and other Commonable Lands and Wafte Grounds :

And whereas the Right honourable *Amabell* Baronefs *Lucas* is Lady of the Manors or Lordfhips of *Flitton cum Silfoe* and *Pulloxhill* aforefaid :

And whereas the Dean and Chapter of the Cathedral Church of *Chrift* of the Foundation of King *Henry* the Eighth, in the University of *Oxford,* and the faid *Amabell* Baronefs *Lucas,* as their Leffee, are entitled to the impropriate Rectory or Parfonage of *Flitton cum Silfoe,* and of the Great or Rectorial Tythes and Glebe Lands thereto belonging ; and the faid Dean and Chapter are Patrons of the Vicarage of the fame Parifh, and the Reverend *John Robinfon* is the Vicar thereof, and as fuch is entitled to the Vicarial Tythes arifing and payable within the faid Parifh :

130   A   And

Plate 11/5 - The front page of the Silsoe Inclosure Act

At the enclosure, roads were listed and while in some parishes they were straightened or new ones built, none seem to have been affected in this way in Silsoe. However, the main purpose was to re-arrange land ownership and this was carried out. So, taking as an example Barrel Hill, the area between Newbury Lane, the River Flit, the Clophill Road and east of Newbury Farm; the earlier map of 1718 shows a total of 45 strips and small fields. At the enclosure it was divided into three allotments: Amabel, Countess de Grey received 27 acres at Warren Hills (Simpsonhill Plantation) and the Rector of Flitton, on behalf of the Dean and Chapter of Christ Church Oxford, received 124 acres. The final allotment was of 2 acres for a gravel pit and there was a new road leading to it. Also, in the middle of this, Firs Farm with its smallholding is retained as a unit.

However, while the allotment fields were large, it seems that they were still subdivided but into more manageable areas. Comparing the old maps from 1718 through 1826 to the current day *Google Earth* (and allowing for different standards of surveying), it can be seen that many of the present day field boundaries follow the old layouts; and even most of the old path from Road Houses to the old common near the Flit, is still today a public footpath.

Several years after the enclosure in around 1862 there was a major programme of works on the order of the Enclosure Commissioners carried out in the village, using their funds. This work included drainage and the erection of farm buildings and cottages.[108] The row of houses, numbers 3 to 7 High Street and blocks of houses at Fielden Farm and Home Farm are from this date, and the year 1862 can be seen on the cast iron ventilation grilles under the eaves. Similar brickwork can be found around the village, suggesting that improvements to houses owned by Wrest estate were carried out at this time.

However, many lost out at enclosure. Even if common rights for the use of marl pits or gravel pits were retained for public use, the common and waste land along with any rights to forage in the stubble after harvest disappeared, and the village poor lost whatever use they had made of this land. If the poor could not have a strip of land they could not keep a cow or other livestock, and accordingly many fell back on the parish to support them. Silsoe may have been more fortunate than many villages, as the Wrest de Greys may have been more compassionate in allowing for their needs, but even so the landscape had changed forever.

The Farms of Silsoe

Newbury Manor Farm

At the time of the Great Survey in 1089 Nigel d'Albini's concubine held 2 hides in this manor, perhaps about 240 acres, with a tenant having about 120 acres. There were 7 ploughs with an eighth possible, so perhaps some land was under-utilised or had never been ploughed. As no woodland is recorded for this manor the unused land may have been rough sandy land, such as that where Warren Wood now is. The manor was the administrative centre for its land, and the fields making up the manorial land were not necessarily around the manor itself, but could have been scattered in the parish or even outside it.

Each plough would have had 8 oxen to pull it, so a good area of meadow would have been necessary to provide feed and to put them out into after

---

[108] BLARS L22/68

work. None is mentioned but adjacent manors at Cainhoe and Silsoe had almost an equivalent area of meadow as pasture.

Nothing is found in the records for the next 500 years for this manor but it is likely that with only minor exchanges, sales and purchases, the land associated with it remained virtually unchanged up to the first major record of the land attached to it. However, we have a long document of 22nd November 1524 relating to the sale by Henry Wayte of the manor and lands to Edward Daniel which lists the land in some detail[109]

At that time it seems that the manor of Newbury had 4 messuages 6 tofts[110], 200 acres of land, 40 acres of meadow, 40 acres of pasture, 20 acres of woods, plus an income of 60s rent for land or messuages rented[111]; a total area of more than 300 acres. However, another document sometime later dated 1573 lists the following manor lands as; " 4 messuages, 6 tofts, 240 acres land, 40 acres meadow, 60 acres pasture, 40 acres furze, 40 acres wood, 20s. rents"[112], this time it totals 420 acres.

The manor lands changed a certain amount in the 16th century with a sale from Henry Wayte to Edward Daniel in 1525 of a field called 'Growts Holmes' of 6 acres and also 'Bockill Grove' (now Buckle Grove), no area given, were conveyed. Then in 1544 1¼ acres owned by Edward west of Cainhoe moor and east of Kenelfurlong was exchanged with a similar area owned by Sir Henry Grey of Wrest which was south of Shefford Way[113].

It appears that Edward died without issue between 1554 (the date of the last document including his name) and 1559 when Sir Henry Grey, as guardian of Stephen Danyell, born about 1547, a minor and the son of Thomas Danyell of London, leased the manor to William Danyell[114]. It is inferred from this that Stephen Danyell inherited from his father Thomas, who was the brother of Edward. The rent was £17 and 8 dozen pigeons.

Throughout the 17th century the Daniels made minor changes to their land holdings such as in 1608 when 2 acres in Red and Barrell Fields were purchased by Thomas Daniel from Thomas Childe,[115] but no major purchases have been found.

We have a further indication of the extent of Newbury land in 1624/5 when in a short document the estate is described as: "… the Manor of Newburye, messuage, dovecote, garden, orchard, 200 acres land, 100 acres pasture, 30

---

[109] BLARS LJeayes 143
[110] A toft was a homestead with perhaps a little land attached.
[111] BLARS L5/345
[112] BLARS L5/350
[113] BLARS L5 /346 & 348
[114] BLARS LJeayes364
[115] BLARS L5/356

acres wood, 50 acres heath, in Flitton, Maulden, Clophill and Silsoe, a total of 380 acres"[116].

It is difficult to find out what farms in Silsoe would be growing or producing at that time, but no doubt as today whatever was profitable in the country would be grown or reared if the land allowed it, and there was a market nearby. There are in some sales or leases of this time an indication of which fields were arable and which were pasture; and in some a penalty if meadow was converted to arable, an indication that there was much animal rearing at the cost of changing arable to good pasture. The inclusion of the word 'Sheepcote' in the name of some fields at Newbury obviously suggests that sheep were kept there.

Just before Thomas died in 1664, in 1660 William Daniel managed to acquire the two Hollington watermills for the manor from the Morgan family for £300[117] in a deal which included their meadows. Late in the previous century the two watermills plus a windmill had been included in a marriage settlement on Francis Morgan and Judith Duncombe by John Morgan the miller[118]; but several mortgages were later taken out on the property in the 1650's and these appear not to have been repaid. No doubt ready for a bargain, William bought them from the Morgan family when an Edmund Morgan was still the miller[119]. This was an important purchase as they would enable the farm to mill its own and others grain for flour, and as it was on the Flit it could operate most, if not all of the year.

In 1658 William Daniel, Thomas's son, was getting married to Elizabeth Mulsoe from Finedon and the manor and land details settled on the marriage, were listed in the marriage settlement document[120]. This was followed soon after by a deed in 1666/7 which included a schedule listing most of the remaining lands not covered by the marriage settlement[121]. Thus a combination of the land in this and the earlier document gives an indication of the land owned by the family and seemingly farmed from the manor in the mid 17th century. This is shown on Plate 11/6.

---

[116] BLARS L5/360
[117] BLARS L5/380
[118] BLARS L5/374
[119] BLARS L5/380
[120] BLARS L5/372
[121] BLARS L5/387

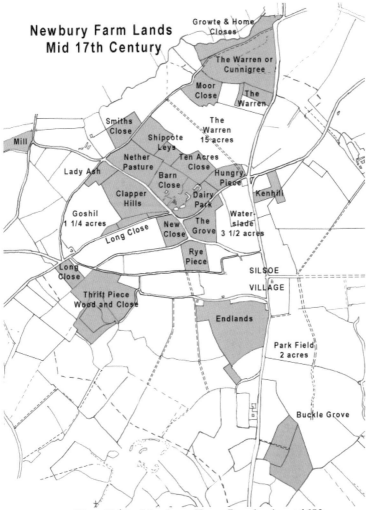

Plate 11/6 – Newbury Farm Lands about 1650

Soon after, in 1668, William took out a mortgage of £200 from the Countess Amabella on 20 acres of Buckle Grove, Rye Piece and Lady Ash Piece, all occupied by Benjamin Pigott. He then, two years later, took out a further mortgage for 500 years of £500 on the same lands plus 15 acres in Barrell Field, 3 acres in Waterslade, Dairy Park and a Pightle next to Frith Wood[122].

He must have been getting even further into debt, as in 1673 a 1,000 year mortgage for £700 was taken out from Sir Charles Scarborough, physician to the King and the Duke of York[123]. This mortgage deed had a further detailed

---

[122] BLARS L5/388, 389
[123] BLARS L5/391

schedule which included the lands in the earlier mortgages, so he had presumably paid them off.

In 1685 William, perhaps as a result of getting over-stretched or perhaps wanted a rest away from farming, sold the manor with its lands to Robert Nicholls of St Albans for £13,000. He did however retain for his use during his life the mansion house with its outhouses, gardens, fishponds etc and for a rent of £25 p.a. the Dairy Park, and New Close[124]. He was to remain there until his death in 1706.

A detailed schedule associated with the sale shows that the estate was not much changed from the earlier surveys, at about 380 acres.

It appears that the manor and farm had descended from Robert to William Nicholls by 1717 as William was at that date, and later in 1722, exchanging a few acres in Beech, Kennel and Park Fields with Henry the Duke of Kent, presumably to rationalise William's holdings and also to consolidate the Duke's holding in Park Field prior to him taking the whole area for the extension to his Park. As part of the exchange, the Duke agreed to give William half a fat buck annually, at Christmas.

The great Wrest Park survey of 1718 was compiled to show only the land owned by that estate, but happily it also has inscribed on it the lands owned by 'Mr Nichols'. The ownerships are detailed in the common fields where the Duke had an interest but only as large blank areas outside of these.

By 1757 the lands associated with the Newbury estate had been divided into smaller, but still quite large, separate tenancies and were being farmed as such. As William Nicholls is said to be from Aldenham in Hertfordshire on deeds, and was thus presumably an absentee landlord, it was perhaps the Nicholls family that sub-divided the property.

Although the manor eventually descended to his mother Sarah in 1736 and to him in 1767, Robert Hucks of Bloomsbury was involved in land deals in the village by 1739; as in that year he obtained a 1½ acres meadow in Lady Ash Mead next to Silsoe Moor from Henry Pearson of Ampthill. [125]

It is provident that in 1757 Sarah had a detailed map drawn up showing her land ownership in Silsoe[126]. The land area totals about 407 acres. Apart from some smaller areas, the estate was divided into three main farms. Newbury Farm was centred on the manor house and was of about 243 acres, and was being farmed by Russell Finney from the manor. Warren Farm of 73 acres was based at what is now Firs Farm on the track between Beaumont's Oak and the A6, and was farmed by Benjamin Goode.

---

[124] BLARS L5/395
[125] BLARS L5/409
[126] BLARS X1/89 Original in private ownership.

England's Farm whose land of about 39 acres was in the south of the village, comprised mainly of the three England's fields south of West End Road, Buckle Grove meadows and a field at Thrift. Later in 1775 the farm was said to include a farm house, barns, stables, outhouses and buildings and was commonly called England's. It seems probable that the farm house was close to the fairly substantial England's fields, and was not then owned by Wrest. The obvious candidate for the farm is the old house in West End Lane, now called Little Gable.

Finally there were 22 acres mainly in Flitton and towards Wardhedges, farmed by Richard Merry who was probably based in Greenfield, plus some 25 acres of woods retained by the owner.

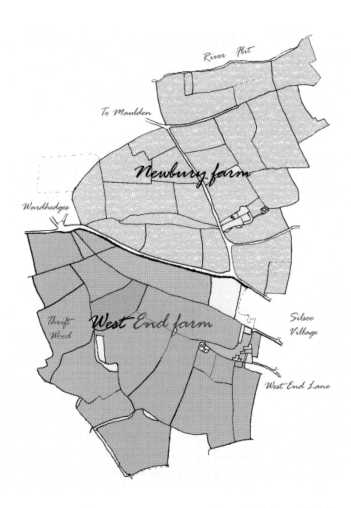

Plate 11/7 - 1845 Newbury and West End Farm Holdings

Eventually the manor and its lands became available for sale. It was purchased from various interested parties in 1775 for £6000 for incorporation into the Wrest estate. While there may have been some rationalisation of the tenancies no details of these remain, and it is not until 1845 that a map of Newbury and West End farms gives some indication of how the lands had been parcelled out. [127].

The main difference is that we are now fully post-enclosure and that as the narrow strips in the large common fields had been incorporated into larger fields, further rationalisation could be carried out. Thus Newbury Farm now has all the land to the north of the Wardhedges Road and west of the old A6, a total farm area of 255ac 1r 32p, with 'W' P Squire as the tenant.

In the 19th century the censuses help us with the names of the farm managers and to some extent the size of the holding, plus how many labourers were needed to operate the farm.

By 1841 the Squire family, who were to remain at Newbury until 1891, had taken over the tenancy. Initially it may have been Joseph Squire, but by 1841 it was William Peppercorn Squire from Stratton with his wife, four children and four servants who were living there. It is said that there were 11 daughters in William's family and each, as the manor house was so large, were able to have a bedroom each. In 1851 the farm is said to be of 273 acres and he was employing twelve men and four boys with two house servants, to manage the farm. Still there in 1861, he was then employing 13 labourers and seven boys on the land but only needed a cook, a domestic servant and a groom to run the house.

Then in 1871, with the acreage now at 274, and William aged 74 years and with only one daughter living with him, he was using 11 men and four boys plus a general servant and an indoor farm servant, who was also a groom.

William died in 1873 and by 1881 Edward Frederick Squire, his son, and born in Silsoe in 1829, had returned from Cross Hall Farm in Eaton Socon (much bigger at 450 acres), with his wife and six children to take over the running of the farm. The farm is still 274 acres and he employed 8 men and 2 boys, there was a cook and housemaid helping his wife in the house. He continued for at least another ten years at Newbury as the 1891 census shows him there with his wife and two children, plus a couple of housemaids.

Edward's death is recorded at St Neots in 1897 and in the 1901 census a new tenant, (previously of West End House Farm in Haynes), Samuel Taylor Maddams, aged 67, has taken on the farm. He is with his wife, a daughter, and a general servant. He unfortunately did not last long there, and on his gravestone it says that he departed this life at Newbury on June 27th 1904 aged 71 years. It also records his Huguenot ancestry as his family is said to have come to England from Normandy in 1685, and settled at Clophill.

---

[127] BLARS L26/457-458

The new tenant was Samuel (Sammy) Paterson a dour and frugal Scot who in Kelly's 1914 Directory is found farming there. In the Wrest Park estate sale in 1918 he, still the tenant farmer, managed to buy Newbury Farm after protracted negotiations for £8,000. A plan attached to the sale document shows the estate unchanged with a total area of 274ac 0r 39p [128].

It is said that Sammy allowed one of his workers the Saturday morning off to get married but as the afternoon was part of the normal working week he had to go back to work.

Samuel is still there in the 1936 Kelly's but in 1939 Hugh (Hughie) Charles Harris had taken over. He was a skilled and gifted farmer and in his hands the farm prospered having at one time a herd of pedigree Large White pigs known as The Silbury Herd as well as a well known herd of pedigree Shorthorn cattle. Unfortunately he had to retire due to ill health and in 1960 Mrs D Clarke and her son Maurice bought the farm.

Under Maurice's stewardship the farm produced a wider variety of crops such as vegetables with some 25 acres of Brussels sprouts, producing an average of 100 tonnes per annum together with 20 acres of mixed variety potatoes yielding 260 tonnes per annum. In addition cereals, runner beans and other root and salad vegetables were grown. Some four full time workers were employed with a causal labour force of three to four women being used at harvesting time.

The present farm bears little relationship to that in existence in the last century. Much of the old manorial lands north of the manor are farmed from Beaumont Farm, on the Maulden Road while the lands west of the manor up the valley have been converted into horse paddocks with a lagoon being constructed at the site of the old St Edmunds Well.

The manor house is now a private residence while the farmhouse is a modern bungalow with the 1840 farm buildings being converted to residential use.

West End Farm

The first indication of a farm in West End appears in the 16th century when in 1521, Hugo Swynnerton granted his messuage with a croft in '*le Westende of Sevelisho*', in which he was living, to various local rectors and Richard Swynnerton, possibly his son. The property extended from West End Road to '*le Churchweye*', the road from Silsoe to Flitton, and also included 7 acres of land in strips lying in the East Field, Park Field and 'Gosehyl'. He had apparently only recently obtained this land from John White of London, 'Fisschmonger', the son of Thomas White, late of Syvelischo.[129]

---

[128] BLARS L23/259
[129] BLARS LJeayes 780 &781

This property then appears to have passed down to Hugo's daughter Agnes, who had married George Fletcher. They then sold the property to Sir Henry Grey in 1548 for 25 marks.

The farm and its location must have been found suitable for basing a substantial farm there, as in 1549 Sir Henry was leasing this messuage and croft for 21 years to Christopher Kynge in the West End of Silsoe, "next the pightle or close of Henry on west and a close called Towne Close to the east" together with 16 ac of land which he had recently bought from George Fletcher and Agnes his wife, in 1548[130]. Included in the lease was an acreage of at least 130 acres scattered mainly in ½ or 1 acre plots throughout the common fields of the village.

Christopher Kynge presumably died or moved on, as in 1563 what appears to be the same farm now with 195 acres of land, is being leased for 21 years by Dame Anne Grey, widow of Sir Henry Grey, and Regnold Grey her son to Robert Lathbury of London, merchant taylor[131]. One would assume that Lathbury installed a working tenant or bailiff in the farm to operate it, as it would seem unlikely that a merchant taylor had knowledge of farming. However, a lease of the mansion house and lands of Norwood Manor dated 1567[132], where one plot is said to be a pightle in West End next to a farm occupied by Robert Lathbury, does suggest that Robert came down from London to farm in Silsoe.

Moving on to 1615, a lease for 9 years[133] of a messuage or croft which was situated in the West End of "Sylveshoo" "lately in the tenure of Henry Eden, deceased, but now in the occupation of Edward Hill together with all barns stables edifices buildings yards gardens backsides pastures meadows arable land and appurtenances". A few years later in 1619 there is a terrier[134], with amendments made up to 1770, in which are described lands which Edward Hill of Silsoe held of Anthoney Grey, they totalled about 206 acres.

Edward was buried in 1635, and there is then a gap in the records as to who the tenant might have been, but it was likely to have been William Caton who died in 1640, as in 1658 the Widow Caton is found in a rent book paying £50 per annum for "the farm house in Silveshoo called Westend farm with divers land pasture and meadows hereunto belonging lying in Flitton Silsoe and Maulden"[135].

In 1674 Nicholas Payne entered into a 7 year lease for West End Farm and buildings plus land for £60 per annum[136]. He was not to plough up or sub-let

[130] BLARS LJeayes 803
[131] BLARS LJeayes 807
[132] BLARS L5/1091
[133] BLARS L5/1097
[134] BLARS L26/445 A terrier, in this context has nothing to do with dogs, it is a schedule in which the details of a land holding is described.
[135] BLARS L26/1384
[136] BLARS L5/1120

and had to leave all the lands due for fallowing and sheep commons in order, when he left. He probably was good at keeping to the letter of the lease as well as keeping an eye on others, as he was, in the 1680's, reporting those who had missed going to church for more than 2 weeks to the Silsoe Petty Sessions Court.

Then, by 1684 at least, the Catons were back. Thomas, a yeoman of Wardhedges, appears in a draft 6 year lease for the farm for which he had to pay Countess Amabella £60 18s 4d a year plus two fat geese at Christmas[137]. Confusingly it says that the farm was lately occupied by William Caton who died 48 years earlier. Some form of lease, now missing, must have been adopted as in 1702 in an account book, Thomas's rent is said to be £92 18s 4d [138]

Thomas seems to have prospered at the farm, or had some other source of money, as in 1700[139] a farmhouse and lands in Greenfield was conveyed to Thomas Caton. In 1702 his rent for the farm was £92 18s 4d. The size of West End Farm had not changed greatly as a terrier of tenants and lands of the Wrest estate made in the 18th century, gives the total at 185 acres[140]. This list also included land in Flitton, but the bulk was in the common fields of Silsoe.

Thomas was still at West End Farm 25 years later in 1718, as a terrier compiled for Wrest Park has him there farming a total area of 196a 1r 33p and paying a yearly rent of £92 18s 4d, (no increase from 1702!). Sadly he died in February that year and was buried at Flitton where the records describe him as a 'husbandman', (another term for a farmer).

Thomas's son Daniel Caton had married Mary Burley in Higham Gobion in 1719, when he was only 19 years old, but at some time he took over the farm, as later in 1747 he is leasing a farmhouse in Silsoe[141] which, by comparing the field names with the West End Farm terrier of 1718, can be seen to be West End Farm. The land included in the 219 acres total, the 8 acre Home close, 25 acre Beechwood close, a 5 acre close at Ward Hedges, 3 acres at Hanger close (in Flitton), 12 acres at Warden Hill close, 3 acres of Corn close, 3 acres of Russells close, 2 acres of Broom close, 45 acres in Beech Field, 61 acres in Red Field, 44 acres in Barrell Field, 1 acre in Fielding mead and 1 acre in Maulden mead. The rent had gone up over the intervening years to £124 9s 10d.

As tenant he could "lop such trees as are usually lopped for repairs and firewood; shall plash quick hedges and scour ditches; shall carry out repairs (except those necessitated by fire, storm and tempest), being allowed £35 for

[137] BLARS L5/1123
[138] BLARS L26/1449
[139] BLARS L5/207
[140] BLARS L26/452
[141] BLARS L5/1127

same with rough timber annually for cart bote and plough bote", the "landlord may inspect and order repairs to be done within 3 months". The tenant had also to use compost on the premises and he had also to make available to any incoming tenant certain rooms in the farm house.

Daniel Caton the elder, a yeoman in his will which was proved in 1768[142], left to his son Daniel Caton the younger of Silsoe, the house in which he lived together with a close and common rights, which he would get after the elder Daniels wife, Mary, died. Daniel could not sell it. To his other son Thomas Caton, he left 5s, and after the death of Daniels wife, Thomas got an occupied house in Flitton with land belonging, which also he could not sell. He left his daughter Elizabeth Larrance, the wife of Edward, 8 acres of common field land in Flitton with reversion to Matthew Caton and his daughter Jane Caton. Another daughter, Jane received £100 and his son George Caton a house in Silsoe with 2 acres in Pulloxhill. Finally, his daughter Sara Caton would receive £60 at the age of 24. The residue went to his wife and at her death to Matthew. It can be seen that Daniel had prospered and was wealthy by the standards then existing.

A schedule of 'Caton's Farm' of 1770 lists the farm holdings which then totalled 196 acres. About a third had been 'inclosed' and the farm included most of the land between the Luton Road and the Wrest Park parkland in addition to areas, still mainly in strips, between Thrift Wood and the farm, and also in Cold Willows and Waterslade.

Although Daniel the elder was buried in 1787 at Pulloxhill, Matthew Caton, Daniel's youngest brother, was leasing the farm in 1772 for 12 years at £125 per annum from the de Greys. Daniel may have taken a back seat by then or the farm was being run by the family[143].

There is a certain laxity in the continuation in leases as shown above (or several have been lost) and this was recorded by the de Grey's agent in 1779 [144] when it was noted that Thomas Caton's leases had been out of date for several years but that this was to be rectified in 1782 – another three years. Neither the original nor the renewal leases survive.

Matthew Caton died in 1806 and the new tenant was a stranger to the village, Richard Eve, who came from Hertfordshire. He was then only about 18 years old but came from a farming family, and was to remain as tenant for some 79 years.

In late 1845 a survey of both West End Farm and Newbury Farm was carried out, a map was drawn up and a schedule was compiled. Farmed by Richard Eve as tenant, West End Farm was slightly bigger than had previously been recorded at some 238 acres 1 rood 25 poles, and extended westwards from

---

[142] BLARS L5/737
[143] BLARS L5/1137
[144] BLARS L26/43

the farmhouse up to and on either side of Thrift Wood, and from the Flitton Road southwards almost to Upbury Farm. The farmhouse and associated yards, gardens and orchards were in excess of 4 acres with about 52 acres of pasture, 3 acres of wood and the rest as arable.

The censuses throughout the 19th century show that he was a major employer of men and boys in the village, probably taking most of the men from the West End area, plus others from the village centre.

The area farmed is given as much more that the 1845 survey shows, and while there may have been some rounding up, it seems that he farmed in 1871, from 450 to 500 acres reducing to about 311 acres in 1881. To assist him he employed 29 men in 1851, 26 men and 21 boys in 1861 and 23 men with 19 boys in 1871; and reducing to 14 men and 8 boys in 1881, with the lesser acreage.

None of Richard Eve's children took over when he died in 1885, and it was Charles Browning who between 1890 and 1891 became the new tenant farmer. He was born in about 1835 and originated in Staughton, Huntingdonshire from a farming household. In the 1871 and 1881 censuses he is the innkeeper of the George Inn in Silsoe, but while there was also farming, 91 acres in 1871 and 121 acres in 1881, employing 5 men and 1 boy.

Charles died in March 1905 aged 74 and his wife Sarah took over, being described as Mrs Charles Browning in 1910, a farmer of West End Farm, and Mrs Sarah Browning in the 1914 and 1920 Kelly's Directories. She died in 1925 also aged 74, although probably her son Francis Timothy took over before that as he is referred to in the 1924 Directory as of the farm.

Thanks to the 1917-18 War Agricultural Committee records there is an indication of how the farm was operating at that time. The farm consisted of 154 acres of arable and 162 acres of pasture in both Silsoe and Pulloxhill and was stocked with 24 cows, 41 other cattle, 7 horses, 6 young horses and 190 sheep. It was operated by 5 men and 2 boys. The owner was still Nan Herbert, Lady Lucas, and the executors of Charles Browning (Sarah and Francis) originally objected to the War Committee ordering the ploughing up of 10 acres due to the heavy and wet nature of the ground. They knew their land, and later claimed compensation due to a failure in crops caused by wireworm and the need to re-seed. They had needed four horses to plough the land due to its heavy nature.

It seems that H C Harris bought the farm after the Wrest Park estate break-up but the Brownings continued to farm there. However, in the late 1930's the Ministry of Agriculture proposed that the County Council buy the farm for it to be used as a demonstration farm with fruit gardens and livestock, with an estimated price of £8,600. The Second World War intervened, but after that the proposal was carried out, and the Council bought the 315 acres farm.[145]

The farm prospered and in 1948 a farm manager, Mr J B Fisher was appointed. In 1952 the farm produced and sold a variety of produce including bulls, cows, pigs, lambs, 33 tons of potatoes, 202 quarters of wheat and 30 tons of sugar beet. In addition many improvements were carried out and new buildings constructed, including a pair of cottages behind West End Road for workers on the farm.

In 1959 and following discussions on the best site in Bedfordshire, the Minister of Education announced that with the agreement of the County Council, a National College of Agricultural Engineering was to be set up at Silsoe. The land and West End Farm was transferred to this establishment and the new college buildings were completed in 1962, at a cost of £35,0000.

Eventually it became amalgamated with Cranfield University and the establishment attracted students from around the world. However, Cranfield decided to leave Silsoe and in 2009 the educational aspects of the farm had mostly now left the village, although some experiments are continuing. While the land is still owned by Cranfield University it is primarily farmed out of Beaumont Farm, Maulden Road.

Park or Home Farm

Although Home Farm is now the major farm in the parish with its operations extending into adjacent parishes, there is a lack of information as to its origin and early development. It seems possible that it may have been the remnants of Braybury Manor which had been retained for use in farming within the Wrest Park estate boundary when the lands at the north of the parish were enclosed, to extend the parkland.

A scattered cluster of buildings appear on the 1718 estate map for 'Rest Park' [146] on the west side of an avenue which extended northwards from the mansion; together with a few other buildings on the east side, but there is no name given, and all the farms in the schedule to the Silsoe village map are all accounted for. At the same time and on another map of the same date, a large farming complex is shown to the north of the church (where The Rowans now is), and which would presumably have been quite able to work the farming in the park area, from that base.

Later in that century in leases of 1775 and 1776[147], John Hill of Flitwick is renting the farm house called Cainhoe or the Park Farm situated in Silsoe, Clophill and Gravenhurst plus about 140 acres of land and paying £130 per annum for the rent. Nathaniel Dennis was in occupation and presumably was

---

[145] BLARS AG/Sub M/7/1 & 2
[146] BLARS L33/286 F3
[147] BLARS L4/387 & 335

the sub-tenant farming Great Ground (63 acres), the Sheep walk (18 acres), Bean Close (13 acres), High field (19 acres), Gravel pit field (16 acres) and New ground (15 acres).

A developed farming complex is shown superimposed on the early 19th century plans at the location of Home Farm, and is named 'Park Farm' or 'Field Farm', and as the farm opposite the church had by then disappeared, it seems that the farming operations had been moved to Park Farm some time before that date.

Unfortunately the 19th century censuses do not provide much assistance in finding out about the acreage farmed or much other detail, but in 1841 there is John Mason, a bailiff, living at Wrest Park Farm with two servants. In 1851 he is said to be aged 39, from Newby Farm in Yorkshire and was there with his wife, also from Yorkshire, their six children aged 8 and under, a governess and a living-in farm labourer. A bailiff was normally someone employed by an estate to ensure that the tenant farmers were using their land properly. The census says the farm was of 770 acres employing 42 outdoor labourers and one indoor labourer. This area is far more than the farm by the church plus other lands mentioned in the schedule, and must have included lands in Clophill and Gravenhurst.

Adjacent to the above entry, and presumably in an adjacent cottage, although also described as Wrest Park Farm, is a farm labourer, John Kemp with his family.

John Mason (the bailiff), did not stay much after the 1851 census and had left sometime between 1854[148] and 1861 to go to a farm in Leppington, Yorkshire.

From here onwards the enumerators may have been confused or overawed by the estate as no farming areas are given and there is no sign of a bailiff. In 1861 John White Burrows is at the farmhouse but is described as a builder from Clophill, aged 40. The only farming connection of Mr Burrows appears to be his mother-in-law who was also there, and who is described as a former farmer. In what is now described as the bailiff's cottage is still John Kemp, a shepherd overseeing three labourers.

It seems likely that John Burrows was concerned with the farm building boom which took place in Silsoe around then as witnessed by the air grills with the 1862 date found on many farm buildings in the Wrest estate and in Silsoe. Home Farm has the appearance of a 'Model Farm' and may well have been extended around that date with the farmhouse, listed as originally being of the 16th century, incorporated in the new works.

In 1871 John Burrows is still there, but is now the clerk of works to the Wrest estate (which was probably his job in 1861) and Archibald Haddow, a

---

[148] PO Directory for Bedfordshire

land agent's clerk is also at the farm house. We do however now have a farm bailiff for the estate one John Frossell aged 38, of Biddenham. He is at the Bailiff's Cottage, but no acreage is given in this census.

John Burrows died in 1876 and for the next three surveys from 1881 to 1901 at Wrest Park Farm there is Charles Robinson, a building surveyor and clerk of works. Archibald Haddow is now an accountant and John Frossell remains there as the farm bailiff until his death in 1915, aged 79.

The break-up of the Wrest estate led to Wrest Park farm being sold to John George Murray, a brewing and mining magnate from Consett, County Durham, as a separate lot within the package that included Wrest Park[149]. At that time, (1917), it was said to comprise of 438 acres, a farm house occupied by the bailiff and a second house divided in two; and the associated plan shows that most of the land was within the Park.

Plate 40 shows the farm land extending northwards from the north side of the main drive up to the then Shefford Road, and from the stone wall on the east side of the village eastwards to about the Brabury Lodges, and then the parish boundary. Part extended into Gravenhurst and part of Cainhoe Farm Lot extended slightly into Silsoe by about 3 acres.

Plate 11/8 -Home or Wrest Park Farm in 1917

Mr Murray eventually granted the tenancy of the farm to Ben Burton in about 1932 who was able to buy the farm in 1947. This he passed to his eldest son Tony Burton in 1967 who still occupies the farm with his wife Rowena and their son Timothy. The farm has grown considerably since the

[149] BLARS L23/999/1

Burtons took over with Cainhoe Manor Farm being purchased in 1971 and other parcels of land being added as they became available. With the growth in field sizes and the consequent joining of the old fields only Home Field and Bean Field retain their original names.

The total area of the farm (not all in Silsoe) is about 1500 acres including woods and contains a dairy herd of some 300 pedigree Holstein plus young stock with some 1000 acres down to cereals and oil seed rape.

Fielden or Fielding

In the far south of Silsoe, beyond the formal parkland of Wrest and Buckle Grove and extending down to the Fann Brook, lies the area known as Fielden. The land would have been originally very wet, it being flat and between two streams, and the fields would have been created initially on drier ridges and then, by digging drains, extending the fields into wetter areas, until all the land had been reclaimed for farming.

A document of 1314[150] refers to the hamlet of "la Felde" as being adjacent to the highway although dwellings or crofts may have been scattered rather than centralised. Early documents were signed at La Felde, which implies a reasonably sized house where the parties to a document could meet, and this may have been the precursor to Fielden House, possibly where an old manor house was sited.

In the 13th century William Jacop and his wife Alice, (the family name is associated with Fielden from at least the early 1200's to 1439 as Jacob or Jecob) were granted a rood of land in the fields east of Sivelsho by Joan le Wodeward of Barton and in 1298 William Jacob is confirmed as renting some more land in le Estfeld for ½ d at Michaelmas [151]. In documents a few years later, he is named as William son of Walter Jacob de la Feld, thus demonstrating how people sometimes took the name of the place they lived in. Associated with the Jacobs from la Felde, were the Totegos of Eye just to the east.

There are at least 32 documents of the 14th century which relate to the land transactions at 'La Felde' which contain some 13 different surnames associated directly with la Felde. Several documents are also witnessed at La Felde indicating a building of reasonable comfort. However, land was slowly becoming concentrated in a small number of owners hands, and not exclusively the de Greys.

The name Millward or Mylward first appears in the hamlet with William Mulward of Feld later Wm. Melleward de la Feelde in 1393 and 1395, having land there. Then later in the 1400's more land is obtained by William and

---

[150] BLARS LJeayes 674
[151] BLARS LJeayes657& 658

Thomas Mylward of La Felde, not only in Silsoe but also in the adjacent parishes of 'Schytlyngdon' and Little Gravenhurst [152].

The Milward family prospered and Richard in his will of 1653, was able to leave both money to his children and grandchildren but also, as was normal then, his house other buildings and land to his eldest son, another Richard. His other son Henry, remained farming the family land at Fielden and in addition, in 1656 was also leasing from the Duke of Kent, a farmhouse in Silsoe, once occupied by Francis Raworth with all the outbuildings and associated land plus 40 acres in Fielden fields for a total of £34 per annum. [153] There is no confirmation that the farmhouse was at Fielden but Francis is said to be 'of Fielden' in baptism records around that time.

The eldest son Richard became the Rector of Great Braxted, near Bishops Stortford in Essex, and was appointed Canon of Windsor, so it was more practical for his brother to farm the land back in Silsoe. The Rev. Richard had married Mary Thomas, the daughter of Sir Anthony Thomas, and they produced a daughter called Mary. She was his only child and heir, and in his 1681 will he left his 'capital messuage' and lands at Fielden to her. A year later Mary married Sir Anthony Abdy whose family held large landholdings in the country, and so through this relationship much of Fielden passed to the Abdy family.

Charles Millward, the third son of Henry, in 1679 is described as of Fielden, a gentleman and single man and was then leasing land in Gravenhurst to increase his farming operations[154]. He was 28 years old and married Margaret Savin in Flitton 6 years later, afterwards having 9 children.

In 1712 an exchange of 11 acres took place between the Duke of Kent and Dame Mary Abdy presumably to rationalise the land holding to form larger plots, a mini inclosure[155]. However, an enormous argument blew up over the quality of land exchanged, with Lady Abdy feeling aggrieved that she had been short-changed. This lasted for many years and may only have been settled in the late 1780's.

Fielden House

The 1719 map of Fielden shows a sketch of a house marked "Mr Millward's" much where the existing Fielden House is now. This map also shows the strip system operating over the whole of Fielden fields with the bulk of the land split between Lady Abdy, Charles Millward and Richard Millward (presumably Charles' brother).

---

[152] BLARS LJeayes105
[153] BLARS L5/1110 & L26/1384
[154] BLARS L6/301
[155] BLARS L5/419

The schedule to another map of the same date which covers most of the remainder of Silsoe, shows that Charles Millward was paying the second highest rent of all the farmers to the Duke for land, £95 p.a., and was farming a total of 106½ acres most of which was in the various furlongs of Fielden. Richard Millward does not appear in the schedule and so the lands marked with his name must have belonged either to him or the Abdys rather than the Duke.

Charles was buried in 1725 and in his will he asked that his lands in Fielden, which he bought, should be sold and the proceeds divided amongst his seven children. While his eldest son Charles got only £50, the executor was another son Daniel and a 1739 conveyance[156] has him, a gentleman of Fielding as party to it. It may be that Daniel took over farming the rented land from his father, carrying on this work until his death in 1770, when he was described as a yeoman of Fielding.

In 1778 a 21 year lease was drawn up for the exchange of land at Fielden[157]. The deed involved Francis Hawkins, Yeoman of Fielden, relinquishing his tenancy on about 65 acres in Fielding north of The Portway owned by the Abdys, in exchange for him leasing 66 acres in Fielding belonging to the Earl of Hardwicke to the south of that road. The plan and schedules show that the land was all in strips. The map also shows several buildings to the east and south of the existing Fielden House, which then belonged to the Abdys, and which may have been from where Francis farmed. No buildings are shown adjacent to the Gravenhurst Road.

In 1813 Dame Mary and Sir William Abdy, were leasing a farm house, buildings and outhouses, and 150 acres of arable, meadow and pasture in closes in Silsoe, Higham and Pulloxhill for 14 years to John Whitbread Tuck, a farmer of Silsoe; with Francis Hawkins being described in the lease as a 'tenant at will', (presumably he was a sub-tenant). [158] That farm may be the buildings adjacent to Fielden House.

Francis Hawkins was still farming in 1822 (with Dame Mary Abdy living at Fielden House) when his rent was £360 p.a., but in that year, and apparently after unsuccessfully negotiating with John Edwards of Silsoe, the Abdy family sold Fielden House, farm and lands to a cheesemonger from Newgate Street in London by the name of Thomas Field, for £10,000[159] and Mr Tuck then surrendered his lease.

In 1841 Fielden House had William Dawson, a clergyman, living in it with his family and servants but at the next census in 1851 there are Thomas Flint Field aged 75, the purchaser of most of Fielden, his second wife, the 38 year old Rose and their two daughters, Rose and Amelia. He was at New Inn

[156] BLARS L5/328
[157] BLARS L5/420
[158] BLARS Z937/3/1
[159] BLARS Z937/3/3

Farm at the previous census, perhaps preparing Fielden House for his use, as his wife was in Rose Cottage at Hutton in Essex. [160]

In early 1861 Thomas was still there with his family but he had died by July 1861, and so in 1871 his wife Rosa is recorded alone with her two daughters, a cook and a housemaid - quite a modest household for those days.[161] She is still there aged 61 at the next census and still with her now middle-aged daughters; and also her grandson William is visiting from the West Indies.

Rosa Field the elder died in 1886, and was buried at Barton and there is no indication that her daughters wanted to participate directly in farming, as they are said to be living on their own means that year at Fielden House.

In 1901 only a coachman is in residence but the Misses Field are registered there until 1924, with Miss Amelia Field on her own in 1928, the year of her death.

Fielding New Farm

It seems that it was decided to build a new farmhouse and farm buildings in Fielden to be called Fielden Grounds, and presumably this was to enable the Wrest lands in Fielden to be farmed more centrally. In 1779 Phillip Earl of Hardwicke was leasing "a new-built farmhouse, cowhouse and barn to be erected called Fielden Grounds, Silsoe" to Enoch Hine and John Burley of Upper Gravenhurst. The lease was for 20 years with a rent of £136 per annum, and there was 145 acres. The conditions were that they could not sow hemp, flax or woad, they could plough up 15 acres in Middle Furlong, North Field, but must not take more than two successive corn crops. They also had to lay down again to grass before expiry of term with hay seeds and Dutch clover; and must employ dung to fertilise the ground. They also had to maintain the land, clearing away banks, mole-hills and small bushes that then encumbered the land.[162]

The 1814 uncompleted enclosure draft award map of the Fielding area shows the name of Charles Burley, John's son born in 1794, not only over most of the Fielding fields to the north of the road and east of Fielding House; but also superimposed over "New Fielding" Farm whose buildings now appear at the location of the present Fielden Farmhouse which lies alongside the Gravenhurst Road. However, the listing schedule suggests that its date is of around 1700, so there may be a point of dispute here.

In the 1841 census the tenant at New Fielden Farm is Fanny Haytred, a 45 year old farmer, with her daughter and two sons: but by 1851 Edward Danns Roberts from Orton near Peterborough, at only 27 years old, with his wife

---

[160] Thomas's second son by his first wife Ann, William Ventris Field, became a judge being created 1st Baron Field in 1890.)
[161] Memorial in Barton churchyard.
[162] BLARS L5/1146

and a young child and with assistance from a house maid, a cook, a nursemaid, a groom and a farm servant are living there. At that time he was the tenant for Mr Thomas Field of a farm said to be of 271 acres, and had the assistance of 19 farm labourers. Then, in the next census ten years later, his acreage had grown to 637 acres and he was farming all of Fielden and employed 22 men and 20 boys. His family had also grown as he had 5 children, a governess and other servants.

Edward is still there in 1871, and then farming slightly more land, 700 acres, and with 23 men and 14 boys to help him. His family now included 8 children aged from 19 to 1 years, but they are now down to three house servants. Some of his men did not have to travel to work so far by then, as in 1861 the farm cottages behind the farmhouse had been constructed, and his groom and a farm bailiff were installed there.

In 1880 Miss Rosa Field of Fielden House, aged 61, had decided to do some farming herself (her solicitor wished her the best of luck in the enterprise) and was farming 270 acres from Fielden House, and in 1881 was employing 7 men and 1 boy. This arrangement had resulted from Edward Roberts writing at the end of 1880 to Miss Field at Fielden House, to say that he wanted to give up the farm by the end of March 1881 which he occupied under the trustees of Thomas Flint Field[163]. Edward, now aged 56, was tenanting only 404 acres from Fielding Farm with the help of only 16 men and 5 boys.

Negotiating on the details of Roberts leaving took some time with both Rosa Field and Danns Roberts employing surveyors and valuations of items such as the hay remaining, and the need to release part of New Inn Farm to John Field being included. One letter also gives an insight into the crops then popular, with beans being particularly mentioned.

Edward eventually moved to Stevenage and it seems that Henry Brown came down from Turvey to take over the farm with his family. Sadly Henry died early in 1891 aged 59, so that in March 1891 his widow Sarah is continuing as a farmer, with the assistance of a 34 year old foreman, Albert Paine, also from Turvey, who is living in. No indication of the area she was farming is given.

Another census, brought another tenant, Leonard Bottoms, who seems previously to have been a bricklayer and then a builder in Battersea, and was presumably at Fielden Farm at least by 1898, as his first wife died that year. In 1901 he is recorded as a farmer with his own and his second wife's children, totalling ten in number. However, he passed away in 1902 aged 59 and although his wife, Anne Bethia, was farming there in 1903, the farm was in 1918 tenanted by Mr Edward Bosworth[164]. He is recorded as being instructed to break up 12 acres of land in 1918 also, as part of the drive for

---

[163] BLARS SFM3/154
[164] BLARS L23/374

more food in the war[165]. The next record for the farm is of him in 1918 rejecting an opportunity to purchase Fielding Farm at the Wrest Park break-up sale.

With Edward declining to purchase it was sold to Benjamin Arthur, Francis Alfred and Stephen Charles Edward Brown (Messrs Brown Bros.), timber merchants of Essex, for £6,500 in May 1918. The map relating to the sale shows the land comprising virtually all the fields between Buckle Grove and the Park down to the Gravenhurst Road, with fields surrounding the Farmhouse and running down to the Fenn Brook. The total area was 291 acres including the cottages, farmhouse and homestead. Of this, some 161 acres were in Silsoe parish.

After the farm was bought by Brown Bros., it seems that it was quickly sold on at an auction held by Brown and Merry at the Lion Hotel in Bedford in August 1919 after they had taken out the best timber[166]. It was Lot 1 and in the auction document there is a detailed description of the farmhouse and buildings where it is said to include a "farm house with seven bedrooms, cellars and a dairy plus a model homestead, 2 cottages, together with 291 acres in Silsoe and Higham Gobion plus 11 cottages at West End" bundled in to the lot.[167]

Throughout the sale and de-forestation Edward Bosworth stayed on as tenant, appearing in the Kelly Directories up to 1931, but in 1940 Anthony Cuthbert Catlin is listed as being there.

Like many other old farmhouses in the parish, it is now a private residence with the model farm buildings also having been converted into residences; the land is now farmed from outside the village.

New Inn Farm

From its name it would appear that the building was at one time an inn, but it is not certain for how long this use lasted. Its location on the A6 near the Gravenhurst Road and near a bridge over the stream, which in the past was narrow and thus slowed down travellers. This location appears good for an inn, but it was away from the village centre, and it may only have been an ale house catering for passing trade. Eventually the appendage 'Farm' was added, but it is possible with the owner in the early 1700s having a brewery in Hitchin, that it continued to serve beer to travellers.

A map of 1715 has a miniature sketch of the building with 'The New Inn' inscribed beside it, so even at that date it appears still to have been more an inn that a farm[168].

---

[165] BLARS WW1/ac/re1/2
[166] BLARS BML10/64/1
[167] BLARS MBL 10/64/11
[168] BLARS L5/286v

Plate 11/9 - The New Inn 1715

A land exchange between the Duke of Kent and Charles Nicholls of 1718 shows that Charles Nicholls, a gentleman of Hitchin, was the owner of New Inn and in addition, a marriage settlement of 1773 between John Field and Frances Flint relates that New Inn was purchased by Charles Nicholls of Hitchin, John Field's grand uncle[169]. Charles Nicholls specialised in lending money to people who had over extended themselves and then foreclosing, taking the land that had been put up as security, when the owner could not pay up. This practice nearly cost him his life in 1709 when John Cripps, to whom he had loaned £2,000, chased him to Bendish (just east of Luton) and threatened to kill him.

It seems possible then that New Inn became his as a result of this legal, but morally corrupt practice. When he died in 1746, the property passed through Thomas Field, Charles Nicholls's nephew, to John Field who eventually transferred it to his son in a marriage settlement. The settlement associated 40 acres with New Inn and this may have then been the size of the farm.

When John Field the elder died in 1759, his will left New Inn farmhouse and his lands to his son John, even though his eldest son Carolus Nicholls Field was still alive. The will, apart from saying that Thomas Day was the tenant of the farm, does not give any indication that the building was being used as an inn.

An account book[170] relating to tenants of the Field family land dated 1749-1759, gives the rent for the farm at New Inn at £41 p.a., and also notes that Thomas Day received a part-payment of £100 from the owner, John Field, for crops at New Inn Farm. On the back of another document[171] there is a note dated 15 Mar 1817, which says that Thomas Day, now 64 yrs of age, "remembers his great uncle Thomas Day occupying New Inn Farm in the parish of Silsoe and Higham also Closes called Barton Pightle and Bray Closes .... it was 50 yrs since he knew his uncle in person who was succeeded by John Hill; Bray Closes always went with New Inn Farm." (Bray Close was a field of 17 acres between Kitchen Field and Great Road Field.)

---

[169] BLARS Z937/2/1 & Z937/2/4
[170] BLARS Z937/1/5
[171] BLARS Z937/1/6

Thomas was still paying rent in 1763[172] to John Field of Hitchin and another document, an Agreement and Memorandum by Thomas Day dated 1762[173] records that "Carolus Nicholls Field of Hitchin let to him Bray Close in Pulloxhill and Flitton for 3 years for £13 pa plus taxes except land tax.", timber excepted. Thomas Day promised to pay Carolus Nicholls Field £2 each half year, the witness was Sarah Field, Carolus's mother.

As mentioned before, in 1773[174] John Field of Hitchin married Frances Flint, the youngest daughter of Thomas Flint, a yeoman of Higham Gobion. Thomas Flint gave John Field £500 through his executors, with more to come on his decease. In addition the rents from a great deal of property was to go to the happy couple viz. This included New Inn with all houses, outhouses, barns, etc. in Flitton cum Silveshoe, and several other closes containing together about 49 acres of pasture including a pasture called Cherry Orchard recently enclosed in Kitchin Field between Kitchen End Road and Southill Fore Brook.

This document also says that the tenant is now John Hill who was paying £58 per annum, and who had recently taken over from Thomas Day.

It is not known when John Hill left, but certainly by 1809 it seems that John Field had moved in, as there are letters to him at that address throughout the year, regarding title to the land so that he could take out a loan on the property of £1,000 and £300.[175] He was also ensuring his rights that year, claiming right of common for horses, cows and sheep in Town Close, Town Orchard, North Field, Redding Corner Field, Kitchen End Field, part of Greenfield Green, and also on all the waste land in Pulloxhill parish.

A few years later, in 1815, an exchange of land took place with Amabel, Countess de Grey, [176] J Malden of Biggleswade wrote to Mr Field saying:

> "the small grass field nearest Silsoe and the wood is exchanged
> for ... the large grass field against the bridge which is much better
> land and you gaine one acre of land cloas to your house .... it will
> make your farm compleat on that side of the road and you will be
> out of the reach of the [hares?] and rabets which devowers a great
> deal of the wood cloase."

In the same year[177] John and Frances Field confirmed that New Inn and the associated property were to go to their eldest son, Thomas Flint Field viz. "40 ac of closes of pasture, the 1ac 1r pightle exchanged with Countess

---

[172] BLARS Z937/1/10
[173] BLARS Z937/2/2
[174] BLARS Z937/2/4
[175] BLARS Z93731/2-4 & Z937/4/32-33
[176] BLARS Z937/2/6
[177] BLARS Z937/2/7

Dowager of Kent, decd, and the adjoining 2 closes, formerly 2 pightles, in Flitton, all formerly occupied by Thomas Day, then John Hill, and now and for many years past by John Field, a close called Cherry Orchard containing 5ac in Kitchen Field, 4ac of which in Pulloxhill and 1ac in Flitton plus all tithes from the 4 acres."

In June 1819 Frances Field of New Inn gave up her interests in her property to her son Thomas Flint Field, a cheesemonger of Newgate Street, London in exchange for an annuity of £200 per annum[178]. He then in December [179] leased New Inn plus the outhouses etc. and around 100 acres of land to John Edwards the younger, a gentleman of Silsoe, at an annual rent of £200, presumably using the money to pay for the annuity. As an indication of the value then placed on good meadow land, the lease required that John Edwards would have to pay £50 for every acre of meadow or pasture which was ploughed, dug, broken up or converted into tillage during his tenure. Fairly obviously, but no doubt to ensure that the farm did not deteriorate, he had to store in barns or set up in stacks, all corn, grain and hay for the use as fodder for beasts and cattle, and manure had to be spread where most needed. The rental also said that New Inn had been lately occupied by John Field, after him his widow, but at the time of the lease it was divided into several dwelling houses occupied by labourers, as undertenants of John Edwards.

The 1831 census still has Frances Field living in the village, but Thomas is presumably still selling cheeses in London.

In 1841 William Arnold aged 40 was at New Inn Farm, a farmer and widower. He was originally from Clophill and had his five children William 15, John 14, Thomas 7, Mary 5 and Susan 2 living with him. There were also three female servants all aged around 25 probably looking after the children, as well as cleaning the house and working in the kitchen. In addition, a living-in farm labourer, Charles Waller was with them. Sadly William was to lose all his sons, William and John in 1850 and Thomas in 1853, and his daughter Mary also died in 1861.

Also living at the same address was Thomas (Flint) Field aged 60, described as a farmer although in addition he was the owner at that time. He was perhaps using his cheese making skills, as other documents refer to a dairy at the house.

William Arnold was still there in 1851 and the census gives the area he was farming 256 acres. This probably comprised the land previously associated with New Inn, plus other land in Pulloxhill owned by Thomas Flint. At that time he employed 9 outdoor labourers and 2 indoor. An 1856 directory has him still there, but by 1861 William Bennett, a commercial traveller in books, was living there, with his wife and ten children. By comparing the land areas

---

[178] BLARS Z937/2/8
[179] BLARS Z937/2/10

recorded in the censuses of 1851 and 1861 it seems that when Mr Bennett took over the tenancy, the land and farming operation was transferred to Fielden House or Farm. At the same time Thomas Field also moved to Fielden.

Strangely, a directory of 1862 [180] describes William Bennet as an innkeeper at the New Inn. This may have been an error based on the name of the house, but it may also indicate that there had been a continuation or resumption of ale selling there.

Mr Thomas Flint Field of Fielden House, a "Land proprietor" died in June 1861 leaving his land, which included New Inn, Fielden Farm and other property nearby, in trust to his second wife Rose Eliza Field the elder, and after her death to his daughters, Rose Eliza Field the younger and Amelia Field.[181].

At that time the land with New Inn Farm was said to be about 126 acres which included "Upper Orchard 2ac, Back Orchards and meadow 12ac, Horel [?] Close 9ac 2r, Home Close 10ac, Bones Close 13ac, Todlake Pightle 2ac 2r, Todlake Close 8ac 2r, Turnpike Closes 17ac 2r, Sluice Hill 9ac, Old House Field 9ac, Bray Field 17ac and Fielden Ground 16ac," all in the parishes of Silsoe, Pulloxhill and Higham Gobion.

By 1871 and still there in 1876 is James Roberts, aged 55, originally from Hockliffe and Chalgrave, a cattle dealer and farmer with his wife and son and a servant, Mary Field. It is possible that he was related to Edward Danns Roberts farming at Fielden in the same period, but as the latter came from Haddon near Peterborough, it must have been a distant relationship.

James Roberts had moved by 1881 to Maulden and the census of that year recorded Charles Shaw originally from Gibraltar Farm, Toddington, a farm bailiff, aged 23, at New Inn with his 38 year old sister. He was probably bailiff for Fielding Farm under Edward Danns Roberts. He was only there for a few years as an 1890 Directory has John Kingsley, another cattle dealer, at "New Ends" (sic) farm but in 1891 only his widow, Lizzie Kingsley plus 3 children, a servant, a nurse and a footman were there.

They also eventually moved on and by 1898 the 31 year old George William Cook, a farmer from Barton with his stepdaughter, Gladys Kingsley, and a housekeeper were installed at New Inn Farm, where he remained until at least 1903[182].

Andrew Harris was there in 1910 while in 1931 the Kelly's Directory records William Saville, a farmer, at New Inn Farm.

---

[180] *Directory of Bedfordshire and Huntingdonshire*, pub Edward Cassey & Co, 1862
[181] BLARS Z937/31/19 & Z937/32/7
[182] *Kelly's 1903 Directory of Beds Hunts & Northants*

New Inn is now a private residence with some of the old farm buildings having been converted into housing and further development taking place in the grounds.

Upbury (Manor of Beeches and Upbury)

Though this farmstead was just outside of the parish, the parish boundary ran and still runs just around the north and east of the farmstead area, bisecting several fields that were farmed by the Manor. Also, one of the main accesses to it was from the north, from the track that still runs south west from the Barton Road.

There are now no buildings on the site, the only indications of the previous occupation being some major earthworks with small paddocks enclosed by hedges, the remnants of ponds and ditches and some high and wide overgrown hedges.

The name Upbiri is found in a 1205 'fine' between Henry de Nordwde and Roger de Bray, probably the first reference to the place, and then in 1298 Adam, the son of Isolda de Hupbury appears. [183]

Upbury Manor, which may have been originally part of Pulloxhill Manor, first appears by name at the time of the Dissolution when it was probably taken from Dunstable Priory and granted to Simon Fitz[184]. The name 'Beeches' is first associated with Upbury (as a manorial name) in 1552, and it seems probable that the name of Beeches was retained in the common field of Silsoe, between the Red Field and Upbury called Beach or Beech Field. The Upbury Farm map of 1768[185] also shows enclosed fields called Further and Hither Beech Fields, to the north west of the homestead.

An extensive and detailed 1519 terrier[186] of "Symon Fitz of certain lands and tenements in Pulloxhill called Upbury" exists which describes a large, (for those days), holding of 154 acres of which part, including 'Bechefield' and other strips lie in what is now Silsoe.

The land passed down to George Fitz who was said to be the owner of Upbury and Beeches and who died there on 15 August 1608. It then seems that Sir William Briers took over the manor. He prospered, and there was even a gatehouse to Upbury perhaps on the lane leading from the A6, and in 1641 purchased from Thomas and Henry Hill for a little more than £500, a capital messuage with approximately 65 acres in the fields of Silsoe.

Sir Henry died in 1653, presumably without sons and in his will, administered by his widow Arabella, the latter purchase passed to William Wheeler. It was

---

[183] BHRS vii p 137, LJeayes658
[184] VCH Pulloxhill
[185] BLARS L33/286I
[186] BLARS L26/804

then transferred to Stephen Shepherd as part of a marriage settlement and was eventually bought by Amabella, the Countess Dowager of Kent in 1674.

As to the manor and its lands, this seems to have been the property of Thomas Cheyne of Luton, gent. and James Smith of London, gent. in 1676 when it was conveyed to John Coppin Esq. of Luton and London. At that time the farm, which had an area of about 220 acres, had been sub-divided, with Thomas Cheyne and James Smith farming part and Thomas Phillip the remainder. Thomas Rawlins apparently occupied the manor house and was there in 1682[187].

The new owner built a cottage adjacent to the manor house, possibly for a bailiff, as Thomas Day was occupying it in 1699, but at the end of that year he sold the cottage and lands for £3,389-3-1d to William Boteler of Biddenham[188]. He seems to have sold the manor itself to Edward Stracey, a scrivener of London earlier that year. Then, although no deed has been found, it seems that the manor then passed into the hands of the de Greys of Wrest in the early 18th century, after which it remained with them for around 200 years.

In 1718 there is a field in Great Road Field of about 7-8 acres marked 'Mr Allen of Upbury'. In 1702 John Allen junior was leasing 83 acres from the duke, and his father, John Allen, the Wrest Park steward, is leasing another 52 acres. As his father was probably nearer to Wrest in order for him to carry out his duties there, it seems likely that John junior is the Mr Allen at Upbury

A terrier of the lands of Upbury of 1750[189] gives a total area of around 160 acres of which probably half was in Silsoe. Then in 1768 a map was prepared of the farm which shows the buildings, the many moats and the fields attached to the manor house.

---

[187] BLARS L4/306
[188] BLARS L12/2 & 5
[189] BLARS L26/807

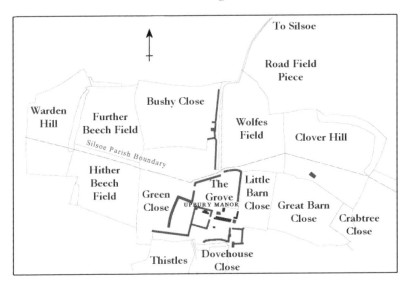

To Silsoe

Road Field
Piece

Bushy Close

Warden
Hill

Further
Beech Field

Wolfes
Field

Clover Hill

Silsoe Parish Boundary

Hither
Beech
Field

Green
Close

The
Grove
UPBURY MANOR

Little
Barn
Close

Great Barn
Close

Crabtree
Close

Thistles

Dovehouse
Close

Plate 11/10 - Upbury Manor Farm and Lands 1768[190]

Early in the next century when the enclosures were taking place, from 1814-1826, the maps still show the farmstead, perhaps even bigger than in 1768 with the name Upbury Farm over it, and the name on the fields is George Whitbread, who was presumably farming from there.[191] In 1821 Mary Lowings, the blacksmith from Silsoe, billed the Wrest estate for ironwork carried out there. There is an advertisement in *The Times* of 24th September 1824 asking those who have a claim on the estate of George Whitbread, late of Upbury Farm, to contact his son.

However, some time after then the old, probably mediaeval, buildings were demolished and the farm split up. Some of its land was being farmed from West End Farm in 1845 and the remainder from other farmsteads such as Gagmansbury, as many of the farm fields were managed from there at that time.

Taber or Tabert Farm

This farm is directly mentioned only four times in Wrest Park documents. Two documents exist of the same date in 1574[192] relating to the sale from "Margery, the widow of Francis Pigott Esq. of Lower Gravenhurst, to Edward Hill, yeoman of Sylsoe, of a messuage called Taberte in Silsoe with two closes adjoining the backside, one called Stocking", plus other, unspecified land for £30. The farm had been lately occupied by James Finche.

[190] BLARS L33/32a&b
[191] BLARS L33/18b Pulloxhill
[192] BLARS LJeayes808 & L5/1092

Sometime between that date and 1615/16[193] the farm became the property of the Earl of Kent as there is a Counterpart lease for 20 yrs at £45 per annum dated 5 February of that year[194] for "… all that messuage tent or ferme house in Silveshoo aforesaid in Beds anntyentlye called or known by the name of Tabert wherein the said William Burden now dwells together with all the lands barnes stables edyfyces buildings yards etc etc with lands in Silsoe and Fielden …" The rent was £20.3.0. per annum and the agreement was between Charles, Earl of Kent, Lord of Hastings, Waysford and Ruthin and William Burden of Silsoe, yeoman. Previously William had been a tenant of the former Earl of Kent, Henry, brother of Charles. As seems common for those times, that the timber was retained by the Earl but he provided William with 'great timber' to carry out major repairs. William was allowed to lop willows but could not sub-let.

Then in 1627[195], in the reign of Charles I, Henry, 8th Earl of Kent and his wife Elizabeth " do lett all that messuage tent or farm house in Syvelshoo antiently called or known by the name of Tabort " for 21 years to William Gamble of Sylveshoo for £40, annual rent of £20, with a requirement that the lessee shall

> "….from time to time as often as the said Henry Earl of Kent shall keep his court or courts in the manor of Silveshoo sufficient warning being given provide and beare the charge of dinner for the Steward and not more than 6 persons not more than once a year"

This arrangement was continued as in 1655[196] Amabella, Countess Dowager of Kent, entered into a 6 year lease with William Gamble and John Greene at an annual rent of £40 and 10 doz. young pigeons. The pigeons and dovehouse are mentioned several times so must have been of an economic significance. The lease is for a farm in Silsoe anciently called the Taber occupied by William with lands in Silsoe and Fielden and lately occupied by William Burden.

An additional requirement, which implies a farm house of some size, was that he had to provide accommodation at not more than once a year for the Manor Court when the Countess summoned it. He also was to be given sufficient warning and had to provide a 'competent dinner' of wholesome meat for the steward and six of his company.

The amount of rent is quite high for that century, about the same as was being paid for West End Farm, and as 60 years later the only other farm with

---

[193] Until 1752 the year started on 25th March, the feast of the Annunciation, rather than 1st January. Our current system, the Gregorian calendar established in catholic countries in 1582 by Pope Gregory, was introduced in 1752 so as to agree with what had been in use throughout most of Europe (and Scotland) for some 150 years.
[194] BLARS L5/1098
[195] BLARS LJeayes819
[196] BLARS L5/1108

a same rent comparable with West End Farm is the one situated north of the Church, where The Rowans was built.

It is suggested in the Manors Chapter that the Manor or Norwood alias Silsoe, was situated to the north of the church just across the Wrest Park drive. There is a rental showing William Gamble and John Greene paying £30 10s to the Earl of Kent's estate as annual rental for "the manor or farm house in Silvesho called Norwoode with divers pasture and meadowes in Silveshoo and Pulloxhill" in 1658[197] . These are the same two renting Taber Farm a few years earlier in 1655 and it is suggested that the site of the 'Taber' farm is the same location as the Manor of Norwood alias Silsoe, under the Rowans development.

Blanes, Rowarths and Sellars Farms

These farm names appear primarily on the map associated with the 1718 survey of the Wrest Park estate and the accompanying schedule,[198] and it seems that the names of these farms appear to originate from their tenants or previous owners, as they can be found in the parish records.

There was a Blane family in the parish in the 18th century when Thomas and Elizabeth Blane were having children between 1707 and 1716. Sadly of the 7 children baptised, 4 at least were buried within one year with apparently only Isabel, Judith and Mary surviving. No other records of the family appear in the parish.

Similarly Francis Rayworth and his family are found to be in the village from 1623 to 1721, and John and Joan Sellars around 1679.

Early references are uncommon but there is a 6 year lease of 1656[199] which relates to a messuage and farm in Silsoe with 40 acres in Fielden all previously in the tenancy of Francis Raworth and now in the occupation of Henry Millward; and a 1696 reference to a 1 ac plot in Waterslade "late of Raworth's farm probably adjacent to the Ampthill Road on which Thomas Burrows the carpenter will build a good and sufficient cottage". One document implies that Francis Raworth is occupying part of the Flitton parsonage so he may not have been resident in Silsoe[200] but merely leased land there.

Francis was buried in 1657 with his widow continuing to pay rental for the parsonage in 1658, and she was buried as of Silsoe, in 1665.

The 1718 schedule has for one farm the title "John Allen late Blanes Farm" with a note that say "Part of late Blaynes Farm and late Sellars etc. " and also

[197] BLARS L26/1384
[198] BLARS L26/292
[199] BLARS L5/1110
[200] BLARS L5/1082

"Some parcels belonging to late Rowarths farm cannot be distinguished" and within the list making up the 217ac total, several plots marked "late Sellars". (Well, if they couldn't decide at that time what the farm included then it is impossible to try now!)

A further document of the same year associates many fields and strips with the three farms, but there is no indication of where the farm houses were.[201]

It seems likely that the three farms were all amalgamated in the early 1700's with the farm situated opposite the Church (The Taber) in the area now occupied by The Rowans housing development.

Warren or Simpsonshill or Firs Farm

This farm first appears as a separate entity in the schedule to the sale of Newbury Manor to the de Grey family in 1775, when it was known as Warren Farm[202]. The Warren was a large area of about 34 acres in 1757, 50 acres in 1658, and was the area occupied by what is now called Simpsonhill Plantation and which now has a sand quarry in it. The name signifies that at some time in the past it was used to provide rabbits as meat for Newbury Farm.[203] In 1525 it was 40 acres and was called The Hethe, and was probably open terrain with scattered gorse bushes.

In 1658 it was occupied by Henry Cells and was called the Warren or Cunnigree. Henry was probably the warrener. The Flitton registers for the 1650's have several entries of Henry and Ann Gellis's children being baptised and we know that it is the same person as the register says of Henry, that he is "warrinour to Mr Daniels". The Burial Register records Henry Gellys, "warriner by Clophill Bridge", being buried in 1682.

The farmhouse is shown on the 1757 map at the western corner of the plantation, and was probably located where the warrener's cottage originally was. There is good access along what was once an important route from Clophill to Flitton and it was well supplied with water from the River Flit, a few metres to the north. In 1775 the farm comprised of the Warren at about 34½ acres together with 37 acres of pasture and meadow, and about 1½ acres of 'waste' alongside the A6. The farm was then tenanted by a Mr Cook who paid £32 a year rent.

The inclusion of the fields with 'sheep' in their name suggests that those animals were the main product of the farm at that time.

At least from 1831 until the 1890's, two generations of Richard Simpson, father and son leased the farm from Wrest Park estate as a market garden.

---

[201] BLARS L26/292

[202] BLARS L5/411

[203] The warren for Wrest Park was on the same hill but further to the east and was associated with the Warren Farm now just in Clophill parish.

The farmhouse must have been spacious – or more likely very crowded – as in 1841 Richard was there with his wife Ann and their 9 children. Ten years later he is a market gardener, no land area is given but it was probably the same area he was farming in 1861 and 1871 - 17 to 18 acres.

Richard's children were used as labourers on the farm whilst they were growing up, as it is recorded in 1851 that five of his sons aged from 24 to 11 were garden labourers; and in 1861 Richard and Henry his unmarried elder sons of 34 and 30, were also listed as garden labourers. By 1871, when they had left, he had only two men to help him and in 1881, 9 years after Richard the elder had died, his son Richard had two labourers living in, to help with the work.

From 1881 onwards the farm was called Simpsonhill after the Simpson family, and this name was retained until at least 1901 where it is listed as 'Simpsons Hill' in the census, and by which time William Billington aged 23 from Silsoe, had taken over the smallholding, as the younger Richard had died in 1899.

Being right on the outskirts of Silsoe and with the main access to the farm being off the A6, (near the present garage), it seems likely that the Simpsons would have based their lives in the more accessible village of Clophill.

In the Wrest Estate break-up in 1918 Ernest Edward Collip Williamson, who was probably living there at the time, bought the farmhouse now known as Firs Farm, together with 38ac 1r 4p of fields on the south side of Simpsonhill Plantation and alongside the Flit for £1,100.[204]

Eventually the farm came into the ownership of the Shephard family and Mr Shephard, who is still there, was at the farm after the war in the late 1940's when it was a market garden, and produce was driven from there directly to London.

England's Farm

The first mention of this as a farm is in a deed of 1666/7[205] when it was described as a parcel of land of about 40 acres and was the large fields immediately south of West End Road. It was also one of three farms included in the land holdings of Newbury Manor.

In the sale of Newbury to Wrest in 1775 it had evidently become a farm in its own right and had as its base a "messuage, tenement or farm house with barns stables outhouse and building belonging commonly called England's" in the occupation of Robert Finney with an annual rent of £44 6s. 8d. However, the farmhouse was in Wardhedges, not in West End Road.

---

[204] BLARS L23/260
[205] BLARS L5/387

At that time the land holding for the farm included "Spring pond pightle, 3r 28p *(near Newbury Manor)*, Hither England, 10a 2r 19p, Middle England 9a 1r 4p, Buckle Grove mead, 4a 2r 24p, Buckle Grove close, 7a 0r 4p; Thrift close and wood, 6a 1r 34p & 9ac 1r 35p and Buckle Grove 15ac 2r 21p".

After the sale to the Wrest estate the farm holdings were probably broken up with the land allotted to other farms owned by Wrest. However, the farm or rather the main field area was remembered for many years in the name of the principal room in Silsoe College, England's Hall.

Village Farm, Silsoe

This farm, according to the plans attached to the sale of the unit in 1918, was based at what is now 43 High Street and which now has the name of 'The Old Village Farm'. The farmhouse and approximately 50 acres was then sold for £1,600 to Mr F W Stanley. [206] The bulk of the land was south of the village including the Upbury Manor site, so the farm may well have been created - or extended - when Upbury Manor farm was broken up. Also included in the farm were two fields in the village behind the farmhouse extending across Vicarage and Fir Tree Roads to the old stone quarry. In addition to the purchase Mr Stanley leased a further 9 acres on the east side of the A6.

It seems likely that throughout most of the 19th century the farm was farmed by the Barnard family as maps of the 1820's drawn up for an enclosure, show fields both at Upbury and behind the farmhouse which extend up to the old quarry marked 'Mr Wm. Barnard'. Then in 1856 the same fields, with the deduction of the land for the Vicarage, have Robert and James Barnard written on them[207]- William having died by then.

The continuing tenancy of the Barnards is confirmed by the 19th century censuses. In 1851 Robert Barnard aged 82, is a harness maker and farmer of 30 acres, employing one man and one boy. His nephew James aged 50, harness maker, and his wife Mary are at the same address. Ten years earlier Robert had been there operating as a harness maker, with James and Mary also listed.

James is shown to be farming 28 acres using two men and two boys in the 1861 census but died soon after then in May. At the census his wife was there together with an uncle, Robert, who was to live for another four years. Robert's tombstone says, possibly in error as there is a Robert Barnard baptised in Flitton in 1769:

> "In memory of Robert Barnard of this parish bachelor who died in the same house wherein he was born more than one hundred and one years. He died December 1-? 1865"

---

[206] BLARS L23/383
[207] BLARS L33/12b Plan & Schedule

By 1871 and continuing through to 1881, Mary Barnard is farming the same acreage and she was employing 2-3 men to run it. She has her niece, Mary Doggett, living with her who is presumably carrying out the household work, while Mary Barnard farmed.

The old farm house itself is listed Grade II and in the description it says that it is of 17th century origin, with a 19th century re-working. It may thus have been inconvenient as in 1891 Mary Barnard had moved into the house, now called Barnards Cottage, built on the site of an old house between Village Farm and Old Woodstock Cottage (No 39), and William Wilde of Hammersmith and his wife Hephzibah have taken over the farm. Hephzibah was born in Silsoe, a daughter of James Pedder from West End Road, and they perhaps met through working at Wrest Park, as William had been a butler there in 1871.

Perhaps his inexperience overcame him as by 1901, George Harris aged 40 from Southill and his wife Emily 27, from Clophill, plus their two young children were installed and running the farm.

As mentioned before, in 1918 the farm was sold to Mr F W Stanley who remained there at least until 1920, then, some time later in the 20th century, the land was sold off and the farmhouse became a residence.

Road Farm, Silsoe

This small farm was created from land behind the Lord Nelson public house in the early 19th century - probably from an initial smallholding. Maps of that day show a building in approximately the same location as the current farm house; and in the 1841 census Thomas Ambridge, a thatcher, and originally from Higham Gobion, is living there with his wife and four children. Twenty years later he is still there, still a thatcher but now an occupier of 7 acres of land. Two of his children, John and Thomas are rake makers.

Ten years on again and in 1871 aged 65, he is a rake maker and farmer employing one man and a boy. His wife Jemima had died aged 64 in June 1870 but his son and daughter are still there to give him a hand. There is a stone plaque dated 1877 under the eaves on the eastern side of the old part of the existing farm house with the intertwined initials 'TA'. No doubt Thomas was able to have the new building constructed for himself but the date also reflects his death in November, and may be a memorial stone rather than a date for the house.

His son James and daughter Charlotte Ambridge took over, and in 1881 they were farming 9 acres employing two labourers and one boy. James was there farming as a market gardener in 1901, but with Ernest Ambridge listed as a 'farmer's son'.

Sadly Ernest died in the Great War in September 1918, and when Wrest Park sold up in 1918, Road Farm and about 16 acres was sold to John Emerton for £700 who remained there until at least 1928. The land at that time included a field to the north west of the house plus Beech Wood Close, off the Upbury turn.

The land attached to the farm was gradually sold off during the second half of the 20th century and the old farmhouse then became a private residence, like many other old Silsoe farms.

The George Inn

Through to the early part of the 20th century, the innkeepers of the George held a considerable amount of land. Initially when the George was at its original location the land was needed to put the drover's animals in, but after that it seems that the new innkeepers preferred to continue to do some farming, and some even increased their holding. The inn had been owned by Wrest Park before it moved to its present site in about 1838, and the land attached to it was presumable rented from the estate together with the inn.

In 1851 Benjamin Carter was farming 130 acres and employed eight men and three boys on the farming operation. This was the fifth largest holding in the parish after Wrest Park, Newbury Farm, West End Farm, Fielden and New Inn. Ten years later James Beaumont was farming a reduced holding of 100ac and only employed four men and two boys.

Then in 1871, with another change of ownership to Charles Browning the farm had further reduced to 91 acres, although the labour needed was now four men and three boys. By 1881 Charles had increased his farming operation having now 121 acres and five men and one boy for labour. About 1891 Charles moved over to West End to take over that farm from Richard Eve when he died. The replacement innkeeper, John Palmer Grey, is not described as a farmer until the 1901 census where he is a publican and farmer.

Charlotte Anderson had been the tenant since about 1914[208] and in 1918 she bought the hotel from Wrest Park together with 29½ acres of arable land and 29 acres of pasture for £3,100.

8, West End Road

In 1719 Frances German was living at what is now No 8 West End Road, and farming both the field alongside Vicarage Road up to the top, plus another 5 acres in the common fields around the village. This farm probably continued, although no details have been found, but in 1841 (and probably in 1831 as William Hubutt) it seems that William Herbett, a butcher, lived there

---

[208] 1914 *Kelly's Directory* has Grey still there.

with his wife and two servants, and it would seem that he was farming several acres.

By 1851 Charles Brightman aged 42 from Maulden, had moved there from another part of the village with his wife, seven children and a labourer. He was a butcher but was also farming 24 acres employing 2 men, his eldest son Leonard aged 19, was also a butcher.

Five years later in 1856 a map and schedule of Wrest Park tenants shows that part of his land extended up from (and including) the house as far as the Almshouses, with another 1½ acres between Vicarage Road and the High Street, abutting West End Road[209].This totals only about 2½ acres so he must have rented other lands in the village.

In 1861 and 1862[210] Charles was still there but his holding had grown to 84 acres, and he was employing 3 men and one boy. He and his son were still butchers with three of his daughters working as dressmakers. By 1871, with Charles now aged 62, he had slightly reduced his land to 70 acres, but still employed 3 men and one boy. His assistant butcher is now Alfred Snoxell and he also has John Olney, a brewer, as a servant. He is missing from an 1876 Directory and by 1881 he is farming in Pulloxhill. In that year the house was then occupied by the wheelwright Robert Upton, who seems to have taken over by 1876 by which time the farming operation had apparently ceased from that address.

Dairy Farm, 56 High Street

Back in 1851 Charles Giddings, 41, together with his wife and four little Giddings, was farming 12 acres from an unknown address in the High Street and was employing one man. He was a wheelwright and farmer. Luckily his address can be fixed a few years later as on an 1856 schedule, the map has his name at No 56, Dairy Farm.

Ten years earlier his father Frederick Giddings had been a wheelwright there, with Charles also practising that trade. Even in 1831 the name was common in the parish and although there is no indication of their trades at that time, the name and the associated trade of wheelwright can be traced back at least to 1706 when Thomas Giddings of Silsoe, wheelwright, is referred to in a marriage settlement,[211] when he may have been in the same house.

Charles Giddings is still at No 56 in 1861 then aged 57, a wheelwright and farmer of 12 acres employing one man, but he died in 1868 aged 59. In the 1851 census he had a ten year old son William, who in 1861 was an apprentice carpenter at Upton, Bucks and later he appeared in London; the wheelwright connection had been broken.

---

[209] BLARS L33/12b
[210] 1862 *Kelly's Directory for Bedfordshire*
[211] BLARS L5/911-912

Thus in 1871 a new family is in residence, it is led by John White, 43, a dealer and farmer of 30 acres employing 3 men and 2 boys, who previously had been in West End Road working as a corn jobber. Ten years later he had expanded his business to be a cattle dealer and farmer of 70 acres employing 3 men and 3 boys. He remained there until at least 1903 when the Kelly's Directory has him as a farmer - he would have been 78 years old that year. He lived on until 1921 dying in March that year, aged 95[212].

It seems that John White had absorbed into his farm the land mentioned earlier run by the Payne family as the 1910 valuation shows Alfred White, presumably John's son, at the house and also having land to the north of The George, land between Vicarage Road and No 3 High Street plus more off the Barton Road.

The schedule of land being bought by J G Murray on the east of the High Street, which was included with his much larger purchase of Wrest Park, shows Christopher A N Harris as the tenant at the Dairy Farm but with no land around it tenanted by him. However, he did in 1918 pay £1,400 for approximately 64 acres of land, the bulk of which was to the south of the village and east of the A6, plus a field near Buckle Grove which gave him a useful holding to operate. It also included a strip of land where the school now is, north of the George Inn which included buildings and yards. [213]

In the ensuing years the farm land was mainly used for housing development and the farm house is now a residence.

10/12 High Street

For many years in the nineteenth and on into the twentieth century the Olney family operated a butchers shop and dairy from the building which was the original Old George Inn. Prior to their arrival, a Joseph Lowe was living at that address in 1851, a dealer and farmer of 20 acres and before that in 1841, he was a pig dealer.

The 1856 map and schedule has Joseph Olney living at that location with fields of about 2½ acres behind the house also in his tenancy, presumably for storage or fattening of stock before slaughter.

He and his family were there in 1861 and in 1871 he is described as a butcher and farmer having 12 acres and employing 1 man and 1 boy. He appears not to have had any sons and in 1881 when he was 62 years old, he had his sixteen year old nephew, Valentine Olney from Hexton, working with him as a butcher's assistant. The same set-up is apparent in 1891 and in 1901, but in those years there is no mention of any land.

---

[212] Graveyard memorial stone
[213] BLARS L23/347, L23/384

Sometime between 1903 and 1914 Valentine took over the business, as Joseph disappears from the Kelly Directories in the latter year.

In the 1918 Wrest Park estate sale Valentine paid £110 for a field on the east side of the A6 opposite Buckle Grove, but at the same time J G Murray, the purchaser of Wrest Park, managed to obtain both the house and the fields behind Valentine's butchery as part of his major purchase.

Valentine Olney remained at that address as a butcher and milkman until at least the 1940's, when the area between the road and the front of the house was open to the High Street, with a small orchard between the house and the road. Subsequently near the end of the 20th century a row of houses, 14 to 18 High Street, and the old house was converted into accommodation.

26 High Street or Yellow House Farm

Apart from the occasional person with a few acres, the only other small farmer of note in the 19th century was Charlotte Bone who lived at 26 High Street. In 1841 she was described as a baker and ten years later aged 61 she was farming 5 acres with one man, as well as being a baker. In 1856 she is the tenant of No 26 but also tenanted the field behind the house which now contains The Rowans. Another ten years on in 1861 she had increased her farming operation to 18 acres and employed 2 men.

She died aged 78 in 1868 and there must have been some domestic re-arrangement as in 1871, there are at No 26 James and Emma Bone, her son and his wife, plus as a separate household but probably in the same house, her two daughters Elizabeth and Charlotte. Both families are in the baking trade and curiously Elizabeth has land in Shillington, which Charlotte senior had perhaps also farmed. The same arrangement applies in 1881 but in 1882 James died, and by 1891 only the second Charlotte is left as a baker, although she had an assistant there.

She died in 1893 and John Harris from Southill apparently took over the business as he was there in 1901, described as a baker and farmer. He probably took over the same fields that the Bones had tenanted, behind what became to be known as Yellow House Farm. In the 1918 estate sale, the house and bakehouse including an area of about ½ acre was sold to J G Murray but John continued as tenant; and at the same time managed to buy for £200 the 7 acres field to the west of the Lord Nelson at Road Houses, and originally called Hungry Piece when it was part of Newbury Manor.[214]

In the late 20th century the land was farmed by his son, another John Harris, as a market garden before being sold for housing, and The Rowans was built there.

---

[214] BLARS L23/329 & 1013

Others (such as Chicken Farms)

Farming and market gardening was carried out from several locations in the village although there is no record of any farm name being attached to those operations.

Thus from 1851 until 1881 a small farmstead north of the George and located approximately where the current school now is, was tenanted by the Payne family and in 1851 William Paine from Billington is farming 23 acres with one man, his wife and two daughters and is 57 years old. At the next census he has 30 acres and employs 2 men and a boy. William was buried in 1866 aged 73, but his wife Elizabeth from Tipperary carried on with her daughters Sarah and Elizabeth.

The holding by 1871 had reduced to 20 acres but they still employed 2 men. Elizabeth senior eventually died in 1873 and the daughters carried on, although by 1881 they were down to 10 acres. Sarah died in 1886 aged 66.

Then in the early 20th century some of the directories between 1928 and 1931, have Captain Edgar Orton as a poultry breeder at Gwent House. By 1940 his son Frank Alfred George Orton had taken over and it is believed that the business carried on into the 1950's. Gwent House at the south of the village is now Taymar house and lies just south of the Nursing Home.

The National Institute of Agricultural Engineering

Originating at Oxford University in 1923, and following changes in name, location and size, this important national and international centre for agricultural engineering research was transferred to Silsoe from its temporary wartime home at Askham Bryan, Yorkshire in 1947-48. It took over the Wrest Park mansion and grounds, then owned by the Ministry of Works. During the next 50 years the Institute expanded on the site, building new research laboratories and experimental facilities of varying architectural merit, and extended its facilities for on-site field research by 190 acres. The Wrest Park site was chosen for several reasons; different soil types available nearby, other agricultural research stations in the neighbouring counties and Bedfordshire had both livestock, arable and horticultural enterprises in the post-war years.

Following further name changes to reflect the relationship with funding sponsors, it was eventually called the Silsoe Research Institute in 1991. It was decided that the name 'Silsoe' was what truly identified the Institute both nationally and internationally. By 1994 SRI was one of the eight grant supported institutes of the Biotechnology and Biological Sciences Research Council (BBSRC).

Research work at Silsoe involved the application of engineering knowledge and expertise to areas such as farm machinery testing and development, farm buildings, crop spraying and grain drying, animal production and welfare and improving the efficiency of small scale farmers in developing countries. Later research concentrated on applying physical, engineering and mathematical applications to agricultural and biological processes and systems. This expertise over the years helped to produce many examples of prototype machinery and processes that were later taken up by industry and helped to put the name "Silsoe" on the map. A commercial milking robot was developed from the original prototype at SRI; image analysis techniques paved the way for a high speed potato grader ; the " Silsoe Whole Farm Model" , used for cropping decisions on arable farms, the Silsoe whole crop harvester, the stripper harvester, the patch sprayer, the blackcurrant harvester, mower conditioners, a vision guided hoe, a poultry harvester, a mushroom robotic harvester…….even a medical trolley for use in hospital operating theatres, all originated from research at Silsoe.

During the latter years of occupation of the Wrest estate, the Institute worked with English Heritage to provide some public access to the house and gardens. With only a small team of approximately six Institute gardening staff, the grassed areas were mown, flower beds kept tidy and as much maintenance work as was possible within tight budgets was achieved to maintain the 91 acres of historical garden. Many of the fields adjacent to Wrest Park were used in experiments for improving crop production. A test track was built to put tractors through their paces and a paddy field was even created to assist with technology destined for warmer and wetter climates. The walled garden was used, as it was in the 19th century, for fruit growing, either in the good fertile soil, sheltered by the high walls, or in instrumented and calibrated greenhouses for tomato experiments.

Due to a change in research direction of the funding body (BBSRC), the core grant to support the Institute was withdrawn and the Institute was forced to close in 2006 after some 59 years of operation in Silsoe. Some of the research was transferred elsewhere whilst some scientists and engineers set up their own Silsoe based businesses at offices and laboratories on the site. The BBSRC retained ownership of some laboratory and office buildings and land until they were later sold.

The presence of both an agricultural institute and an agricultural college in the small village of Silsoe helped to make the name of the village known throughout the agricultural world. Many international students, especially from developing countries came to study or undertake research here, hopefully taking back expertise gained and friendships made.

Chapter 12 – The Growth of Silsoe

The Building of Silsoe

If Silsoe has existed since well before William the Conqueror's invasion then where did the people live? We are not in a rocky area so houses would have been made out of wooden beams and struts with lath and clay/mud/horsehair infill. Houses made of these materials do not last well, and so any evidence of them can only be found with modern archaeological techniques. The houses might leave evidence of where the posts supporting the roof had been and possibly the drip line, (a trench caused by water dripping off the thatch, and probably used to take the water away from the hut).

The archaeological digs carried out near West End Road farmhouse as a result of the proposed housing was one of the most thorough performed in the village and found evidence of early mediaeval occupation, and structures in the form of trenches and post holes, plus bricks and pot sherds.

It would require excavations of this standard in central village locations to prove the existence of very early or mediaeval occupation there. However, it is likely that houses were built and rebuilt many times over the centuries, with the result that very early structure evidence might have been destroyed.

We know roughly where the manor houses were, and the servants and labourers huts would have been nearby. The evidence of the early hovels associated with Wrest have probably disappeared during the many remodellings of the park land; and rebuilding that has been carried out in gardens abutting Newbury Manor in Newbury Close have turned up many bits of pots and other articles, proving residence there.

At the centre of the village it is a shame that there was not more archaeological work carried out when The Rowans was built, as if that was the site of a manor then there may have been other habitations around it and also, perhaps, evidence of much older habitations. Unfortunately the archaeologists got there when house footings were already in, and could only discern some post holes and ditches.

Plans are available for the village from the early 18th century onwards by which time the form of the village had been established. The estate plan of 1718 shows many houses at Silsoe village but, when comparing this plan to more modern surveys, it is evident that a certain amount of licence has been used by the surveyor; and also some houses have been omitted as they did not belong to the Wrest Park estate.

The various plans drawn up for the enclosure and dating from about 1814 vary between each other, but show Silsoe in greater detail and accuracy. Plate 12/1 shows the buildings in around 1826.

Following the Enclosure maps, a schedule and plan of houses owned by the Wrest estate in the village was prepared in 1856. After that came the Ordnance Survey maps which were of a high accuracy but were not available in large scale until well on into the 19th century.

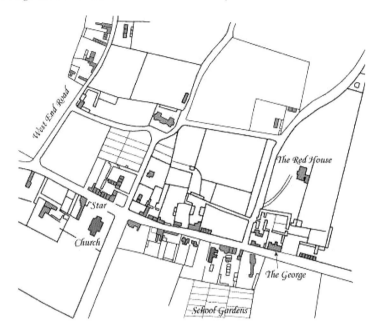

Plate 12/2 - The Village in 1856

During the surveys carried out when buildings were considered for listing by the relevant Government department, now English Heritage, broad estimations of their ages were made and where they are available they have been used as a basis for placing the building in the timeline for the development of Silsoe. There are a total of 99 listed buildings in the village but most of these are garden features at Wrest Park such as statuary.[1]

To set out in detail the progression of development in the park and gardens at Wrest would need another book but as a summary the following gives an indication of the erection of the main buildings there:-

Banqueting House /Pavilion	1709 - 1711
Bowling Green House	1720 – 1721, remodelled 1735
Bath House	around 1770
Brabury Lodges	1816
Silsoe Lodges	1826
The new Mansion	1834-39
The Orangery	1835
Ice House near Home Farm	early 19th century.

---

[1] http://www.heritagegateway.org.uk/

Development after the turn of the 19th century resulted in the epicentre of Silsoe moving northwards when several new roads were constructed at Newbury Lane, and by filling in the spaces between the old village centre and the village stone quarry in Ampthill Road. Eventually even the quarry was built on, and the fields between Ampthill Road and Newbury Lane and east of the old A6 up to the Wrest Park stone boundary wall were also developed, leaving only the allotment land undeveloped.

Even now building continues with the planning authority's 2007 decision to consider the Cranfield Agricultural College site as 'brown' land and thus developable. The first houses there were constructed in 2008 adjacent to West End Road and the remainder of the old campus will be built on eventually increasing the population in Silsoe considerably.

Very Old buildings – 16th century or perhaps earlier, 1500 – 1599

There are four buildings which were said to be of 16th century origin, and these are Home Farmhouse, 39 High Street (Old Woodstock), 21/23 West End Road (Little Gable), some of 17 to 25 High Street and Newbury Manor house.

Obviously over 500 years there have been some alterations and upgrading to the current standards but the basic structures originate in that century. Little Gable for example was, during the 19th century and for most of the 20th century, two dwellings and was only changed back into a single house relatively recently. Its early history is a mystery and as it was not owned by the de Greys in 1718 it did not appear on their maps. This suggests that it may have belonged to Newbury Manor.

Many old buildings in the village appear to have had work carried out on them in the 19th century, probably around 1861 when the enclosure commissioners provided finance for estate improvement, and this may have happened at Home Farm where the oldest part of the house has 19th century wings attached.

Newbury Manor fortunately did not have any such improvement and stands as a good example of 16th century manorial construction, probably built by the Daniell family, the Lords of the Manor at that time, and possibly by Edward who bought the manor in 1524. No doubt however, a much earlier manor house was knocked down to enable the 'new' house to be built.

It is not known where the name for 39 High Street, Old Woodstock Cottage, comes from, which dates from this time, although there is also an old cottage in Flitton that is also called 'Woodstock'. It has known many changes either side: on the north side there used to be another old building which was demolished probably in the 1870's to enable Barnard's Cottage to be built. On the south side is a Georgian-style house which was also probably built on the site of a much earlier building, as there in no gap shown there on the 1718 map.

The house in the Maltings Yard separate from and built at an angle to the others is now divided in two, but was once a single house of the 16th century and has been described as a farmhouse. The grotesquely huge chimney stack is a later addition, as is the 19th century extension on the west.

Finally, while some of the range of picturesque buildings opposite the church are dated to the 16th century, others are from the 18th and there have been 19th century additions and improvements - see the chimney stacks in yellow brick.

Not so old, relatively – 17th Century 1600 - 1699

There are more buildings remaining in Silsoe from this century than the previous one as might be expected, and especially farms. Fielden House dates from the 17th century with later additions and re-working, and was possibly built on the site of an earlier house and farmstead.

West End farmhouse is said to be late 17th century even though there was certainly a farmhouse in West End Road dating back to mediaeval times. The old house at the end of West End Road, in an area once called West End Green, was also built around that time, being made with a timber frame on a stone or brick plinth. It is probably the last evidence of the old hamlet of West End where some of the farm workers for West End Farm lived.

Finally in West End Road, the block of three houses nos. 18, 20 & 22, date from the 17th century but have had 19th and 20th century modifications.

Apart from the thatched houses at Holly Walk, (numbers 7-11), the only other buildings of this date are in the centre of the village. They are 20 High Street (Church House), 43 High Street (Village Farm), 46 High Street and Malting House Cottage (they were once one building) and the Old George at 10 & 12 High Street.

The Wrest Park estate map of 1718 shows many buildings in the centre of the village, most of which can be assumed to be from the 17th century or before.

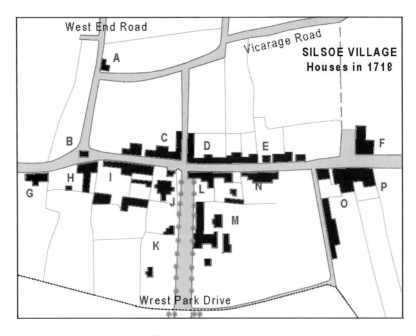

Plate 12/4 – The Village in 1718 – Key

A   Now 8 West End Rd, not listed but is known to have a beam with a date from the 17th century carved into it.

B   Forge or smith's shop in the middle of road, now gone.

C   The row of houses opposite church, numbers 17 to 29 plus part in Church Rd.

D   The Ragged Staff Inn and probably part of the building which became the old village shop.

E   The detached house is possibly the old house knocked down to build Barnard's Cottage, the next house on the north would be the Old Village Farm House while to the south the house which is now Old Woodstock Cottage.

F   Site of Ruthyns Cottage which although dated later is suggested to contain an older building.

G   Now 2-4 High Street

H   This shows a large house of which perhaps only remnants remain which may have been incorporated into what is now Amabell Cottage.

I   The old George, its shape differs from later maps and there are buildings fronting the High Street here which have either disappeared or became the

Star & Garter.

J Silsoe chapel is shown in its original shape and with possibly a lytch gate at the corner of the road.

K The old parsonage or workhouse or tithe barn. All these buildings are mentioned in various documents but the precise location of each is not discernible.

L Church Cottage before amendments and with contiguous building to the north, now gone.

M This farm complex was possibly the old Silsoe manor site but the buildings have been demolished, probably in the late 17th century but certainly before 1814. No reason is known, perhaps the upkeep was expensive or they may have been unsightly and taken down with the mansion house build.

N Perhaps 26 High street.

O The Maltings area was bigger then and it is difficult to relate those shown with the present layout.

P The location of the Dairy Farm, it is possible that all the old building shown here have disappeared.

Not shown on the above extract but existing on the full copy, are a row of houses situated behind where the Nelson public house stood. Three are shown at this date but the plans of the next century show a row of tenements there, abutting Newbury Lane at right angles. These later plans also show a block on the southern side of Newbury Lane at the High Street. In the 1881 census there were a total of ten families at this location, so the tenements would have been rather crowded by today's standards. The 1948 OS map still shows those houses together with infill that had commenced in Newbury Lane, so their demolition must have occurred within the last 50 years.

Fairly Old – 18th century 1700 - 1799

The front block of Fielden farmhouse is said to have been built around 1700 although it also has 19th century additions, such as the parallel block behind it. It may be that the 'New Fielding Farm' note on a map of around 1814 applied to a separate block adjacent and to the east of the old house. On the 1826 map both the east and west houses are shown and it is not easy to read the western one as having two parallel wings. The old house is not shown on the 18th century maps, there is only a thumbnail sketch of Fielden House which described it as Mr Millwards.

Other houses from this time are 2-4 Church Road and it may well be possible that these are the remnants of the Ragged Staff Inn, which was on this site until at least about 1826 and which was probably demolished when the Almshouses were constructed, to provide the Earl de Grey with a better vista when he drove from his mansion through the village to Flitton.

In a mortgage of 1737 an inn called The Bell, together with three brick messuages or tenements were said to be lately erected by John Allen.[2] The location in the document places them at the site of what became the Old George. These buildings are shown on the various enclosure maps of the 19th

[2] BLARS L5/323

century, although the plot containing The George was smaller and it was not until later that some of the outbuildings associated with Silsoe House were demolished, and the land thrown into the George's domain. The cottages remained for many years, being shown on the 1948 OS map, but were eventually knocked down at the time when the development known as The Oaks was constructed which included several houses being built at that location fronting the High Street. The George has apparently not been listed, presumably because it has been amended too many times.

The old white painted houses facing on the High Street, (numbers 40 – 44), when entering the village from the Ampthill Road, are said to be of the 18th century with 19th century additions. The southern part of this building was used for many years as the head teacher's house when the school was in the School Mews.

27 – 29 High Street & 1 – 3 Church Road may have been a reworking of an earlier structure according to the listing schedule, although there were 19th century improvements as witnessed by the fancy yellow brick chimney stacks. Although not listed, the row of cottages on the west side of the High Street near Ampthill Road have a certain charm, and possibly date from around 1726, if a recent estate agent's sheet is to be accepted.

The 18th century Star and Garter was altered in the 19th century and more recently in the late 20th when the connecting link between the main pub and the old house on its south side was built.

Finally, the village lock up has a plaque stating that it was built in 1795 although where this provenance, and a suggestion that it was moved from an earlier location near the quarry, come from is unknown.

Into the Nineteenth century

The New Inn is considered to have been built around the turn of the century, about 1800, but may have been constructed over an earlier building and could contain parts of this older structure inside. Similarly, the two storey house at 26 High Street is dated at around the same time, but is almost certainly a reworking of an earlier building, as a similar sized block is shown on the site in 1718.

The early 19th century and the 1856 maps show a building alongside the Barton Road approximately where No 1 High Street stands. It is reasonable to assume that this was built at around the turn of the century even though it is not listed. Also shown on these maps, but not on one from the earlier 18th century, is the row of cottages at the rear of the almshouses.

There was a small building boom in Silsoe in the early part of the 19th century associated with the construction of the new mansion although not all dates are known, There is a date for the church of 1829 – 1831, the Silsoe Lodge's gates of 1826 and for the mansion of between 1834-1839. However, no dates have been found for 5 to 11 Church Road, the Almshouses, 31 to 37 West End Road and the Red House.

In 1718 Ampthill Road did not exist, there was only a short close alongside what is now known as No. 53 High Street, Ruthyn Cottage. In the listing schedule this is suggested to have been built over an earlier structure and is suggested to be the 18th and 19th century reworkings of an earlier structure. The shape drawn in 1718 suggests a large wing to the west which does not now exist, so presumably the later reworking took place after that year.

Also relating to Ruthyn Cottage, the east end of Ampthill Road was a hive of activity during the latter part of the 18th and early into the 19th centuries when it was the site of a thriving carrier business.

In 1718 William White (document) paid £5 for "2 roods of land with warehouses, stables & other outhouses lately built thereon which was sited in Waterslade abutting south on the highway near the pound and which had recently been part of Gwyn's farm". After William's death in 1746, his daughter-in-law Elizabeth Edwards, conveyed to Edward's brother John White of Tottenham in 1747, the land previously mentioned plus "1 acre of land abutting west on the highway near the pound in which were a messuage or tenement with outhouses, barns, stables warehouses yards gardens orchards etc."

Henry Sharp, a carrier from Bedford, had obtained this land and buildings in 1764 and 19 years later devised part of it as a marriage settlement on himself and his wife when it was described as a cottage and a butchers shop. Upon his death in 1791 he left "….all that Messuage or Tenement with the Buildings Lands and all other the appurtenances thereunto belonging or therewith usually occupied situate standing and being in Silsoe aforesaid and commonly called by the name of The Waggon House …. unto my son in law the said John Edwards…" It seems that Henry lived there with his wife, but had improved the house while using the area as a carrier's depot.

In 1807 & 1809 another John Edwards purchased 2½ acres on land in the same place and both early 19th century maps prepared as part of the Inclosure, shows Ruthyns with to the west of that house the range of stables and the house known as the Waggon House. It also seems that Waggon House, now known as Silsoe House, had been constructed at the end of that range of buildings, possibly by Henry Sharpe and was used by him as his house and then by his wife after his death, in 1791.

Ruthyns had also been owned by Sharpe and at his death William and Elizabeth Burridge lived there.

The third John Edwards died as a result of a hunting accident in 1823, and in 1828 his trustees were leasing " … a new built mansion-house with garden &

plantation (3ac.), at Silsoe, late occupied by William Humbly and now by J.R.Henderson ...... with cottage at end of same land ...."[3] to Mr Henderson who with the lease obtained the use of a pew in the Chapel of Silsoe and a cottage for his gardener at the end of the garden, now called the Round House.

This mansion house, now the Red House, was evidently constructed before 1828 and probably even before John Edwards died in 1823, although it is not shown on the 1826 or 1828 plans of the parish.

Between where the old pond used to be opposite West End farm and the Battle of Alma ale house, now No.15 West End Road, old maps show a warren of houses and buildings. Now only Little Gables and numbers 31-37 remain. Immediately east of the latter was a small "mews" running back to the fields comprising of a courtyard surrounded by tenements, which early on accommodated upwards of 9 families in probably very poor conditions. It was sold to the Wrest Park estate in about 1856 when it was said to contain two cottages now converted into 4 cottages plus 6 other cottages newly erected by John Croxford.[4] They were sold to the Essex Timber Company (who also bought Fielden Farm for its standing trees) in 1918, and after that they were in various ownerships, probably being demolished in the early 1960's when they were uninhabited, so that the present houses could be built.

The western section of this hamlet seems to have been sold by the Wrest Park estate in the 19th century, at an auction in 1883 at the White Hart, Ampthill. The auction included The Alma, two thatched cottages (of which one was let as a chapel) two more brick and slate cottages, a house divided into two tenements and five freehold cottages, including a bakehouse and a large oven.

The Almshouses at the end of Church Road were probably erected as part of the general improvements in the village in the 1830's which related to the building of the new mansion; and included such projects as moving Church Road northwards and chopping off of a third of Church Cottage. This nicely designed amenity provided a suitable backdrop to the entrance to the village from Wrest and happily included shielding from view the row of old cottages now in The Orchards, which were probably not then very salubrious. That row of cottages is shown in the maps of 1814-1828 and were thus constructed earlier, possibly late in the 18th century. It was in existence in 1812 and were originally 2 cottages with apple stores at each end, and with the front door facing east rather than west as they now do.[5]

There must have been considerable disturbance for the village with all this work going on with no doubt many strangers employed on the construction being accommodated in the inns, or living in the village houses.

---

[3] BLARS L5/949-950
[4] BLARS L5/989
[5] Information from owner of No 2

The Old Vicarage was built to accommodate the new vicar who was needed when Silsoe became a parish in its own right in the 1840's, and while no firm date has been found, the land for it and the adjacent stone built cottages to its rear, was being bought around 1845.[6]

Also around this time the pairs of cottages nos 28 & 30 and 32 & 34 High Street were being built. The latter pair was built probably before 1841 as the inhabitants in that year's census are still there in subsequent censuses when the address can be more certainly established. In 1851 the census has the note '*two houses building*' at the location of numbers 28-30, so it is safe to assume that they were completed that year.

**Plate 12/5 - West End Road about 1940 looking West.
Vicarage Road on the right with The Alma straight ahead.**

Pear Tree Cottage in Church Road appears to have been in existence since before 1841, when a Mrs Macintosh was in residence, and lived there for at least another 20 years. Its style suggests construction early in the 19th century, but it does not appear on the early maps of that century.

Later in the 1860's there was another mini-building boom with money from the enclosure commissioners being used to improve building in Silsoe but also to build the row of houses, numbers 3 to 13 High Street, most of No 15 High Street, plus pairs of semi-detached houses at Fielding Farm and Home Farm. The old ventilation grilles visible on these buildings can be seen to carry the date 1862.

---

[6] BLARS L5/787

The Twentieth Century

There has been an enormous amount of infilling that has taken place over the past 100 years and it would be too much to date each individual house or small groups of houses, so only the developments associated with new roads or major infilling have been considered.

Two buildings that were constructed early on the 1900's but which have had a significant impact on the village were the village hall and Wrest Park Lodge which was located where the first houses of The Beeches now stands. The village hall was built by Mr John George Murray, the owner of Wrest Park, in 1926[7] for the use of the village.

Wrest Park Lodge is believed to have been built for the use of Mr Cecil Argles, Baron Lucas' agent. It is shown on the 1918 sale plans but not on the 1892 OS map, so was evidently constructed between those dates.

Apart from scattered individual houses the first major developments in the 1900's were the row just inside Wrest Park, which was constructed for workers at Wrest Park; and the Grove, which was constructed as council housing, both in the early 1950's.

There was no master plan for the development of Silsoe, a field became available and with planning permission being obtained, housing was erected. Also, starting in the 60's the new roads were named after trees rather than using local landmarks, their location or historic references. They could therefore be anywhere in the country rather than specific to Silsoe.

The dates below are of when people living in the major street developments of Silsoe started to appear on the electoral register, construction of these developments would typically have been commenced a year or so earlier.

Row inside Wrest Park, tragically built within the Wrest Park stone wall
 1949
The Grove, named after the Newbury Manor field in
                                                which it was built   1952
Bedford Avenue first phase   1956
Newbury Close, constructed adjacent to the manor   1962
Poplar Close   1965
Fir Tree Road   1967
Elm Drive   1973
Holly Walk   1974
The Sycamores   1976
The Oaks   1982
The Orchards   1983
The Grove – bottom end   1984

---

[7] See '*Silsoe News*', Jan 1985, article by Bob Thurman.

Plate 14/1 – The Old George Inn from the south

Plate 14/3 – The "new" George Hotel or Inn

ix

Plate 14/5 - The Lord Nelson in the early 20th Century

Plate 14/6 - The Alma about 1940.

Plate 14/8 - The Ragged Staff Window in Silsoe Church. Emblem of the Earls of Kent and probably why the lost pub was so named.

Plate 15/2 - Silsoe Village Hall

Plate 15/3 – Wrest Park Croquet Lawn

Plate 15/4 – A Silsoe   Drama Club Production

Plate 12/6   The Vicarage .

Plate 15/5   Maypole dancing in the 1950s, Wrest Park.

SILSOE MAY FAIR

AND

Traction Engine Rally

Organised by the Silsoe Church Restoration and Improvement Fund Committee in conjunction with the Bedford Steam Engine Preservation Society

WEST END FARM, SILSOE

(By kind permission of the Beds. County Council)

Saturday, 9th May, 1959

ADMISSION BY PROGRAMME   PRICE 2/6

Plate 15/6   Poster for the 1959 Traction Engine Rally

Plate 15/7   Silsoe Harvest Supper in the Village Hall 1969.

Plate 17/2 – The Old Silsoe Workhouse in West End Road

Plate 17/3 – The Silsoe Almshouses in Vicarage Road

Plate 17/4 – Firemark in West End Road

The Maples, constructed in the old Silsoe stone quarry in Ampthill Road
1984
Hawthorn Way   1985
The Rowans, constructed in market garden land opposite the church 1986
Bedford Avenue second phase   1987
Juniper Close   1987
The Fairways, High Street, next to the school   1987
Yew Tree Close   1990
Silbury Court   1992
The Beeches   1999

The Twenty-First Century

In the 21st century building has continued unabated, both by infilling gaps with individual houses being squeezed in between existing houses, or constructed in large gardens to the rear of existing properties such as in Newbury Lane. In some cases, such as at the end of West End Road, development was permitted virtually in open countryside.

Work started early in this century in 2000 with the construction of 13 houses at Apple Tree Close behind the Post Office, in Newbury Lane. Several single properties have been constructed as infilling off the same road, and a small group of 3 houses were inserted into back gardens on the north of Newbury Lane, when Willow Close was built in 2006. This process looks as though it may continue given the size of other back gardens in that road.

Starting in the previous century but continuing into this, development of the redundant farm buildings on the north side of Newbury Manor together with the insertion of new housing there was allowed by Mid-Beds Planning Department. This is known as Silbury Court, a somewhat contrived name, and following completion in about 2006, totalled about seven houses.

Moving southwards, the two semi-detached houses on the left when West End Road is first entered, were constructed about 2002 and won an award for their sensitive design. However, by way of contrast, some larger houses have been permitted nearby in West End Road in small plots with others being built at West End Green.

The departure of Cranfield University from their site south of West End Road enabled them to apply for and, despite much local opposition, gain planning permission for around 180 houses. Construction started in 2008 and the houses are being occupied with the initial phase nearly completed. The details for the development of the remainder of the site have yet to be fully agreed. While the original consultants for the developers suggested in their 2007 Planning Consultation Document that there will be up to ten ways the development could help serve the needs of Silsoe; it will result in a huge increase in the village population, changing the feel and appearance of the village forever.

Silsoe Conservation Area

In 2004 the Mid-Beds District Council invited comments on their review of the original Conservation Area document. The intention of this was to designate areas of special architectural or historic interest in the village, the character or appearance of which it is desirable to preserve or enhance. The area included the High Street from No 1 to Bedford Avenue, Ampthill Road including The Oaks to the Old Vicarage, Wrest Park Drive and Church Road from the lodge gates to and past the Almshouses, and West End Road up to the Old Farm House. As can be seen, it does not just comprise of the older areas, but consists of a large section of most of the centre of the village which includes some newer areas such as The Oaks.

The establishment of a Conservation Area also enables the planning authority to ensure that any new development within the area, including extensions and alterations, contributes to the character of the village; and that new development on green spaces in the area should be resisted. Thus, outside of the normal planning permission requirements, there are additional areas where permission is required such as for the demolition of walls, the installation of satellite dishes, the felling of trees and changes to roofs. It sets out a policy for development of the rest of the village and, hopefully, that is where the Silsoe Parish Plan would come in.

Silsoe Parish Plan

A new initiative to encourage communities to interact more with the local planning process was set out in 2000 in the Government's Rural White Paper "*A Fairer Deal for Rural England.*" It proposed that, with the encouragement of the parish Council, the whole community be asked by means of meetings and questionnaires to set out its priorities for different aspects of their life in the village such as traffic, amenities, employment and development.

From these early stages, and the process took about two years, a parish Plan document was produced in 2008 which set out broadly the results of the consultations and in its action plan suggested a timetable for those items which could be programmed; always of course, subject to available finance.

The Housing and Development chapter proposed that all future development should maintain the village character and that further development would be limited to brownfield sites and infill, with priority given to local people where possible. It also sought to limit to business use only, any proposals for development at Wrest Park now that the Research Institute has left.

A further proposal was to draw up a design statement, which would be adopted by the District Council as a guide that would set out design parameters, and considerations for all future building. The Parish Plan

Committee after this work was to continue to assist the parish council by monitoring the progress of the action plan and to update the plan when necessary.

The principles behind this initiative are good and it is to be hoped that all councils involved follow the suggestions contained in it which are, following the extensive consultations, a compilation of the wishes of most of the village community.

Chapter 13 - Transport and Communication

Road Travel

From very early times, when the population was very mobile, there would have been tracks criss-crossing the country to enable groups to get to and from good hunting grounds. After small farms sprang up and the people became more settled, tracks would still have been needed to enable the local farmers to get from manor to manor, village to village or more practically, to transport goods to markets. In addition, some of these routes were used to move troops around to counter invasions, or to quell rebellions. Gradually mobility increased and the roads became established with the more strategic ones such as the Icknield Way, running along the chalk hills from the north-east to the south-west becoming established as major routes, even remaining in use after the Romans had built their more direct roads.

No Roman roads have been found through or even very near to the parish of Silsoe, although with a settlement to the west at Ruxox near Flitwick and other occupation sites to the east at Gravenhurst and Shefford, there would no doubt have been tracks linking them. There has been a suggestion that a Roman road can be discerned running north from the Roman settlement at Limbury towards Streatley[8] and beyond, but this may have been a link to Ruxox rather than part of a north – south route along the A6 alignment through Silsoe.

With the need for a north south route from Limbury to Bedford and a suitable crossing of the Flit at Clophill, there is the possibility that what is now the A6 was an old pre-Roman route linking those towns.

With Roman sovereignty gone, invading groups associated with the frequent Saxon and Viking invasions coming mainly from the east, would have used existing tracks and waterways. Therefore, Silsoe was perhaps fortunate in not having a significant east – west road or river through it.

With the development of the manors after the Norman invasion there would have been many tracks in and around the village, some of which became public roads and others that remained as private tracks within farms or major landholdings. Thus in 1359 a field at Little Cainhoe was said be alongside the road leading from "Broibury to Sylvelesho"[9] which was probably the track that still runs from Home Farm to Silsoe, and which continued through to Warren Farm at Cainhoe.

After the Norman invasion and with the imposition of their laws, roads were maintained by the parishes through or in which they ran, and the local people were required to work on and maintain the roads. Much later, with the

---

[8] *Roman Roads in the South East Midlands*, The Viatores, Gollancz, 1964 & *The Roman Period*, Angela Simco, Beds CC, 1984
[9] BLARS LJeayes 322

increase in national prosperity and the greater use of heavier waggons to transport goods, the upkeep of the roads through this system of paid and unpaid labour did not work well, with many roads becoming impassable in bad weather. Nothing new there then!!

That the need for good all weather roads were taken seriously is shown by a form[10] of 1691 issued by the Quarter Sessions, for the appointment of surveyors to view or inspect the highways. Local habitants were to work six days every year on the highways and the form also stipulated the width of cartways and 'horse-causeys', the penalties for damaging horse- and foot-causeys, duties regarding nuisance hedges, mending the highways before harvest time, penalties for not keeping ditches open, limits to number of horses drawing a hire waggon and penalties for tyres less than 2" wide, except on carts used in husbandry.

Some private initiative appears to have been carried out by the Silsoe carrier William White at the notorious Barton Hill, as in a 1718[11] deed he gives permission "for the Duke's coaches, chariots, chaises, horses, carts & waggons to use the new road and way up Barton Hill lately made by me & Matt. Stevens." At that time it still ran up the escarpment to the east of the present alignment, as it was not until about 1831 that the new Barton Hill toll road alignment was built, running up the valley to the west.

Toll or Turnpiked Roads

As the village maintained road system evidently did not work for major roads, a new method of road maintenance was introduced from the 17th century, that of the turnpike trusts. The trust's boards, composed of the local great and good, would petition Parliament to take over sections of the road network, and if successful would introduce tolls, collected at toll gates, with which money the trust would maintain, or improve the roads. An Act for Amending and Repairing the Roads from Luton in the County of Bedford, to Westwood-Gate in the north of the county, the trust which covers the Silsoe section, Turnpike 7, was passed in 1726/27. Turnpike gates were constructed near the Speed the Plough and north of Maulden Hill.

Despite various comments by locals, no mention of a toll gate at Road Houses near the Lord Nelson has been found in the archives.

An act of 1774 extended the Luton Road Trust to include the St Albans to Maulden section of the A6, known as the 'Luton District'. The trustees met every 6 months, sometimes in Luton but also at the George in Silsoe.[12]

Despite all the good intents and pressure from carriers and local nobility and sub-nobility, the condition of the turnpiked roads was not good (and not all

---

[10] BLARS Z937/36/1
[11] BLARS L5/933(1)
[12] William Austen, *The History of Luton*, 1928, p 84.

roads were turnpiked so what their state was heaven knows). Some idea of the condition of roads even in the summer, can be found in a letter of June 1775[13] from Wrest where Amabel, Countess of Grey writes that she "had a fair Overturn this Morning" on the way back from Southill, "The Roads not bad nor the Coachman Careless. We were talking on when we found the Coach very gently laid down on one side; we would scarce believe ourselves in so unusual a situation, however we did not exert our Voice till we found them attempting to set the Coach up again with us ????? in it."

Only a few years earlier in 1772[14] she had written that "The Road to Barton was very dirty: that on Luton Downs still worse perhaps, from the Deepness of the ruts, but as hard as Stone; from St. Albans to here very tolerable; upon the whole I rather think this Journey was pleasanter than from Wimpole to Wrest, but I am sorry to see our Turnpike in a very neglected state".

Heavy rain also caused problems, as today, and in 1795 there was a flood in Luton and when a Silsoe waggoner tried to cross Bridge Street his waggon got stuck and he had to leave it there and return to Silsoe.[15]

Plate 13/1 - A Long Stage Coach – for 15 travellers you would need one this size [16]

The poor state of the roads probably continued for some time as in 1827 there was a bad accident, when the Pilot Coach to Bedford turned over near Silsoe and all 15 of the passengers were injured to some extent, with one receiving severe cuts and another having a skull fracture.[17] This was said to be down to excessive speed as the coach was said to have been travelling at a

---

[13] BLARS L31/106
[14] BLARS L31/13/12/5
[15] William Austen, *The History of Luton*, 1928, p 94.
[16] Taken from Luton Museum 1972 book *The Turnpike Age*
[17] *The Times* 15 August 1827

rapid rate round a corner. The Pilot Post Coach ran from the Three Cups Inn in Aldersgate, London, every Tuesday, Thursday & Saturday morning starting at 8 o/clock and passing through St Albans, Luton, Silsoe and Ampthill to Bedford.

At this time, around the 1830's, there were several coaches which made the Bedford – London return trip. There was The Peveril of the Peak: which was daily from Manchester to London via Bedford, Ampthill, Silsoe & Luton. The Pilot: which left the Fountain, High Street Bedford at 7 a.m. on Monday, Wednesday and Friday, and travelled to London via Ampthill & Luton. It returned on Tuesday, Thursday and Saturday.

The Post Coach was a daily coach to London starting either at Kettering or Bedford, and also going through Silsoe and finally The Umpire: which left the Red Lion at Bedford on Sunday, Tuesday and Thursday at 9 a.m. also going via Ampthill and Silsoe to London.[18]

As can be seen, Silsoe was an important stop for several coach routes in the 19th century, bringing wealth and news to the community. However, with the coming of the railways such traffic and hence the toll income reduced due to profitable traffic diverting to the trains. Many trusts were unable to function, some even becoming bankrupt, and the last turnpike trust in the country closed in 1895.

The responsibility for highways was from the late 19th century settled upon the town and district councils, and the country and rural district councils. With some 1900 councils involved then and no national standards, the road conditions were variable to say the least, and with the increase in motor traffic national standards were eventually imposed. To provide some standardisation the government took over the main highways routes in 1936 through the Trunk Roads Act.

In Silsoe the A6 had been a trunk road for some time until recently when it was handed back to the county council to maintain, and even more recently that road plus all other roads and footpaths in Silsoe passed to the new Central Bedfordshire Council. Perhaps the next stage will be for the parishes to maintain them again!

Roads in the Village

In early times it may be that street names were rare and if they existed, they described their function or where they led to such as High Street or Ampthill Road, while in older documents the more important roads were given the term "The Kings Highway". It is unlikely that signs were erected naming the roads until outsiders became more frequent or the post office required a formal location in order to deliver the mail. The enumerators, who tended to be local men, used names in the 19th century that they knew and, for example,

---

[18] Pigot & Co, *Directory for Bedford and Northamptonshire*, 1830

the main road through the village was variously described in that century as Silsoe Town, Church Road, Village Street and finally in 1901, High Street.

The North South, A6 route

A road from Luton to Bedford through Silsoe can be shown to have existed for many hundreds of years, with the first reference being to the "King's Road which leads thro' the village of Silsoe as far as Barton" in a document of about 1270[19]. It is well shown on maps dating back to the late 17th century and early 18th century.

From Barton northwards where the ground is clayey and there are several east – west streams, the route follows slightly higher ground to avoid the damp areas before turning towards the east near where, until a few years ago, there were some cottages on a site west of the place called Toglake (Doglake on early OS maps). There was, until a recent bend improvement, a sharp bend towards the north and Silsoe, following which the road crosses the stream by New Inn Farm, known as Kitchin Brook in 1712[20].

From New Inn Farm the road meanders gently up to the village following high ground, and from the centre it runs straight to Road Houses at its junction with Newbury Lane. This straightness suggests that it was, at a very early time, cut through the common fields north of the village centre, with Waterslade on the west and Dowdel on the east, perhaps to avoid a meandering route up Vicarage Road down towards Newbury Manor and back down Newbury Lane.

It is believed that the straight section of the road north of Road Houses is due to the Wrest steward of 1807, Lewis Harrison, who on his arrival decided to improve its alignment by removing the old trees and fencing it.[21]

After the area known as Road Houses, the road heads towards Clophill crossing over the ridge of sandy ground now planted with chestnut trees. Originally it then turned east and then north to cross the River Flit into Clophill, at what used to be called Sluts Green. Presumably this was the best crossing point of the Flit and the shortest route across the marshes, but the dog-leg may have been to do with avoiding a steep slope down the sand hills, as south of the crossing in Warren Wood on an 1814 map, there is a line indicating a track on a direct line, and even today there are earthworks showing the old alignment.

In the late 20th century the increase in traffic caused great problems in the narrow centre of the village, with damage caused to houses by large vehicles and the near-squashing of pedestrians, and so the road was diverted in 1981 with the construction of the new by-pass by Bedfordshire County Council.

[19] BLARS LJeayes 653
[20] BLARS L5/419
[21] Mary Phillips etc etc

The chosen route was around the east side of the village over a length of about 2.6km (1.6m) including a cutting between Wrest Park and the village all costing about £1.6 million. More recently in 2006, the junction at the southern end of Silsoe has had a new roundabout constructed to provide a safer access to the village, and to cope with the new housing development at the old Cranfield Campus.

Flitton to Shefford - direct

To get from Dunstable[22] to Shefford the natural route would have been through Toddington, Flitton, Westoning and Silsoe and then remaining on the south bank of the Flit to avoid crossing the river, or the low lying marshy areas.

Entering Silsoe at Wardhedges, the initial alignment used is shown on the 1718 Wrest Park estate map as running from Wardhedges down the little valley towards Newbury Manor and then along Newbury Lane past Cainhoe Castle, and on to Shefford.

At the time of the enclosure in the 19th century, when the ancient field systems or small plots were replaced with bigger fields and many roads in the country were improved or downgraded to make better use of the land, this route down to Newbury Manor became a track and eventually a footpath, with the road being diverted onto the route it follows today.

The first alignment also passes by the ancient well known as "Edmundewelle" in the 14th century[23] which later became "Admannys well"[24] in the 16th century. A well or earlier, a spring, would have provided good, safe water for the thirsty traveller and his horse on this route.

There is a slight dog-leg adjacent to Newbury Manor which prevents Newbury Lane from lining up with the route down from the well head. In the section on Silsoe in the *Victoria County History for Bedfordshire* there is a note which may explain this, as in 1323 Ralph Fitz Richard, then at Newbury, received royal permission "to inclose a lane 63 perches long by 1 wide, leading from the King's highway, below his dwelling-place, in order to enlarge his house, on condition of replacing the road by one on his own land"[25]. This length, relates very well to the length of Newbury Lane at the west end where it deviates from a direct route to the old valley alignment.

---

[22] Two documents of 1314/1315 refer to a plot of land abutting the Kings Way leading to Dunstable. However, this seems to be in Fielden and accordingly would be the Portway referred to in (5). There is no obvious cross country route from Fielden to Dunstable except perhaps via Sharpenhoe & Sundon so this reference is unclear. (BLARS LJeayes 674 & 678)
[23] BLARS LJeayes 672
[24] BLARS LJeayes 781
[25] VCH footnote refers to:- Calendar of Patent Rolls 1321-4 p.364

After reaching the A6 the route followed the now stopped-up road, which led towards Cainhoe and eventually Shefford. Even as late as 1826 the road is annotated as the Dunstable – Shefford Road east of Road Houses.

Flitton to Clophill & Shefford

The second alternative between Flitton and Shefford, and one which provides a better access to Clophill or even Bedford, is the route which followed the Hollington Road up out of Flitton, turned eastwards at the top of the hill, went over the hill and then descended to the Beaumont Oak at the Silsoe-Maulden road. The part or this route over the hill down to the public footpath is now ploughed up.

A possible variation has the route starting at Wardhedges and following the line of the existing footpath down to the oak. This may have been a side road, but it has persisted longer that the first line.

As early as 1567 Lady Ashe Lane is mentioned, which was the early name for the track running from Beamont Tree down to the A6, and this name persisted into at least the mid 18th century. The former name may have derived from a very early tree on the site, which perhaps was replanted and became Beaumont's Oak.

After crossing the road from Silsoe to Maulden at the oak, Lady Ash Lane is still operational as a farm track, with a footpath along it all the way through to the A6, where it emerges from the woodland at the garage south of the roundabout. It presumably would have joined the Silsoe-Clophill road at the Flit crossing and the last section between the A6 and the crossing point was evidently used for the part of the dog-leg mentioned above, on the old A6.

The road then carries on towards Shefford on the Silsoe side of the Flit, meeting the other route from Flitton at Warren Farm, near Cainhoe Castle.

Silsoe-Maulden Road

Another important local route was the road which led from the Newbury Manor area towards Hollington Mill, and which nowadays crosses the Flit to provide a direct route to Maulden and Ampthill. It takes the 'best' line for crossing the Flit at a narrow point away from marshes, and utilises the high ground where possible.

The mills belonged for several centuries to Newbury Manor and no doubt served both Flitton and Silsoe, and so this road may have started initially as a route to get to the mills. Then when the Flit valley was drained for agriculture and flooding became less of a problem, the road was extended towards Maulden.

The Portway, the A6 to Gravenhurst

This route which commences at the old corner in the A6 just south of New Inn Farm and runs north - eastwards towards Gravenhurst, finds its way along what was once probably a drier ridge through what was most likely a fairly damp terrain, lying as it does between two streams. It is probably of considerable antiquity and is the only road with a significant old name. The word Portway relates to an important road or track linking to a market or even a port, and it does seem to be another route from Dunstable to Shefford, both market towns.

The earliest reference so far found to the name is in a grant of the late 12th century where land is described as abutting the "Portweye"[26]. However, references to the Portway continue in land grants, leases and sales or on maps through to the 18th century, after which the name 'Gravenhurst Road' or more boringly in the enclosure, 'The Fielding Road No 7', took over.

Apart from the A6 it is the only other road in Silsoe which was turnpiked, having its own toll gate which was situated at its western end at the junction with the A6, and inside the parish boundary.

The first direct mention of the toll gate in censuses is in 1851 when it is called the Wheel House where Ann Wheeler, the 17 year old unmarried daughter of agricultural labourer Alfred Wheeler, is said to be the "Toll collector, (side gate)". Alfred does not appear in the village on the earlier censuses so may have only recently been installed there. It was common practice for toll collection to be auctioned annually, with either the person successful at the auction living at the toll house, or his agent being installed. There is no reason for a 'wheel', normally associated in those times with water pumping, to be there, so it may be a contraction of Wheeler's House.

In 1861 the house is called Fielden Bar, and Mary, the wife of Henry Burley aged 35 from Clophill, is the toll collector. Bar was a common name for the tollgate where the gate barred the passage.

The Burleys are still there in 1871 at Fielden toll bar when Henry is the turnpike gatekeeper and also a farm labourer. Mary is a straw plaiter but it would have been she who collected the tolls while Henry was out in the fields labouring. In 1881 it is called "New Inn, the Wheelhouse" but no mention then is made of toll collecting by the head of the family, Absolom Page. 1891 has Tollgate Cottage occupied by Jude Wilton, a farm labourer, but in 1901 the property is temporarily unoccupied, while in the 1910 valuation it is occupied by Alfred Ansell. The site of the demolished house can still be seen in a wooded copse to the south of the old junction of the A6 with The Portway.

---

[26] BLARS LJeayes 630

Silsoe to Wardhedges

Originally the main route from Silsoe towards Flitton ran along Holly Walk (known as Mount Pleasant in the 19th century); and then past the horticultural centre, to run along the sandy ridge of land up to and past the site of the old Windmill north of Thrift Wood, before descending to meet the tarmacked road at Wardhedges. This was the route used to get to Flitton church by the de Grey family and, before Silsoe chapel was consecrated as burial ground in 1845, by countless villagers taking their dead to be buried at the church.

The use of the high land in Silsoe indicates that the route may have been of some antiquity, and it may have been the original route from Flitton through Wrest Park to Gravenhurst. If that was the case, then it has probably been much amended and straightened by landscaping and other works at Wrest Park, but the alignment at the eastern end near Upper Gravenhurst can be picked out on the early editions of the OS and other maps.

It is probably the road described in a lease of 1563[27] as the "waye to wynmell hyll" and also in a deed of 1521 as "… le Churchwey leading from Sevelisho to Flytton …" or perhaps in the same document "Prescessyon way" or "Prestessyn Way".[28]

It became the main access to Wrest Park and in 1836, when it was a bridleway, there was a proposal to divert the alignment from this route to one which emerged onto Silsoe High Street, further to the north by the old school house. The implication of this is that it was an established route.[29].

At its east end where it meets Vicarage Road, and where there is now a dog-leg to reach the High Street; there is a property boundary which can be traced on the early maps which suggest that it may have originally extended along that line to the High Street.

Ampthill Road - High Street to Vicarage Road.

This road was constructed after 1718 and before 1809. On the early map it appears as only a stub alongside what is now Ruthyn Cottage but with, perhaps, a track alongside the southern edge of Waterslade initially providing a short cut to Flitton or Ampthill from that part of the village. However, with the growth of the carrier business established at what is now Ruthyn cottage, and the outbuildings of Silsoe House by Henry Sharpe in the late 18th century, and later John Edwards, the track was probably upgraded to a road to allow better access for the business to the west. In detailed maps such as that of 1826, it is shown as quite wide for the first 50m from the High Street, perhaps to allow the waggons to be parked there.

---

[27] BLARS LJeayes 807
[28] BLARS LJeayes 781
[29] BLARS L33/211

After 1856, when it is still shown on a map as alongside the southern front of Silsoe House, it seems that the occupant of Silsoe House, then Mr Trethewy, the Wrest Park estate manager, wanted a bigger front garden and so for his convenience the east end of the road was shifted some 40 metres to the south[30]. There is a Quarter Sessions Road Diversion Order relating to Ampthill Street, Silsoe, dated 4 January 1860 in the parish records, so presumably the diversion took place later that year.

Ampthill Road - Vicarage Road to Newbury Lane.

On the 1718 map this is an extension of what is now Vicarage Road, and interestingly its alignment cuts diagonally across a field of 3 acres comprised of 12 lands which seems to have been the south-western corner of Waterslade common field. The same map and the later Newbury Manor map of 1757, show a track heading north through Waterslade from the northern end of Vicarage Road directly to Newbury Lane. It is suggested that this was the original alignment for Vicarage Road through to Newbury Lane and that the part of Ampthill Road under consideration was cut through at a later date, to provide a direct route to Newbury Manor.

West End Road or Lane

The section of West End Road beyond West End Farm up to the group of houses in what was called West End Green, was probably originally a farm access track to farm workers cottages and fields, but the road from the High Street to the farm was much older. The farm house building is said to be of late 17th century origin[31], but it was probably built over a farm of a much earlier date, as there are records relating to the farm dating back to at least the 16th century.

The road runs alongside the stream running from the fields near Thrift Wood to the east, which until the 1950's also filled the large pond opposite the farmhouse. The stream was culverted from the pond alongside the early 18th century thatched cottages where the road narrows, and later from there to pass under the A6.

Although now West End Road, it was in the 19th century called West End Lane.

---

[30] BLARS L5/1002 plan attached to deed of sale of Ruthyn Cottage
[31] Listed Building description

Vicarage Road

The name may be quite new, the vicarage in Ampthill Road was only constructed in the early 1800s, but the road is shown on the 1718 map, and especially at its southern end it would seem to be far older. At this location, between Church Road and West End Lane it is more reminiscent of the deep lanes of Devon, which became that way due to use over many centuries by waggons and farm animals.

The suggestion above that the road to Flitton is of some age may account for the bend in Vicarage Road where it meets the former. If the Flitton Road had priority, then the northern half of Vicarage Road could have been aligned along a separate boundary.

Church Road

On all early maps up to and including 1826 this is shown as running alongside and close to the houses on the south side, now numbers 1 to 9. Then, in 1828, it is shown some 20m to the north and is in line with the Wrest Park Drive. If you were an earl who owned most of the village, would you want the road from your nice new mansion to head directly towards a public house?

This is suggested elsewhere to have occurred in association with the re-building of Wrest Park house when in order to give a more acceptable approach to the estate, the Ragged Staff Inn on the north western corner of the crossroads was demolished as was part of Church House, and Church Road was moved northwards to line up with the Park Drive. The almshouses were constructed at the end to the road which proved an attractive 'stop' to the view.

The Maltings

This was originally just a track serving the maltings on this site and it is now a cul-de-sac containing several houses. When the Co-op had a branch there, it was locally known as the Co-op Yard.

The Road to Upbury

As late as the early editions of the OS maps, surveyed around the 1830s, a road is shown running from a point on the A6 about mid-way between West End Road and the nursing home, south westwards to and through Upbury to emerge on the Pulloxhill / Barton Road, at the foot of the hill. Buildings are shown at that time on this ancient manor site, but sadly nowadays all that remains are some ponds and earthworks, and the old road is now either a farm track or a footpath.

Kitchin End Road

On a 1774 map relating to New Inn Farm and detailing only areas within the parish, Kitchin End Lane is shown and named; yet on the earlier 1718 map only a simple field division marks the route. It may be assumed therefore that the road was cut through (or at the very least improved) to the Pulloxhill Road, between those two dates.

Housing Estate Roads

As the village developed over the last century, roads were built into fields to enable houses to be constructed. So, in approximately the order in which they were built, there were Fir Tree Road, The Grove, with its later add-ons of The Sycamores and The Hawthorns; Bedford Avenue, Newbury Close, Elm Drive, The Fairways, The Orchards, Holly Walk, Yew Tree Close, Juniper Close, The Maples, The Rowans, Appletree Close, The Beeches and Silbury Court, with many more to come.

Given the history of Silsoe it is perhaps unfortunate that the roads were not given names more relevant to the village rather than trees, but as we seem to be running out of the more common trees then perhaps new developments will show more imagination. The first phase of the new development in the old Cranfield University site is in 2010 advertising their new properties as being in 'Archers Fields', (without the apostrophe!) and while this does seem to end the arboricultural road naming, how on earth does that name relate to Silsoe?

Other Roads

Some road or track names have appeared in documents but their location has not yet been found. It is probable that they were early names for roads that still exist. Thus there is Watelondwey[32] of 1362 in the South Field of Silsoe (probably at Fielden and perhaps deriving from 'wheatland') and Scallards wey[33] of 1373 near Little Cainhoe, possibly to Shefford or a side track. Newbury Lane was called the "way from Newbury to Shefford" in 1549[34] and the same document also refers to Chantrye Leyne, possibly what is now Church Road, and Waywynnunge which may or may not be a road.

To maintain the roads John Hill of Silsoe left 6s 8d towards the upkeep of the high ways between "Sevellshoo and Sowthend Brege" in his will of 1546[35], presumably meaning the A6 down to New Inn.

As suggested above, there may have been other roads that ran through what is now the park which have, through landscaping and other works, been

---

[32] BLARS LJeayes 723
[33] BLARS LJeayes 332
[34] BLARS LJeayes 803
[35] BLARS ABP/R11/240

stopped-up or diverted. One may have been a route from Pirton heading northwest through Ion up to Clophill. Even now there is a road which runs directly from Pirton past Shillington and which terminates at the Ion entrance to the park, on the Gravenhurst Road. The alignment is continued along the private road to Whitehall, and if followed through would have run past the mediaeval Wrest House and along the farm track past Home Farm to Warren Wood, and then Clophill.

Until the 19th century the main access to Wrest was from the Clophill direction, running down the avenue in front of the mansion and then to the east of Home Farm. The access to Silsoe, as indicated by an avenue on the 1718 Wrest estate map, may have been joined the Barton road south of West End Road but by that date there was a road to the mansion from Silsoe where the current alignment is.

Footways, Paths and Tracks

There are several footpaths in the village registered as public rights of way, and fairly obviously fewer in the Wrest Park area. Probably most are of some antiquity, enabling farm workers to reach their places of employment, but not many are recorded in old documents.

One old route which mostly remains intact is a footpath originating at Newbury Manor which terminates near West End Farmhouse. It lies under the first stretch of Elm Drive after which it is a footpath until Ampthill Road. After that the development of Fir Tree Road and the adjacent quarry has obliterated the original line, but it re-emerges as a footpath at the southern end of Holly Gate before it reaches West End Road as a footpath.

A second important path found in a document of 1674 and later in 1819 is the footpath which enabled workers in Silsoe to get to Fielden, and which ran through Buckle Grove[36]. Initially it seems to have commenced on the A6 near the track to Upbury before heading directly towards Fielden. Another footpath also providing access to Fielden starts near Kitchen End Road and provides a perfect route from New Inn Farm to Fielden House.

Other footpaths follow the lines of old tracks which are not now public roads. Thus the footpath from Wardhedges to Beaumont Oak which has already been mentioned; and also the footpath which runs from behind the old Lord Nelson northwards up and over what was Barrell Field and terminates on the footpath near Firs Farm. This probably enabled villagers to reach the old village common moor, by the Flit.

Finally there is are a group of footpaths west and south west of West End Farm giving access to Wardhedges, Pulloxhill, Upbury Manor site and to Gagmansbury Farm.

---

[36] BLARS L5/83 1674 & Z937/2/1

Waterways

The nearest canal to Silsoe is the River Ivel Navigation which opened in 1823, and ran from the River Ouse at Tempsford to end at Shefford. The original Act of Parliament of 1757 allowed for it to extend as far as Hitchin but due to objections based on the lack of trade to make it viable, the construction of the section from Shefford to Hitchin was delayed, and eventually cancelled. The Tempsford to Shefford Navigation was closed by the 'Ivel Navigation Abandonment Act' in 1876 with debts of £14,350.

Later in 1823, a meeting was held in Hitchin where it was decided that the company should extend the Shefford line west, to meet the Grand Junction Canal. This would have run up the Flit valley past the northern edge of Silsoe. It was acknowledged that this would be a very lucrative stretch of water, as it would create a link from the main inland waterways system to Bedford, Ely, Cambridge and King's Lynn on the River Great Ouse network. However within a few years the railway system started to extend over the country and the westerly extension, which would have provided a local link to the waterways system was never started.[37]

Railways

The nearest railway still operating is the old north – south Midland Railway line with the station closest to Silsoe being that at Flitwick This route was opened in 1868 as part of the Leicester to London line and continues to be important to Silsoe providing a route to London via the Thameslink line which runs from Bedford; and which also passes through or rather under London to Brighton via Gatwick. This line was also used in World War 1 with casualties for the Wrest park hospital being brought to Ampthill station for collection.

However, until that route opened, the main London route from Bedford was the Leicester to Hitchin line that passed through Shefford which then had a station. This station had full passenger facilities, and Shefford even had a crane of 1 ton 10 wt capacity for goods work. The Midland Railway obtained powers for this line on August 4th 1853 and it was opened throughout, on May 8th 1857.

Unfortunately that line always lacked a strong industrial base to provide continuous revenue, with the only real local industries being the gas works and scrap yard at Shefford, a quarry at Henlow, plus the ever present agricultural produce. The line closed to passengers on January 1st 1962 and to freight services on December 28th 1964.

Interestingly for Silsoe, there were two proposals which nearly brought the iron horse much closer to Silsoe. Plans were drawn up for the construction

---

[37] *Canals & Waterways: Roots & Routes*, Peter Hardcastle,
http://www.canals.btinternet.co.uk/index.htm

of a railway from Towcester to Hitchin in 1865, and again in 1871 by the engineers, James & Joseph Burke for the East & West Junction Railway Hitchin Extension, both of which followed the same route crossing the A6 just above New Inn Farm and leaving the parish to the west of Fielden House.[38]

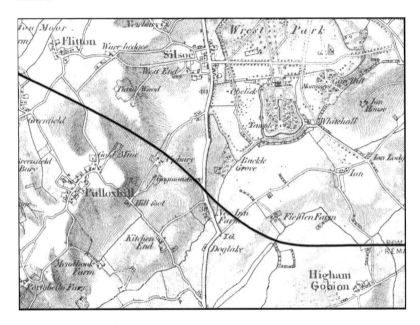

Plate 13/2 - Route of Proposed Railways, 1866 & 1872

Plans show the alignment in detail and include a section showing the intended cuttings and embankments. There is also a schedule of the land owners along the route. This implies that surveyors would have worked along the route, and no doubt their actions were much discussed locally in the pubs and elsewhere by the locals.

In addition to the above route a letter exists dated 1845 in which a line from Shefford to Clophill was proposed, and which further suggests that Earl de Grey was anxious to have a railway nearby. That alignment was probably not even surveyed as no map has been found.[39]

---

[38] BLARS PDR12/1/1 & PDR17/1/1
[39] "The Railway Age in Bedfordshire", F G Cockman, Beds Hist Records Socty, Rev. 1994.

Chapter 14 - Silsoe Ale Houses, Inns and Pubs

The village in 2010 has only two public houses or inns which remain open; the George on the High Street just north of Ampthill Road and the Star and Garter next to the church. There were three but the Lord Nelson, which was situated on the corner of Newbury Lane where it joins Clophill Road (in a part of the village once known as Pork End) was closed in 2003 and, like so many other pubs in the country, is now converted into a private house.

However, in previous centuries, when work was more strenuous and farm labourers drank prodigious quantities of, admittedly weaker, ale, there were more places around the village where thirst could be quenched. There was also probably at least one malt house or brewery open in the village at any one time, so that stocks could be kept fresh and many inns made their own ale.

Only one inn has remained in its original location, several have disappeared and one has migrated from one end of the High Street to the other; some have also changed their names.

The two remaining continue to provide centres of activity for villagers to chat, to play darts and other games, to provide a place where the various clubs active in the village can hold meetings and in addition they provide food and drink for the villagers, those visiting the village, or just passing through.

The George Inn, Original and New.

Although the Georgian frontage of the George Inn makes this perhaps the most imposing building of the two pubs now remaining in the village, the George was not always in its present location, and has probably been extended several times where it now stands. It was originally south east of the Star & Garter behind what is now 14a-14b High Street.

The original inn could not have been named after any of the King Georges as the George I commenced his reign in 1727, 100 years after the first mention of the inn in documents. There was, however, a George Grey, the 2nd Earl of Kent, who died in 1503 and after whom the inn may have been named. If this is correct then this implies that the George would have been in existence many years before the name first occurs in documents.

The first mention found of the inn is in a sale document of 1613 when a messuage called the George was sold to Richard Daniell of Newbury Manor for the sum of £240-10s-6d in performance of the will of John Child, a yeoman of Silsoe. This included the backside and adjacent close of 3 acres plus about 8 acres of arable land elsewhere in the fields of Silsoe[40].

---

[40] BLARS AD1101 23 Nov 1644

Edward Daniell, citizen & dyer of London, bought the property from Richard Daniell in January 1615/16 and sold it on in 1628 for £285 to Benjamin Hale of Flitton and his wife Ann[41]. The sale included the adjoining close of pasture of 3 acres plus other land in the village, as in the earlier sale. The occupant in 1628 was said to be Joseph Sticklin, presumably the tenant innkeeper at that time.

Benjamin Hale left the George and the adjoining pightle plus 5 acres in Colewillows close to his daughter Ann in his will, which was proved in 1631/32[42]. She seems to have married William Wheeler, as Ann Wheeler, his widow, left the property in 1672 to her daughter Mary[43]. Ann was living in the George at the time.

On a more joyful note, a year later, Francis Roworth, probably a farmer, married Elizabeth Creke "ye Georg maid" at Flitton in November.

The George and the associated lands were conveyed to Thomas Arnald of Ampthill in 1673 for £310 by William Wheeler and Mary Wheeler, yeoman and spinster[44], two children of William and Ann. Mary had the right to remain in occupation, but in March 1676 Amabella, Countess of Kent, bought the property from Mary and Thomas Arnald for £360, (not a bad profit over three years).[45]

In 1679 a Thomas Godfrey alias Cooper of "ye Georg at Silsoe" was buried at Flitton. He is recorded as occupying "a capital messuage" in Silsoe in 1672, which is presumably the George Inn where he was probably the innkeeper[46].

However, is seems that William Moses took over later in that century as he is described as an innkeeper in a lease of 1687. He is not at the Ragged Staff as John Allen is there that year, and neither the Bell nor the Star and Garter appear to have been in existence then.[47]

A William Moses was buried in 1717 (there was another one to confuse matters) and a terrier to the survey of the Wrest Park estate of 1718 has Humphrey Fletcher at the George Inn as innkeeper. In association with the George he is renting land to the extent of 47a 1r 13p, and for both the inn and the land he was paying to the estate, £53 a year. [48]

Humphrey Fletcher was probably still there in 1739 when in several documents relating to a lease and a mortgage he is described as an innkeeper.

[41] BLARS L5/8
[42] BLARS L5/10
[43] BLARS L5/11
[44] BLARS L5/14
[45] BLARS L5/17
[46] BLARS L5/74
[47] BLARS L5/1056
[48] BLARS L33/286/folios1-43 "A terrier of the Lands in the Mannor of FLITTON cum SILSOE" 1719

There is some interaction between the George and the Bell as that mortgage relates to the Bell Inn at the opposite end of the village.[49]

Fletcher was still in the village in 1750, as a Land Tax schedule says he is paying no taxes, but there is another item for "Jn Fann ye George Inn" who paid £24 that year. The Rev. Rouse in 1764 quoted Mr Low, the Wrest Park gardener, as saying that together with Mr Finney, "he usually went up to Fanns in the evenings about seven or eight at night and returned home about ten or soon after, seldom exceeding that time, and Finney confirms same."

Silsoe's location on one of the main roads leading to London made it a favourite stop for drovers taking their cattle and sheep to market and it is probable that the several acres of fields behind the George and Fletcher's other fields towards Barton, were used for pasturing overnight. The drovers paid eightpence a score a night for pasturing their sheep, and fourpence a head for oxen. The innkeeper would provide food, lodging and a small beer for the drovers, and fodder for their horses, plus in some cases a drove mug of ale for each drove of cattle, and the men were allowed a penny in the shilling for their patronising of the inn.

Another more alarming event relating to the George occurred on Monday, April 21st 1751 when three strangers put up at the Flying Horse at Clophill, from where, after settling their bill of twelve shillings with the landlord Abraham Perrin, they set out in the morning. They dined with a butcher who kept a public house at Houghton Conquest, left at four and started to rob people on the Ampthill to Bedford road and also near Millbrook, taking about £68.

Before the hue and cry could be raised they had regaled themselves with gin at a Maulden alehouse and proceeded to the George at Silsoe, where they drank three pints of wine and ate a crust of bread at the door without dismounting. About a quarter of a mile out of Silsoe on the road to Luton it is thought that they quarrelled over their booty. One of them was shot in the back with a blunderbuss, dragged into a close and shot with a pistol through the head. The remaining two carried on in the Luton direction, stopping to pay their toll to the turnpike man for themselves and the loose horse, and even waiting for their change. Early next morning the corpse was discovered, taken back to Silsoe, and exposed to view for several days after which it was then buried in Flitton churchyard as a "Highwayman name unknown". A turnpike ticket from Maidstone was found in his pocket showing how far he had travelled in his trade.[50]

Henry, Duke of Kent, had been granted a charter for a weekly market at Silsoe and for an annual fair on September 10th in 1715. The market died out

---

[49] BLARS L5/331

[50] Bedfordshire Magazine, Vol. 7, No 54 Autumn 1960. Silsoe Village by Mary Phillips. Also CRT 100/27/3/ for Rev. Birts letter to the Earl of Hardwicke detailing the events.

about 1729 but was revived in 1765 when it was held in the yard of the George Inn, but was again discontinued. Until recent years the fair was held in May.

There is an interesting survival of a bill for £4 10s from the George of 1774 for the entertainment of the Silsoe tythe renters by the tythe owners. They were charged £2 for food, £2. 4s. for drinks with the remaining amount being spent on servants and corn. Edward Goodale signed as received, and he was presumably then the innkeeper.

In 1781 the George Inn was taken over by John Gough, who had been butler to the late Lord Polwarth[51].

However, Mr Gough's character turned out not to be acceptable to the park steward or his Lordship. In March 1786 Thomas Gostelow, the estate gardener, wrote to the Earl of Hardwicke to say that some of his school friends had unexpectedly arrived and he had drunk some liquor with them. Later on they had gone to the George for some more and he had become totally drunk. During this he accused Mr Gough of murdering Bet Odell four years ago. Elizabeth Odell had then been a living-in servant at the George and when she became 'ill' Mr Gough sent her to Leighton to recover. The landlord at Leighton, suspecting something more than a simple illness, had sent her back to Silsoe.

Upon her return Mr Gough treated her with his own remedy and put her in another house in the village. While there, a surgeon Mr Bolding had inoculated her against smallpox and had accused her of being pregnant despite her denials. She died two days later in labour. Her burial is recorded but not that of any child. Gough was said to have tried to implicate Gostelow so that he did not have to face his wife.

The agent Mr Pawsey presumably having received a response from Philip, Earl of Hardwicke, on the matter said that Gostelow was due to be dismissed as soon as his accounts had been made up and that John Gough had been given notice to quit the inn at next Michaelmas (29 September) . He was upset as he had a wife and five children plus one on the way. There was a follow up in September when William Stuart of Luton wrote to the Earl to say that his tenant, John Gough, was so notoriously profligate and abandoned, that the magistrates would not licence his house for the sale of beer the next year.

Mr Pawsey wrote to the Earl in October that year to say that the justices would licence Benjamin Carter from Lady Day and, as the season from then until Lady Day is known as a dead season for travellers, there will be no great loss.

---

[51] *Northants Mercury* 16 Jul 1781

It is fortunate that John Byng of Southill stopped several times in Silsoe on his rides and wrote in some detail in his *"Torrington Diaries"*[52] of his visits to the George Inn.

HON. JOHN BYNG

Plate 14/2 - John Byng, later the 5th Viscount Torrington

In 1789 he recorded that,

"A short road back brought me, at 2 o'clock to the George Inn, Silsoe, a tolerable noon stop, free from noise, close to the park, and with a neat garden; where on a seat in a yew bush I enjoyed the fragrance of a sweet briar hedge, sheltered from the rain; I but just escaped.

The stable here is very good and the people very civil. Unluckily I was too late for their egg and bacon, so was obliged to have a bad fry'd beef steak – but I brought a good sauce with me.

I made a longish, tedious stay here, my horse faring better than I did, in a good stall, and with good food. But my charge was very cheap, and the brown bread excellent (white I always discard) nor was the sage cheese amis…

I allways think of Dinner for half an hour before my arrival at the Inn, which gives me an appetite and a hurry for eating; and I now eat with so much good

---

[52] *The Torrington Diaries*; containing the tours through England and Wales of The Hon. John Byng (later fifth Viscount Torrington) between the years 1781 and 1794 Eyre & Spottiswode 1934. Portrait from http://www.wgma.org.uk/Articles/Torrington/article.HTM

will , as when I come in heated, and can have my meal quickly; for then both body and mind are instantly refreshed and recovered

	d
Eating Beef steaks and Drinking	8
3 glasses b & water	6
Horses, hay & corn	5
Feeding – 2 servants	<u>4</u>
	1s 11"

He was back again in 1790 to look at Wrest Park gardens,

"but the rain falling fast , hurried us along under an avenue of trees, to the George Inn, Silsoe where we housed ourselves and stabled our horses. C. thought of a good dinner but I confined his wants to the situation, and to a half eaten, half-hot leg of mutton; to which were added eggs and bacon: C. praised the ale and I quaffed brandy and water.

Such a deluge of rain fell as to drive even the drovers into shelter; once I ventured out into the garden and from a seat well sheltered in a yew bush took this drawing.

George, Silsoe	s	d
Dinner	1	6
Beer	0	3
Brandy	1...0	
Tea	1...4	
Horses corn and hay	<u>1...4</u>	
	5...5	

The misery of the Inn and the misery of the day could not but gloom us; C. had no great coat and mine could only make a short defence aginst the weather. We were obliged to drink tea; and to stay as long as possible."

The drawing he made is reproduced in the book and appears to show the eastern elevation of what is now No. 10 High Street, the half-timbered building lying behind Nos. 14a-c High Street. Droving, the movement of herds of cattle or sheep from farms to towns or cities was at its height at the end of the 18th century and the beginning of the 19th century but slowed and stopped, with the introduction of the railways in the mid-19th century.

In 1794 he travelled again to Silsoe this time to see the repairs to Wrest House;

"More rain coming on, hurried us to the George Inn, a small public house at Silsoe (oft mentioned in my tours). Here in the back room towards the garden, we employ'd ourselves in blowing the fire and in waiting for something to eat. The day was cold and rainy and this house is only for a hot summers lounge.

The people and their best room were taken up by a post chaise company. The stabling is tolerable and the hostler very attentive. The chops at last burnt up and our bad dinner came in. But all these rides became pleasant in the eagerness and gratification of my cade lamb – and as the world appears so young to him it presents my feeling it so old, as I should if I were above.

George, Silsoe

Eating	2.0
Beer	0.3
Brandy	1.3
Fire	0.6
Horses corn & hay	<u>1.6</u>
	5.6

The expence was not high for three people? Tho' they screw'd up hay 1d per horse.''

As an important building in the village, the George was often used for auctions and other sales as, for example, in August 1814 when 1½ acres of arable land in Silsoe belonging to Mary Porter were sold by auction.[53]

The census for 1831, which is more of a list than a detailed schedule, shows two persons being an innkeeper or publican in the village but no names are given. There were two, possibly three public houses in the village at this date, the Star & Garter, the George and perhaps the Ragged Staff if it was still standing. The Lord Nelson, if operating then, was only an alehouse, so would not count as an inn. However, as the census of that date only counted males, any female innkeeper would not be shown. In another part of the census there is a Carter household, the head of which is Widow Carter aged 30-40 with three others in the household, including a male of the same age. This name is mentioned as in the later 1841 census the Carters are at the George.

In 1838 Alfred Russell Wallace who was a draftsman involved in the building of the new Wrest Park house, boarded at the inn kept by Mr Carter "whose wife and 2 daughters, nice well educated people, took an active part in management". It was apparently very full due to the rebuilding of the Wrest Park mansion and he could only find for his use a small empty house opposite the inn in which to do his drawings.[54]

"Here we used sometimes to sit of a summer's evening with one or two friends for privacy and quiet conversation, Mr. Clephan, the architect, and his clerk being our most frequent companions. My brother supplied them with gin-and-water and pipes, and I sat by reading a book or listening to their discourse. Sometimes they would tell each other stories of odd incidents they had met with, or discuss problems in philosophy, science, or politics. When jovially inclined, the architect's clerk would sing songs, many of which were

---

[53] BLARS L5/680
[54] BLARS CRT476

of such an outrageously gross character that my brother would beg him to be more cautious so as not to injure the morals of youth."[55]

Perhaps as a result of its overcrowding and also no doubt due to the need for a newer building, the records of the Petty Sessions of 20 December 1838 says that proof was given of the untenantability and irreparability of the old building and that following proof of service of the relevant notices, a licence was granted for the new building. The liabilities while acting under the licence were explained to the tenant and innkeeper, presumably Benjamin Carter, and his agent Mr Brown. Thus the George moved from near the church to its present location north of Ampthill Road.

What remains of the Old George are to be found in what is now a private house, or perhaps houses, behind numbers 14a-14c, the High Street, see Plate 14/1. Recent refurbishment of the half timbered house at the rear uncovered evidence of the earlier use of the building with parts of an old bar being found behind a partition.

There may be other things left to remind us of its earlier use as in the mid 1990's someone looking out of the rear window of the new houses in front of the George saw, in daytime, a 'highwayman' ride through the garage towards where the George was, he wore a large hat and was mounted.

Pigot's Directory of 1839 confirms the move with the statement that there is in Silsoe, the George, a good inn and lately built there with Benjamin Carter the Innkeeper. The Petty Sessions show that Benjamin was not above turning people away he did not like as there are two instances, in 1839 and in 1840, when he was fined for not putting up a sailor and a soldier as required by their 'billet' - a ticket issued to enable members of the armed forces to travel. In addition, in 1837, he charged John Clark with breaking an earthenware jug who was fined 3d with £1 1s 1d costs.

The Carter family remained at the George for many years. In 1841 Elizabeth Carter aged 45-50 is there with 9 children and two servants, Sarah Kempson aged 11, and Harriet Newbury. Benjamin may have been away for the night as he is at home in 1851 when he was then aged 58 and was not only the innkeeper but also the postmaster. In addition he is farming some 130 acres employing eight men and 3 boys. His wife Elizabeth is there as is their daughter Harriett, a servant Harriett Lewis aged 20 of Diddington, and a tap boy Edward Chiswell aged 18 of Woburn. A visitor there is Fanny Heighington 23, also of Woburn, a milliner.

The 1854 Post Office Directory (and also the 1862 directory) has The George down as an inn and posting house. Benjamin Carter is a receiver for letters which are dispatched at 6pm by hand cart to Ampthill. He also received letters at 8am from Ampthill and delivered them at 9am.

---

[55] Autobiography of Alfred Russell Wallace (Brit Lib X809 7455)

Benjamin Carter's gravestone in the village cemetery says that he was 35 years at the George and was respected by all who knew him. He was 63 years old at his death in 1856 and must therefore have started at the inn in 1821 aged 28, probably at the old George.

James Beaumont, born at Flixton, Suffolk in 1820, took over the George from Benjamin moving from the White Hart Inn at Ampthill, and in 1861 with his wife Elizabeth and ten children he was ensconced there. To help him he had Eliza Pratt a housemaid and Sarah Goss a nursemaid. In addition, at the time of the census William Wacher a messenger at the House of Commons and his wife Sophia, were staying there. He also continued the farming tradition of the George innkeepers having 100 acres and employing 4 men and 2 boys to farm the land.

He must have found the farming life more to his taste as in 1871 he is a farmer at Pinner in Middlesex, and Charles Browning aged 35 from Great Stoughton had taken over running the George. He also farmed, having 91 acres with 4 men and 3 boys. It seems likely that most of the land was transferred to new innkeepers along with the inn.

Charles was unmarried with a housekeeper, Martha Turner from Lincolnshire. He also had a general servant, Jane Rainbow aged 23 of Clifton, and also Frederick Beaumont a butcher, the son of the previous tenant was staying there.

Charles got married in 1875 at Ampthill to Sarah (probably Church) from Higham Gobion and was still at the George in 1881 by which time they had had two children, Francis and Sarah. Their servants were Hanna Elmore 22, a general servant of Marston, and Isabel Garner 13, a nursemaid of Shefford. He had built up his farm and now had 121 acres and employed 5 men and 1 boy. However, as his predecessor, he too turned entirely over to farming and in 1891 he was at West End Farm.

At what was then called the George Hotel was John Gray of Marston Moretayne, aged 26, with his wife Florence, child Harold aged 4 months, a nursemaid Kate Sharpe aged 12 of Clophill and Charlotte Evans a general servant of Flitwick. No mention of farming this time, John is described as a publican.

William Treacher, the teacher at Silsoe school from 1883 – 1922, says in his introduction to *"A stroll in Wrest Park"*,

"A large house on the right side of the road, with 'The George Commercial Inn' over the porch, is the principal 'hotel,' and the words 'posting house' reminded us of the time when 'iron horses' were little known - the old coaching-days, when the villagers would crowd around and eagerly inquire the latest news from town. The porch we found decorated with geraniums, and the hall well furnished with the products of the .artist and taxidermist, to suit the taste of the sportsman. Having refreshed' the inner man in the good old-fashioned style, we strolled up the village, which, if not a model one, is certainly very picturesque. Tidiness' seems to be the motto.

Adjoining the churchyard stands the only inn besides the one we have mentioned within any reasonable distance of the Park and Gardens, boasting of the sign of the 'Star and Garter.' This is as much frequented by visitors as the 'George', and on most Mondays during the summer months vehicles of all descriptions may be seen, either standing in the enclosed yard or under the large chestnut tree that lends its thick shade around. There companies are entertained by the genial landlord at very reasonable charges, and if the open air is preferred to the large club-room, an awning is quickly brought into use on the lawn attached."

John Gray is still at The George in 1901, but is now listed with his middle name and is John Palmer Gray, a publican and farmer. At that time horse transport was still important and he probably leased several acres to pasture horses overnight and perhaps to enable him to carry out a bit of farming. He still has with him his wife Florence, his son Harold John aged 10, and also has Mary Everett, a general servant.

Even after being charged for the third time in 1902 with selling watered down brandy (he had a fine of £2 with £1 6d costs) he remained there[56] and the 1903 Kelly's Directory describes the George as a "family and commercial hotel" with John a farmer and coal merchant. In the 1914 Kelly's Directory, John Palmer Gray is still at the George.

During the sale of the Wrest Park estate, in 1919 the George's tenant Charlotte Anderson bought The George Hotel, the half acre site on which it sits plus about 58 acres of pasture and arable land scattered around the village for £3100[57].

Charlotte sold on the George in November 1924 to Higgins & Sons of The Castle Brewery, Bedford, together with the garden, homestead and outbuildings for £3000 presumably holding on to the fields elsewhere in the village[58]. Higgins was taken over by Wells & Winch in 1931 who were eventually absorbed by Greene King in 1961.

In 1928 Frank Carthew was the innkeeper while three years later Major Reginald Philip Cork, OBE, was the proprietor of The George with at the same time Frank Hinson using the George Hotel garage for his wireless, general and motor engineering business.

The present George Inn or Hotel still provides accommodation, while in 2007 an Indian Restaurant had taken up residence in the dining area and then

[56] *Beds Times* 25 April 1902
[57] BLARS L23/1007/20
[58] BLARS GK85/1

in 2009 it became a Chinese restaurant and take away. It also holds band nights, karaoke and other events notably the St George's Day feast when a suckling pig roast is available complete with morris dancing.

It does however boast a ghost: that of a young woman dressed in grey with an impressive hat, which was creating so much disturbance by opening and closing doors in 1959 that the resident landlady called in an exorcist. A psychical research team turned up but, as so often happens, they did not experience anything. It is said that a Lady Elizabeth Grey had been using the George to hide from her father, as she wanted to marry a coachman at the inn, but while fleeing after her father found out her whereabouts their coach overturned into a lake and they were both drowned.

Now the present George has only been in existence at its current location since 1838 when the family surname of the Earl de Grey was Robinson so no Lady Elizabeth Grey could have existed then. If the story is of an earlier Elizabeth Grey then unless ghosts follow an inn's licence around, any earlier ghost would have remained at the old George's location. Also, no burial record of an Elizabeth Grey has been found at Flitton.

The "Angell Inn", then the "Duke of Kent's Arms" finally the Star & Garter.

Mary Phillips in an article for the *Bedfordshire Magazine*[59] on Silsoe says that The Star and Garter belonged at one time to the Wheeler family and was possibly their private house. The Wheelers were an important family in the village in the 17th century and appear many times in land conveyance documents of that time, one of which is for the sale by Mary Wheeler of The George to Amabella, Dowager Countess of Kent in 1676.

The survey carried out at the time of the listing of the building describes it as of 18th century date with re-working in the 19th century, so there must have been a building on the site before then, possibly the one shown on the 1718 plan.

Although in 1765 the pub was known as the Star & Garter, at the break up of the estate in 1918 when the land was sold, it was stated that it had been originally called the 'Angell Inn' and then the 'Duke of Kent's Arms'. The second name is also found in a letter of 29 January 1767 from Hadley Cox, the Vicar of Flitton, who said that a Mr Basset had been arrested for burglary and had been kept at the Duke's Arms at Silsoe[60]. No other source for these names has been found but evidently the names had been recalled from somewhere as late as the 20th century.[61]

---

[59] *Bedfordshire Magazine*, Vol. 7, No 54 Autumn 1960
[60] BLARS CRT 100/27/3 p97
[61] L23/381

Plate 14/4 - The Star and Garter pre 1910

At some time the Wheelers sold the pub after it had passed through several hands. One record shows that in 1781, half the ownership, with the residue of a 950 year lease then belonging to Philip Morris, was bought by Henry Ashley, Ann Morris & Jane Morris.[62] Prior to 1765 the inn had been previously owned by John Morris, an Ampthill innholder.

In 1765 the inn had been run by a Mr Sharpe and his brother who had replaced Humfrey Clarke when he died in 1763.[63] At the time of the 1781 sale it was occupied by John Hatred although it had been previously occupied by John Sharp and then by Mary his widow. A John Sharp, "gent of Silsoe and Chief Constable of ye Hundd of Flitton" was buried in Flitton in March 1775, presumably he had been the innkeeper of the Star.

It is surprising that the Star and the George co-existed for so long, given that they were so close to each other that their boundaries even touched. But maybe the George concentrated more on passing trade such as drovers and coaches, given that it had much land attached, with the Star being a more local pub.

When the residue of the 950 year lease was in the hands of the Henry Sharp and John Morris in 1781 the inn was by then called the Star & Garter although the document implies it had recently been called the Duke of Kent's Arms[64].

---

[62] BRO X21/629
[63] CRT100/27/3 Note by Rev. Hadley Cox dated 1/6/1765
[64] BLARS X1/629 Sheet 27

In the same manner as the George, there are references to the Star & Garter being used as an auction place and this is recorded in 1790 when cottages were auctioned there[65] and in 1804 when a further property was sold there, to George Whitbread. [66]

It seems that the occupancy of the Star and Garter in the early 19th century was still in the Haytread family. In 1807 John Haytread is described as an innkeeper when selling cottages and land in West End,[67] and similarly there is a reference to John Haytread as a victualler in a conveyance of January 1812, where he is selling a house in West End Lane to Amabel, Countess de Grey[68]. In a declaration of 1839 when he was 73 years old[69], he says that he had been in Silsoe for 41 years so he may have been the innkeeper there as early as 1798.

An inventory of 1827 of property belonging to John & Joseph Morris Esqs includes The Star and Garter. It is described as a freehold public house, occupied by John Haytread, with a stable for six horses, granary, cart shed, four stalled stable, two stables for two horses each, a yard and a well planted garden. The property is leasehold for the term of 950 years; it is therefore considered equal to freehold. It also held an allotment of about 3/4 of an acre of pasture land situated about 1/4 mile from the house.[70]

The 1831 census, which unfortunately does not associate people with property, has a John Hayhead (sic) aged 50-60 with two other women in his family. In a separate schedule to the census it is said that there are two 'Publican Hotel or Innkeepers' in the village, these are presumably the Star and Garter plus the George, (the Ragged Staff must have been discontinued as a public house and probably demolished by then). A schedule of this year of various public houses and inns owned by the Morris family, describes it as a cottage in Silsoe with outbuildings, stables, yards, orchards barns etc called the Star and Garter with allotment or pightle of pasture of 3 roods held for remainder of term of 250 years and in the occupation of John "Hayhead".[71]

In the 1841 census, (although the pub's name is not directly mentioned), is John Haytread 75, victualler, with his wife Mary aged 60 from Hinton in Hertfordshire. Also recorded there are Louisa Lucas 20, dressmaker, Charles Jeeves 9 and Elizabeth Lucas 6. There is also a female servant, Jane Beaumont aged 15 and Joseph Toothill, a smith, aged 30. [72]

Perhaps Haytread was not able to carry on the business profitably or his land speculation landed him in trouble, as in 1846 a review of his bankruptcy was

[65] BLARS L5/991
[66] BLARS L5/760
[67] BLARS L5/728
[68] BLARS L5/616
[69] BLARS L5/968
[70] BLARS Z 1043/1
[71] BLARS WB/M/4/1/VP1
[72] Note that in the 1841 census the ages are rounded down to the nearest 5 years.

carried out. [73] He did not last long after that and he was buried in the Silsoe churchyard in December 1847. However, his wife carried on and in 1851 she is a victualler aged 69 still at The Star and Garter. Her grandson Thomas William Geeves, aged 16 and born at Hitchin, is assisting her and there are two servants, Elizabeth Whiteman, a house servant, and Thomas Whiteley an ostler. The 1854 Post Office Directory shows Mrs Mary Haytread still at the 'Star & Garter'.

In an 1856 estate map of the village the name 'John Morris' is inscribed across the location of the Star & Garter on the map, confirming his ownership. There is unfortunately no name in the attached schedule and therefore no indication as to the innkeeper.

However the 1861 census, (the first census in which the pub's name is used), has Mary Haytread's grandson, Thomas William Jeeves, aged 26, as the innkeeper along with his mother Mary Ann who was born at Cheapside. No burial for Mary Haytread his grandmother has been found at Silsoe although her death was recorded at Ampthill in 1859. Thomas had a 17 year old domestic servant, Mary Cawcutt of Upper Gravenhurst and a 'Hostler', Charles Eddy of Silsoe. There were also three lodgers, two Joseph Lipscombes, father and son and a William Lyred. All three are sawyers and of Princes Risborough. No doubt they were working in the Park and if three were staying at the inn, there must have been quite an amount of felling taking place on the estate at that time.

By 1871 Thomas W Jeeves, having married Emma Brightman (whose father was a butcher), had moved away to the Wellington Inn at Welwyn, and the innkeeper of the Star is now the 34 year old Henry Bailey, born at Turvey, with his wife Louisa and three little Baileys, Henry, Walter and Arthur. Ten years earlier Henry had been a police constable at Cranfield so no doubt he was quite able to keep order. This time the general servant is Dorcas Hyde of Shillington and a single lodger is Benjamin Slipper of Rotherhithe, aged 21, an articled pupil to a surveyor.

Henry Bailey moved on to become a baker at Stevington and by 1881 mine host was the 65 year old John Barker of Biggleswade. John had been living in West End Road and was an ostler at the George ten years earlier and no doubt considered he could run the smaller Star & Garter. He was living there with his wife Anne and their 18 year old daughter Mary. There were no lodgers. They were still there in 1891 when he was 75 years old.

John died in 1893 and the pub was taken over by his 45 year old son also called John Barker, born in Ampthill, but who seems to have previously worked in London as a gardener. This second John was there in 1901 with his wife Elizabeth, his mother Ann aged 84 and his sister Ann who was a hospital nurse. Also at the inn was a timber hewer / woodman called Elijah Soaffe who came from Minsfield, Hampshire.

---

[73] BLARS L5/807

In the 1910 and 1914 Kelly's Directory Thomas Lancaster is the publican at The Star and Garter.

Then in 1919, the Wrest Park estate sold "All that messuage and Inn with outbuildings stables yards and appurtenancies thereto belonging formerly known as the "Angell Inn" afterwards as the "Duke of Kent's Arms" but now known as the Star and Garter to J G Murray, the purchaser of Wrest Park, in a job lot including many other small plots in Silsoe.[74] In 1933 J G Murray sold his interests in the Star to J W Green.

The Kellys Directories for 1920 &1924 have Thomas Miller as the publican at the Star but in July 1927 Frank Agar, the son of Charlotte Anderson from the George, became the tenant there. In 1956 Tom Mackay, who had been at The Alma, took over the tenancy from his father-in- law and he remained there until he died in 1969 when his wife Joan took over, staying there until 1970. The new tenants then were Ron and Peggy Lawson who remained there until 1974, after which there were six other tenants until Mark and Linda Hewitson came in 1991.

The cottage to the south of the main public house which was separated from it by a narrow driveway, had at one time been used as accommodation by Tom and Joan Mackay but in the mid 1990's it was joined to the Star and an extension constructed to the rear so as to provide a larger ground floor dining area and bar space. The upstairs of the cottage is accessible from the bar and is used for meetings and other groups.

More recently the steadily increasing rents imposed by the brewers on tied houses has resulted in a more frequent change of tenants and a change from reliance on beer sales to beer plus food, with emphasis on the food. The current publicans, Mark and Linda Hewitson have now created a balance between the restaurant and the bar and since coming have raised its popularity both in the village and to outsiders.

The Lord Nelson

The earliest reference to the building, possibly before it became an alehouse, is in a conveyance of 1822 when John Francis Bird, a currier, and Mary Bird, widow, sold the property to William Clark, a carpenter of Silsoe. It was subsequently re-mortgaged for £140 in 1833, to William Hogge and Robert Lindsell of Biggleswade Bank. When William Clark died intestate in 1843, the property passed to his eldest son Benjamin who promptly re-mortgaged it to the bank for £100 in 1844 at an interest rate of 5 per cent. Little of the interest seems to have been paid and when Benjamin Clark died in 1858, leaving the property to his widow Charlotte for the benefit of her three

---

[74] BLARS L23/381

children, the Bank foreclosed and the £300 purchase money of the purchaser, Earl de Grey of Wrest Park, was paid to them.[75]

In the 1831 census the two people included in the 'Publican, Hotel or Innkeeper' in the village are presumed to have been the tenants at the George and the Star & Garter. There is however a Clarke family headed by William who if a beerseller would not have been included in the innkeeper category.

In 1841, when thankfully it was decided to collect more details for the national census, we find William Clarke with three children at Road Houses, aged 55, whose occupation is described as a 'Victualler'. His wife Fanny Clarke had pre-deceased him being buried in 1840 aged 56 from Road Houses. A victualler in those days generally described someone selling both food and drink so presumably he was then selling ale.

William himself died in 1843 aged 57 and his son Frank Clarke, being described as a publican in 1851 had obviously taken over at the alehouse. With him were his wife Sarah and their three children, Joseph, Frank & Love. Benjamin, the owner, was also living at Road Houses and was a bricklayer. An 1854 'Post Office Directory of Berkshire, Northants, Bedfordshire etc' confirms that The Nelson was run by Frank Clarke and it has him down as a 'beer retailer'.

The Lord Nelson first received its licence in 1857 as a public house, prior to then it could only sell beer, being only an alehouse.

A copy of a plan attached to an 1859 conveyance, when Earl de Grey became the owner of the property, buying it from Mrs Charlotte Clark(e) and her mortgagers Hogge & Lindsell, shows the pub with three tenements to the rear, fully occupied.[76]. The property is described as a beer house and on one side was a blacksmiths shop which became a shoemakers. It may be that the Nelson was not sufficiently well patronised as in 1861 Frank Clarke is still there but is now a publican and a bricklayer's labourer. His wife probably ran the pub and looked after their now seven children while Frank went off bricklaying.

The occupant had changed by 1871 when Joseph Billington born in Flitwick was the publican and also a dealer; in what we are not told. He remained there for at least another ten years with his wife Ellen and family as they were still there in 1881 with six children. It was a tied house to Wells and Winch although still owned by Earl Cowper.

By 1890 Joel Martin, originally from Flitwick, was there as a beer retailer[77] and licensed victualler. The 1891 census shows he was also a carpenter and 53 years old. The inn is also described as a tied house of Wells & Co who

[75] Letter of BCC to Greene King 1 Sep 1977
[76] BLARS L23/285
[77] Directory 1890.

held the lease, the Countess Cowper still being the owner. Joel was also from Flitwick and was a carpenter as well as a licensed victualler. He may have been previously in London as his two children had been born in Kensington.

In 1895 Alfred Brown, born in Maulden, and his wife Sarah Brown were there, his main job was a shepherd with no doubt his wife pulling the pints. In 1901 Alfred Brown, aged 55 and born in Maulden was listed as the innkeeper, helped by his wife Sarah, and they had by then a daughter Clara aged 12, born in Silsoe. He was still there in 1914, as is recorded in the Kelly's Directory, but by 1916 Charles Mondin, Alfred's son-in-law, had taken over. He was an engine driver but his wife Emma Mondin probably ran the pub.

In 1898 the lease of the Lord Nelson, as part of a job lot of pubs owned by Wells Brewery at Biggleswade, was bought by a solicitor, Charles Winch, for his son. The controlling company eventually became Wells & Winch which merged with Greene King and Sons in 1961. In 1918 at the break up of the Wrest Park estate the Lord Nelson was sold for £665 by Lady Lucas to Messrs Wells & Winch, brewers of Biggleswade[78]. Eventually Greene King became the owners when they acquired Wells and Winch in 1961.

In 1920 Charles Mondin still was the 'beer retailer' but when he died in 1929, his widow Emma Mondin (Clara) carried on and was still there in 1940.[79] She died in 1967 aged 91 years, having given up her innkeeping job in 1952 when George & Rene Anstee took over.

After the Anstees came a total of thirteen tenants with the last being Bob and Koidula Crumpton who were installed in 2002.

The Lord Nelson remained a public house until 2003 when the brewery/owners, Greene King of Suffolk, closed it in order to obtain planning permission to convert it into a residence. After an appeal against this, the inevitable happened and it was converted in 2005.

The Battle Of Alma

This small alehouse was on the southern side of West End Road about half way down, now number 17, where it also doubled as a local grocers. Currently the shop window is still preserved but the door onto the street through which access was gained to the beer shop is now blocked up. At the time it opened in the early 19th century West End Road was a small, almost separate community with no houses on the road between Vicarage Road and the High Street and none in Vicarage Road, it thus served as the 'local' for the west enders.

---

[78] BLARS L23/287
[79] Kelly's Directory 1940

It had no inn sign and was familiarly known as 'Cook's Place', and, for a time after that, as 'Tom Mackey's Place' in the days when it was frequented by Luton Football Club supporters from the village. It was also affectionately known as the Mouses Hole.[80] Currently the large shop window has been retained but the door to the tiny bar to the right has since been bricked up and is now a window. A photo in the Whitbread collection shows the shop front before it was changed with 'J W Green Quality Ales & Stout' on the boards above the window.

It seems that the Alma developed from an inheritance by William Cook in 1837/38 of a leasehold cottage and garden in Silsoe owned by Mrs Mary Porter who was a relative of Frances Cook, his wife. William and Frances had the lease for their lives after which it went to their son Isaac. William was a tailor, originally from Harlington, and developed his business with his wife as in the 1851 census he is called a shopkeeper and publican and is probably living at the cottage which became the Alma. This building seems to have been extended up to the road and another building built on the site by 1856, so the shop and tailoring seems to have flourished.

Isaac Cook, William and Frances' son was born in Silsoe in 1820 and probably lived his life entirely in West End Road. He was trained as a tailor by his father William, and in 1841 is living in West End Road with his parents and their family aged 20, and is a journeyman tailor. In 1851 with his wife Louisa and children, he is fully a tailor and is also described as a draper in West End Road, living a few houses up from his parents.

The military operation called the Battle of the Alma took place during the Crimean campaign in 1854, and no doubt the alehouse was named after the action in the fervour of patriotism, and if there was a name before this, it has not been found.

Ten years later in 1861 his family has grown to include five children and Isaac is a tailor, draper and grocer. No mention of any ale selling then but in 1871 he is a tailor, draper, publican & grocer with his daughter Louisa being the house and shopkeeper. He perhaps stopped tailoring later on and in 1881 is a grocer, draper & publican in 1881, aged 60.

There may have been financial problems around then as in 1883 the Alma plus 9 adjacent cottages (one having a bakehouse), a former chapel and a house were put up for auction at the White Hart, Ampthill[81]. It appears that Earl Cowper purchased the lot for £900 and presumably leased the premises back, as Isaac is still there in 1891 but described as only a grocer. He was buried in August of that year.

---

[80] BLARS WB/Green4/2/5
[81] BLARS WE1278

In 1901 Louisa Cook, his wife, now a 79 year old widow was the grocer and beer shop keeper and had her son George, a carpenter, and daughter Louisa living with her.

Louisa died aged 88 in 1910 but on the break up of the Wrest estate in 1919 Miss Louisa Cooke, Isaac's spinster daughter, then aged 61, of Alma Inn, West End Rd, bought the house and allotment ground in West End Lane, Silsoe for £350 [82]. The conditions of the sale were that she had the use of, but had to help maintain, the local water supply. This referred to Thomas Case's well in the grounds of No 8 West End Road opposite, and that access be allowed to Annie Mann, who had bought the house behind the Alma.

George Cooke, Isaac's eldest son, has taken over by 1914 and is a carpenter and beer retailer in a directory of that year and, with his brother Charles, remained there for many years with both the bachelor brothers being featured in the *Luton News and Bedfordshire Advertiser* of about 1939 when George was 90 and Charles 85. The article reported that George retired from active management of the Alma when he was 87 years old!

Plate 14/7 - George and Charles Cooke, 1939

Charles remained the licensee until 1946 when Jessie Rust took over. Jessie married Arthur T Bottoms and she continued as licensee until 1951, a year after Arthur's death.

Some time in the mid 20th century the Alma was sold to J W Green Ltd. but it had a limited trade as it served only ale and no other alcoholic drink.
In March 1951 Tom and Joan Mackay moved to The Alma and remained there until 1956 when they moved to the Star. The subsequent licensees were Roy Ansell, Joseph Halliday and George Reed but the business closed in 1970.

---

[82] BLARS L23/1007/21 & L23/306

The Bell

There are only a few historical references to the Bell Inn in Silsoe, and there is also the possibility that at one time there were two of the same name and adjacent existing at the same time.

In 1721 John Allen of Silsoe, the Earl's steward, bought from William Bourne of Middlesex three roods of land with a cottage occupied by John Bird. This was said to be sited with the road to Clophill on the east, the common field of Waterslade to the north and William White's land to the west[83]. From examination of the 1718 map this would place it at about the location of the present George.

Then, included in a mortgage 16 years later in 1737[84], there is reference to a messuage called the Bell Inn plus three brick cottages, all lately erected by John Allen on a pightel of 3 roods formerly bought from William Bourne of Westminster. Apart from the land of Thomas Bishop being to the south, the other adjacent properties are as described in the 1721 document.

The Bell was said to be occupied by Mary Bird, a widow in 1737, presumably of John Bird, and in 1739[85] it is still occupied by widow Mary Bird. There is a record of a Mary Bird marrying Thomas Herbert in 1745 and in 1774, when the Bell Inn is again mentioned, Mary Bird is said to be a previous occupant and Mary Bust, widow, now the occupant[86].

The suggestion that there was another Bell Inn in the village at about the same time and in direct competition rests on an agreement made by James Poulton with Joseph Coles, the Earl of Hardwicke's agent, in August 1773 to discontinue using his house called the Bell as a public house. If he stopped that practice then land to the value of £20 a year was to be attached to the house in which he then lived.[87] It is possible that Polton started his venture in direct competition in the hope that he would be bought off!

Maps from the early 19th century show a building at the site of the present George with a row of brick cottages to the north which were only demolished in the last century, and which were sited where numbers 59 to 61a High Street are today. No mention of the Bell Inn after 1775 has been found and it may be that it closed after that date, and also that when The George moved from behind the Star & Garter in 1838 it took over the Bell buildings, and in the process changed its name.

---

[83] BLARS L5.321
[84] BLARS L5/323
[85] BLARS L5/331
[86] BLARS L5/335
[87] BLARS L5/343

The Ragged Staff

This hostelry, now lost to us, had the most prominent position of all the inns in the village, being located at the crossroads in the centre of the village directly opposite the church. The name the Ragged Staff probably derived from one of the emblems of the de Grey family, which can be seen in one of the stained glass windows in the church, Plate 14/8, and with the emblem dating from the early 15th century, the inn may have been of some antiquity.

The earliest mention of this inn is in a 21 year lease of 1635 for a messuage called the Ragged Staff from Henry, Earl of Kent, to the widow Elizabeth Newman and her son Richard Allin for £6.00 and an annual rent of £7.00[88]. The lease also included a total of some 7 acres of land in various fields around the village presumably for stabling and pasture.

A counterpart lease of 1656 for 10 years between Amabella, Dowager Countess of Kent, and Richard Alline, a brewer of Silsoe, is also for the Ragged Staff Inn including an orchard and a pightle plus the same land as in the earlier lease and for the same rent.[89]. Richard would receive rough timber from the Countess for building repairs and stakes for hedging. He died in 1658 but the inn remained with that family, as a Wrest Park estate rental book of the same year has "John Allen for the inn called the Ragged Staff in Silveshoo and 6 acres of land and one acre of meadow £7 00 00". John was probably Richard's brother.

Later in the same document there is a record of a Richard Cawne renting a cottage in Silsoe "beinge the signe of the wayfer and Ragged Staff and a pightle adjoining about 4 acres of arable land for £2 00 00 p.a.'[90]. It is not known what 'the signe of the wayfer' means.

Another tenant who comes down to us through the parish records is Philip Allen as on 11 December 1679 he is buried at Flitton as 'of the Ragged Staffe, Silsoe'. Then, in a 1687 lease for 26 acres of land John Allen, probably Philip's brother is described as an innholder and this is presumably the Ragged Staff.[91] He was probably there in 1681 when he prosecuted Henry Johnson for stealing glass bottles and knives.[92]

In the records of the Silsoe Petty Sessions of the 17th century that remain, many were held in Silsoe and one in 1681 is recorded as being held in the Ragged Staff[93]. The building must therefore have had a room of sufficient size to accommodate the constable, witnesses, magistrates and other court

---

[88] BLARS L5/1103
[89] BLARS L5/1107
[90] BLARS L26/1384
[91] BLARS L5/1058
[92] BLARS HSA1681/S/23 & 26
[93] BLARS HSA1681/S/14

staff. No doubt other sessions for which the records are lost, would also have been held at the inn.

Apart from the above, there is no other direct reference to the inn until 1718 when in a terrier attached to the Wrest Park atlas, (a survey of the lands belonging to the estate); Thomas Cox of the Ragged Staff is included. This building is described as "A messuage with barns stables etc called the Ragged Staff with a homestead adjoining 1ac 1r 30p". In addition to the building Thomas rented about 6 acres of land scattered around the common fields of Silsoe. For the land and the inn he paid an annual rent of £12 5s.[94]

Luckily there is a map associated with the terrier and shown on this, in the north west corner of the junction of the High Street with Church Road, is a plot with 'Cox's Close, 1ac 1r 30p' running from the High Street back to what is now Vicarage Road. There are substantial buildings shown in this plot running along the High Street frontage and partially back along Church Road. The Ragged Staff was thus in a prime location in the centre of the village and no doubt in competition with the George and the Star and Garter to the south.

The size of the main building in 1718 and on later maps of the 19th century, put it equivalent in area to the church so it was of some size and presumably from its age, a half timbered mediaeval construction.

Reasonably accurate maps dating from the early 19th century show that Church Road was at that time not directly in alignment with the Wrest Park Drive, and was in fact several metres to the south running close to what are now numbers 1 to 11 Church Road. The maps also show buildings on the corner forming what was probably The Ragged Staff so no doubt it continued to operate in the next hundred years or so.

As mentioned elsewhere, t seems likely that in association with the rebuilding of Wrest Park house in the 1830's and probably by 1831, Church Road was moved northwards to line up with the drive and with the Ragged Staff in the way of this scheme it was demolished.

Given their location and age it is a possibility that numbers 2 to 4 Church Road are all that remain of the inn or its outbuildings.

The New Inn

A map dated May 1715 shows a building marked as the New Inn on the site of the current New Inn Farm, south of Silsoe village just before the Gravenhurst turn off and west of the A6. The existing building is listed and said to be of around 1800 and the listing documents suggest that it may contain an earlier structure.

---

[94] BLARS L33/286

With a name like that, it seems likely that it was at one time an inn or possibly an alehouse. However, with the inns just up the road in Silsoe and at Barton, it is possible that trade was poor and eventually it became a farm house. Certainly no occupants named in the 19th century censuses are said to be innkeepers.

The White Horse

There is a glimpse of what might have been another public house on the 1718 estate map and terrier, where Charles Millward leases from the estate a messuage or tenement called the White Horse together with about 102 acres. Unless this is mis-transcribed from the 'White House', (and it is unusual for houses to be named at that time), then we have the only mention of this pub.

The map of that date has it situated at about where numbers 26 – 32 High Street are now, although there is no trace of a building there on the maps of the early 19th century.

Malthouses

Malt is made from dried barley grains which have been soaked for a few days to encourage their sprouting after which it is very roughly crushed or ground so that the husks are just starting to break away from the grains. The grains are then dried in the malting house for several days. Since the 13th century the flavour of beer has been obtained through mixing the malted grains, hops, water and yeast which is then allowed to ferment. Hops could have been obtained locally as in 1784 an entertainment at Sir George Osborn's hopground at Chicksands was mentioned by Rev. Ezekial Rouse[95] of Clophill with tea, coffee and chocolate and then dancing on the lawn.[96]

With Wrest Park[97], local inns and also farms brewing their own ale, malt was a valuable commodity and in the 15th century it was even left in wills to people or the Church. Thus Thomas Prest of Silsoe left in 1359 4 bushels of wheat 1 quarter of malt plus 1 mark to make his funeral procession[98] and John Smith of Eyen in 1435 left quantities of malt to several local churches.

An indication of the construction for a brewery is gained from a conveyance of 1696 when the cottage of Rebecca Fenner of Greenfield is described as having in a yard a chimney with a small addition annexed to a bakehouse or brewhouse[99].

---

[95] Ezekiel Rouse MA, 24 Apr 1754 died 27 Feb 1792, aged 84; Rector for 57 years; - William Rouse MA, 24 Jul 1792 died 18 Nov 1792, aged 58; - Ezekiel Rouse MA, 30 Mar 1793 died 13 Apr 1799, aged 60.
[96] BLARS CRT 100/27/4(I)
[97] BLARS L31/252
[98] BLARS Jleayes2 1359
[99] BLARS L5/229

John Alline of the Ragged Staff in 1635 was referred to as a brewer so no doubt he also brewed his own beer on the premises.

There are also other maltsters mentioned in documents relating to Silsoe in the 17th and 18th Centuries: Christopher Whitamore of Silsoe is said to be a maltster in a mortgage document of 1673[100], and in the 1718 terrier of lands of the Wrest estate William White was leasing a malting house etc. for £11 per annum[101].

Edward Lawrence of Silsoe was a maltster in 1728/29[102] and his will of 1757 allowed for his wife to continue or sell 'the business I am now in' – maltster. Edward is also described as a farmer in 1757[103] so was presumably brewing at the farmhouse. He died in 1757 but his widow carried on, as there is a draft agreement of 1772 letting to Widow Laurence a farm malting office in Silsoe. It is believed that this farmhouse is the building to the right as you enter The Maltings off the High Street. The Maltings is the cul-de-sac opposite to and just to the north of where Ampthill Road meets the High Street.

In 1740[104] Lord Hardwicke leased to Humphry Fletcher, the innkeeper at the George, a house or cottage in Silsoe previously occupied by John Else together with about half an acre of land, a dove house, a malting together with other buildings and one bay of a barn still in the occupation of Edward Lawrence. With this he also rented six cow commons. The rent was for £15 a year but as John Else seems to have let the buildings deteriorate badly, Humphry was given three years free of rent in exchange for paying the local builder, Thomas Bishop, £43 17s to repair the cottage. He had to keep it in repair himself after the main improvements had been carried out, winds and fire excepted and he seems to have added a cow hovel, a bottle rack plus a hen house and a necessary house.

Then in 1758 John Beaumont, a gentleman of Silsoe, rented from Viscount Royston and Jemima, Marchioness Grey, a cottage, malting, dovehouse, sheep & other commons in Silsoe[105] of which Jemima Beaumont, his mother, was occupier. In a further document of 1755 he is said to be a maltster[106] and in 1771 a lease referred to his widow Jemima Beaumont renting the maltings, (John had died in 1768.[107])

In the crime mentioned in a preceding chapter, two brothers, who were later executed, stole a ladder from Beaumont's maltings in 1754 to help them carry out a burglary[108].

---

[100] BLARS L5/55
[101] BLARS L33/286
[102] BLARS L5/793
[103] BLARS L5/1134
[104] BLARS L26/1429
[105] BLARS L5/1129
[106] BLARS L5/263
[107] BLARS L5/1136
[108] BLARS L29/15

At his burial in 1785 William Beaumont is described as a maltster of Silsoe. He was probably the son of John and Jemima being baptised in 1759 and was thus relatively young at his death.

Confirming that what is now 'The Maltings' was the locus of this operation is a plan dated 1813, obviously of this location, which shows a "farmhouse and offices" occupied by John Field in the village of Silsoe and which includes a malthouse, millhouse, dovehouse & wheelwright's shop.[109]

---

[109] BLARS L26/459, 460

Chapter 15 - Social Life, Fairs and Markets

Having Fun

Since most records of the past dealt mainly with business or land deals not much has been found of how the previous inhabitants of the village spent their leisure time. Of course, there was not much spare time, as for hundreds of years the average labourer was worked hard by his master and any time he did have, was probably spent on his own land ensuring he and his family had enough food to survive.

It could be said that the equivalent of hunting for the working classes was poaching, but this was more practical than sport, and involved a severe penalty if caught. However it was a necessity sometimes and there are cases recording the sentencing of poachers even into the last century.

Far more is known about the landed classes' relaxation. As mentioned elsewhere John Edwards, the carrier from Ampthill Road, managed to drown himself while fox hunting in the north of the county, and there were kennels at Wrest, established by Lord Polworth husband of Amabel, for the de Grey hounds. An early hunting reference was in 1692 when a list of clothes included red hunting breeches[110], and this sport obviously remained popular for many years as letters in the Wrest archives are peppered with references to it. Thus in 1772 Amabel wrote from Wrest to discuss foxhunting, and a year later about both hare and foxhunting, while in 1774 she visited the kennels which had been built by Lord Polwarth at Warren Farm a year or so earlier (and which remained there into the 20th century according to Mary Phillips).[111] In 1775 she commented that her husband "is too good a friend to the Sport, to destroy the Enemies of his Poultry-Yard by any other way than the fair War of Hunting".

Also in 1774,

"A report was spread that a fox had been seen by the Pavilion, upon which all the bow-wows were brought into the garden and ran yelping about the woods to no purpose. The horses all stayed at the bottom of Cainhill, the huntsmen ran about on foot, and Lord Polwarth and Sir Francis walked about the terrace and grumbled, and I made acquaintance with one of the dogs who seemed to like a bit of bread better than a fox-chase. Friday the wind was too high and they lost. At last yesterday they killed a fine old gentleman with a huge brush."

Other field sports included shooting and fishing and in the 19th and 20th centuries the Earl de Grey and his keepers introduced pheasants and partridges for the sport. They had a great deal of time in which to read and a large library at Wrest was built up due to the interests of Jemima, Philip and

---

[110] BLARS L31/129
[111] BLARS L30/13/12/4 and others.

Amabel. But, while many by the 19th century had bibles or tracts in their houses, but how many could read? Many documents, including marriage certificates from this era have an 'x' where they were required to witness.

John Stow in 1603 listed the *Sports and Pastimes of London* of that time and while these may be of a more urban nature no doubt many were carried out in Silsoe.[112] Most related to Christian festival days, but some went back much earlier and related to pagan festivals.

May Day was celebrated in a far more boisterous way then than now, and one of the few references to Silsonians enjoying themselves comes in the Hon. John Byng's notes of 1789 when after gratuitously insulted the local peasants he refers to Morris Dancing viz:-

"The cottagers every where, look wretchedly, like their cows; and slowly recovering from their wintry distress: Deserted by the Gentry, they lack Assitance, Protection and amusement; however, my landlord says that in May there are Mayers (alias Morris Dancers) who go about with a Fool, a man in Womans Cloathes (the Maid Marion) and Musick".[113]

Archery practice at 'the butts', usually located near the local parish church, was initially a voluntary occurrence in all English & Welsh towns and villages as men, young and old, would test their bow skills at regular weekly meetings. A bit like darts, but on a larger scale.

However, in the 15th century newer sports such as an early variety of cricket and then football, became too popular and in 1515 a law was imposed by King Henry VIII that his subjects should keep a long bow in his house, and should provide bows for his children between 7 & 17 years of age. It also required butts to be set up in every city, town or place as used in ancient times, and that the inhabitants should exercise themselves with long bows on holy days and other convenient times.

(It is believed that this Act has never been repealed so just remember, fathers with male children over the age of 7, you may be fined if you have not provided them with a bow, two arrows and taught them how to shoot!)

An act of 1542 established that the minimum target distance for anyone over the age of 24 years was 220 yards (the modern competition maximum is 80 yards!). A trained archer could shoot 12 to 15 arrows per minute and hit a man-sized target at a minimum of 200 yards.

---

[112] *'Sports and pastimes of old time'*, *A Survey of London*, by John Stow: Reprinted from the text of 1603 (1908), pp. 91-99. URL: http://www.british-history.ac.uk/report.aspx? compid=60025

[113] *The Torrington Diaries*; Containing the tours through England and Wales of The Hon. John Byng (later fifth Viscount Torrington) between the years 1781 and 1794 Eyre & Spottiswode 1934

The bow used was the longbow, up to 78 inches in length and made of yew, elm, or ash. The draw weight was up to a remarkable 120 pounds, with the bow drawn "to the ear" rather than to the corner of the mouth, as is common in modern archery. At short range, an arrow could drive into 4 inches of seasoned oak, and could penetrate the armour of a knight at 200 yards. This was no toy!

Although there is a location in Clophill called Butt Hills, no field has been found in Silsoe with the word 'Butt' attached. However, there is one reference in a 1663 conveyance to some land being east of "Flitton Butts".[114] Perhaps the archers of Silsoe had to walk across to Flitton to practice, carrying their bows and arrows, but maybe, somewhere in Silsoe, there is a site at least 220 yards long where this practice was carried out.[115]

Fairs and Markets

As there was no easy way of keeping food fresh, and with slow transport making it difficult to get to distant centres to sell or buy fresh food and other products, most sales were made in local markets and had been for ages. Market towns had been in existence since Saxon times with some being specialised concentratin perhaps on perhaps poultry, clothing or in the 19th century straw plait. Bedford had a market from before the Norman conquest while Ampthill market commenced in 1219. There waa short lived one at Westoning from 1304 and the Shefford market started in 1229. No doubt many from Silsoe went to those events to buy, sell or just have a good time.

Markets and fairs were strictly controlled by the Crown and were only permitted by Royal Charter. These were granted as a reward to nobles and landowners for services rendered to the sovereign, and the grant of a Royal Charter to a landowner was of great value, as he was allowed to charge rents and tolls to those sellers attending the markets. Also, it gave protection to the holder of the charter from disturbance by other market operators. This protection still exists as, under common law, the holder of a market charter is entitled to take action against any rival market operator who opens a market, or attempts to open a market, within 6 and 2/3 miles of its charter market.

Thus, when at York in November 1319, King Edward II granted a market and a fair to Ralph of Silsoe[116] it was made clear that it was not to be prejudicial to other existing markets ;

"Edward by grace of God K of Eng, Ld of Ireland, Duke of Acquitaine etc

---

[114] BLARS L5/166

[115] Purely a suggestion but the tree known as Beaumont Oak near Hollington Basin is on the 1794 plan of Flitton called 'Bowmans Tree, possibly where the bowmen stood to practice?

[116] He owned Newbury Manor as in 1324 he was given royal permission to divert the Kings Highway there.

Know that we have granted and by this our charter confirmed to our beloved & faithful Ralph fil Rudulphi fil Ricardi, that he & his heirs may have forever one market every week on Wednesday clos to his manor of Silsoe in Cty of Bedford and one fair in the same place every year which shall last 2 days to whit on vigil and day of Apostles Philip & James (30 Apr. and 1st May) unless either market or fair shall be to the harm of neighbouring fairs or markets ....

Witnesses. W(illiam de Welton) Archbishop of York, Primate of England. J(ohn) Hotham, Bishop of Ely, 'Our Chancellor'; R(oger de Martival) Bishop of Salisbury; Thomas, Earl of Lancaster 'our cousin'; John de Britannia, Earl of Richemund; Adomar de Valencia, Earl of Pembroke, John de Grey, John de Moubray, John de Butetourt."[117]

There is no indication where these great social events were held, but if Silsoe Manor was near the church, then by the crossroads would seem the best location.

Also, it is not known how long 'forever' turned out to be. Silsoe is not best placed nor was very big, and as mentioned above there were other markets and fairs at Ampthill, Luton, Shefford, Bedford and Dunstable. Both the market and the fair in Silsoe, held by Ralph son of Ralph son of Richard, were recorded in 1330 when he produced the charter to prove he had the right to hold them, but no other reference after then has been found of this early market.[118]

That the fair lapsed is backed up by the fact that the Duke of Kent, also no doubt after a bit more cash, managed to obtain a new Charter from King George II for a weekly market and a fair on 13th September, in 1715/16.[119]

In 1765 the Earl of Hardwicke was enquiring about the history of Silsoe market. The vicar of Flitton and Silsoe, Mr Cox, wrote to him reporting that Mrs Caton, probably of West End Farm, said that it had been discontinued about 36 years before, due to lack of business. A month after that letter however, the local farmers were reported to have assembled at the market place to discuss a proposal to move the market about a furlong from its present location. This location is not given, but it was thought that the new location would be too far from the George inn. Later when it was suggested by his Lordships agent, Mr Cole, that it could be held in the yard in front of the George (the George's old location, that is), this was said to be convenient both for that inn and also for the Star & Garter so the people at the market could use whichever public house they wanted. The Earl of Hardwicke agreed to erect a shelter for the market people as long as it was not in the

[117] BLARS L26/1427, LJeayes682

[118] *Samantha Letters*, Online Gazetteer of Markets and Fairs in England Wales to 1516 <http://www.history.ac.uk/cmh/gaz/gazweb2.html>: Bedfordshire, last updated 23 July 2007

[119] BLARS L26/1426, Vol. 7, No 54 Autumn 1960 *Silsoe Village* by Mary Phillips, The National Archives | Catalogue | Reference C 202/103/3

avenue leading to his park gates. If this was done, it is not known where, but the logical location would appear to be in the George's yard.[120]

A letter of the 13th May 1812 from Wrest Park dealing with documents, said that one had not been attached to the file as that day was Silsoe Fair, and the writer was very busy. On the date in question it was a Wednesday.[121]

In the 1820's J D Parry in the *Gentleman's Magazine* said that there were two fairs held each year, one on 12th May and another on 21st September. This is corroborated in Cooke's 1820 itinerary, although he said that the first fair was on the festival of Saints Philip & James, 1st May. The 1843 - 44 *Parliamentary Gazetteer*[122] said that the weekly market was no longer held but fairs were held on 13 May and on 21 September for cattle of all sorts.

The fair was certainly there in 1823[123] when William Brunt of Biggleswade, mercer and draper had items stolen from a stall at Silsoe Fair.

"Between six and seven in the evening a lady said to him "Mr. Brunt some persons are stealing your Goods" he then missed three parcels of worsted stockings from his stall containing about eight parts in each. "I jumped out of the stall, and saw a person of the name of Lowe standing near the place where the Goods were missed. I said to him "Lowe, do you know the Men who have robbed my stall"? he said "No" - my Brother and I then went in pursuit - About eleven o'clock the same Evening, Joseph Lowe came to me at the George Inn at Silsoe where I slept and told me that he could not rest - he knew the two men... they were William Page and James Page... The following morning, I was told by a little Girl whom I met in the street that she had seen William Page with a Bundle of Stockings under his arm, and that if I was to go up, I should find him drunk in a Barn belonging to a Mr. Hatred of Silsoe" In custody Page denied all knowledge of the robbery but later when Lowe came as a witness at the Flying Horse, Clophill he confessed to his share and said that they would find others in the possession of others who he named. Page said "that it was the first time that he had ever got into the Gang" and "I was completely drawn in by James Page my fellow Prisoner, to commit the Robbery... I am sorry for it" James Page says "There was a hole cut at the corner of the stall... and I picked up a Bundle of the Stockings, and gave them to William Page"".

How long the market lasted for is not known and William Treacher, when writing a short pamphlet on Silsoe and Wrest in 1899, said that while the fair was still held on 13th May, the market had been long discontinued.[124] He had

---

[120] BLARS CRT/100/27/3
[121] L30/11/132/123
[122] BLARS CRT 130 Flit13
[123] BLARS QSR/26/1823/330
[124] W Treacher, Headmaster of Silsoe school 1883 – 1922, 1899, "*Wrest and its Surroundings*"

been in Silsoe at least since 1883 so it seems likely that the 13th May was the correct date for the fair or the date had been changed.

The May 13th fair was apparently still being held in 1931 according to the Kelly's Directory of that year but may well have ceased at the time of the Second World War.

The fair was briefly revived in the 1950's and again in 1970, when it became for many years the main social event of the village with the proceeds being used to help with the upkeep of the church. The first fair in 1970 was opened by Ron Montague, who still (2010) lives in the village, and formerly was the Pearly King of Kensington with his wife, Bet the Pearly Queen. It was always held on August Bank Holiday Monday and at its height in the 1990's attracted up to 4000 people and was able to provide the church with a substantial amount of money each year.

The fair was held around the cricket square in Wrest Park and had many side shows such as coconut shies, stalls selling all sorts of things and attractions such as smashing up old pianos, bands and the Royal Air Force Memorial fly past of a Lancaster, Spitfire and Hurricane.

Unfortunately it was so big and involved so many from the village in its organisation and running that it became difficult to find enough new villagers to help and so, with the falling off of helpers and with the competition of large commercial events such as craft fairs being held on the same day in Wrest Park it was decided to abandon the event in 1997.

Other Village Pastimes & Celebrations

It seems that when it was time to pay tithes or rents, to soften the blow, and perhaps to encourage people to pay on time, food and drink was laid on. In the mid 18th century a letter from the Rev. Rouse to the Earl of Hardwicke mentions the reason that some of his chief servants had been out late was that " It had been a custom for the waggoners and carriers of Silsoe about Christmas time to invite their customers to a fish feast" It is likely that the fish was well washed down with the local or home-brewed ale.

There is no doubt that at times of celebration for the de Grey family, marriages and the like, the villagers were encouraged to join in, with money donated for parties to be organised. At times of national celebration such as coronations, this also took place and there is a record in the Wrest letters of a party being organised for the Coronation of George IV in 1821.[125]

In addition, Earl de Grey held theatricals at Wrest park and also balls linked to his role as Lord Lieutenant of the county.

---

[125] BLARS L30/11/20/17

By the end of the 19th century it is evident that life had improved a great deal in Silsoe and taking the *Bedfordshire Times'* reports of 1901 and 1902 as an example, it can be seen that there were many occasions when people could let their hair down.

Early in May 1901 there was the first run of the season for Silsoe Cycling Club when they went to Old Warden on a Saturday evening. There was another run in June to Barton with " a capital tea prepared by Mr Jn. Harris of Silsoe" for their return.

Also in June there was a cricket match with Silsoe playing Luton Cricket Club, unsurprisingly we lost by 48 runs – we only scored 37! (Apparently the Rev. Robert Lang, Vicar at Silsoe from 1873 – 1887 "…was well known in cricket circles as the great Harrow and Cambridge bowler."[126] - perhaps he managed to get a side together when he was here!)

The next month Silsoe church members went on an outing to Dover via Flitwick, where it is reported they saw the castle & the pier.

Then there was a big day in August when the Silsoe & Ampthill Show held their 61st event in Wrest Park. It was said that 10,000 people attended and there was dancing, a fruit, produce & flower show in addition to exhibitions of work. In the tug of war event, Robinsons Mechanics beat Silsoe Gardeners & won a sovereign. There was no baby show.

If this was an annual event then it must have started in about 1840, although no report of such an event at that time has been found.

The next year on 10 January 1902 there was a bagatelle match in the Reading Room in the village, when Silsoe beat Clophill by 4 to 1. However, there was a return match on 17th at which Silsoe was beaten by the same score.

There is some dispute over the location of the Reading Room. One villager has suggested that it was in the old school building which was situated where the village newsagents now is, while the May 1985 issue of *The Silsoe News* has it in the other old school, that is, the building on the left at the entrance to the village hall. Its full title was the Working Men's Reading Room (no women?) and it is pleasing to read that at the AGM on 31 January it was reported that there had been a vast improvement in the conduct of those using the room – what had they been doing before? At the same meeting, with the vicar in the chair, Mr Treacher, the teacher, said that 45 books had been added and that books of a more elevating nature were to be acquired. The reading room was supported by the Earl who gave a substantial annual donation towards the cost of purchasing new books.[127] Amongst the committee members were J Rich, H Walker, H J White, C Bottoms, E Ambridge and F Carvell.

---

[126] *History of The Church Missionary Society*, Eugene Stuck 1836-1928
[127] *Beds Times* 24 Jan 1902.

It must have been a hard winter as the 21 February brought a new sport with skating on the frozen lake and the new pond at Wrest.

Later that year in April the Cricket Club held its annual concert in the Reading Room, it may have had to have have discontinued it there, but maybe the singing has continued in the Star.

In August 1902 Edward VII had his Coronation and Earl Cowper gave £10 with Mr Trethewy donating £3, towards the village celebrations. Before that however, the British Women's Temperance Association had held a summer fete in July, tea was taken in Mr Harris's close, behind No 26 High Street, and in a speech it was said that those girls thinking of marriage should avoid young men who frequented public houses which should all be closed.

Also that year The Maharajah of Koihapur and his suite visit Ampthill Park for a picnic. They arrived from London on the 4th August, and detrained at Millbook Station. They were met by Earl Cowper and Lord Alwyno. The band of the Bedfordshire Regiment played for them in Ampthill Park and the inhabitants of the villages of Ampthill, Clophill, Silsoe and Flitwick took part in sports.

This was apparently a good year for celebrations as although the Ampthill & Silsoe Agricultural Fair had to be held at Ampthill rather than Wrest Park, on 8th August Viscount Kitchener of Khartoum visited Wrest. The flags were out, the church bells were rung and the local men took the horses off the carriage and pulled it by hand to the mansion - patriotism was more evident then.

More festivities again on 22 August when the Earl and Countess entertained children of those connected to Wrest Park with punch and judy, swing boats and other things. Other years of that era give a similar story, so life had improved since John Byng's sour comments on the populace a hundred years earlier.

While on the subject of royal celebrations, it was remembered by the villagers for many years that on 24th July 1909 King Edward VII visited Wrest Park as a guest of the American Ambassador, Whitelaw Reid, who rented the mansion from 1906 to 1912. The *Times* reported that earlier that day the King had lunched wearing the Cullinan diamond (value about £200 million), but no doubt he left that behind before coming to Silsoe. Various local lords and ladies attended the evening event, as did the Deputy Mayor of Bedford who gave a loyal address. The event created a great deal of excitement in the village and around, as can be seen from the photograph of the event.

Plate 15/1 - King Edward VII's visit to Silsoe 1909

Silsoe Village Hall

The hall was built in 1926 by the then owner of Wrest Park, John George Murray. It was originally of red painted corrugated iron and was used two or three nights a week for film shows, (the projector room is still there), and at the weekend for dances. There were two gasometers at the back, which supplied gas for lighting.

During the Second World War soldiers were billeted in the hall, and they presented a shield thanking the people of Silsoe for their hospitality.[128]

By 1946 Mr Murray was living in Buntingford, Hertfordshire, and in that year he sold the hall to the village for £1,800. The Carnegie Trust donated half the sum with the proviso that the village found the rest. The original trustees were John Miller of Church Cottage, Benjamin Burton of Home Farm, Aubrey Sampson, Aubrey Boutwood, Herbert Mason, Henry Mann and Horace Godrey.

In the early 1960's the iron cladding had begun to leak and it was replaced with rendered metal lathing. Toilets were also added, replacing the use of buckets in outhouses to the rear!

The village hall became a charity in 1968 when its object was stated to be ".. the provision and maintenance of a village hall for the use of the inhabitants of the parish of Silsoe and its neighbourhood without distinction of political, religious and other opinions including use for meetings, lectures and classes

---

[128] Most information on the Village hall history is contained in the January 1985 *Silsoe News* written by Bob Thurman.

and for other forms of recreation and leisure time occupation with the object of improving the conditions of life for the said inhabitants." And so it has.

The management committee continued to improve it and a committee room was added in the early 1970's, the stage was widened in 1976, and in the early 1980's a major renovation costing well over £100,000 was carried out. This provided the range of storage rooms on the north side, a bar area, the deepening of the stage area and other improvements, such as better toilets. This work was partly financed by holding money-raising events, but mainly by selling off land to the rear for housing. It is difficult to balance the cost of the maintenance needs of the hall with the revenue obtained from hiring and at the present, additional finance is obtained from the "100 Club" where members pay an amount each year with the hope of winning a prize in a monthly draw.

Modern Day Societies and Clubs

With the availability of even more leisure time over the past 50 years or so, those who do not just want to sit in front of the television have a great choice of activities, both physical and cerebral to choose from. Most are centred around the village hall, which is a valuable community facility and which continues to be well used. Plate 15/2.

On the sports side, the Icknield Cycling Club meets every week at the village hall as does the Karate Club and the Springboks Trampoline Club; and there is also a dance school which practices at the hall regularly. The more traditional sports of football and cricket are well catered for in the village, and there are teams for both which shared the sports field just inside Wrest Park as their venue. The cricket club celebrated its 100th year in 1999 and has been playing in the village on the ground just inside Wrest Park either though the generosity of the Wrest Park owners or through a licence, latterly from English Heritage. However, due to problems both with damage to the pavilion and the pitch and the lack of a permanent tenure of the ground, the cricket club decided in 2010 to leave that pitch and become a touring or 'rambling' team. The football club then became responsible for the pavilion and the pitch.

For many years there was a tennis club which initially used a court halfway up the hill of Vicarage Road, managed by trustees. When facilities at Cranfield Agricultural College became available this was abandoned, and is now overgrown, but with that organisation having now fled back to Cranfield and development of the site in view, there are now no courts available in the village for this sport.

Other sports such as golf and croquet are available, with the latter using the immaculate lawns in Wrest Park for their sport, holding championships and other events there. See Plate 15/3

The Golf League uses the course at Beadlow Manor Golf and Country Club as its base, while members occasionally head abroad to Portugal or Wales for more adventurous courses.

Occasionally dances and other fund raising events such as table top sales or bazaars are held at the village hall which nowadays are usually organised by the various village societies plus others such as the Young Farmers. In addition concerts or special events such as the country and western singer Kevin Montgomery from Nashville, are arranged.

One other big user of the village hall is the Drama Club which was formed from the Women's Institute drama group in 1971 and which has put on productions since then, both in the hall and at Wrest Park where many thousands have come to see the 'Shakespeare in the Park" events. Other shows have been varied from pantomime and musicals through to plays by Denis Potter, Noel Coward and Alan Ayckbourn. Currently it puts on at least two shows a year, and involves many people in both acting, backstage and production. See Plate 15/4.

Prior to the village school being able to take 3-4 year olds, parents ran a playschool there for the toddlers, while for the older youths the village hall has on and off been used as a youth social club for many years, although its viability does depend on the willingness of helpers to spend time with the more energetic section of the population.

Also available in the village to those of a more literary mind, is a mobile library provided by the district council, the reading group and the poetry group. There are also the Derby and Joan Club and Chatterbox, both aimed at the less young in body and another group, SOS (Silsoe Offers Support) was formed to provide assistance in getting to the doctor's or other places and in addition a weekly open-door event at the village hall was organised for the 'senior citizens'.

The Silsoe Women's Institute group was formed in 1946 and has carried on ever since meeting about once a month to listen to speakers, to discuss current problems and learn how to make good jam (No, honest, I did not mean to write that!).

Once almost a necessity to provide cheap food for labourers, allotments were at the end of the 19th century provided for his estate workers by Earl Cowper. The village allotments, which were created on land obtained by the County Council at the Wrest Park estate sell-off, are now available to all, and are very popular. The present Waterslade Allotments Association not only runs an annual produce show but also gives growing advice in the *Village News,* as well as selling gardening necessities such as seeds, fertiliser and other items from its new shed on the allotments, to its members.

The *Silsoe Village News*, published every month provides a list of most of the clubs and associations that are currently active in the village, in January 2009 they were:-

Busy Tots Toddler Group	Christian Aid
Chatterbox	Darby & Joan
Drama Club	Friends of Silsoe Church
Icknield Cycling Club	Karate Club
Lace Making	Rotary Club
Silsoe Cricket Club	Silsoe & District Young Farmers
Silsoe Dance School	Silsoe Golf League
Silsoe Horticultural Centre	Silsoe Lower School Parent Teachers Assn
S.O.S.	Springboks Trampoline Club
St James' Church Choir	St James' Guild of Bell Ringers
Waterslade Gardeners Club	Women's Institute
Wrest Park Croquet Club	Yam Kai Shotokan Karate Club
Youth Social Club	

25 years earlier in January 1985, although probably not all clubs were mentioned in the *Silsoe News* for that date (for example the croquet club was formed in 1961) the following were mentioned:-

Baby Sitting Circle	Silsoe Drama Club
Pre-School Playgroup	Darby and Joan Club
Mother's Union and Young Wives	Waterslade Gardeners Club
Women's Institute	Workers Educational Association

Other Activities

Many in the village enjoy their spare time in an unorganised way by using the public footpaths, or keep fit by jogging in the morning or evening. In addition the Millennium Green, a public space created with the assistance of a £46,000 grant from the Countryside Agency to celebrate the millennium, is used as an informal space to relax in, or take dogs for a walk.

The Future.

With a quantum increase in the village population expected in the future with the proposed development of the old Silsoe College site, the current village facilities will certainly be insufficient to cater for the needs of the numbers of incomers.

The developers were strongly advised at their consultations that the present population expect there to be a good provision of new services and facilities, and while a final plan has yet to be presented, the "Masterplan" issued in 2008 included play areas, a community woodland, a soft sports area for cricket and a hard one for tennis or handball , 5-a-side pitches plus a sports hall, and the relocation of the school to new premises.

These facilities are also included in the *Silsoe Parish Plan* which was released in 2008 by the planning committee and the parish Council, and which contains many proposals made by the villagers at the consultation stage of the plan for sports and leisure activities.

Chapter 16 - People and Families

Introduction

"And some there be, which have no memorial; who are perished, as though they had never been; and are become as though they had never been born; and their children after them.

But these were merciful men, whose righteousness hath not been forgotten.

With their seed shall continually remain a good inheritance, and their children are within the covenant.

Their seed standeth fast, and their children for their sakes.

Their seed shall remain for ever, and their glory shall not be blotted out.

Their bodies are buried in peace; but their name liveth for evermore.

The people will tell of their wisdom, and the congregation will shew forth their praise."[129]

Unfortunately, as most ancient documents related to land purchase and as the average peasant did not have any land, most of the older information on families is heavily biased towards the land owners.

It is only from about the 16th century when the church started to keep records of births, marriages and deaths that the appearance and disappearance of families in the village can be traced. And even then, as the parish was Flitton cum Silsoe, it is difficult to prove that people were at one or other of the population centres. Also, while the bald facts of their existence can be made out, some evidence of their actual character is hard to find.

The owners of Wrest Park and the other families who owned the manors, or were major farm tenants have been mentioned in those sections, so this chapter will deal mainly with those families of whom we have more information, those of the 19th and 20th centuries.

The Eve Family

It is believed that the Eve family, one branch of which found itself in Silsoe early in the 19th century, originated with the Eves that can be traced back to Abbess Roding, which lies midway between Chelmsford and Harlow, in the 1540's.[130]

Richard Eve, who was born in 1788 at Lanark Farm, Weston, Herts, came to Silsoe in 1806 aged only 18, where he rented West End Farm from Amabel, later Countess de Grey. He made a great success of farming there, and lived

---

[129] *Ecclesiasticus / Sirach* Ch9 Vss 9-15

[130] Most information regarding Eve descendants was taken from www.evetree.co.uk

in that house until he died in 1885, having had 10 children from two wives.[131] He married his first wife, Sarah Caton, almost as soon as he got to Silsoe[132], in 1807, and they had seven children. When she died in about 1817 she left seven children alive, Charlotte Caton born 1808, Richard born 1810, Charles born 1811, Henry Thomas born 1816 and three others.

How he cared for his children while farming a large area for nine years is not known, but Richard obviously needed another wife to look after his brood and he was married for the second time to Mary Trustram of Shillington in 1828. She produced a further three for him, Eliza born before 1833, John Richard Eve born 1833 & William Eve born 1835. She died in the same year as her husband

He would recount the story of the collapsing of the tower of the old church at Silsoe during its construction, and that the West End farmhouse was extended by Earl de Grey (to accommodate Richard's growing family?) using materials from the old mediaeval house in Wrest Park when that was being demolished.

During his life he was a member of the Board of Guardians[133] and an original member of the Luton Turnpike Trust. He was appointed as churchwarden in 1811 at Flitton, when only 23 years old, and remained as a churchwarden for some 74 years until he died, having seen off 10 vicars of Flitton or Silsoe.

He also took a leading part in starting the Silsoe and Ampthill Labourers' Friend Society, in which he always continued to take a great interest.

Several prominent people are descended from his son, John Richard Eve. They include John Richard's second son Arthur Stewart, who attended Pembroke College, Cambridge, and became a professor at McGill University, Montreal, in 1903. He was a Fellow of the Royal Society of Canada in 1910 and served in the Great War, 1914-19, becoming a colonel in 1918. After the war he was Director of Physics at McGill University and President of the Royal Society of Canada. He wrote a several books on applied geo-physics; college physics; and the life of Lord Rutherford with whom he worked and was a friend. He returned to England after he retired and settled at Overponds Cottage, Shackleford, near Godalming, Surrey where he died in 1941, he is buried in Silsoe churchyard near Richard, his grandfather.

John Richard Eve's third son, Herbert Trustram Eve, born 1865 in Ampthill was a London Kings Councillor and was knighted for his services. His son,

---

[131] Most information from the obituary of Richard Eve, *Bedfordshire Standard*, Nov 14 1885.

[132] There is no record of the marriage at Silsoe but Caton is a Silsoe name

[133] The Boards of Guardians were created by the Poor Law Amendment Act 1834 and replacing the parish Overseers of the Poor established under the old poor law. The boards administered workhouses within a defined poor law union consisting of a group of parishes.

Arthur Malcolm Eve, born 1894, was created a Baronet in 1943 and Baron Silsoe in 1963. He also lies in the churchyard.

His son, David Malcolm Trustrum Eve was a QC and the 2nd Baron Silsoe. He was leading counsel in several important public inquiries such as Heathrow Terminal 4, Gatwick North Terminal, Sizewell B and Hinkley Point C nuclear power stations and finally the Heathrow airport Terminal 5 expansion inquiry. He died in 2005 being succeeded by Simon Eve, the 3rd Baron.

Finally, John Richard Eve's fifth son, Frank Cecil Eve, attended Emmanuel College, Cambridge in 1890 becoming a M.D. in 1903. He became consulting physician at the Victoria Hospital for Children, Hull.

In the past it was not easy to attain a position of importance if born of an unconnected family, but some people managed to reach positions of importance due to their inherent merit, thus we come to one of these:-

Henry Trethewy[134]

A representative of the Trethewy family who, like Richard Eve, came to Silsoe to work for the Wrest estate was Henry Trethewy. He was born in 1814 in Probus, Cornwall not far from Truro, where his father was also a land agent, and by 1836 he was witnessing documents as agent for the trustees of the will of Earl de Grey.

It is not known when he came to Silsoe, and he is not mentioned in the 1841 census, but he was involved in the Gravenhurst Enclosure of 1847, and at his marriage in Northampton to Emma Barwell in 1850, he was said to be of Silsoe. He probably moved into Silsoe House when it was built, and was instrumental in getting Ampthill Road moved, to give himself a bigger front garden.

As an important member of the Silsoe elite he needed many servants to maintain his standard of living, and in 1861 with a family of four children he needed a nursemaid, a cook, two housemaids and a page boy. He and his wife had a total of ten children but as he was wealthy enough to send them away to be educated, only once is a teenager found in the censuses.

He found Bedfordshire to his liking, and presumably through his family contacts his nephew, Alfred Tresawna Trethewy came to this area, and with Mark Sharman founded the group of solicitors, Sharman and Trethewy who started in Ampthill but whose heirs, Sharman Law, are still practising in Bedford today.

---

[134] This name, originally from Cornwall, is spelled differently in different documents but Trethewy is used here.

Henry and his family were evidently kind to their workers as is shown by the memorial to Thomas Mann who worked variously as a cowman at West End farm and as a gardener, probably at Wrest park.

"Thomas Mann entered into rest May 31st 1896 aged 78 years
This stone is erected by Mr Trethewy and family in remembrance
of 48 years faithful service."

Henry's wife was found neither in the censuses for Silsoe in 1881 nor in that of 1891, when he was at Silsoe with two unmarried daughters and his son Arthur. She died in London in 1900 and had maybe moved there. Henry had continued his interest in the land when of some age and in 1890, *The Times* reported that he had given an address to "The Farmers Club" in London on the subject of tythes; he was also described as a J.P. in 1901. He was buried at Silsoe in 1908, aged 94.

In the latter half of the 20th century, David Manby, who worked at Silsoe Institue, and his wife Mabs lived in the house and she informed *The Luton News* in 1987 that she often saw the ghost of a little girl, apparently named Sarah. It quite often crossed the hall and had been seen by others. It also seems that a hundred years earlier when the house was lived in by a Mrs Hallam that a lodger, Bill Turner, was woken by the stairs creaking, he got out of bed, lit a lamp and outside his bedroom door saw a fair haired little girl in a pinafore, who ran past him in distress, and disappeared by the bed.

The Fields of Barton & Fielden

The first mention of the Field family name is found in 1558 in the Barton parish register, but they were probably around for much longer and may have taken their name from La Felde of Lower Gravenhurst as there is reference to "… John son of Silvester de la Felde (now Fielden) and Agnes, daughter of Augustine de Kechinge his wife…" in a 12th century document.[135] Agnes probably came from the now disappeared Manor of Kitchen just south west of the parish, so it would have been a fairly important family.

In 1694, John Field married Mary, the sister of Charles Nicholls, a Hitchin gentleman who inherited his father's estate in 1692, and added to it mainly by lending money with property as security, and foreclosing on the 'mortgages'. When Nicholls died unmarried in 1746 all his estates descended via John Field's wife to their three sons, two of whom, like their uncle, were attorneys with chambers in London, and homes in Hitchin. Working with the law seems to have been uppermost in the families' minds, as it seems that they used it for many matters, with almost every will or bequest appearing to be contested in the courts.

John's son, John, eventually inherited most of the estate through his brothers dying without male children, and in his will of 1757, the property passed to

---

[135] BLARS LJeayes 630

his eldest son, Carolus. This son had also gained in 1763 by way of a marriage settlement, property including the White Hart at Ampthill. Carolus had been indentured as a draper to George Gurney, of Ampthill, for 7 years from 15th July 1754, during which time he was not to use alcohol or go gaming, etc, and must not contract matrimony during the term. Sadly Carolus died early after only a year of marriage, and a third John Field, Carolus's brother, was the beneficiary.

This John Field 3rd, when he married Frances Flint of Higham Gobion in 1773, had, like Carolus, benefited from a marriage settlement from his father-in-law. This was New Inn with 40 acres (mainly in Pulloxhill), plus another 8 acres in that area and he earned £58 a year rent from John Hill, the tenant. It seems that John lived at New Inn as several documents refer to him as being of that place.

Following tradition, the eldest son Thomas Flint Field inherited the bulk of the estate from his father in 1815 with the two other brothers, Charles Nicholls and John Fesh[136] receiving £60 & £30 pa respectively for life.

Around this time it seems that John Fesh went off the rails, as in 1812 John his father, had to agree to pay a debt via a solicitor, to ensure that one of his sons was not arrested for defaulting. There were also many loans taken out on the property totalling £1,900.[137]. This son was probably John Fesh Field, as his brother Thomas Flint is said to be a cheesemaker in London, and Charles seems to have settled in Hitchin.

There was a more serious matter involving the family which took place in 1818, 3 years after John Field 3rd's death. A report in *The Times* of 22 December 1818, taken from the *Northants Mercury*, runs as follows:-

"On Friday night, 6th November last, a desperate gang of poachers, (About twenty in number), known by the Bedfordshire Poachers or Robin Hood's gang, headed by a farmer named Field, of New Inn, near Silsoe, who called himself Robin Hood, attacked the woods and estate of Joseph Latour, Esq., of Hixton, near Hitchin. The keeper, Dalby, and his assistant Godfrey, on finding Field and his companions advancing near them, concealed themselves in a hedge; the gang, however, crossing the hedge near the spot discovered them, when, without any attack or provocation whatever on the part of the keepers, they formed a line around them, when four or five of the party most cruelly beat them, leaving them for dead. Field held his dog by the ear, while it licked the blood from the head of Godfrey.

Much credit is due to Mr Latour, for his spirited exertions in sending immediately to Bow-street for assistance, when an active officer of the name

---

[136] In Deborah Fields will of 1787 there is " to Revd John Fesh six teaspoons marked M.F. and 1 guinea to buy a ring to wear in testator's memory". He has not been traced.
[137] BLARS Z937/1/20 & Z937/4/31 - 35

of Holyland was sent down, who soon ascertained that the gang consisted of at least 40 men, with Field at their head, and that they were encouraged by a number of gentlemen and farmers. Two of the men, Senly and Brown, were speedily apprehended, and sworn to by the keepers, but neither of them would impeach their accomplices.

About a week after, the officer had information on one of the party named Usher, whom he succeeded in taking after four days and nights severe labour, in a ditch, where he had a violent struggle for nearly half an hour, when a young man came to his assistance, and they handcuffed him. Usher is a very stout bony man, six foot one inch high; he defended himself with a spade, till the officer wrested it from him, who was much hurt by the blows he received.

In less than an hour, Usher gave a clue to the whole gang, when Holyland proceeded to apprehend Field as the ringleader, in doing which he was exposed to great danger, as he found him at a public-house surrounded by 20 of his colleagues, who had pledged themselves to die to a man rather than suffer Field to be taken. He entered the room, assisted by two of Lady de Grey's keepers, who, to their credit, stood by him until Field was taken. The officer was assaulted, and had his warrant torn from him, when he drew his cutlass, and by a spirited and well-timed plan he carried Field off.

Three of the ringleaders in the assault have been sent to Bedford Gaol to take their trial at the ensuing sessions. Field, Usher, Senly, Brown and Roberts, are committed for trial to Hertford gaol; and the officer is now in pursuit of the others.

This gang has been for some time a terror to the whole neighbourhood, and Field has frequently given notice to the gentleman whose park he was going to attack. Some idea may be formed of the depredations committed by Field's gang, when it is pretty correctly ascertained that Field has paid from 60/- to 70/- a week to his men, and employed a cart to carry away the Plunder."

John Fesh Field may have nearly been apprehended earlier that year as in The Quarter Sessions Rolls he was bound over to keep the peace towards John Butcher, a gamekeeper from Tingrith.

At the Epiphany (January) Bedfordshire Quarter Sessions an indictment for The King against Simon Mullin, Thomas Adams, William Nash "for neglecting and refusing on 3 December at the parish of Barton in the Clay to aid and assist Francis Holyland in the apprehension of one John Fesh Field to answer a charge of felony and robbery and for an assault upon the said Francis Holyland at the time and place aforesaid and attempt to rescue the said John Fesh Field out of the custody of the said Francis Holyland".

They pleaded 'not guilty' but there is a note on the page saying "Removed by certiorary to the Court of Kings Bench" so presumably they were tried at the higher court elsewhere. The result of this trial has yet to be found, and it is not known what the sentences given were, but with a family full of lawyers it may be that he got off lightly, as was indicated by an 1826 agreement where it is said, that John Fesh Field was discharged from prison on 9 Feb 1825 as an insolvent debtor.

Thomas however, was a respectable cheesemonger from Newgate Street and was 38 when he inherited. He had money and paid off his father's debts, so presumably cheese dealing was a profitable job at that time. His mother Frances, who was previously at New Inn Farm, gave up all her interest in it and the land there in 1819, to her son Thomas, in exchange for £200 a year. It appears that at that time New Inn Farm was divided into several dwelling houses, which were occupied by labourers as undertenants.[138]

Thomas married his second wife, Rose Eliza Armitage, late in life when he was nearly 60 and she was only 26. Initially they lived at Hutton near Brentwood in Essex, but by 1851 they were installed at Fielden House. He died in 1861 and was buried in Barton churchyard leaving all his " .. household furniture, pictures, plate, trinkets, jewellery, wines and liquors, horses and carriages .." to his wife with all his estate etc being put into trust to pay her expenses, and to educate his two daughters Rose Eliza Field and Amelia Field.[139]

These two never married with Rose dying in 1916 and Amelia in 1928 aged 82, both from Fielden House, perhaps where the family originally came from many centuries before.

Other Village Families

Like many others, people came into the village to work, had families which increased the numbers bearing that name and then either had girls, small families or left the area. There almost seems to be a 200 year rule which sees the family names disappearing after that length of time. However, this rule is disintegrating nowadays or even earlier, with personal mobility becoming easier.

A name which was associated with Silsoe at an early period was Allen. This name first appears in a baptism of 1597 but had left the village 200 years later. The family produced innkeepers for the Ragged Staff and the George, and in the late 17th century John Allen became one of the major farmers and the estate manager or steward, for the de Greys. He went to Crudwell in Wiltshire to manage another of the de Grey's estates, but the family is last found in the 1841 census where Philip Allen, a farm labourer, and his small family are living at 44 High Street. He is not in the village ten years later.

---

[138] Z937/2/10
[139] See memorials in Barton Churchyard for dates etc.

The Bonner family was also much the same, appearing in 1584 and generally tending to be tradespeople or artisans. Thus in Flitton many were carpenters such as John of around 1655 or Joseph 50 years later, but in Silsoe there was Nicholas Bonner, a butcher, who seems to have operated from south of the Star and Garter. They appear to have left the village at around the turn of the 19th century.

The Giddings were baptising children in Flitton from about 1663 and continued through until about 1850 when Matilda, the daughter of Charles was baptised at Silsoe. This family expanded over the years with sons and daughters moving away and there are none shown in the census for the 1881 and subsequent censuses. There are however, Giddings being buried in the churchyard from 1868 to as late as 1919. As mentioned elsewhere, the Giddings family were wheelwrights, and passed on their trade from generation to generation; but as there was only room for one or two of that trade in a village, the second and other sons tended to become labourers, or left the area to work elsewhere.

Around 1830 Thomas Ambridge from Higham Gobion found he could ply his trade as thatcher from the village and set up in the area behind where the Lord Nelson was, with his wife and seven children. Two of his sons became rake makers and he was also farming seven acres there. The family prospered and after he died in 1877 his son John took over farming a total of 9 acres for which he needed the help of two men and a boy. The family had been able to build the house that is now called Road Farm, and which carries the date 1877 and the initials TA.

John seems to have remained single but he remained there with a 'farmer's son', Ernest Ambridge, helping him until the First World War when Ernest was called up, and sadly died in 1918. His name can be found on the War Memorial in the churchyard.

The Manns

The first person bearing the name of Mann who appears in the records for Flitton cum Silsoe is Thomas Mann, who set about having what was then a normal number of children, seven, starting in 1788 with Joseph. Most of his sons were equally prolific, the four of them having a total of 21 children. By 1881 there were a total of 45 members of the clan still in Silsoe not counting those who had left to live in Clophill or Islington, London. Isaac Mann, the blacksmith at West End Farm, seems to have lived in what is now 20 West End Road with his wife and eight children, while Arthur & Arabella with their six children were at 34 High Street. It must have been really crowded inside those houses, as it must have been for other families.

The name continued in the village well into the 20th century, but today although the name can be found in the area around, it has gone from the village. (However, Dora Brazier, born in Silsoe, had the maiden name of Mann.)

The Croxfords

John and Sarah Croxford's son Joshua, who was born in Maulden in 1759, moved southwards across the Flit into Silsoe, where he married Mary Hewes and had several children. Joshua must have prospered, or his wife had some money, as in 1809 for £130 he bought the old courtyard with cottages in West End Road where nos 25 & 27 now are from John Haytread innkeeper at the Star[140]. He was then described as a yeoman.

John, their eldest son had two wives, Ann and Lucy, and they produced a total of 11 children between 1806 and 1836. In the 1841 census John & Lucy Croxford were living in West End Road with their eldest son of 20, Joshua, and another son John 8 with Lucy's other son, Joel, away from home in Hertfordshire.

John the elder was described as an agricultural labourer in 1841, and he was buried at Silsoe in May 1849 aged 66, leaving his 64 year old widow Lucy with two unmarried sons, John 15 and Joel 12 years old to look after her. The rest of the children, mainly girls, were already married or living away from home.

John had received the courtyard from his father in 1817 and on his death he left it to Lucy for her lifetime. She also received John's cow and the household goods. Joshua the eldest son was to get the courtyard on his mother's death, but he also received the horses & carts & implements of husbandry. This John had also improved his 'station' to being a yeoman by the time of his death.

Joel, the third son of the family, had only received a small sum of money on his father's death but had enough initiative to improve his life, (or perhaps it was an adventure), and decided to emigrate. Thus at the age of 19, in 1855 Joel was an assisted migrant on the vessel "Speedy" to Australia. The assistance was probably from the Ampthill Union, or maybe his brother loaned him the money.

The trip probably lasted about three to four months with most emigrants travelling in the cheapest class of accommodation, known as steerage. This was similar to a dormitory with bunks down the sides and tables in the centre. It was frequently overcrowded with poor ventilation, and diseases such as cholera and typhus frequently caused the deaths of many on the voyage.

On his arrival Joel evidently went prospecting as he wrote home in November 1864:

---

[140] BLARS L5/974

"I must tell you it was I who sent those too newspapers I was on a new gold field at the time and doing very well but we gold diggirs are never satisfide for we hear of a new gold fields braking out in some other country wher they say people are making rapped fortune so I must tell you that I have had a trip to newcelond since then which I must say was a pleasure trip for I went with the mailboat and called in every habbour in that country but newzealand was to cold for me so I sone return to melbourn and made my way back to the lambing flat whear I stade about 18 months and from there I came to the ironbarks these wear the first gold feilds I wear every on and I found my ould and respected mate John Smith there and comfortably settle in life and I must say I wear well received for he sold me a share in his pugmill and bought me a good horse and carte too work with him... My dear niece Hephzibah... I have found a smol nugit of gold to day which I will make a present to you for a keepsake for me." November 1864

There still is at Barraba, north of Tamworth in New South Wales (the Australian country music mecca), the Ironbark Gold Field where you can 'fossick' for gold and it is probable that this is the area where he worked for a period.

He settled down eventually marrying Margaret Hills in 1866 and they lived at Wellington, near Dubbo, having at least seven children. He eventually was buried at Wellington in 1900.[141]

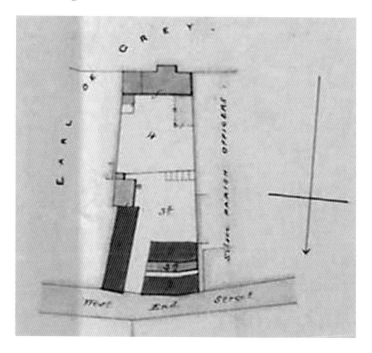

Plate 16/1 - The Croxford Property in West End 1856

---

[141] Australian information from A. Bradshaw, Quirindi, New South Wales

Back home in Silsoe, the West End property had been improved over the years and in 1856 Joshua sold it to the Earl de Grey for £500. It then included 4 cottages plus 6 other cottages newly erected by John Croxford, and these were occupied by Joshua Croxford, George King, William Swannell, John Croxford, Richard Peddar, Elizabeth Cherry, James Sutton, Mary Mann, Thomas Eddy and Mary Bell.

The last record of a Croxford in the village seems to be John Croxford who, aged 66 was living in the Almshouses in 1901.

Recent and Earlier Reminiscences

When I started this project I thought it would be a good idea to capture the memories of those whose earlier years had been passed in the village in the last century, and that I would catch up with some of them later. However, I have unfortunately missed some people by being too late, and so there are probably some anecdotes which are lost forever.

To those who did contribute many thanks, the dryness of history disappears when their history is recounted.

John Worker

Firstly, however, the Worker family. They were in Silsoe or Flitton from at least the early 1700's and provided the village with their postman, John, for about 40 years in the 19th century. His grandson, John H Worker, wrote in 1975[142] that John, who was born in 1819, "fetched the mail in his pony and trap from Bedford and at each village blew his post horn so the villagers could collect their mail". The horn eventually came into the possession of Ken Scott in the village, his cousin. John H Worker's uncle, Sam Ashton was a coachman and before he died[143] Lady Cowper would bring him invalid food and read books to him.

John H's earliest memory was of the visit of Lord Kitchener to Silsoe[144] on his return from the South African War. Most of the villagers met him at the Park gates and the men fitted trace ropes to the carriage and pulled it to Wrest House.

He said that oil lamps, wells and cesspools were in regular use, and transport over the four miles to the Midland Railway was by pony and waggonette. When the fields were cleared at harvest, loose corn was gathered by gleaners who took it to the miller to grind for winter use, while the bread was made by the baker. On Sunday many villagers took their joint of meat with a jug of batter and a fruit pie, to be cooked in the baker's oven for midday lunch.

---

[142] BLARS crt 130 SIL 31
[143] Samuel Ashton died in 1893 aged 45.
[144] 8th August 1902

The steward was in charge of agricultural policy, tree cutting and disciplining bad behaviour for the estate. A saw pit was used to cut planks with one man on top and the other underneath operating a two-handled saw.

He said that education at the village school cost 2d per week.

Violet Armstrong

Violet wrote about her family at Wrest Park and Silsoe in 1984 for the *Bedfordshire Magazine*[145] and this provides an interesting earlier reminiscence of life early in the 19th century. Thanks are due to the Bedfordshire Historical Record Society for allowing us to print this article

"Well over a hundred years ago my late mother, who died in 1932 in Norwich, was sent to work in Bedfordshire. Her father was a small farmer at Harleston, Norfolk, until the Agricultural Revolution split up farm lands under the enforced Enclosure Acts, which resulted in the hedging-in and restriction of personal properties. Of his five children, two boys opened a grocery shop and a post-office in the same county; one girl had a boarding house for professional people in Harleston and another did dressmaking at home until she married in the same county. My mother, Frances Matilda Dade, the third child, in her early teens was sent to join the huge staff of the Earl and Countess Cowper, at Wrest Park, Silsoe.[146] There were many servants of all grades including elaborately attired footmen. At first, seeing these men and in complete ignorance of the high life, she assumed they were dressed specially for a party but soon became accustomed to this everyday scene. Until she rose in rank to have a room of her own as second to the housekeeper, she took meals with others in the fascinating 'Still Room'.

A source of wonder to her was the vast variety of foods concocted and decorated there; creams, custards and sweets all elaborately prepared; joints of meat, poultry and game decorated in remarkable guises to entice the appetite, and a wonder to behold. Mother was naturally artistic and thrilled to see priceless tapestries covering most of the walls in the main reception rooms. The huge staircase in the main hall was hung with paintings of famous ancestors of the Cowper family, etc- some of the paintings remain today.

The first years of mother's service in this great mansion were extremely hard, Early each morning her task was along cold and unheated corridors upstairs and into the many bedrooms where fireplaces and implements in them, made of pure steel, had to be brought to a fine polish each day, Not being very robust my mother was relieved as time went by to be moved to less arduous

---

[145] *Bedfordshire Magazine* Vol. 19 No. 149 Summer 1984
[146] 1881 census has Fanny Dade 17 at Wrest Park, Housemaid, of Harleston. In 1891 she was still there aged 29

work, though at the same time she admired the beautiful workmanship of the steel.

Earl Francis Cowper was a descendant of the de Grey family, He was Lord Lieutenant of Ireland, and his home a natural target of rebels, Once when the family were away, taking the housekeeper with them, and mother was left in charge, she was alarmed to see a crowd of men walking briskly along the drive towards the front door of the mansion, Her first thought was of the 'Fenians' and she was much relieved when they asked only alms for a charity, The de Grey family seat is at Panshanger, near Hatfleld, Hertfordshire and the Earl and Countess would sometimes go there to stay, taking the first housekeeper with them.

My father, Charles William Armstrong, was a much travelled man working for an English company introducing the new electricity to Canada and America, He was there for seven years, mostly in Toronto, with his first wife, They then returned to England and stayed with the wife's family at Silsoe Post Office, she became an invalid and had to be pushed along the village paths in a bath-chair.

Later the lady died and my mother and father met, according to the rules at the big house the senior staff of ladies were addressed as 'Mrs' but it did not take father long to unravel that problem and to propose marriage.

They came to mother's home at Harleston for the wedding where Wrest Park was represented by a pretty bridesmaid and magnificent flowers.

Although there was no facility for specially arranged study at the mansion, seniors could read and work on hobbies in their private sitting rooms by the light of oil lamps: until quite recently I possessed mother's old oil lamp, There was every stimulus for study in the beautiful library. Although mother did not compose verse herself, she kept a large writing book (which I still have) in which she copied poems by famous poets. Mother also left me her album of photographs taken at Wrest Park: ancestors of some readers may be pictured there!"

Violet Samway nee White's (previously Pepper) recollections
Interviewed on 19th September 2005

Vi was born in 1914 at Vicarage Cottage, Ampthill Road, Silsoe, which was then two cottages. The White family occupied both cottages. Vi was one of 11 children (6 girls and 5 boys), but her mother actually brought up 14 children. The other 3 were grandchildren. One of Vi's sisters-in-law died, followed by her brother (of a broken heart) and the 3 orphaned children went to live with their grandparents.

Her father was the church sexton for 20 years and not only looked after the church but also dug the graves in the churchyard. A new vicar, the Rev'd

Black came to Silsoe, and brought with him his own sexton, and Vi's father was out of a job. The family moved to West End, where they again occupied two church cottages and her father went to work at Wrest Park for the rest of his working life. She had two brothers who served in WW1 and both survived. The family then moved to 29 High Street.

Vi began school at the infants school, which was where the newspaper shop is today. There was just the one class for multi-aged children. She remembers a teacher there, called Emily Mann, who, when the children were reading, used to go to sleep standing up, and then used to wake up with a start! (Her daughter Janet also remembers a teacher called Miss Barker, who used to do exactly the same when she was at school.) Vi at the age of seven went to the school near the village hall, where she stayed until she was fourteen. The girls' playground was at the front and the boys were at the back, behind the wall. Vi remembers a teacher called Mr Teacher (sic) and another, Mr Bond of whom she was fond. She used to collect his *Bedfordshire Times* every Friday"

Vi recalls a very happy childhood, and can only once remember being in trouble when she didn't set the family table for her mother. Christmases were wonderful. The children had to go to bed early on Christmas Eve, and a fire would be laid in her parent's bedroom, ready to be lit on Christmas morning. They would go into their parent's room to show them what they had in their stockings, which was usually an orange and a few nuts. One of her brothers would dress up as Father Christmas, but Vi guessed it was him when she noticed his trousers under the red suit. With her father being the sexton, the family had to attend church three times on Sunday, wearing their Sunday best clothes. The longhaired Vi had her hair tied up in rags on Saturday night, ready for Sunday church.

She recalls naughty boys hiding the village policeman's bike for a lark. The village children had great fun playing in the sandpit (now 'The Maples') on a mound of sand there, known as Mount Zion. It was also the village rubbish dump, and Vi loved rummaging through what others had thrown away. Vi, who was only allowed to go to the pit with her brother, used to sit in an old frying pan and slide down the steep slopes. It used to make her laugh so much that she weed herself, and that was blamed for giving her pneumonia, when she was twelve years old. She had to have all her hair cut off and her brother gave her a doll (her first ever) to make her better, which at some time later came to grief by being dropped in a chamber pot!

Picking wild flowers was a happy pastime but gleaning the cornfields to feed the chickens (the newly cut stubble scratched the legs), and the constant gathering of wood for the fire (even when Vi had an abscess on her tooth) were considered chores.

Although Vi didn't visit the seaside until she was 17 or 18, the annual fetes held at the vicarage are remembered fondly. They had games, tea and danced to an old fashioned gramophone in the gardens. Vi recalls the tea-rooms that

312

were opposite the village hall moving to Pear Tree Cottage in Church Road, and taking the Sunday roast to be cooked in the baker's large oven, at the cost of 1d. After Mr Olney's butchers closed in the village, a Mr Ingle, from Ampthill brought meat for sale on Saturday evenings in a horse and cart.

When she left school, she went to work in various hat factories in Luton, travelling there by buses which ran from Clophill to Luton, costing 10d return. Vi's mother and sister had been to Luton to find her employment before she left school. She became a hat trimmer and was paid 2/6d for trimming a box of 12 hats. She married Lawrence Pepper in 1934 at Silsoe church, when she was 20. They went to live at West End and had three boys and one girl, all delivered by Nurse Brightman.

When Vi was having her first child her midwife was on holiday so they engaged a private nurse, and she went on to deliver the three-later babies. Vi recalls a Dr O'Donnell from Barton, who was a very kind, caring and much-loved local doctor. Lawrence worked with horses for Dunhams of Clophill, and then went to work as a gardener in Luton. He then worked for Harris Market Gardeners in Silsoe, where he learned to drive a lorry (no driving tests were taken then). (Vi also did backbreaking seasonal work on the village market gardens.) Lawrence ended his working life as a crane driver, but failed to come to terms with retirement and died in 1979.

World War II didn't seem to affect Silsoe too much. Soldiers were camped in Clophill Woods and American GI's seemed to be around. When Vi was living in West End, she remembers a bomb being dropped near the Speed the Plough one evening and that they all dived under the table! Lawrence was in the Home Guard and one of his duties was to check for lights. He saw one in an upper room of Timmy Brown's farmhouse in West End and shot it out, much to the consternation of Mr Brown!

She recalls an eccentric character called Bert Fry who had a wheelbarrow that he used to wheel about upside down. He used to go back and forth to Clophill to get coal, and when he died the whole house, even upstairs, was full of coal! Last but by no means least Vi has had contacts with the village ghosts! When courting Lawrence in Wrest Park, they saw a pony and trap with lights coming up The Avenue, they heard the clip-clop of the pony, which then stopped and then vanished. Another time at Buckle Grove, which was then a field with trees around, they saw a figure coming up the path towards them. Vi's brother-in-law, who was a night watchman at Wrest Park house, was sitting at a table one night when the Grey Lady appeared out of one wall, glided past and vanished through another wall. Janet, Vi's daughter during her time working there, did not see her, but smelled her perfume.

May Cooper née Martin
Interviewed on 7 June 2005

May was born in July 1912, into a family of eleven children at 13 High Street, Silsoe, which was, at that time, a house belonging to the council. She remembers a strand of barbed wire running along the top of the wall running from numbers 3 to 13 High Street, and two large elm trees grew by that wall. Opposite those houses and in front of 10 High Street, where the Olney family lived, there was a small orchard where pear and plum trees grew. She remembered the fire at Wrest Park during the time it was used as a hospital in World War I, although being only 4 years old then, she may have been told about it.

May's eldest brother Eustace Charles Martin, was killed in action on 1st December 1917 around Cambrai, in Northern France. Charles, as he was known, enlisted at Bedford and joined the 16th Battalion Middlesex Regiment; like so many, he has no known grave, but is commemorated on the Cambrai Memorial. May does not remember much of her brother, but does remember her mother crying when news came of his death. Christmas was not much fun that year in the Martin household.

Freddy Olney was a butcher and he slaughtered all his stock at No 10 High Street, and stored it in the cellar of the house. Christine, May's daughter, used to go into the cellar with Dolly Olney and bring up large pans of milk with cream floating on the top. The house behind No 10 was the Old George Inn, and apparently when 'knocking it about', the inn counter was discovered hidden in the wall.
A cobbler was at 39 High Street. Clifford White lived at No 48/50, and Michael Halfpenny was at No 23. A rather eccentric character called Bert Fry occupied No 21 High Street, who was fanatical about collecting wood and coal, and filled his house with it. May remembered taking him Christmas dinner one year, (she said 'he was a bit odd!').

May's sister also lived in the High Street, in the house with the steps, opposite the church, that she paid £100 to buy *(the year is unknown!)*. May's grandma, Mrs White lived at No 25 and another relative, Maureen Collyer lived at 1 Church Road. At the entrance to Church Road was a large, old walnut tree, and as a child, she remembered that they were told off for throwing things to knock the nuts down. May also remembered the almshouses, named Park View selling for about £100.

Numbers 2-4 Church Road housed her mother's family, and she has an old photograph picturing her grandma, granddad and her three youngest siblings, 'all dressed up', on the doorstep. A blacksmith called Mr Lowings was in Church Road and he made Christine, May's daughter, a hoop. Two spinsters, Miss Eve and Miss Rogers lived at The Birches at the end of Church Road, and they gave presents to the village children at Christmas. May said that one year she was given a book, but she would have rather had a doll!

May went to school where the papershop now is, and there used to be another near the village hall. The policeman lived at 9 High Street.

Her father, brother and sister all worked at the Co-op shop in The Maltings. Her father, Charles Martin was a baker there for forty years. The bakery was in the yard to the left of the Co-op. According to May, her sister nearly ran the Co-op on her own because the manager was over at The George most of the time! There were two one-bedroomed houses at the bottom of The Maltings, one of which was occupied by a Mrs Lomax. Hobbity Walker lived at the bottom of the Co-op yard.

Buffom Clarke lived in West End Road, as did Enid Lilley at number 8. Just around the corner from Enid's house in Vicarage Road, stood the tin roofed building of The Mission. May played the organ there and it was attended by Sammy Brightman, the churchwarden, who lived in Ampthill Road. There was a white-bearded milkman by the name of Brightman too, she recalled. George Cooke had The Mousehole in West End Road and he sold 'four Spanish for 1d' which was liquorice, a Miss Rust was also there. Mr Mackie took it over and then went on to run The Star and Garter in the High Street.

There was a now demolished cul-de-sac in West End Road that was a courtyard with small houses around it, where Doreen Docknell and Miss Dickens lived.

Timmy Browning lived at West End Farm, with the duck pond being opposite the farm. That was filled in when the college was built. There was another pond further up with frogs, (just about where the last house is, opposite the old farm buildings).

The area behind 3 West End Road, where the college was, was called 'Englants', and not 'Englands'. Fred Martin lived next to No 3 and he had land at Upbury Turn. There was an obelisk on Wrest Park land, opposite the college that was moved to Trent Park. Gladys Gee lived at the Hostel behind the church, which was demolished to allow The Beeches to be built.

Wrest Park had the American Ambassador, William Whitelaw in residence and he was followed by Mr & Mrs Murray[147]. The village children used to run to open the Park gates for them, hoping to be given a sixpenny tip. Bill Bailey, a character from Wardhedges also used to open those gates, doffing his cap at the same time. May recalls that he used his hymn book upside down! When the Murrays moved out, the Sun Insurance company took over the mansion.

There was also a regular knife grinder that visited Silsoe, and ice cream was served from a bicycle.

---

[147] There was a 5 year gap between the ambassador leaving and Mr Murray taking over occupancy.

She worked for just one year making hats in Luton, and then during World War II went to Kents (also in Luton), making tank impellers. The workers were bussed back and forth from Silsoe.

Apart from two years in Osset when her husband, Bob, was doing National Service, she lived for forty years in the cottage now known as Annabel Cottage at the southern end of the High Street. Then Annabel Cottage was semi-detached and 'a little Welsh woman' lived in the other half.

Dora Brazier née Mann
Interviewed on 14 June 2005

Dora, that lovely lady that we all know and love, was born in 1929 at Leaside, no.1 High Street, Silsoe. She was the only child of Ruth and Harry Mann, who met whilst both working in service at Windsor Castle. Harry served in the Great War, and afterwards through a shortage of employment, came to Silsoe to live with Ruth's parents, and he became a bus driver. Dora's parents were great cinema-goers, often going to the Granada Cinema in Bedford in their Austin 7.

Dora began school just before her 5th birthday at Silsoe School, which was then situated at the entrance of the village hall (later to be relocated where it stands today). It was a church school, with a Miss Fullerton as the headmistress, assisted by a Mrs Woodhead. There were three classes and morning assembly was a very important part of the school day. Maypole dancing featured in the school year. Dora was 10 years old when World War 2 was declared, and she remembers an air raid shelter being built next to the school building.

She remembers food rationing being an inconvenience, but being a typical rural community, Silsoe residents did not go hungry during World War II. A girls' school from Walthamstow, London, was evacuated 'lock, stock and barrel' to Silsoe. They came with their own teachers and set up their school at Silsoe House in Ampthill Road, with the girls being billeted with the villagers. Dora's mother said she would take one, as their cottage was fairly small, and was given three!

They were all a few years older than Dora, and one poor girl had to go home when her mother died. Dora kept in touch with one evacuee until she died a few years ago. There were some other evacuees (boys and girls) and they attended the village school.

Soldiers were billeted within the village with the inevitable consequence of romance! (No Americans seemed to have been in Silsoe, although one village girl married a Canadian.) The soldiers were billeted at the village hall and Wrest Park, and manned guns and searchlights on strategically high local buildings.

The Sunday school was run by two spinsters, Miss Eve and Miss Rogers who were related to Lord Silsoe[148], and Dora was a teacher. Miss Eve was known for her very deep voice; and although she did not interfere, used to stand behind the junior teachers to make sure they were doing a good job! Reputedly when Dora was suggested as a teacher, it was said, "Dora Mann is too frivolous!" However, she must have done a fairly good job, as when she married Des, from Flitton, in 1950, the Sunday school bought her a dinner service as a wedding present. Misses Eve and Rogers invited her to choose a wedding present from them and Dora selected a brass bell in the shape of a crinoline lady, which is still well polished and much treasured.

She remembers that the Sun Insurance Company bought Wrest Park from the Murrays (who had bought from the Lucas's in the Great War). Hubbards the well known Luton hat manufacturers bought the hostel (now the Beeches) which had previously housed the estate workers.

The original police house was opposite the Star & Garter, the white one on the end (not West End side). Constables remembered were PC's Wood and Greenwood.

Yellow House Farm (next to the paper shop) was a private school, run by the parents of John and Tom Harris. The paper shop was a hall where snowball whist drives were held.

In West End was a small pub called The Battle of Alma. Two Mr Cooks ran it (one had a long white beard) and it was also a hardware shop but sold sweets as well. The pub had a six day licence and was unable to sell spirits. The Agar/Mackay family ran the Star & Garter for 43 years and Tommy Mackie, the father of John the ex-postmaster, played football for Luton Town.

Two sisters, the Mondins, ran the Lord Nelson and brought beer up from the cellar in a jug.

The main shop and post office were opposite the paper shop and was run by Reg Batt. Another small shop was run by Norman Harris in the cottages opposite the church – a speciality of his was cooked meats.

Mr Dunham was a cobbler and a hairdresser regularly visited Yellow House Farm. Mr Olney (Geoff's father) had a butchers shop and dairy behind the Star & Garter. The Co-op was opposite the George, as was the bakery in the Maltings, until it moved to the village hall yard.

---

[148] See the Eve family.

Doreen Lodge née Fossey
Interviewed in 2005

Doreen Fossey was one of six sisters and two brothers. Two of her sisters were born at 'Ivy Cottage', No 2 High Street, Silsoe, one of two semi-detached cottages. Three of the sisters, including Doreen still reside in the village.

Her father was the postman for the area, and delivered mail to Silsoe, Gravenhurst and Shillington on his bicycle. Her mother was a postlady who delivered mail in Silsoe.

She has many reminiscences of the Silsoe she enjoyed when young. She remembers particularly parts of the High Street. Olney's yard where there was a butcher's shop and milk was also sold. The oldest building in the yard was the original George Inn. A Miss Fossey lived in the added-on part of the Star and Garter.

There were several shops, and Ramsey Harris sold fruit and vegetables from his in the terraced houses opposite the church. The newsagent living accommodation had been a school from 1880, and the long house next to the newsagents sold haberdashery (and was possibly also another butchers shop). Another Harris owned that shop and the yard behind the shop was cobbled.

There was a men's club somewhere by the old school, but Doreen is unsure exactly where it was. The other school was near the village hall, and the schoolmistress lived in the end Mews Cottage. The Co-op was in the Maltings, and at one time the village fair and market was held in the field where Bedford Avenue was later built.

When Doreen was young, there were no houses between the Lord Nelson (which stood in the area known as Pork End), up to the corner of the Ampthill Road/Newbury Lane junction. The manor house was close by and was owned by another of the Harris family.

In the area opposite the old quarry in Ampthill Road, some small terraced houses were demolished to make way for the larger ones that are now there[149].

Pear Tree Cottage in Church Road was used as a tea rooms, and the Alma public house in West End Road was know as the 'Mouse House'. Doreen also remembers a chapel in the village where services were held every Sunday, but she cannot remember exactly where it was located.

---

[149] These have not been found on either the 1927 or 1938 OS maps.

The entertainment was provided by dances in the village hall, and the hourly buses to get to Bedford and Luton enabled trips to visit the cinemas in those towns. Doreen enjoyed a day out every Sunday in Bedford.

Eleanor Woodward née Bottoms:
Interviewed in February 2006

Due to poor health, Mrs Woodward was unable to speak personally, here follows a transcript of telephone conversations with Mr Woodward on her behalf:

She was born as Eleanor Bertha Bottoms in 1920 at 7 Newbury Lane, Silsoe. Her father, Herbert, worked at Wrest Park and her mother, Mary Jane was a parlourmaid for Mr Whitelaw Reid, the American Ambassador. She was one of five children (two boys and three girls). One sister worked in a hat factory but died at the early age of 22 years from tuberculosis, and her eldest brother William, was killed at the end of World War II (see the Roll of Honour). Eleanor is now the only child surviving.

The family lived very close to the Lord Nelson public house, and although it was always very busy, Eleanor does not ever remember any disturbances there. The landlord was Charlie Mondin and after his death, his wife, assisted by her sister who was affectionately known as Auntie, ran the pub.

She attended Silsoe Church of England school, which was where the village hall stands today; and whilst playing in the playground, broke her leg on a conker. That resulted in 6 weeks of lost schooling (as in those days children stayed at home with a fracture). She passed the 11+ examination, but was unable to go to the High School (Luton) because her parents were unable to afford to send her. She attended Sunday school and enjoyed the yearly 'Sunday school Treat' of a day at the seaside on a coach. She was a member of the church choir up until her marriage, and went to Buckle Grove every Good Friday to collect primroses for the decoration of the church on Easter Day. She was a member of the Girl Guides, and during World War II was trained as a first-aider. As an older girl she went to the socials in the school and the dances in the village hall - which had the reputation of being the best hall in the district!

When she left school she worked as an assistant at the Silsoe Co-op. At that time the Co-op served a wide area around Silsoe; and much of Eleanor's time there was spent weighing and wrapping goods ready for delivery - sometimes until 8 o'clock at night.

As far as she can remember, Silsoe like many Bedfordshire villages didn't really suffer from food shortages during WWII, although the nuisance of rationing was the same as everywhere else. She remembers flying bombs falling on Maulden Woods, and recalls one bound for Silsoe hitting telephone wires on the road between Clophill and Silsoe.

Despite the war, in 1943 there was a horse show and gymkana in a field where The Grove is today.

She married Dick Woodward, a farmer, in 1943, and went to live and work alongside him in Maulden. She returned to Silsoe with Dick in 1996 after their retirement.

Finally

Many people when asked would say, and have said, that their lives were mundane and of no interest to others. However, the 'others' would probably say that all lives are interesting, especially to those who have lived differently, and maybe they would have liked to have had more in this book. If everyone in the village had been asked to provide a short history and had done it would have filled another book and maybe this could be done in the future. It is perhaps an empty hope that people will now write down how they have lived, what they did, who they knew and what happened in their lives if only that those in the future can be amazed at how we lived and how things have changed.

Chapter 17 – Health and Safety or Swords can be Sharp

Keeping Healthy and Avoiding Accidents

Life was hard and dangerous in early times at Silsoe with few facilities if a person became ill or had an accident. It was only with the introduction of the National Health Service in the 20th century that care became available for all, without the need to check the wallet before going to the doctor or hospital. But even before then medicinal knowledge had been increasing, and the effect of the ownership of most of Silsoe by one prominent family had its beneficial effects, with some care being provided for their servants and workers.

Before the 19th century, knowledge of herbal medicine gained from experience and presumably experiment, would have been available to treat illnesses; and before the Dissolution of the monasteries there were also hospitals at those religious institutions, the nearest to Silsoe being at Chicksands, Woburn and Bedford. In a small village like Silsoe there would also have been local experts, or perhaps 'wise women' to whom the villagers would have turned. Of course, if the medicine didn't work or people became ill without evident reason, then at some periods the 'wise woman' was just as likely to have been burned as a witch!

'Herbals' such as Nicholas Culpepper's would have been available to physicians in the 17th century, and they would have applied their knowledge in the attempt to affect a cure.

As for accidents, no doubt if infection didn't set in, the patients were in for a long period of recuperation during which no sick pay would have been available. They would have had to survive on small payments from the village poor overseers.

And as for toothache, if a tooth hurt, out it came with no anaesthetic.

The Smallpox, Plagues etc

The people of Silsoe suffered like others in the country from recurring diseases such as smallpox, typhus, cholera and influenza. Although for the times before the keeping of burial records in parishes commenced in the late 16th century, it is difficult to assess the effect of these major diseases on the village. Even after those records were kept it is only occasionally that we learn of deaths from those illnesses.

The first major epidemic recorded in the UK is of course the Black Death, or the plague of the mid 1300's. This probably arrived in the south of England from France in the middle of 1348, and such was its speed of infection that it was at St. Albans in April 1349, and would have been at Silsoe at around that time. It is generally held that on average, about one third of the population died through catching the disease, and even the efforts of the 'qualified' apothecaries to stem the epidemic by bleeding, purging, and giving mercury or arsenic had no more success than traditional herbalists.

Imagine the effect of the death of one third of the present population of Silsoe: the constant burials, the loss of friends, of whole families and those involved in running the village. At that time Cainhoe as a village probably disappeared, and it also seems that the vicar of Flitton and Silsoe, John le Beister, may have succumbed as John Tyndel, the chaplain, was installed in 1350 as "Vicar of Flytton with the Chapel of Syvelesho".

There was also a breakdown in law and order, as an inquiry taken at Shefford records that " ... fireplace stones, timber, furniture and tiles were taken away from the great chamber and gatehouse at Cainhoe Manor by John Kirkeby and John Cane in addition to which they did a great deal of damage, destroyed the rabbits in the warren and the fish in the pond." That this could be done without anyone stopping it, also says something about the depopulation of the area.

It should not be thought that after this disease swept through the country it totally disappeared, as there are records of other outbreaks of the plague following on from the first outbreak in the 14th and 15th centuries. The plague also erupted again in the country in 1645 and in 1665, when it was known as the Great Plague, and then it was recorded in London by the diarist John Evelyn who was kinsman of Amabella of Wrest Park, Countess of Kent.

In 1657 an epidemic of some disease affected Bedfordshire and especially in this part of the county. In August that year the Dowager Duchess of Devonshire wrote about "this time of universal sickness" and in September wrote "I find Bedfordshire much infected by this new disease". Thirteen adults were buried that year in Clophill while in Flitton/Silsoe, the total numbers of burials were in 1656 – 16, 1657 – 32 (5 are identified as son or daughter) and in 1658 – 7. She would probably have been aware of bubonic plague, as there had been outbreaks in the united kingdom throughout that century, so to call it new indicates that it was something else, one schedule of epidemics refers to "Great epidemics of agues, with influenzas, 'Hot agues'" for that year.[150]

Other epidemics

Throughout the centuries England has been visited with diseases other than the plague, with influenza being a recurring fatal problem as was cholera, typhus and smallpox - most resulting from poor hygiene or general health. Also prevalent were the childhood diseases which are thankfully now rare such as scarlet fever, measles, mumps, polio and diphtheria. Lady Amabel

---

[150] http://www.fraser-courtman.co.uk/*list_of_famines_&_pestilences_england*.html

Polwarth writing in 1774 asked if the Bishop and Mrs Yorke had taken precautions against their children catching measles. [151]

Once parish records began to be kept, an indication of the epidemics around can be seen from the peaks that arise if deaths are plotted over the years. There were also some years when there is a huge rise in infant mortality with, for example, the period from August 1779 to February 1780 having eight infants or children being buried. Also in 1793 there are 12 infant /child deaths for the whole year with only four adults; this was a year when there was a diphtheria epidemic in England so that may have been the cause.

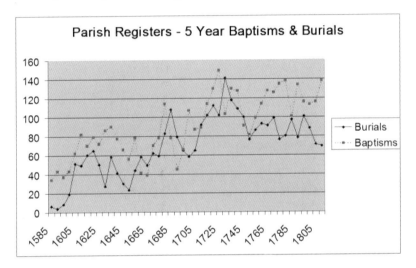

Plate 17/1 – Baptisms and Burials 1585 to 1810

Very occasionally the parish registers state the cause of someone's decease but this is rare. The vicars recording the death were more likely to be concerned with the status of the deceased than the cause of death.

The most recognisable disease and one greatly feared was smallpox identifiable by its rash of festering spots with around 40% of victims dying. It is no surprise that the first cause of death recorded in Flitton burial records is of that disease, with Mary Woodwarde dying of the 'smallpoxe' in 1639.

A few other cases are recorded with in 1665 William Child's son dead at Fielden, and two more in 1674, when Nicholas & Susannah Crouch, Quakers of Flitton, both died of it and were buried in a corner of Broom Close Field, just east of the church. The pox returns in 1685 when two more cases are mentioned, and the last mention of a fatality from smallpox is in 1782 when Elizabeth Bayley died.

---

[151] BLARS L30/13/12/22

Inoculation had been seen in Constantinople / Istanbul in 1717. However, it was not until 1774 that a farmer, Benjamin Jesty, carried out the first (known) inoculation in England; and not until 1794 that Dr Jenner of London showed to established medical practitioners that the process worked, and even later in 1813 that compulsory vaccination was introduced.

In Silsoe in 1786, there is a reference to a surgeon, Mr Bolding, inoculating Elizabeth Odell against smallpox only two days before she went into labour – or did the inoculation cause premature labour?[152]

In the middle to the end of the 18th century the vicars of Flitton and Silsoe, notably the Rev. Philip Birt (1722 - 1763) and the Rev. Hadley Cox (1763 – 1782)'s, took it upon themselves to regularly report to the Duke of Kent or the Earl of Hardwicke the happenings in the village[153]. In these notes there are mentions of smallpox in 1746 and also in 1765, when Hadley Cox said that James Poulton the baker's son had smallpox and had become so deranged that he had attempted suicide -he was later consigned to 'the madhouse'. Also in 1767 a lodger at the schoolhouse was found to have smallpox, and had been put in the care house which had last been used in 1763.

Then, in January 1782, Hadley Cox reported that smallpox was found to have spread to three houses in Silsoe with five people ill, but that it had not spread to Flitton. The population was then 240 of whom only 90 could afford to pay for inoculation. (The cost for inoculating the remaining 150 would be £40, which the parish would have to pay.) It seems the Earl paid towards this cost, as later in January the Rev. Cox thanked him, and said that upwards of 300 people had been inoculated between one month and 80 years old, and none had died. The disease broke out again in 1788, but thanks to the general inoculation very few were at risk.

A later case occurred in 1801 when John Swannell caught it, it is said, from Edwards the waggoner coming from London. The family was sent to Barton Smallpox Infirmary but was sent back by their parish officers! [154] The disease presumably returned later that century in the area, as in 1881 the Silsoe Benevolent Society made a donation to the Ampthill Smallpox Fund, and in 1902 the *Bedfordshire Times* recorded a proposal for a smallpox hospital at Maulden.[155]

It may seem surprising that malaria was quite common in the southern half of England in marshy areas, especially in north Kent, until the 19th century and it is quite possible that this disease, then called 'The Ague', was present around Silsoe perhaps in the boggy areas near the River Flit, where

---

[152] See also Inns & Pubs section, reference comes from Mr Pawseys letters to the Duke
[153] BLARS CRT 100/27/3
[154] BLARS L30/11/215/144
[155] BLARS P54/28/15-18 & Beds Times 7 February 1902.

mosquitoes could breed.[156] Many local remedies, some bordering on magic, were used to ward off the ague and it has been suggested that the practice of nailing hair or toe nail clippings to the Beaumont Oak may have been for this purpose.

Another old, now thankfully rare, infectious disease was tuberculosis or consumption which was prevalent in the 19th century, and which was probably transmitted via infected meat or milk. In Silsoe churchyard there is an 1850 inscription to John Arnold, the 23 year old son of William and Elizabeth which reads :-

"Twas pale consumption gave the fatal blow
and laid my cherished hopes .. low
No power could wrest the mighty hand of death
nor longer stay my last expiring breath
and I had sunk in anguish and despair
but the good shepherd made my soul his care."

Typhus also occurred, and there was an outbreak in the 1860's when the Dowager Countess Cowper's de Grey's daughters distributed blankets and ensured that infected cottages were whitewashed, presumably on the inside. They did however, take precautions against infection by only visiting healthy cottages, but when they left for London they took the opportunity of visiting the village again, to see if the poor wanted for anything.

Accidents and Suicide

Safety at work was initially down to the individual or his workmates: if you saw a tree falling or an out of control carriage bearing down, you yelled and ran. Also, when harnessing working horses or oxen, great care had to be taken not to get trodden on. However, accidents happen and the first record found in the burial records is of the un-named "John Greens man of Flitton, having an hurt in his leggs which brought him to death", 1664.[157]

More relevant to Silsoe is the death of Thomas Gurnett in 1681 who was "killd in levying the great court at Wrest. " With no heavy machinery at that time, it is difficult to see how he died, but he may have been crushed by a waggon.

The next century provides more records of death by misadventure. In 1763 John, the infant son of William and Sarah Saunders, drowned; and in 1771 Thomas Rowe aged 15, was "killed by a waggon going over his body". The

---

[156] The last major outbreak occurred in Queenborough on the Isle of Sheppey during the First World War when servicemen returning from Macedonia carried malaria parasites in their blood. The infection was picked-up by local mosquitoes biting the convalescing soldiers which then went on to infect 32 local people over a period of several years.

[157] Flitton cum Silsoe parish records & Hadley Cox's letters.

Rev. Hadley Cox records that the accident occurred near Silsoe quarry pit when the boy got his clothes caught up in the waggon and was run over. He was particularly concerned that this occurred on a Sunday when work should not have been going on, and was perhaps suggesting divine retribution.

There is also in Silsoe graveyard a memorial to Arthur Walker aged 13, who was killed accidentally in 1854 in Wrest Park, although no details are available.

Suicide occurred even in those days when we like to think there was little stress. The attempt at suicide by James Poulton, affected by smallpox, has been mentioned above; and in 1775 Elizabeth, the wife of Thomas Stratton a farmer, killed herself *'non compos mentis'* or not of sound mind. This was important to be said as otherwise a suicide could not have been buried in consecrated ground.

In the time of coaches there were accidents as have been mentioned in the Transport chapter, but the coming of the motor car created more opportunity for accidents, and even bicycles were a menace. An accident to Sidney and Emily Mann's 4 year old daughter made news in the *Bedfordshire Times* on 4 July 1902, when a cyclist collided with her as she was leaving the infant's school at lunch time, and broke her arm. The rider did not stay on the scene but reportedly made off at high speed towards the Park.

With the speed of the car came accidents, and in the early days of the motor car these were reported nationally. There is an early report in *The Times* of a fatal accident on the bridge, (then probably narrower but now just an unnoticeable culvert), by New Inn Farm. In 1927 late at night, Alfred Howe from Bedford, was motorcycling to Luton with Bessie Braine aged 19, as a pillion passenger. He hit a car driving in the opposite direction and his passenger was killed instantly, with him dying later in hospital.[158]

More recently, the *Bedfordshire Times* of August 1958 records that two men were struck by lightning while working a mechanical shovel in a sand pit at Silsoe. Luckily they escaped with burns and shock only.

Care for the Sick

It is not known how the sick were cared for in Silsoe in early times, or whether there were medical experts or later doctors, readily available (and who paid for them). For the poor, whether or not they received medical help seems to been entirely as a gift of the local landowners as in 1784 Hadley Cox informed his Lordship that doctors had been found who could be used if his servants became ill – what happened to the average labourer is not said.

The estate even exercised control in who could provide care, as in the same year William Harrison, the Silsoe schoolmaster, who lived in Silsoe, had to

---

[158] *The Times* 22 March 1927.

apologise for allowing his house to be used by a Dr Dominicetti, who apparently had the impertinence of setting up his practice at Flitwick. His The Earl was upset that the practice had been set up without asking his permission and asked if the doctor had advertised. The doctor apparently left soon after.

There are no early records of doctors living in the village except perhaps Thomas Thomson, a "Surgeon late of Kg's ships", who was buried in 1811 and who may have applied his skills in the village. Even in the 19th century none are recorded in the censuses for the village. They were probably called in from larger towns such as Ampthill if they could be afforded, and even then cures which worked were few and far between. There is an apothecary recorded in the burial records for 1748, Matthew Crouch, but there is no proof that he worked in the area dispensing medicines.

Bleeding was quite common for fevers and other illnesses where the local barber or barber-surgeon, opened up a vein to remove a pint or so of blood. In 1758 the Rev. Birt said that he had been ill recently and had been bled; where or by whom is not recorded.

That doctors were available at a cost is shown by the following: in July 1797 George Swannell, a shoemaker of Silsoe, wrote to the clerk of the Petty Sessions complaining about his apprentice, John Carter, who at the last Sessions had said he was 18 years old, but George now believed him to have been only 17. However, the real complaint was that John had been ill, and George now had a "great Doctors bill to pay for doctoring him when he was lame and ill last winter." He couldn't pay the bill as he had also been ill for seven weeks, and could not do much work.

While a proper doctor may have been called in for severe cases, local people with some expertise were used, and receipt of 1859[159] refers to Jane Baldwin "As Doctress" for seeing to the Silsoe poor - presumably she was also cheaper. Jane lived with her daughters at where the newsagents now is and in 1851 she was referred to as a midwife, late schoolmistress, whilst her daughter Emma was an assistant midwife.

In the same year there is mention of an infirmary being completed at Clophill, so there may have been some medical care available there for Silsoe residents. After 1803 however, when the Bedford Infirmary opened, there was care available for the really ill and although there is no record of any Silsonian being there in the censuses, no doubt it was used for urgent cases.

In the 19th century from 1852 the enumerator for the censuses was supposed to enter whether someone was either blind, deaf of dumb and from 1871 further categories of (a) an Imbecile or Idiot and (b) a Lunatic; no political correctness then. This first year provided more information than all the rest, with William Bowles stating he suffered from fits and Ann Sale said to have

---

[159] BLARS L28/63

had fits from birth, (possibly both suffered from epilepsy). Only in 1881 is another mental illness recorded that of Alfred Eddy who had been an imbecile from birth. All of these were, however, either still working or living with their families in the village.

In the same year, 1871, other complaints are also recorded. One person had been bedridden for ten years, another had been lame from birth, George Swannel was blind in one eye, Charles Denton was dumb and Richard Eve of West End Farm was rather deaf. Mary Ann Cook was blind. Finally, in the Sale family James, the head, had been lame for 30 years, his wife had been blind for 7 years, and their daughter Ann has been mentioned above as having fits. This list is probably typical for that century even though the other censuses did not go into so much detail.

It was only in the 20th century when medicine became more effective and available, that the posibility of being treated by a doctor increased, even though there was still a direct cost. For example in the 1930's each visit by a doctor cost 7/6, the present day equivalent of this is £44. Then, when after the Second World War the desire to change the old systems was implemented with the formation of the National Health Service, doctors and hospitals became freely available to all, together with care for the elderly and the mentally disturbed.

Of the available surgeries within easy access, the doctor's surgery in Barton became the most easily available and used by the villagers and it currently provides a modern medical service with nurses, several doctors and a pharmacy all available for Silsoe residents.

In addition, the village has at its southern end, the Taymer Nursing Home which was started by the late Dr Taylor and his wife and which still provides long or short term nursing care for up to 33 patients.

Mental Healthcare

As for the mentally ill, it is probable that as long as they did no hurt to themselves or others, they were cared for at their home. In 1771 the Rev. Hadley Cox after thanking his Lordship for £5 for the poor, said that a poor girl in Silsoe had twice thrown herself into the pond opposite the George and was now tied to her bedpost with a chain!

A few years later when Hadley Cox had reported that James Simons, an apprentice to the shoemaker William Crouch, was in the poor house but was due to go to Bedlam, the Earl of Hardwicke wrote that he had had more applications regarding mad people in Silsoe than from any other part of his estates.

In the next century with the new Poor Law, the Overseers became responsible for the care of the insane and they were ordered in 1836 to prepare a list of insane paupers in the parish.

The Bedford Lunatic Asylum was opened in 1812 for the county and in 1851 there is "SN" aged 36, a shoemaker from Silsoe, there. However there was a lack of knowledge about how to treat the mentally ill effectively, restraint was used generally and a report of 1834 said that the institution had 18 straight coats, 12 wrist locks and 11 police handcuffs available to restrain the inmates. In 1860 the Fairfield Asylum just outside Arlesey, was opened and the Bedford Asylum was closed down as being unsuitable. The censuses which include Fairfield do not provide us with the inmates' origin, so it cannot be established that there was anyone there from Silsoe, for that the asylum records would need to be trawled through.

Fairfield grew to be able to care for around 1100 patients in the mid 20th century, but following changes in Government policy it was closed in 1999, and the buildings are now flats with the grounds containing luxury housing.

In Silsoe the Horticultural Centre at the end of Holly Walk, provides work for about 50 adults with learning difficulties. They can participate in learning skills in horticulture incorporating numeracy, literacy, hygiene and social interaction, assisting staff in the care and maintenance of gardens in the community, and are able to interact with the public who call in to buy produce or have a cup of tea.

Other more severe cases are now either back home taking medicine, in smaller specialist hospitals or perhaps in gaol.

Care for the Poor

Much illness was no doubt caused by the poverty in which many families lived in the early centuries, and many burials have notes perhaps indicating indifference to people not of the village, such as in 1603 "an old poor man of Bedford" or 1604 "a strange beggar", 1615, "a daughter to a poore stranger", in 1632 "a poor mayde died at Flitton and was buried", 1669 "a poor travelling man" etc.

But local poverty also caused early death, and thus in 1699 Mary Miller is just described as "poor" while in 1717 after their father Robert Raddice, a labourer, died in October, a month later Thomas and Elizabeth Raddice were buried as "poor orphans".

One would hope that the de Greys gave their surplus or worn bedding to the poor, and they certainly had a great amount of it as in 1691 a survey of the contents of Wrest recorded 68 feather beds & 172 blankets etc.[160]

---

[160] BLARS L31/179

The problem of what to do for, or with the poor remained. To quote a much earlier source "There will always be poor people in the land" [161] and this is still true. In 1765 a local vicar, the Rev. Rouse, gave his opinion to the Earl of Hardwicke on a proposed act for the better relief of the poor that " The purchasing, hiring, renting, and enclosing Land and houses of reception, especially if any buildings should be erected anew, must necessarily require vast sums of money..", not much sympathy there. He continued with " The poor are everywhere increasing, and must, I think, for several reasons which might, I allege increase daily, and not only in number , but in wickedness and vice…" A year later he seems to have softened his opinion saying "The poor in general throughout the nation …….are more than ordinarily distressed by a universal scarcity or rather dearness of all the necessary provisions of life" He then expressed the hope that his Lordship's and others charity would be sufficient to prevent any insurrections. A more practical proposal was for the baking of bread from potato flour which, he said, the poor did not dislike.

Concern was also expressed about the amount of poverty and need in Silsoe in about 1790[162] with a note in the file recording the following cases.

William Stapleton, aged about 60, and his wife needed bedding or a blanket. Then there was John Wilmer with 10 children of whom 6 were at home with two who couldn't walk, one being a cripple. They had three "poor dirty flock beds" one with no blanket "others only threed bare worn & thin. Their poor rags of sheets wonderfully white & clean and patched as the coverlids. Nothing but the greatest notability as industry could have kept them together and there appears … in extreme poverty. Man works as a carpenter under Buncker at 9/- per week."

William Chamberlain had 6 children with 5 at home and all were sleeping in three beds. They needed blankets as they had only four very old ones. He was a labourer but had recently broken 2 ribs. He was supported by club at 7/- per week and was attended by the Apothecary.
Nathaniel Bottom and his wife were elderly, with 2 daughters aged 12 & 13 who were lace makers. They had one poor ragged blanket to their bed and a coverlid. The "Girls lye in a little bed close to them with bits of old flannel to cover them. In great want."

Thomas Odle his heavily pregnant wife and 3 children were ".. all of them nearest to savages that anything can be. Bits of bedding & 1 blanket between them all with a fleays of ruggs & filth ."Thomas was a labourer being paid 6s a week.

James Arnold, another labourer, his wife & 5 children were clean and industrious but very poor. They had had one sheet stolen from them recently. John Notingham his wife, both about 60, and their 14 year old son had very little bedding. John had recently broken his leg recently and was "on

---

[161] *Holy Bible*, Deuteronomy 15:11, about 1400BC.
[162] BLARS L29/118

the parish". Rainbow, a widower since 1784, had 4 children and was "in wretched want of bedding only has rags to sleep in."

Finally there was Widow Chapman and her 4 children who "slepped on heaps of straw on the earth floor. They were ignorant and uncivilised but chearful and as in good health more contented than others." (Education would have made them unhappy!)

From 1598, under Elizabeth I, various Acts had been passed to ensure that relief was available for the poor and infirm such as those above. This was initially carried out at a local level with each parish having to appoint Overseers of the Poor, who were responsible for finding work for the unemployed and setting up parish houses for those incapable of supporting themselves. A later law increased the parish's responsibility requiring it to relieve its aged and helpless, bring up unprotected children in "habits of industry", and provide work for the able-bodied who could not work in their usual trade.

To pay for this the parishes had to raise money by taxing those in the parish such as landowners, tenant farmers and trades-people - those who could afford to pay. This tax was known as the Poor Rate, and eventually became a local tax levied on those who owned or rented properties above a certain value in a parish

Problems arose as what to do with those who did not 'belong' to a parish such as beggars, vagrants and others, and further laws were passed which defined a persons place of 'settlement'. Those not of a parish such as the above or newcomers who became ill or unemployed could be removed to their original place of settlement, to avoid a parish paying for them.

In 1691 another Act defined settlement, for which a certificate could be issued, as being acquired by
* birth – a legitimate child took its father's parish of settlement, even if this was not where it was born. An illegitimate child claimed settlement in its parish of birth.
* apprenticeship, by the parish or privately.
* service. A hiring agreement of a full year or more (i.e. continuous employment for at least 365 days), each subsequent settlement replacing the previous one.
* marriage or remarriage. A woman took her husband's place of settlement on marriage.
* renting property worth at least £10 a year (well beyond the means of a labourer), and paying parish rates
* election to a parish office (e.g. overseer or church warden) for a year

In 1795, the protection against removal to another parish was extended to all poor persons not claiming poor relief, except pregnant, unmarried women. parish overseers made that category least welcome as they were considered

331

the most expensive to support, and they were commonly removed from any parish they entered, back to their place of settlement.

As the cost of the poor was down to the parish who like today, wanted to keep their expenditure low, there are many examples in the records of people being moved from Silsoe to other parishes and vice versa.[163]

Thus in the Overseers of the Poor settlement papers, there is for October 1817 William Worker, his wife and one child being carted (probably a correct term) off to Upper Gravenhurst; and in November 1826 Jane Baldwin, her daughter Jane Blatherwick & 7 other children were repatriated to All Saints, Hertford .

Another unfortunate case was that of Jane Plowman, the wife of Joel Plowman, brickmaker, late of Silsoe, who had deserted her and their 5 children, George, 11, William, 9, Augustus, 7, plus their twins Jane and Minnie, aged 7 months. They were all transported back to Lower Gravenhurst in 1864.

Coming in the other direction were in April 1809, Elizabeth Francis, the wife of George Francis a private in 14th Regt. of Foot and one child, who were moved from Higham Gobion; while in January 1826, St. Neots, Hunts sent William Odle and his wife Susan, plus one child all the way to Silsoe. Susan was initially unable to travel, so they waited until she had recovered and she was then returned.

All of this transporting of the poor backwards and forwards cost money, and in the late 18th century, John Field of New Inn received a bill from his solicitor for the prosecution of the Overseer and Constable of Luton, for the removal of a poor woman from Luton to Silsoe where she immediately gave birth and soon after died[164]. Another record is of 1847 when John Greene of Ampthill sent his bill to the parish for removing Sarah Giddings, a widow, from Baldock to Silsoe.

Not all cases were straightforward as the rules proving settlement were complex and so settlement examinations were held, quite often with legal representation, to establish the person's legal settlement

James Kitchener, a carter, aged 33 was examined in January 1809, when it was said that about 16 years ago he was hired as yearly servant by Robert Finney of Newbury Farm where he earned £3. He worked there for a year but had not since gained any other settlement by servitude. He had a wife called Ester to whom he was married on 21 Feb 1800 at Ampthill church. They had 3 children, Ann 8 yrs, John 6 yrs and Thomas 2 yrs old. He was at the time of the examination an unemployed bricklayer in Middlesex, and was

---

[163] See Silsoe parish records in the series P54/13
[164] BLARS Z937/1/15 It is impossible to ascertain her name from the Flitton burial records as so many people dying were described as paupers.

therefore unable to maintain his family. His covering letter asked for £2 and said that he had already pawned his watch and clothing.

The overseers were also very keen to ensure that the father of an illegitimate paid for its upkeep, and filiation orders were made naming the father and requiring him to pay. One order was made in February 1826 concerning the female child of Lucy Seymour of Silsoe, the father was stated to be James Barnard of Silsoe.

The overseers also chased up defaulters. In March 1826 a warrant was issued to apprehend Robert Hicks, late of Toddington, who was said to be the father of the female child of Mary Janes of Silsoe, born in 1825. And it was not only child maintenance that the overseers were concerned with, as a summons was issued against Samuel Sturgeon of Silsoe for disobeying an order made at the Petty Sessions in December 1835 to maintain his father, John Sturgeon of Silsoe.

In addition, it was found to be financially worthwhile to send people who, though healthy were costing the parish money, to the colonies such as Australia. This was agreed at a meeting in Silsoe in 1848 and it is possible that this is where Joel Croxford found the money to go to Australia, a few years later. There is a record in the Silsoe vestry book of 1836-1849 that £20 had been raised to aid the emigration of Edmund Squire 26, a married labourer, to South Australia with his wife Elizabeth aged 28, together with James Bryant aged 8 and Susan Bryant aged 6 months, his wife's children.

Although the official procedures took care of the poor, or should have, there was still a need for providing for special cases and from at least 1835 until about 1922, the Silsoe Social and Benevolent Society was in existence. This met initially in the school room and considered deserving cases that the existing system had excluded, and was not exclusively for Silsoe residents.

So, amongst the many recommended to the Benevolent Society as in need of assistance, there was Sarah Savage of Ampthill, a young widow with a child born the day after her marriage whose husband had died of fever three weeks after that, and who had been excluded from charitable distributions in Ampthill because of those facts; and also Elizabeth Smith, a widow aged 69, with two idiot daughters of Steppingley, who was ill and needed food.

Also in existence in the 19th century were, according to the Silsoe parish records, the Silsoe and Ampthill Labourer's Friend Society, the Silsoe Bread Charity and the Fuel Fund Charity. The former was established in 1841 and the latter two funds operated in the mid-19th century, although details of these charities and how they operated are not known.[165]

Also, there were older charities endowed mainly in the wills of the donor which helped keep starvation at bay. A plaque in Flitton church records that

---

[165] BLARS P54/25/

William Daniel (of Newbury, died 1706) gave £100 to purchase land, the rent of which was to be used to purchase bread for the poor of Flitton and Silsoe, 2/5 to Flitton and 3/5 to Silsoe. Similarly, Widow Cox gave £20 with the same conditions while Henry Sharp also gave £100 but required his monument to be maintained from the revenue with whatever was left over being given to purchase bread for the poor. Finally, for Silsoe, "some of the Earls of Kent" gave a total of £170 for the education of poor children, 2/5 to Flitton and 3/5 to Flitton.

It is interesting that in the late 1880's poor London children were sent to Silsoe for a country holiday, apparently organised under the aegis of the Bishop of London. The vicar of Silsoe, Joseph Hargrove, wrote to *The Times* in 1885 praising the scheme and saying that it had taken place in the three preceding years with families being paid a small amount, 4/- and 5/- , to board the children.

Even in 1902 a soup kitchen was opened at Wrest House for the poor of seven parishes including Silsoe, and 170 families were supplied with vegetable soup and bread.[166]

The Silsoe Workhouses and Almshouse

What was known as the "poor house" eventually became known as the "workhouse" and the "Town House" was originally situated in the chapel yard according to Mary Phillips. In 1603 Mr Daniell of Newbury and others "of the better sort of ye inhabitants" desired to place a poor widow "in a part of the Towne House which ye smith hath hired to keep his coale in."[167]

Silsoe had a recognised workhouse in the 18th century, as a Parliamentary Report of 1776-7 listed the one at Silsoe as being capable of holding 22 persons. If the building existed in 1718 then the buildings shown in the Chapel Yard on the map of that date, are not large and for that number to be held there, the conditions would have been cramped and not particularly pleasant.

It seems that this had been noticed and the Rev. P Birt commented in 1763 that he would like to see a good school and a comfortable workhouse. The Rev. Hadley Cox[168] a year later spoke about the ill accommodation of the poor in the old house in the Chapel Yard and proposed that it be demolished and rebuilt at a new site, near the pound on the road to Newbury (now Ampthill Road).

However, it was decide to repair the old building and that took place later in the year. Poverty still abounded though, despite 'charity' and Cox suggested

---

[166] *Beds Times* 31 January 1902.
[167] Mary Phillips etc
[168] Hadley Cox was also a magistrate but how this was reconciled with his duties as a priest to care for others is not known.

in 1769 that a workhouse manager be found. He did find someone, Frank Titmus of Stevenage, yeoman, and the agreement between him and Hadley Cox, vicar of Flitton with Silsoe; Matthew Caton the chapel-warden and Russell Finney & John Porter, the overseers for the poor for Silsoe ran as follows:-

"Titmus will provide for the poor of Silsoe with a wholesome and sufficient diet of all sorts with a proper quantity of good small beer, and decent and necessary apparel; so that they shall be in no ways chargeable to the hamlet. Anyone not in the workhouse who breaks a limb, or catches an infectious distemper (smallpox, venereal disease, scald head[169], the itch) should be kept until recovered at a convenient place provided by the parish, and not brought into the workhouse until so recovered; when, if unable to support themselves, they may be so brought in. If the workhouse is not large enough to contain all the poor, the parish shall provide one or more house or houses. The parish will pay Titmus £95 p.a. for 3 yrs., but they may discontinue Titmus as manager of the poor at the end of 1 yr., on paying him £5. Titmus will supply the poor with beds, bedding and other necessary furniture, and provide those who can work with necessary implements and materials. A valuation is to be made of the furniture and apparel (excluding that of such of the poor as are in the gift and charity of the Marchioness de Grey). At the end of the term the parish may purchase at a valuation the furniture installed by Titmus for not more than £31 10s. Anyone catching an infectious distemper (other than those above) and removing with household goods into the workhouse may take such goods out again on recovery. Joint efforts shall be made to secure a runaway, but if he cannot be recovered his family shall be cared for as above."[170]

A similar agreement for Maulden a few years later required the manager also to bury the poor who died at the workhouse, and to share the expenses of a doctor.

On 2nd June 1807 Amabel, Lady Polwarth, received a letter from her friend Mary about the removal of the workhouse " the old one not being an ornamental entrance to your Ladyship's park ….. a small close on the west side of the village near Eve's farm being owned by the parish" should be taken for a new building. Apparently there had been five attempts to relocate the workhouse over the preceding 30 years.

With the building of the brand new workhouse at Ampthill early in the 19th century, there was no need for Silsoe's and the old one was conveyed to Thomas Philip, Earl de Grey, on 25 January 1838 for £155 by the Guardians of the Poor of the Ampthill Union[171]. This is described as "a messuage at

---

[169] 'Scald head' was an infectious eczema of the scalp and 'the itch' was probably scabies.
[170] BLARS L28/29
[171] BLARS L28/31

West End, Silsoe, Flitton with barn and garden, about 1 rood", and was the white painted range of buildings, now numbered 18-22 West End Road[172].

Thus the workhouse, or house for the poor, described by the Rev. Hadley Cox in 1764 as being in the chapel yard and which had been moved to what is now 18-22 West End Road in about 1807, must presumably have been made redundant with the occupants being transferred to Ampthill. The row in West End Road is said to be of 17th century origin in the listing schedule, and so may have been used as a workhouse after renovation. Interestingly, three buildings are shown behind the church on the 1826 map, presumably the old parsonage, the house for the poor and possibly a tithe barn, suggesting that the old workhouse had not by then been demolished.

The Almshouses in Church Road, constructed about 1835, may have been part of the village improvement associated with the new mansion house but may also have been connected with the removal of the workhouse. Perhaps the Earl was benevolent enough to realise that it would be preferable for the older villagers to remain in the village, rather than move them to Ampthill away from their friends and families.

The Joint parishes Workhouse at Ampthill

In the early 19th century it became possible to set up shared workhouses for the old and infirm for several parishes. The law of 1834, known as The New Poor Law was enacted principally to exert control on expenditure and had the following principals in mind:

(a) no able-bodied person was to receive money or other help from the Poor Law authorities except in a workhouse;
(b) conditions in workhouses were to be made very harsh to discourage people from wanting to receive help;
(c) workhouses were to be built in every parish or, if parishes were too small, in unions of parishes;
(d) ratepayers in each parish or union had to elect a Board of Guardians to supervise the workhouse, to collect the Poor Rate and to send reports to the Central Poor Law Commission.

The Ampthill Union was formed in April 1835 which included in its area the parish of Silsoe, and the proposal was to build a large workhouse in that town.

However, in May 1835, the Ampthill area was the scene of serious anti-Poor Law demonstrations, which were triggered by resentment at the proposed

---

[172] The maps of about 1809 to 1828 all show this building, one having the words 'Work House, parish of Silsoe' inscribed on it.

replacement of cash relief by a system of payment in kind.[173] The proceedings featured in a *Times* report on May 19th, part of which is reproduced below.

The relieving officer who had ridden over to Lidlington on a Monday to talk to the overseer found a large group at the gate shouting;

"We don't want you here, and we'll have money or blood, and before you leave this we'll have either the money out of your pocket, or the blood out of your veins."

This continued and he went into another room where some of them found him, and one of the women said she knew he had got money and while he was surrounded, she put her hand into his pocket and took some out. Some of them also complained about the hardship of being obliged to leave their families. A similar event took place at Millbrook the next day where the paupers had collected in such numbers such that the officer remained concealed until night after which he slipped away home.

On Thursday the guardians collected at the Ampthill House of Industry for a meeting but they had not been long in deliberation

" when the paupers, men, women, and children came flocking in from all quarters in great numbers, many of the men armed with bludgeons, sticks, &c. Several of the men told the Guardians that they wanted work, and to be paid for it in money, but that they would not take relief in bread. They were told that their demand for money could not be complied with, when they commenced a most desperate attack upon the windows with stones, brick-bats, cabbage-stalks, and every missile that could be found."

When the windows had been demolished the guardians left the building with Mr. Morris having to defend himself with an umbrella.

Despite trying to talk to the mob of about 200 - 300 the stones continued to fly and several of the guardians were hurt. Then early in the afternoon the Riot Act was read by a magistrate which partially pacified the crowd, but the mob moved where fighting took place between the special constables and the mob. A Mr Adey went off express for London to request assistance from Government who apparently promised him that the Household Troops from Windsor would be sent down on the shortest notice whenever the magistrates felt their presence necessary. Mr. Graeme, the auditor to the Union, was also sent at 5 a.m. on Thursday for a body of the Metropolitan Police, who arrived, 22 in number, on Friday morning. They were shortly afterwards despatched, together with a number of special constables on horseback, in search of the ringleaders.

---

[173] Taken from the website http://www.workhouses.org.uk/ which contains a great deal of information of workhouses and the Poor Law.

Law and order prevailed, although several were tried with the capital offence of continuing to riot after the act had been read and eventually, in 1835-6, a new Ampthill Union workhouse was built at a site on the eastern side of Dunstable Street to accommodate 400 people, for which the Poor Law Commissioners authorised an expenditure of £6,400. The architect happened to be James Clephan who had been involved in the building of Wrest Park mansion a few years earlier.

The 19th century censuses record a few people from Silsoe staying at Ampthill Workhouse. In 1841, amongst others, Ellen, Caroline and Samuel Taylor were there aged 15, 13 and 10 years old. Their parents are not there, so perhaps they had died and their children were sent to the workhouse. Elizabeth Rich aged 80, who probably had no family to support her was also there.

In both 1851 and 1861 Fanny or Frances Dalton (aged 50 in the latter census), a lacemaker is there and in 1861 and 1871 Elizabeth Squires, a straw plaiter but also labelled as 'an idiot', is inside. In 1901 George Mann born about 1821 is there, an ex gardener, together with Thomas Denton about 80 years old, who had been there in 1891.

Fires

Fires would have been a constant risk in Silsoe with houses mainly roofed with thatch and the walls of timber. The first noted instance of this is in a conveyance of 1644 which has a reference to ground near the track to Upbury in the "South End of Silsoe" on which two cottages stood, recently burned down.[174]

Fire insurance was available from the 18th century and those who could afford the premiums were given a fire mark or fire plate to put on their house, to show the fire brigade that they were insured. It is suggested that if a brigade arrived on the scene and found it was not their office that insured the risk, and that no surrounding property in which they were interested seemed to be in danger, they went home again and left the fire to be fought by the public. A fire mark still exists on the road side of No 33 West End Road for the County Fire Office which was formed in 1807 by an "association of noblemen and gentlemen", Plate 17/4.

Apparently in the late 18th century there was a fire at Wimpole Hall, Cambridgeshire, another of the Earl of Hardwick's houses, and this prompted the Rev. Hadley Cox to inspect the fire engine at Wrest – the first mention of such a facility. In the same year, 1780, there was a fire at gardener Edward Charles's house at Wardhedges, when his thatched house was completely levelled. As might be expected the family was quite dejected at this catastrophe, and a subscription was raised to help them as the damage to their goods was estimated to be £8-9.

---

[174] BLARS L5/71

It seems that until quite recently Wrest continued to have had its own fire engine and certainly it existed in the early part of the 20th century as this old photograph shows.

Plate 17/5 - The Wrest Park Fire Engine and Firemen about 1910

This appliance, or an earlier model, was probably used in 1838 when Alfred Russel Wallace, who was helping his brother with the new mansion house recorded that once while the architect Mr Clephan was away, there was a fire at a farm quite near the George where he was staying. This burnt some stacks and outbuildings but the local fire engine after some time, put it out.[175] It was certainly used in May 1902 when a fire was put out by it in 25 High Street, which was then occupied by the 84 year old George Edwards, a retired shoemaker and chapel clerk.

A major fire occurred in Wrest Park mansion in September 1916 while it was being used as a hospital for wounded soldiers from the First World War. A *Times* report of September says that the cause of the fire had not been ascertained, but that the eastern wing and part of the main roof were practically destroyed.

Fire brigades initially arrived from Ampthill, Shefford and Woburn Abbey to deal with the blaze with more engines coming from Bedford, Luton and Hitchin and a 'powerful' engine arrived even from London.

All 200 wounded were evacuated safely with lightly wounded helping to carry out the limbless and other cot cases. They were then all taken to Woburn Abbey on a succession of motor and horse vehicles. The valuable works of art were also saved and it was hoped that repairs of the damage caused by the

---

[175] *Autobiography of Alfred Russell Wallace* (Brit Lib X809 7455)

fire and the water could be carried out. In fact the repair work was carried out quickly and the mansion sold the following year.

More recently, in 1970, the thatched roof of number 2 High Street caught fire.[176] Luckily only the roof was badly affected but the replacement roof was in tiles rather than thatch, which is a pity.

---

[176] BLARS FSD/PC11

Concluding Comments

Well, that's over then. No more staying up nights tapping away on the computer, or hours spent in the Archives Library at Bedford and checking out references. I hope it has been worthwhile for those who manage to get this far and I am aware that there are gaps all over the place, and probably some errors. If there weren't then it would be about ten volumes thick and even more tedious.

Again I would like to thank those who contributed whether by small comments or by providing me with sources and photographs. I had not anticipated how much easier it was going to be to write the early history than that for the last century, but thanks to the restrictions on recent documents that's how it is.

It has been jokingly (I hope) said that I should now write a history of our new village of Poulx, here in France. No thanks, there's too much wine and cheese to sample yet.

Roger Bradshaw

Bibliography

Agricultural Engineering: the Wrest Park story 1924 –2006" edited Bill Day, Liz Field, Anne Jarvis, Elsevier 2009

Austin, William; *The History of Luton*; 1928.

Brown, John; *John Bunyan, His Life and Times*; Archan; 1967

Blundell, Joseph Hight & Hight Blundel MD, The *Blundells of Bedfordshire & Northants*, 1912, private subscription

Carter , Paul & Kate Thompson; *Sources for Local Historians*; 2005; Phillimore.,

Dazeley, R A & Paul Trodd; *An Atlas of the Breeding birds of Bedfordshire 1988/92*; 1994; Beds Natural History Society. ,

Dony, John; *Flora of Bedfordshire*; 1953, Repr 1978; EP Publishing.

Field, John; *A History of English Field Names*; 1993; Longman.,

Godber, Joyce; *History of Bedfordshire 1066-1888*; 1969, Beds CC.

Hodgkin, RH; *A History of the Anglo-Saxons Vols 1 & 2; 3rd* ed 1959, OUP.

Marshall, Hilary; *Palaeography for Family & Local Historians*; 2004; Phillimore.,

Phillips, Mary; *The Clophill Story*; 1988; By subscription.,

Pretty, Jules N; *Sustainable Agriculture in the Middle Ages: The English Manor*,

Reaney, P H; A Dictionary of English Surnames; Rev. 1997; OUP,

Reay, Barry; *Rural Englands, Labouring Lives in the Nineteenth century*; 2004; Palgrave McMillan.

Rogers, Alan; *Approaches to Local History*; 2nd Ed 1977; Longman.,

Simco, Angela; *Survey of Bedfordshire – The Roman Period*; Beds County Council; 1984.,

Steele – Elliott, J; *The Vertebrate Fauna of Bedfordshire; 1897-1901*; Repr 1993; Beds Natural History Society.,

Taylor, Christopher; *Roads and Tracks of Britain*; 1979; Dent,

Trodd, Paul & David Kramer; *The Birds of Bedfordshire*; 1991; Castlemead Publications.,

Victoria County History, *A History of the County of Bedford*,

Wallace, Alfred Russel, *My Life A Record Of Events And Opinions*, London, Chapman and Hall, 1905

Ziegler, Philip; *The Black Death*; Repr 1982; Penguin Books.,

Name Index

Name Index

Name Index

Name Index

Name Index